Why Are These Books in the Bible and Not Others?

Volume Two
A Translator's Perspective on the Canon of the New Testament

By Gary F. Zeolla

Translator's Perspective on the Canon of the NT

Copyright © 2016, 2023 by Gary F. Zeolla (www.Zeolla.org).
All rights reserved.

This version of this book published in 2023 is a corrected text, not a full new edition. Only minor corrections have been made, plus the cover and appendixes have been updated.

Table of Contents

Introductory Pages: 5
Preface 7
Analytical-Literal Translation 8
New Testament Texts 9
Terminology Notes 10
Chronology 11
Church Fathers 12
Abbreviations and Other Notes 13

Chapters: 19
1 – Overview of the New Testament Canon 21
2 – Overview of the Four Gospels and Acts 51
3 – The Synoptic Gospels and Acts 79
4 – The Gospel According to John 113
5 – The Epistles of John and The Revelation 145
6 – The Pauline Epistles – Part One 179
7 – The Pauline Epistles – Part Two 229
8 – The General Epistles – Part One 273
9 – The General Epistles – Part Two 313
10 – Conclusion on the New Testament 353

Appendixes 355
1 – Bibliography 357
2 – Additional Books by the Author 363
3 – Author's Websites, Newsletters, and Social Sites/
    Contacting the Author 377

Translator's Perspective on the Canon of the NT

Why Are These Books in the Bible? Volume Two

Introductory Pages

Translator's Perspective on the Canon of the NT

Preface

Christians claim the Bible is the Word of God, that it is the final authority in all matters relating to Christian faith and practice, and that it is absolutely reliable in all that it teaches. But to put such confidence in the Bible requires that we have the correct books in the Bible. But do we? Why are the 66 books in the Bible in the Bible, and why were other books that could have been included not included?

This subject is very important and complicated, so complicated it takes three volumes to fully cover it. Volume One studied the books included in the Old Testament (OT) and considered other books that could have been included but were not. This Volume Two will cover the books included in the New Testament (NT). Volume Three will then consider the writings of the Apostolic Fathers, some of which were considered for inclusion in the NT, along with other writings, orthodox and Gnostic, that many wonder why they are not included in the NT.

In this second volume, each of the 27 books included in the NT will be reviewed in detail. Who wrote them and when, their theology, and other pertinent background information will be discussed to explain why they were included in the NT. Arguments against the traditional viewpoints on these books will be addressed.

The author is the translator of the *Analytical-Literal Translation of the Bible*. The ALT consists of translations of the Old Testament Greek Septuagint, the OT Apocryphal/ Deuterocanonical Books, the New Testament Greek Majority Text, and the Apostolic Fathers. He is thus very familiar with all of the books to be discussed in this three-volume set, having translated most of them. He is also the author of many other books related to the Bible. Working on this distinct translation of the Scriptures and these other Bible-based books gives the author a unique perspective on these topics.

Translator's Perspective on the Canon of the NT
Analytical-Literal Translation

Unless otherwise indicated, all Bible verses in this three volume set are from the author's *Analytical-Literal Translation* (ALT; see Appendixes One and Two). The ALT is published in seven volumes.

Volumes I – IV are the Old Testament (OT). One unique feature of the ALT: OT is it is translated from the Septuagint (LXX) rather than the Hebrew text. The LXX is a third century BC Greek translation of the Hebrew Bible. The name and abbreviation comes from the tradition that 70 (or 72) Jewish scholars worked on its translation, six from each of the twelve tribes of Israel.

As such, the wording of some OT verses quoted in this book might differ from Bible versions based upon the Hebrew text, which most versions are. In cases where there is a difference between texts affecting the subject of this book, the verses will also be quoted from version(s) based on the Hebrew text.

Volume V of the ALT contains the Apocryphal/ Deuterocanonical (A/D) Books. These are the "extra" books found in Roman Catholic and Eastern Orthodox Bibles as compared to Jewish and Protestant Bibles. The debate as to whether these books should be included in the Bible was addressed in Volume One of this three volume set.

Volume VI of the ALT is the New Testament (NT). It is translated from the Majority Text. This Greek text differs slightly from the other two Greek texts used in Bible translation: the *Textus Receptus* (used by the KJV and NKJV) and the "Critical Text" (NASB, NIV, NLT, and most other modern-day versions). Thus, again, the wording of some verses quoted in this book might differ from the wording in other Bibles. If a textual variant affects the interpretation of a verse, then that point is mentioned.

However, more often than these textual reasons, the wording of the ALT differs from other versions due to the ALT being a literal translation while many Bible versions use a less than literal translation method. These textual and translation differences are addressed in this writer's book *Differences Between Bible Versions* (see Appendix Two).

Volume VII of the ALT is the Apostolic Fathers (APF). These are the writings of the Church leaders of the late first through mid-second centuries, some of which were considered for inclusion in the Bible. These writings will be discussed in Volume Three.

These seven volumes contain most of the writings discussed in this three-volume set. As such, the writer is very familiar with them.

New Testament Texts

"There is more manuscript support for the New Testament (NT) than for any other body of ancient literature. Over five thousand Greek, eight thousand Latin, and many more manuscripts in other languages attest the integrity of the New Testament" (*Parallel*, p.xxiii). Moreover, "No other document of antiquity even begins to approach such numbers and attestation. In comparison, The *Illiad* by Homer is second with only 643 manuscripts that still survive" (McDowell, p.39). Furthermore, "to be skeptical of the resultant text of the New Testament books is to allow all of classical antiquity to slip into obscurity, for no documents of the ancient period are as well attested biographically as the New Testament" (John W. Montgomery, quoted in McDowell, p.40).

These manuscripts consist of: 88 papyri from the second to the eighth centuries, with 41 being from the second to the fourth centuries, 290 uncials from the early fourth century on, 2,800 minuscules from the ninth to the fifteenth centuries, and 2,200 lectionaries from the ninth to the fifteenth centuries. There are also quotes of the NT in the writings of the Church Fathers and early translations of the Greek NT into other languages. The latter includes early Latin translations from the second century on, the Latin Vulgate translated by Jerome in 382 AD, with 8,000 extant manuscripts, the earliest from the fourth century, and translations in Syriac, Coptic, Armenian, Georgian, Ethiopic, Gothic, Arabic, and many others.

By comparing all of these manuscripts, a very reliable NT text can be determined. There are variants about which there are debates, but significant differences are indicated in most Bibles, as will be done in this book. And this writer's *Companion Volume to the ALT* provides a list of significant variants between the three major published Greek texts mentioned on the previous page. But these variants are few and far between, with the vast majority of the text of the NT being identical in all published Greek texts.

Much more details on this issue can be found in this writer's book *Differences Between Bible Versions* (see Appendix Two), and God-willing I will elaborate further in in my proposed book *Texts and Translations of the Bible* (see Appendix Three). But here, the reader can be assured that overall the text of the NT is well attested and can be read with confidence.

Translator's Perspective on the Canon of the NT

Terminology Notes

This three volume set will use the era markers of BC and AD (or B.C. and A.D.). The former means "before Christ" while the latter means *Anno Domino*, which is Latin for "In the year of the Lord." These are the traditional markers for the turn of eras, with the eras being separated by birth of Jesus. This writer is fully aware that Jesus most likely was not born in 1 AD but in about 5 BC. But that does not negate that His birth has traditionally been used to separate the eras.

The markers of BCE and CE (or B.C.E., C.E., meaning "Before the Common Era" and "Common Era," respectively) are now often used. But these markers make no sense. The only reason to separate the eras at this point in history is the birth of Christ, as nothing else of sufficient significance happened at that time to cause a change of eras.

Also, the term "conservative" will be used in this volume to refer to traditional beliefs and those who ascribe to them as to the authors and the dates of the writing of Bible books. These will generally be the beliefs that have been held by Christians from the earliest times down to the 1800s. The terms "liberal," "critical," and "critics" will be used for the opinions that originated in the 1800s and for those who ascribe to these opinions that deny these traditional beliefs.

The term "orthodox" will be used to refer to the historic doctrines of the Christian tradition and those who ascribe to them, while the term "heresy" and "heretics" will be used of doctrines both old and modern that are contrary to these orthodox doctrines and for those who subscribe to these heretical doctrines, respectively. It is recognized these are strong terms, but they best express the concept.

The term "Apostolic Church" refers to the Christian movement of the first century, while the term "early Church" refers to the Christians of the second through fourth centuries AD.

The term "Apostolic Fathers" (APF) refers to Christian leaders and writers immediately after the apostles, who were direct disciples of the apostles and who lived in the late first through mid-second centuries. The term "Church Fathers" refers to Christian writers and leaders after the Apostolic Fathers from the mid-second through fourth centuries, although the Apostolic Fathers are sometimes also included in this term.

Chronology

This chronology presents important dates to know for this study. Some dates are approximate.

B.C.
63 – Romans under Pompey conquer Jerusalem/ occupy Judea
5 – Birth of Jesus
4 – Death of Herod the Great

A.D.
26 – Start of the ministries of John the Baptist and Jesus
30 – Death and resurrection of Jesus
33 – Conversion of Saul/ Paul
50 – Council of Jerusalem (Acts 15)
50-68 – Most New Testament books written
64-68 – Peter and Paul executed under Nero
70 – Destruction of the second temple and of Jerusalem
90s – John exiled to Patmos under Domitian/ John's writings
200 – Muratorian Fragment
313 – Conversion of Emperor Constantine
325 – Council of Nicaea (First Ecumenical Council)
350 – Codex Sinaiticus/ Codex Vaticanus
364 – Council of Laodicea
381 – Council of Constantinople (Second Ecumenical Council)
382 – Vulgate, Latin translation of the Bible
397 – Council of Carthage
400 – Peshitta, Syriac translation of the Bible
1945 – Discovery of Hag Hammadi documents in Egypt

The sources for this chronology are found in the Bibliography in Appendix One.

Translator's Perspective on the Canon of the NT

Church Fathers

The following early Christians leaders of the late first through fourth centuries are referred to throughout this book. All dates AD.

Clement of Rome – born first century in Rome. Bishop of Rome: 88 to 97.
Ignatius – born first century; died 107-117 in Rome.
Polycarp - born first century; died 155. Bishop of Smyrna.
Irenaeus – born c. 120 /140, Asia Minor; died c. 200 /203.
Justin Martyr – born c. 100 in Flavia Neapolis, Palestine; died c. 165 in Rome.
Clement of Alexandria – born 150 in Athens; died 211/ 215.
Tertullian – born c. 155 /160 in Carthage (now in Tunisia); died after 220 in Carthage.
Hippolytus of Rome – born c. 170; died 235.
Origen – born c. 185 in Alexandria, Egypt; died c. 254 in Tyre, Phoenicia (now Ṣūr, Lebanon).
Cyprian – born 200, Carthage; died September 14, 258, Carthage.
Denis (also spelled Denys, Latin Dionysius) – born, Rome? Died 258? in Paris.
Eusebius of Caesarea (also called Eusebius Pamphili), born c. 260; died before 341. Bishop of Cæsarea in Palestine, the author of *Ecclesiastical History*.
Athanasius - born c. 293 in Alexandria; died May 2, 373 in Alexandria.
Cyril of Jerusalem – born c. 315, Jerusalem—died 386? In Jerusalem.
Basil – born c. 329; died January, 1, 379. Bishop of Caesarea.
Jerome – born c. 340 in Stridon, a town on the confines of Dalmatia and Pannonia; died September, 30, 420 at Bethlehem.
Cyril of Alexandria – born c. 375; died June 27, 444.

Heretical Writers

Valentinus – Gnostic leader and writer from 140 to his death in 160.
Marcion – born c. 110. Promoted duelist theology of a creator god distinct from the Christian God.
Celsus – Platonist. Literary activity 175-180.

The Sources for these dates are found in the Bibliography in Appendix One.

Why Are These Books in the Bible? Volume Two
Abbreviations and Other Notes

Following are the meanings of abbreviations seen in this book.

Abbreviations in the ALT

[the] – Words added for clarity are bracketed (e.g., Gen 1:1). But note: very often the definite article ("the") is not used in the LXX with the word *kurios* ("LORD" or "Lord"). But the added article is not bracketed in this case as its frequency made it prohibitive to do so.

[1Cor 15:45] – Reference for when the OT is quoted in the NT (e.g., Gen 2:7).

"father of a multitude" – Meaning of a proper name, placed in quotation marks (e.g., Gen 17:5).

About – Modern-day equivalent for measurements and monetary units (e.g., Gen 6:15).

cp. – Compare. A cross reference (e.g., Gen 1:27).

fig. – Figurative. Possible figurative meaning or paraphrase of preceding literal translation (e.g., Gen 1:2).

Gr. – Greek. The Greek word previously translated, with the Greek letters transliterated (changed) into English letters (e.g., Gen 3:20).

Heb. – Hebrew. Indicates the reading of the Hebrew OT when there is a notable difference between it and the LXX. But note, no attempt is made to indicate all differences between these two texts (e.g., Gen 2:6). Also used for when the LXX omits a verse, but it is included by the translator translating it from the Hebrew text.

i.e. – Explanatory note ("that is" or "in explanation") (e.g., Gen 2:23). Also "Note" for longer notes.

lit. – Literal. Indicates the literal rendering when the text uses a less than literal rendering (e.g., Gen 1:6).

Translator's Perspective on the Canon of the NT

LXX – Septuagint. Third century B.C. Greek translation of the Hebrew Bible. Very often, the spelling of proper names in the LXX differs from how the name is commonly spelled. For notable names, the common spelling is used in the text, but the first time it appears in a book, the LXX spelling is also given (e.g., Gen 2:8). But note: no attempt is made to give the common spelling for all names.

omits –The LXX being used is *Codex Vaticanus*. If it omits a verse, the translator's rendering of the Hebrew is given (e.g., 1Kings 12:2).

NT – New Testament.

OT – Old Testament.

or – Alternative, traditional, or slightly less literal translation (e.g., Gen 1:8).

see – Cross reference (e.g., Gen 25:34).

Notations in the ALT

But – Indicates the use of the Greek strong adversative (*alla* – e.g., Gen 15:4) instead of the weak adversative (*de*, translated as "but" when used in an adversative sense – e.g., Gen 1:2).

LORD – Lord – The former indicates the Hebrew OT has *Yahweh* (the Hebrew proper name for God – Gen 2:8). The latter indicates the Hebrew OT has *adonai* (the general word for "lord") or that there is no equivalent in the Hebrew OT for the LXX's use of "Lord" (Gr., *kurios* – e.g., Gen 6:22). When the LXX has "God" (Gr., *theos*) where the Hebrew has *Yahweh*, "GOD" is used (e.g., Exod 4:11).

you – Indicates the pronoun is emphasized in the Greek text (also, he, she, etc. – e.g., Gen 4:7).

you* – Indicates the original is plural (also, your* – e.g., Gen 1:22). With no asterisk the second person pronoun is singular (e.g., Gen 3:9).

{…} – Encloses "extra" passages found in the LXX but not in the Hebrew text (e.g., Gen 46:20).

Why Are These Books in the Bible? Volume Two
Additional Abbreviations

a – Only the first half of the verse is being quoted or referred to (e.g., Exodus 15:22-25a, only the first half of verse 25 is quoted or referred to).

b – Only the second half of the verse is being quoted or referred to (e.g., Exodus 15:25b-26, only the second half of verse 25 is quoted or referred to).

c – Circa. About. Used with approximate dates.

f – And the following verse (e.g. Psalm 22:9f means verses 9 and 10 are quoted or referred to).

ff – And the following verses (e.g., 22:9ff means verse 9 and several following verses are quoted or referred to).

Abbreviations for Bible Versions

ALT – *Analytical-Literal Translation.*
ESV – *English Standard Version.*
HCSB - *Holman Christian Standard Bible.*
KJV – *King James Version.*
NAB – *New American Bible.*
NASB – *New American Standard Bible.*
NET – *New English Translation.*
NIRV - *New International Reader's Version.*
NIV – *New International Version.*
NLT – *New Living Translation.*
NKJV – *New King James Version.*
NRSV – *New Revised Standard Version.*

Quotations Notes

Much of this book consists of extended Scripture quotations. These have not been put in block quotes (indented) as is normally done for extended quotes due to the length and number of them, as to do so would have made this book even longer than it already is in hardcopy formats and difficult to read in electronic formats. But the superscript verse

Translator's Perspective on the Canon of the NT

numbers are retained, so Scripture quotes are easily identified. All bolding in Scripture quotes is added for easy identification of the point being referenced.

However, extended quotes from sources other than the Bible are indented for easy identification. The sources are cited after the quote in parentheses by the first word or two of the main title of the source, followed by an article title in quotation marks if applicable. The full biographical data is then given in Appendix One.

The LORD

Throughout the ALT, I use "LORD" (written in all capital letters) to indicate when the Greek word *kurios* is a translation of the Hebrew Divine Name (*YHWH*; traditionally pronounced "Jehovah" but more likely pronounced "Yahweh"). As a result, I have gotten in the habit of using "LORD" in all my writings. That is why "LORD" is used throughout this book. But whether LORD, Lord, or God, the reference is to the one true God, the God of the Bible.

Abbreviations for Bible Books

The Old Testament:
Gen – Genesis
Exod – Exodus
Lev – Leviticus
Numb – Numbers
Deut – Deuteronomy
Josh – Joshua
Judg – Judges
Ruth – Ruth
1Sam – 1Samuel
2Sam – 2Samuel
1Ki – 1Kings
2Ki – 2Kings
1Chr – 1Chronicles
2Chr – 2Chronicles
Ezra – Ezra
Neh – Nehemiah
Est – Esther

Why Are These Books in the Bible? Volume Two

Job – Job
Ps – Psalms
Prov – Proverbs
Eccl – Ecclesiastes
Song – Song of Solomon
Isa – Isaiah
Jer – Jeremiah
Lam – Lamentations
Ezek – Ezekiel
Dan – Daniel
Hos – Hosea
Joel – Joel
Amos – Amos
Obad – Obadiah
Jon – Jonah
Mic – Micah
Nah – Nahum
Hab – Habakkuk
Zeph – Zephaniah
Hag – Haggai
Zech – Zechariah
Mal – Malachi

The New Testament:

Matt – Matthew
Mk – Mark
Lk – Luke
Jn – John
Ac – Acts
Rom – Romans
1Cor – 1Corinthians
2Cor – 2Corinthians
Gal – Galatians
Eph – Ephesians
Phil – Philippians
Col – Colossians
1Th – 1Thessalonians
2Th – 2Thessalonians
1Tim – 1Timothy
2Tim – 2Timothy
Tit – Titus
Phlm – Philemon
Heb – Hebrews

Translator's Perspective on the Canon of the NT

Jam – James
1Pet – 1Peter
2Pet – 2Peter
1Jn – 1John
2Jn – 2John
3Jn – 3John
Jd – Jude
Rev – Revelation

Why Are These Books in the Bible? Volume Two

Books in the New Testament

Translator's Perspective on the Canon of the NT

Why Are These Books in the Bible? Volume Two

Chapter One
Overview of the Books in the New Testament

Volume One of this three volume set studied the 39 books contained in the Old Testament (OT) of the Bible. It also studied other books that could have been included in the OT but were not. It explained why each book was or was not included in the canon (list of authoritative books) of the OT. This Volume Two will study the 27 books contained in the canon of the New Testament (NT). Below is a list of these books in their traditional order and groupings.

New Testament Books

The Gospels and Acts:
Matthew
Mark
Luke
John
Acts

The Pauline Epistles:
Romans
1Corinthians
2Corinthians
Galatians
Ephesians
Philippians
Colossians
1Thessalonians
2Thessalonians
1Timothy
2Timothy
Titus
Philemon

The General Epistles:
Hebrews
James
1Peter

Translator's Perspective on the Canon of the NT
>2Peter
>1John
>2John
>3John
>Jude

>The Revelation

This order corresponds with the natural progress of the Christian revelation and was universally adopted by the church, with the exception of a difference in the arrangement of the Epistles. ... Most of the ancient Manuscripts, Versions, and Catalogues arrange the books in the following order: Gospels, Acts, Catholic [General] Epistles, Pauline Epistles, Apocalypse [Revelation]. Some put the Pauline Epistles before the Catholic Epistles. Our English Bible follows the order of the Latin Vulgate (Schaff; 8149-8153).

Reading the New Testament

Before proceeding, it would be good to mention that this book will assume the reader is familiar with the contents of these NT books. If you are not, I would strongly encourage you to read the NT. In today's world, there are many ways to do so.

The complete Bible (OT and NT) is widely available in traditional hardcopy formats: paperback, hardback, and leather-bound. These can be purchased at brick and mortal bookstores and via online bookstores, both Christian and secular.

The complete text of the Bible is also available in various software programs for desktop and notebook computers. The one I utilize is *BibleWorks*. It is an excellent program and the one I used in working on my translation of the Bible and in writing this three volume set. But it is rather pricy and geared towards the serious Bible student. Less expensive or even free software programs are also readily available.

The Bible can also be read in various eBook formats, such as Acrobat Reader, Kindle, and ePUB formats for iPads and Nook readers. The Bible is also available in various apps for smart phones and tablets. The ones I use are *Blue Letter Bible* and Olive Tree's *Bible+*. Both of these are free, excellent, and easy to use apps. For the latter, additional study aids can be purchased. There are also various websites that offer the text of the Bible freely online.

There is a myriad of different translations of the Bible. Mine is the *Analytical-Literal Translation* (ALT). It is available in both hardcopy and eBook formats (see Appendix Two). Other versions are available in all of the preceding formats. My favorite of the popularly available versions is the *New King James Version* (NKJV). My reasons for preferring it are detailed in my book *Differences Between Bible Versions* (see Appendix Two). But many of the other available versions would also be worthwhile.

But however you read the Bible, please do so. The rest of this book will make much more sense if you do so before proceeding.

Overview

The early Christian movement was composed solely of Jews. As such, they held to the tenets of the Jewish religion. Note that "tenet" means, "a principle or belief, especially one of the main principles of a religion or philosophy" (Oxford). Most important among these tenets was accepting the traditional Jewish beliefs about the conception of God and of nature as articulated in the OT and detailed in Volume One.

But to summarize here: the Hebrew conception of God and of nature is there is only one true God, that this one true God directly created the real physical universe and thus this one true God is sovereign over and intimately involved with His creation and especially with human beings, who are the pinnacle of His creation, that this universe as it was created was good, but it is fallen and thus suffering and death now exist in it, but there is the hope of a future Redeemer and thus of a better world, as God is still sovereign over His creation.

The early Christians also accepted the Jewish OT canon and all that those books teach. As such, any books to be included in the developing NT canon would have to uphold this conception of God and be in accordance with the other teachings of the OT. As the *Encyclopedia Britannica* puts it:

> The Hebrew Bible is as basic to Christianity as it is to Judaism. Without the Old Testament, the New Testament could not have been written, and there could have been no man like Jesus; Christianity could not have been what it became. This has to do with cultural values, basic human values, as much as with religious beliefs ("Biblical literature").

But the early Christians would modify some of the other standards for books to be included in the OT canon for the books to be included

Translator's Perspective on the Canon of the NT

in their canon. Rather than books being written by Hebrews in Hebrew as for the OT canon, books for the NT canon had to be written in Greek by an apostle or a direct associate of an apostle. Being written in Greek was important as Greek was the universal language of that time, and the Gospel was to be for all peoples everywhere.

Being written by an apostle or direct apostolic associate was important as the apostles had the closest possible relationship to Jesus. As such, their teachings would be in accordance with the teachings of Jesus Himself. This was extended to direct associates of the apostles, but no further. In other words, although the early Christians might respect the writings of an associate of an associate of an apostle, they would not extend canonical status to their writings. They wanted to be sure accepted books were as close to Jesus as possible.

> The apostles all drew their doctrine in common from personal contact with the divine-human history of the crucified and risen Saviour, and from the inward illumination of the Holy Spirit, revealing the person and the work of Christ in them, and opening to them the understanding of his words and acts. This divine enlightenment is inspiration, governing not only the composition of the sacred writings, but also the oral instructions of their authors; not merely an act, but a permanent state. The apostles lived and moved continually in the element of truth. They spoke, wrote, and acted from the spirit of truth (Schaff; 7315-7319).

Given this standard, any book to be accepted into the NT canon had to have been written in the first century A.D. Jesus' death and resurrection occurred in 30 A.D., so by seventy years after that, anyone who was old enough during Jesus' ministry to have heard and understood His teachings personally would have passed away.

Moreover, for books to be accepted as being canonical they had to be well-known throughout the churches. This is important as it prevented locally produced forgeries from being accepted. And once the first few books had been accepted, any additional books had to conform to those books. This standard maintained a consistency of teachings and doctrines in the early Church.

And finally, the books would have to bear the mark of being inspired. This is subjective, but as I mentioned in Volume One, translating the OT books was a very spiritually and emotionally uplifting experience. However, while working on the OT Apocryphal/ Deuterocanonical Books and reading the OT pseudepigraphical books I never felt so uplifted. The early Christians probably also had this experience and thus could apply it to their developing canon.

Using these standards, by the early to mid-second century, 20 of the 27 books in the traditional NT canon were universally accepted: the four Gospels, the Book of Acts, the 13 epistles of Paul, 1Peter, and 1John. These books were called *homologoumena*, which means "spoken the same" indicating the Church as a whole "spoke" the same positive opinion of them as being authentic and being included in the canon.

The other seven books were disputed. They were: Hebrews, James, 2Peter, 2John, 3John, Jude, and The Revelation. These books were called *antilegomena*, which means "spoken against" indicating some in the Church spoke against their authenticity and inclusion in the canon. But these seven books were accepted by the middle of the third century for reasons that will be discussed in this book.

It was Thus, not a council but the universal acceptance of the churches that determined the canon, but a later council confirmed this list. There were other books that were considered but were eventually rejected based on these standards.

I learned the preceding points when I attended Denver Seminary back in 1988-90. They are verified in the following quote by Allen D. Callahan, Associate Professor of New Testament, Harvard Divinity School:

> Sometimes when the New Testament scholarship discusses the matter of canon formation, the story implied is that there are some smoke filled rooms somewhere in the 2nd century and a bunch of these cigar smoking Christian big shots got together, and they decided who was going in and who was going out and then... it was a wrap, they closed up and then everything else was on the cutting room floor.... I think precisely the contrary is closer to a more responsible historical reconstruction, and that is that there's some kind of consensus among people in the Jesus movement as to what constitutes reliable tradition, reliable literature -- literature that they want to read or they want to hear over and over again, and other kinds of literature that they don't want to hear... That was a development... from the bottom up, as opposed to from the top down (PBS; ellipses in original).

Moreover, Church historian Philip Schaff writes:
> Hence seven and twenty books by apostles and apostolic men, written under the special influence and direction of the Holy Spirit. These afford us a truthful picture of the history, the

Translator's Perspective on the Canon of the NT

faiths, and the practice of primitive Christianity, "for teaching, for reproof, for correction, for instruction in righteousness." [see 2Tim 3:16]

The collection of these writings into a canon, in distinction both from apocryphal or pseudo-apostolic works, and from orthodox yet merely human productions, was the work of the early church; and in performing it she was likewise guided by the Spirit of God and by a sound sense of truth.

It was not finished to the satisfaction of all till the end of the fourth century, down to which time seven New Testament books (the "Antilegomena" of Eusebius), the second Epistle of Peter, the second and third Epistles of John, the anonymous Epistle to the Hebrews, the Epistles of James and Jude, and in a certain sense also the Apocalypse of John [The Revelation], were by some considered of doubtful authorship or value.

But the collection was no doubt begun, on the model of the Old Testament canon, in the first century; and the principal books, the Gospels, the Acts, the thirteen Epistles of Paul, the first Epistle of Peter, and the first of John, in a body, were in general use after the middle of the second century, and were read, either entire or by sections, in public worship, after the manner of the Jewish synagogue, for the edification of the people (Schaff; 8104-8114).

Further evidence of these points is the Muratorian Fragment. It is:

> a late 2nd-century CE fragment of a Latin list of New Testament writings then regarded by Christians as canonical (scripturally authoritative). It was named for its discoverer, Lodovico Antonio Muratori, an Italian scholar who published the manuscript in 1740. The list mentions two of the four Gospels (Luke and John, in their traditional order), the Acts of the Apostles, the 13 letters attributed to the Apostle Paul, the Letter of Jude, two letters of John, the Wisdom of Solomon, and the apocalypses of John and of Peter. The Shepherd of Hermas was listed as a book for private devotions (Encyclopedia Britannica; "Muratorian Fragment").

I learned about this fragment at Denver Seminary. And it is just that—a fragment. Part of the text is missing, including the beginning. The extant portion begins with the mention of the Gospel of Luke. Given that the Gospels of Luke and of John are mentioned in the traditional order, it is very possible the Gospels of Matthew and of Mark were mentioned before this in the lost portion. Also the word "apocalypse" is another word for "revelation." Thus, the "apocalypse of John" would be a reference to The Revelation. As such, this fragment verifies that 23 of the 27 books were already accepted at that time.

As for the other books mentioned, the Wisdom of Solomon is one of the Roman Catholic deuterocanonical books and was discussed in Volume One, and the Shepherd of Hermas and the apocalypse of Peter will be addressed in Volume Three.

Further evidence comes from the Church Father Origin:

> Origen (185-254) mentions the four Gospels, the Acts, the thirteen Paulines, 1 Peter, 1 John, and Revelation as acknowledged by all; he says that Hebrews, 2 Peter, 2 and 3 John, James and Jude, with the 'Epistle of Barnabas,' the Shepherd of Hermas, the Didache, and the 'Gospel according to the Hebrews,' were disputed by some (Bruce, F.F., Chapter 3).

Thus, Origin gives 21 books among the *homologoumena*, adding The Revelation to my list of 20. But he mentions Jude and 2John as disputed, contrary to the Muratorian fragment, and he mentions four books that were not included and that will be discussed in Volume Three.

Moving a little later in Church history:

> Eusebius (c. 265-340) mentions as generally acknowledged all the books of our New Testament except James, Jude, 2 Peter, 2 and 3 John, which were disputed by some, but recognized by the majority. Athanasius in 367 lays down the twenty-seven books of our New Testament as alone canonical; shortly afterwards Jerome and Augustine followed his example in the West. The process farther east took a little longer; it was not until c. 508 that 2 Peter, 2 and 3 John, Jude and Revelation were included in a version of the Syriac Bible in addition to the other twenty two books (Bruce, F.F., Chapter 3).

Thus, Eusebius tells us five books were still disputed in his time, while by the time of Athanasius all doubts on these books had been resolved in the west, through this process took a little longer in the east. As such, there was a process for a few books, but for the most part, there was general agreement throughout early Church history on most of the books of the NT.

Translator's Perspective on the Canon of the NT
Creeds and Hymns Imbedded in the NT

Many early Christian creeds or hymns are embedded within the pages of NT books. The creedal or poetic nature of these passages is determined by the structure of them. In the case of creeds, they are worded as creeds are usually worded, while the hymns have a poetic character to them, and both have clearly identifiable lines or stanzas. The style of the Greek is also different from the rest of the book they are contained within. As a translator, I will say that in most of these cases, that difference is very obvious.

These creeds and hymns show core Christian beliefs were already written down and being memorized prior to the actual writing of the NT books. Since these creeds and hymns predate the writing of the NT, they were probably written within just a couple to a few years after the resurrection of Christ.

The importance of this for our topic is that in addition to being in accordance with the doctrines about God from the OT, any books to be accepted into the canon of the NT would need to also be in accordance with the doctrines contained in these creeds and hymns.

But before getting to the embedded creeds, so the reader knows what is meant by a "creed," the following is the Apostle's Creed:

1. I believe in God the Father, Almighty, Maker of heaven and earth.
2. And in Jesus Christ, His only begotten Son, our Lord:
3. Who was conceived by the Holy Spirit, born of the Virgin Mary;
4. Suffered under Pontius Pilate; was crucified, dead and buried: He descended into hell;
5. The third day He rose again from the dead;
6. He ascended into heaven, and sits at the right hand of God the Father Almighty;
7. From thence He shall come to judge the quick and the dead.
8. I believe in the Holy Spirit.
9. I believe in the holy catholic [universal] church; the communion of saints;
10. The forgiveness of sins;
11. The resurrection of the body;
12. And the life everlasting. Amen (Christian Classics).

Note that the Apostle's Creed most likely was not actually written by the apostles. It instead developed from questions asked of baptismal candidates starting in about 200 AD. Its current form is similar to baptismal creeds of the 3rd to 4th centuries.

> The bishop would ask, "Dost thou believe in God the Father almighty?" and so forth through the major Christian beliefs. Stated affirmatively, these statements became a creed.

This creed reached its current form by the 7th century (Encyclopedia Britannica). But as will be seen, this creed for the most part reflects doctrines that were believed very early in Church history. The reason it is being quoted here is to show the creedal form. It consists a series of short, pithy statements, with each line (or article) asserting a specific doctrine or tenet. This format will be seen in the embedded creedal lines to follow.

Matthew 16:15-16:

^{15}He [Jesus] says to them, "But who do you* say Me to be?" [or, that I am?"] ^{16}Then answering, Simon Peter said, "You are the Christ, the Son of the living God!"

The creedal line is Peter's answer in the second verse. Peter ascribes to Jesus the titles of "the Christ" and "the Son of God."

On the first title, the Greek word for Christ (*christos*) is equivalent to the Hebrew for Messiah (*meshiah*). As such, Peter is asserting with this title that Jesus is the Messiah, the Redeemer promised long ago, first in the Book of Genesis and then throughout the Hebrew Scriptures. It was acceptance of this claim of Jesus being the Messiah that separated the Christians from the other Jews then and still does down to this day.

On the second title, Peter declares Jesus is the Son of God. This is an earthshaking statement for a Jew to make. The OT God is one; He does not have equals. But a son is equal in essence to his father. Thus, with this title, Peter is declaring Jesus' equality with God the Father. It was this claim that would later get Jesus crucified (Luke 22:70), and this doctrine would also separate the early Christians from the other Jews of the time and down to this day.

> The germ of his [Peter's] doctrinal system is contained in his great confession that Jesus is the Messiah, the Son of the living God. A short creed indeed, with only one article, but a fundamental and all-comprehensive article, the corner-stone of the Christian church (Schaff; 7433-7435).

Translator's Perspective on the Canon of the NT

Note also that Peter asserts that God is "living." This is in accordance with the OT conception of God.

Luke 24:33,34:

^{33}And having gotten up that very hour, they returned to Jerusalem, and they found the eleven having been gathered together, and the [people] with them, ^{34}saying, "The Lord was indeed raised, and He was seen by Simon!"

The "they" are the two men to whom Jesus appeared on the road to Emmaus (verses 13-22), while "the eleven" refers to the apostles, minus Judas (who had already defected and committed suicide). The creedal statement in verse 34 is spoken by the eleven apostles and "the people with them." It Thus, represents a common saying that circulated among the early Christians. As such, very early the resurrection of Jesus is another fundamental doctrine of the early Christian movement.

Moreover, the reason for mentioning Simon specifically is that by appearing to him, someone who knew Jesus better than anyone, this demonstrated that it was in fact Jesus Himself in a form that could be easily identified as being Jesus, which is to say, in the same body He had when He was alive, who appeared to Peter. Jesus was not just a phantasm after His resurrection. He had been raised bodily from the dead. This belief was another cornerstone doctrine of the early Christian movement. Any and all writings to be accepted as canonical had to reflect this central doctrine.

Romans 1:3-4:

^{1}Paul, a bondservant of Jesus Christ, a called apostle, having been separated [or, appointed] to the Gospel [or, Good News] of God, ^{2}which He promised beforehand through His prophets in [the] Holy Scriptures, ^{3}concerning His Son, the One having come from [the] seed of David according to [the] flesh, ^{4}the [One] having been designated Son of God with power according to [the] Spirit of holiness, by [the] resurrection from [the] dead, Jesus Christ our Lord, ^{5}through whom we received grace and apostleship for obedience of faith among all the nations on behalf of His name, ^{6}among whom you* also are called of Jesus Christ (Rom 1:1-5).

The creed is most likely contained in verses 3-4. The other verses are quoted for context. And in these two verses is contained several important doctrines.

First, Jesus is a descendant of David. That is important as the OT prophesied the Messiah would come through David.

Second, His descent was "according to [the] flesh." This meant two things. One, that Jesus was a literal, physical descendant of David, while some false messiahs at the time claimed Davidic descent based solely on legal not biological grounds. Two, that Jesus was a real physical Person, not just a spirit or phantasm.

Third, Jesus is the "Son of God." The import of this title was already discussed.

Fourth, this designation was "with power according to [the] Spirit of holiness." Thus, the Holy Spirit is now mentioned, completing the early Christians conception that although one, in some way God was also three. As such, the conception of God's three-in-oneness was a part of the Christian faith from the start.

Fifth, once again we have mention of Jesus' "resurrection from the dead." Again, this doctrine is central to the early Christian movement.

Finally, Jesus is being called "Christ" and "Lord" very early in the Christian movement. These two titles carry great importance. The first was already addressed, but on the second, the Greek word *kurios* can be used of God and of human rulers. As such, the title does not necessarily indicate a claim for the deity of Christ, though it could. But at the very least it shows the early Christians were submitting themselves to the Lordship of Christ.

Romans 4:25:

[23]But it was not written on his [Abraham's] account alone, *"it was accounted to him,"* [24]but also on account of us, to whom it is about to be accounted [or, imputed], to the ones believing on [or, trusting in] the One having raised up Jesus our Lord from [the] dead, [25]who was handed over because of our transgressions and was raised up because of our justification [or, our [being] declared righteous] (Rom 4:25).

The creed is in verse 25. Here we see the early Christians' belief that there was a reason for Jesus' death beyond human politics and religion. It had a divine purpose. It was because of our transgressions and our justification. The former point was prophesied by Isaiah:

[5]But He was wounded because of our iniquities and was softened [fig., bruised] because of our sins; [the] discipline of our peace [was] upon Him, [and] by His wound[s] we were healed. [1Peter 2:24; cp., Rom 4:25; Heb 5:8; 9:28] [6]All we as sheep were led astray; [every] person was led astray in his [own] way, but the LORD gave Him up for our sins. [cp. 1Peter 2:25] (Isaiah 53:5-6).

Translator's Perspective on the Canon of the NT

As can be seen from the cross-references in the ALT, these verses are quoted or alluded to quite often in the NT, as they clearly prophesied the purpose of Jesus' death on the cross.

The second half of this creedal statement has confused many, but the idea is, Jesus' resurrection was because of God's acceptance of Jesus' sacrifice for our sins, to show to us that the sacrifice had been accepted. Thus, very early, a central belief of the Church was that Jesus' death was a sacrificial death and a fulfillment of OT prophecy and that His resurrection showed this sacrifice had been accepted by God the Father.

Romans 10:9:

⁸But what does it say? *"The word is near you, in your mouth and in your heart"* [Deut 30:14]—that is, the word of the faith which we are preaching, ⁹that if you confess with your mouth [the] Lord Jesus [or, [that] Jesus [is] Lord], and believe in your heart that God raised Him from [the] dead, you will be saved! [cp. 1Cor 12:3] ¹⁰For with the heart it is believed to righteousness, and with the mouth it is confessed to salvation (Rom 10:8-10).

The creed is in verse nine. The first clause demonstrates once again the early Christians' belief in the Lordship of Jesus. It also shows that confessing Jesus as your Lord is essential to salvation. The second clause shows once again the importance placed on the resurrection of Jesus, with belief in it as being essential for personal salvation.

1Corinthians 15:3-7:

¹Now I make known to you*, brothers [and sisters], the Gospel, which I myself proclaimed to you*, which also you* received, in which also you* have stood, ²through which also you* are saved, if you* hold fast to which word [or, that word which] I myself proclaimed to you*, unless you* believed thoughtlessly [or, without reason].

³For I handed down [or, delivered] to you* first what also I received, that Christ died on behalf of our sins according to the Scriptures ⁴and that He was buried and that He had been raised on the third day according to the Scriptures ⁵and that He appeared to Cephas [i.e., Peter], then to the twelve. ⁶Afterwards, He appeared to over five hundred brothers [and sisters] at once, of whom the greater part remain until now, but some also fell asleep [fig., have died]. ⁷Afterwards, He appeared to James, then to all the apostles.

⁸But last of all, as though to the [one] untimely born, He appeared also to me (1Cor 15:1-8).

Why Are These Books in the Bible? Volume Two

The creed is found in verses 3-7. The surrounding verses have been quoted for context. The stanzas would be:

1. Christ died on behalf of our sins according to the Scriptures
2. He was buried
3. He had been raised on the third day according to the Scriptures
4. He appeared to Cephas [i.e., Peter], then to the twelve
5. He appeared to over five hundred brothers [and sisters] at once
6. He appeared to James, then to all the apostles

Even if you do not accept the previously quoted passages as being creeds, there is no doubt about this one. This is definitely a creedal format. It clearly parallels the format seen in the Apostles' Creed, with lines 4-5 of the Apostle's Creed echoing the early creed Paul is quoting.

Moreover, the material is not original with Paul, as it contains non-Pauline elements. Namely, nowhere else does Paul specifically refer to the burial of Jesus, and nowhere else does he use the phrase "on the third day," despite the fact that these terms would fit into Paul's discussions on the death and resurrection of Jesus elsewhere.

Before looking at each stanza, it would be good consider the background to this creed. Paul begins by stating, "For I handed down to you* first what also I received." When did Paul "receive" this creed? To answer this question and for future discussions, we first must consider when Jesus died, then work from there.

> Pontius Pilate is known to have ruled Judea from AD 26–36. The crucifixion took place during a Passover (Mark 14:12), and that fact, plus astronomical data (the Jewish calendar was lunar-based), narrows the field to two dates—April 7, AD 30, and April 3, AD 33. There are scholarly arguments supporting both dates; the later date (AD 33) would require Jesus to have had a longer ministry and to have begun it later. The earlier date (AD 30) would seem more in keeping with what we deduce about the start of Jesus' ministry from Luke 3:1 (GotQuestions.org; "In what year did Jesus die?").

Either the 30 or 33 AD date is possible, but the earlier date is more probable and is the date that will be used in this book.

Note that Paul is also known as Saul (Acts 13:9). The former is probably his Greek name, while the latter is his Hebrew name.

Translator's Perspective on the Canon of the NT

In any case, Paul's conversion is recorded in Acts chapter 9. An exact date is not given, but it most likely occurred within three years of the death and resurrection of Jesus, Thus, at the latest in 33 AD. We are told that after his conversion, "immediately in the synagogues he began preaching the Christ, that this One is the Son of God" (Acts 9:20). Thus, from the start Saul/ Paul was proclaiming two creedal tenets already discussed. The Jews are outraged by this proclamation, so Saul/ Paul is forced to flee from Damascus:

[23]Now when many days were fulfilled [fig., after many days], the Jews plotted among themselves to execute him. [24]But their plot became known to Saul. And they were watching the gates closely both day and night, in order that they should execute him. [25]But the disciples having taken him by night, they let [him] down through [an opening in] the [city] wall, lowering [him] in a large basket (Acts 9:23-25).

Paul mentions this incident himself in 2Cor 11:32,33. Then Acts tells us:

[26]Then Saul, having arrived in Jerusalem, was attempting to be joined to the disciples, and they all were fearing him, not believing that he is a disciple. [27]But Barnabas having taken him, brought [him] to the apostles and described to them how on the road he saw the Lord and that He spoke to him, and how in Damascus he was speaking boldly in the name of Jesus. [28]And he was with them at Jerusalem (Acts 9:26-28a).

It is this meeting with the apostles that Paul is most likely referring to in Galatians:

[18]Then after three years I went up to Jerusalem to visit with Peter and stayed with him fifteen days. [19]But I did not see [any] other of the apostles, except James, the brother of the Lord (Gal 1:18f).

Thus, the "many days" of Acts 9:20 were actually "three years." But it is possible that it is three calendar years not three full years and thus closer to two actual years. We are thus at 36 AD at the latest. Paul does not meet with the other apostles again until fourteen years later (Gal 2:1). But that meeting concerned whether Gentiles needed to be circumcised (Gal 2:3). As such, Paul most likely "received" this creed during his first meeting with the apostles or by 36 AD, six years at the most after the death and resurrection of Jesus.

Moreover, Paul refers to this creed as being "the Gospel" (verse 1). That term is first applied to the Christian message in Acts 5:42, "And every day in the temple and in every house, they were not ceasing [from] teaching and proclaiming the Gospel [or, Good News] of Jesus the Christ."

The "they" is "the apostles" as can be seen from the earlier context of this chapter (verse 18 on). And this event occurred very early in the growth of the early Church. An exact date is not given, but it was probably less than a year after Jesus' resurrection. As such, what Paul gives us in 1Corinthians is the original Christian message which he received less than six years later. There was Thus, little time for this Gospel to have developed or changed. It contains the essentials of the Christian message from the start of the preaching of the apostles.

The first stanza we have seen before, "Christ died on behalf of our sins according to the Scriptures." That Christ died was an historical fact well-known to those living in Jerusalem at the time, so that is not a monumental statement, but its interpretation is—He died "on behalf of our sins." Jesus' death was very meaningful to the early Church. It was the fulfillment of prophecy in the OT Scriptures that the Messiah would die for our sins, as seen in the passage from Isaiah quoted previously and in other OT Scriptures, like Psalm 22. His sacrificial death was also seen as the fulfillment of the whole Jewish sacrificial system. This is monumental indeed.

The second stanza is also very important, thought it might not sound like it. "He was buried." The importance is, if Jesus was just left to rot on the cross, then His body could have been easily taken down and hidden. But it was buried in a known place, and guards were placed before the tomb (Matt 27:62-66). This leads to the empty tomb on Easter morning, as recorded in all four Gospels (Matt 28:6; Mark 16:6; Luke 24:6; John 20:1-8).

The third stanza then records the incredible event, "He had been raised on the third day according to the Scriptures." The Scriptures the apostles appealed to were Psalm 16:8-11, among others. Thus, the death, burial, and resurrection are all connected together as being historical events that were prophesied in the OT to occur.

The proof of the resurrection is then seen in the next three stanzas:

4. He appeared to Cephas [i.e., Peter], then to the twelve
5. He appeared to over five hundred brothers [and sisters] at once
6. He appeared to James, then to all the apostles

Translator's Perspective on the Canon of the NT

There were Thus, multiple eyewitnesses of the resurrected Christ, most of which were still alive when Paul wrote this epistle in 56 AD. That eyewitness testimony was also part of the early Christian creed, as it was proof of the incredible claim of the resurrection of Christ.

Paul's mention of Jesus' appearance to him was not part of this creed, as can be seen from the use of first person pronouns, but it does establish his authority as an apostle that will be important in later discussions.

Philippians 2:6-11:

⁵Indeed, be letting the frame of mind [or, attitude] be in you* which [was] also in Christ Jesus, ⁶who existing in the nature of God, did not consider being equal to God something to be held onto, ⁷but He emptied Himself, having taken the nature of a bondservant, having come to be in the likeness of people, ⁸and having been found in appearance as a person, He humbled Himself, having become obedient to the point of death—even of death of a cross. ⁹And so God highly exalted Him [or, put Him in the most important position] and gave to Him a Name, the [Name] above every name, ¹⁰so that at the Name of Jesus every knee shall bow, of heavenly [ones] and of earthly [ones] and of [ones] under the earth, ¹¹and every tongue [fig., person] shall confess that Jesus Christ [is] Lord to [the] glory of God [the] Father! [cp. Isaiah 45:23; Rom 10:9]

This passage could be a hymn rather than a creed. The first verse is not part of it but has been included for context. The first line of the hymn/ creed then declares Christ Jesus exited before His earthy life "in the nature of God." Thus, His deity is asserted. But He "humbled Himself" and took the nature of human beings. Thus, the full humanity of Jesus is asserted. This part might not sound important today, but it was at the time, as will be seen later.

Then once again His death on the cross is asserted. But now we see a reference to something we haven't seen before, "God highly exalted Him." This would be a reference to His ascension and His sitting at the right hand of God, as the Apostle's Creed would later assert.

Then very powerfully, the creed asserts that every knee will bow to Him and declare Him Lord. This is powerful as it is taken from Isaiah 45:23, which is a reference to God. As such, the creed asserts Jesus receives the same worship as God the Father.

Thus, in this creed or possibly hymn we see asserted the full deity and full humanity of Jesus, His death, and His ascension. This means none of these points are later developments but were very early, being incorporated into an early creed or hymn of the Church, which is now being repeated by Paul.

Colossians 1:15; 2:9:
who is [the] image of the invisible God
in Him dwells all the fullness of the Godhead [or, Deity] bodily

These two lines could be from a hymn or creed, and together they assert the full deity and full humanity of Jesus.

1Timothy 2:5f:
⁵For [there is] one God and one Mediator [between] God and people, a Person, Christ Jesus, ⁶the One having given Himself [as] a ransom on behalf of all, the testimony in its own times.

Here we have a new doctrine introduced, that of Christ being a Mediator between God and people. This concept is elaborated at length in the Book of Hebrews, but here it is asserted in creedal format. Then we have asserted another element of importance of Jesus' death—it was as a ransom. This idea might be alien to us today, but in Biblical times it was not. A ransom was paid by a close relative to redeem a person who was in debt or to redeem a slave to freedom. Both ideas would apply to the work of Christ. We owed a debt to God for our sins, which we could not pay, but Christ paid that debt with His death, Thus, freeing us from our slavery to sin.

1Timothy 3:16:
¹⁶And confessedly, great is the secret [or, mystery] of godliness:

God was revealed in [the] flesh, justified [or, shown to be righteous] in spirit [or, by [the] Spirit], seen by angels [or, messengers [of the Lord]], preached among [the] nations [or, Gentiles], believed on in [the] world, taken up in glory!

This is another passage about which there is little doubt it predates the epistle it is contained in, as it is clearly hymnal in form. That is why most Bible versions format this verse in the same manner as they do poetry, such as the Psalms. I did not do so for the first edition of the ALT, but later I did so as it is clear this passage is poetic in nature. As the footnote in the NET Bible states, "This passage has been typeset as poetry because many scholars regard this passage as poetic or hymnic."
The hymn begins with the word "God" in the indented part of the passage, but it with this word that there is some controversy as there is a textual variant here. Some manuscripts have "who" rather than "God."

Translator's Perspective on the Canon of the NT

If "God" is original, then the early Church would be singing "God was revealed in [the] flesh" Thus, asserting the deity and humanity of Jesus. If "who" is original, then only Jesus' full humanity is being sung about, but even that is important, as will be addressed later. Also, if "who" is original it lends further credence to this passage being quoted from a hymn, as "who" makes no sense in this context, indicating the writer quoted verbatim from the hymn without changing it to fit the context. But most versions based on a Greek text with "who" change it to "He" as the context would require.

The next line is difficult both in its translation and interpretation. But this again shows this passage is being quoted and was not originally written by Paul, as the rest of 1Timothy is not so difficult. Jesus was "justified." This word in Scripture generally means to be declared righteous by God forgiving us of our sins, such as in Romans 3:24, "being justified [or, declared righteous] freely by His grace through the redemption [or, setting free], the [one] in Christ Jesus." But here, it more probably has the meaning of "shown to be righteous" as Jesus did not have sins He needed to be forgiven of (2Cor 5:1).

The next phrase could be "in spirit" indicating Jesus was shown to be righteous in His spirit, or it could mean He was shown to be righteous by the Holy Spirit. If the former, it shows Jesus was wholly righteous, if the latter, then we have an attestation to the triune Nature of the one true God in this very early Christian hymn.

The import of the next phrase, "seen by angels," is hard to determine, but it possibly shows Jesus was considered important not just by human beings by also by angelic beings.

The next phrase is historical in nature, "believed on in [the] world." This is a reference to Jesus' earthly ministry and the many who believed in Him at that time. The last phrase, "taken up in glory" is a reference to His ascension and thus the end of His earthly ministry.

Overall, this is a doctrinally filled passage, with some hard to understand assertions, but it shows the early Christians did not shy away from doctrine nor even from hard doctrines, but actually sung about them. How unlike this is with so many Christians today, who have little concern for doctrine and who sing hymns that are emotional rather than doctrinal in nature.

But for our purposes, there are several clear assertions in this passage: Jesus was fully human and (depending on the text) fully God. He was righteous, He was known and believed in by both angels and people, and He ascended in glory.

1Timothy 6:13-16:

[13]I am giving strict orders to you before God, the One giving life to all [things], and [before] Christ Jesus, the One having testified before Pontius Pilate the good confession, [14][for] you to keep the commandment spotless [and] blameless [or, above reproach] until the Appearing of our Lord Jesus Christ, [15]which in His own times [or, at the proper time], He will reveal, the blessed and only Sovereign, the King of the ones reigning as kings and Lord of the ones exercising lordship, [16]the only One having immortality, dwelling in unapproachable light, whom no one of people saw nor is able to see, to whom [is] honor and eternal might [or, dominion]! So be it!

The creedal nature of this passage is not so clear, but Paul seems to have incorporated various creedal lines into this discourse.

First is the line, "God, the One giving life to all [things]." This is a clear reference to an attribute of God taken over from Judaism: God is the Creator and Life-giver.

Second, "Christ Jesus, the One having testified before Pontius Pilate the good confession." The mention of Pilate here is probably why the Apostle's Creed would later mention Pilate as well. The importance of mentioning Pilate is to demonstrate Jesus' trial and resulting crucifixion were historical events, not mere legend or myth.

Third, "until the Appearing of our Lord Jesus Christ," would be a reference to the Second Coming of Christ. This doctrine has not been seen in these creeds before, but it is so important that it would also be included in the Apostle's Creed.

Fourth, the creed proclaims several attributes of God: His sovereignty, kingship, lordship, immortality, and incorporeality. These attributes are all taken from the Jewish conception of God. Thus, we see clearly how Christianity follows Judaism in its conception of the nature of God.

2Timothy 2:8,11-13:

[8]Be remembering Jesus Christ having been raised from [the] dead, of [the] seed of David, according to my Gospel, …

[11]Trustworthy [is] the word: For if we died with [Him], we will also live with [Him]. [12]If we endure, we will also reign with [Him]; if we deny [or, disown] [Him], that One will also deny us. [13]If we are unfaithful, that One remains faithful; He is not able to deny Himself.

The first verse is similar to the preceding passage in which creedal elements have been incorporated into a wider context. The possible creedal line is, "Jesus Christ having been raised from [the] dead, of [the]

Translator's Perspective on the Canon of the NT

seed of David." Both of these assertions have been seen before. Jesus was raised from the dead and was biologically the descendant of David.

But the next paragraph has a clear hymnic form to it and thus is formatted as such in many versions, "The following passage has been typeset as poetry because many scholars regard this passage as poetic or hymnic" (NET Bible).

This poem or hymn first asserts that we must "die with Christ" so that we can "live with Him." Paul elaborates on this idea in Galatians 2:20:

[20]I have been crucified with Christ, but no longer do I live, but Christ lives in me! But [that] which I now live in [the] flesh, I live by faith in the Son of God, the One having loved me and having given Himself [or, having handed Himself over] for me.

The idea here is of giving up your life to the control of the Lord. This attitude has proven effective in dealing with addictions, but it is in fact a good attitude for all of us to have as it will enable us to forge through life's difficulties in whatever from they might come. This means the early Church was not only doctrinal in creeds and hymns but also practical.

The next phrase is "if we deny [or, disown] [Him], that One will also deny us." This echoes Jesus's own words, "But whoever denies [or, disowns] Me before the people, I also will deny him before My Father, the [One] in the heavens" (Matt 10:33). Thus, it is clear these words of Jesus were well-known in the early Church. This point will be important later.

The final line declares God is more reliable than we are, "If we are unfaithful, that One remains faithful; He is not able to deny Himself." This again shows the high view of the nature of God that was taken over from Judaism.

In sum, these creedal and/ or hymnal lines assert Jesus' resurrection and descent from David, along with our need to give ourselves over to God and not to deny Him, as He is much more reliable than we are.

Jude 1:20f:

[20]But you*, beloved, building yourselves up in your* most holy faith, praying in [the] Holy Spirit, [21]keep yourselves in [the] love of God, waiting for [or, expecting] the mercy of our Lord Jesus Christ to eternal life.

Jude is one of the later books of the NT, so this one would not be as early as the preceding ones. But the style of Greek of these verses differs from the rest of Jude, so it is apparent Jude is quoting from an earlier source. But in this case, rather than being a creed or hymn, it was probably a benediction that was commonly said in early church services. The important lines are:

1. Praying in the Holy Spirit.
2. The Love of God.
3. The mercy of our Lord Jesus Christ.

This means the early Christians were reciting in church services a three-fold formula associating God the Father, Jesus Christ, and the Holy Spirit together. As such, very early there was a concept of a triune nature to the one true God.

Conclusion on Imbedded Creeds and Hymns:

Taken together, these creeds and hymns assert:

1. Jesus existed before His earthy life.
2. Jesus is fully human.
3. Jesus is the Son of God.
4. Jesus is fully God and worthy of worship.
5. Jesus died on the cross.
6. Jesus's death was a sacrifice for our sins.
7. Jesus redeemed and ransomed us from our sins.
8. Jesus was buried.
9. Jesus was raised from the dead.
10. Jesus was seen by many, including Simon Peter and the rest of the apostles, after His resurrection.
11. Jesus' death, burial, and resurrection were foretold in the OT Scriptures.
12. Jesus ascended in glory.
13. Jesus is Lord.
14. Jesus is the Christ.
15. Jesus is the Mediator between people and God the Father.
16. Jesus will come again.
17. Through Christ, we can deal with difficulties in life.
18. God the Father, Jesus Christ, and the Holy Spirit are associated together.
19. The nature God is as asserted in the OT.

The importance of all of this is that for any book to be included in the canon of the NT it would have to be in accordance with these basic tenets of the early Church. That does not mean every document had to

Translator's Perspective on the Canon of the NT

assert each of these tenets, but it does mean any document that in any way contradicted any of these points would be rejected on that basis alone.

Now some might deny the creedal or hymnal nature of some of these passages, but for three there is little doubt: 1Corinthians 15:3-7; 1Timothy 3:16; and 2Timothy 2:11-13. The dating of the last two creeds is hard to determine, but the former was shown to have its origins shortly after the birth of the Church. Thus, if you take just the tenets of these three passages or even of just 1Corinthians 15:3-7, that still gives us a several doctrines by which to test any book to be considered for inclusion into the NT canon.

Baptism and the Lord's Supper

From the beginning of the Christian movement, all Christians have participated in two ceremonies (also called ordinances or sacraments). These are baptism and the Lord's Supper (also called communion or the Eucharist, from the Greek word *eucharistia*, "thanksgiving" – e.g., 2Cor 9:11f). Both of these ceremonies have their roots in Judaism, but they were infused with new meaning by Christians.

Baptism:

That Jews engaged in baptism can be seen in the baptisms by John the Baptist before Jesus started His ministry:

¹Now in those days [ca. 26 AD] John the Baptist [or, the Immerser] arrives, proclaiming in the wilderness of Judea ²and saying, "Be repenting, for the kingdom of the heavens has drawn near!" …
⁵Then Jerusalem and all Judea and all the surrounding region of the Jordan [River] were going out to him, ⁶and they were being baptized [or, immersed, Gr., *baptizo*] in the Jordan [River] by him, confessing their sins (Matt 3:1,5f).

These baptisms Thus, represented the repentance of the people being baptized. John the Baptist then explains further the purpose of his baptisms:

¹¹"I indeed baptize you* in water [or, with water] to [or, because of] repentance. But the One coming after me is mightier [than] I, of whom I am not worthy to carry His sandals, He will baptize you* in [or, with] [the] Holy Spirit" (Matt 3:11).

Thus, John recognized his baptisms were looking forward to the greater baptism to be performed by Jesus, that of baptizing in the Holy Spirit. But that would be later. First, Jesus's disciples also baptized by water:

²²After these things Jesus and His disciples came into the land of Judea, and there He was staying with them and was baptizing....
¹So when the Lord knew that the Pharisees heard that Jesus is making and baptizing more disciples than John ²(although Jesus Himself was not baptizing, but His disciples), ³He left Judea and went away into Galilee (John 3:22; 4:1-3).

The baptism in the Holy Spirit would come on the day of Pentecost:

⁴And being assembled together, He gave strict orders to them [the apostles] not to be departing from Jerusalem, but to be waiting for the promise of the Father, "Which," [He said,] "You heard from Me; [Luke 24:49] ⁵because John indeed baptized [or, immersed] in [or, with] water, but you* will be baptized in [or, with] [the] Holy Spirit after not many [of] these days [fig., in a few days]." ...
¹And when the Day of Pentecost [had] come [ca. 30 AD], they were all with one mind at the same [place]. ²And suddenly [there] came from heaven a sound like a violent rushing wind, and it filled the whole house where they were sitting! ³And [there] appeared to them tongues as of fire distributing themselves, and [one] sat on each one of them. ⁴And they were all filled of [or, with] [the] Holy Spirit, and they began to be speaking with different tongues [fig., foreign languages], just as the Spirit was giving them to be declaring boldly! (Acts 1:4f; 2:1-4).

After this baptism in the Holy Spirit, Peter preached a sermon to the multitude who had gathered due to commotion. As a result, "the ones having gladly received his word were baptized, and about three thousand souls were added on that day!" (Acts 2:41). Thus, the apostles continued the practice of baptizing converts in water. They continue to do so throughout the first decades of the Apostolic Church (Acts 8:12,38; 9:18; 10:48; 16:15,33; 18:8; 19:5).

This baptism would carry over the idea of representing the repentance of the one being baptized, but it would also represent the reception of the Holy Spirit. Paul would later indicate that it had additional new meanings:

³Or do you* fail to understand that we, as many as were baptized [or, immersed] into Christ Jesus, were baptized into His death?

43

Translator's Perspective on the Canon of the NT

⁴Therefore, we were buried together with Him through the baptism [or, immersion] into death, so that even as Christ was raised up from [the] dead through the glory of the Father, so also we should walk about [fig., conduct ourselves] in newness of life (Roman 6:3f).

¹²For just as the body is one and has many body parts, but all the body parts of the one body, being many, are one body, in the same manner also [is] Christ. ¹³For also by one Spirit we all were baptized into one body, whether Jews or Greeks, whether bondservants or free persons, and we were all given to drink into one Spirit. [cp. Eph 4:1-7] (1Cor 12:12f).

²⁶For you* are all sons [and daughters] of God by means of faith in Christ Jesus. ²⁷For as many as were baptized [or, immersed] into Christ put on [or, clothed themselves with] Christ. ²⁸There is not Jew nor Greek, there is not bondservant nor free, there is not male and female, for you* are all one in Christ Jesus. [cp. Col 3:11] (Gal 3:26f).

³making every effort to be keeping the unity of the Spirit in the bond of peace: ⁴one body and one Spirit, just as also you* were called in one hope [or, confident expectation] of your* calling; ⁵one Lord, one faith, one baptism [or, immersion], [cp. 1Cor 12:13] ⁶one God and Father of all, who [is] over all and through all and in us all. (Eph 4:3-6).

¹²having been buried together with Him in baptism [or, immersion], in which you* also were raised together [with Him] through faith in the supernatural working of God, the One having raised Him from the dead (Col 2:12).

Peter mentions baptism in his first epistle:

²⁰having formerly refused to believe, when the patience of God kept eagerly waiting in [the] days of Noah, while an ark was being prepared, in which a few, that is, eight souls, were saved through water; ²¹which [as] an antitype baptism [or, immersion] now also saves us (not [the] removal of [the] filth of [the] flesh, but an appeal to God for [or, a pledge to God from] a good conscience) through [the] resurrection of Jesus Christ (1Pet 4:20f).

Putting all of this together, water baptism was performed on new converts in the Apostolic Church. It represented repentance and forgiveness of sins, the reception of or baptism in the Holy Spirit, the death, burial, and resurrection of Jesus, converts dying to their old selves and rising to a newness of life, salvation, and the unity of the early Christians regardless of social status. This unity was based on common essential beliefs, including the belief in "one God and Father of all."

The Lord's Supper:

The Lord's Supper was a carryover from the Jewish Passover. That ceremony had been established by Moses right before the Exodus in 1446 BC. Exodus 12 describes the procedure of and purpose for the Passover.

'On the tenth of this month let them take each one a lamb [lit., sheep, but see verse 5] according to the houses of their fathers, each one a lamb for his household....
5'It will be to you* a lamb unblemished, a male of a year old; you* will take it of the lambs and the young goats. 6And it will be kept by you* until the fourteenth of this month, and all the multitude of [the] congregation of the sons [and daughters] of Israel will slaughter it toward evening. 7And they will take from the blood and will put it on the two doorposts and on the lintel [i.e., the horizontal beam above the door] in the houses in which they shall eat them in them. 8And they shall eat the meat in this night roasted with fire, and they will eat unleavened [bread] with bitter herbs....
12'And I will go throughout in [the] land of Egypt in that night, and I will strike every firstborn in [the] land of Egypt from humanity until animal, and on all the gods of Egypt will I execute vengeance. I [am] the LORD. 13And the blood will be for a sign to you* upon the houses in which you* are there, and I will see the blood and will protect [Heb., pass over] you*, and there will not be on you* [the] plague of utter destruction when I strike in [the] land of Egypt (Exodus 12:3b,5-7,12f).

Thus, the Passover involved the blood of a lamb, and it was so that the LORD would pass over the houses of the ones who by faith in the command placed the blood on the lintels of their doors.

Jesus was celebrating the Passover with His disciples when He instituted the Lord's Supper. But He infused it with new meaning:

26Now while they were eating, Jesus having taken the bread and having given thanks, broke [it] and began giving [it] to the disciples. And He said, "Take, eat; this is My body." 27And having taken the cup and having given thanks, He gave [it] to them, saying, "Drink from it, all [of you], 28for this is My blood, the [blood] of the New Covenant, the [blood] poured out on behalf of many for forgiveness of sins (Matt 26:26f).

Translator's Perspective on the Canon of the NT

[19]And having taken bread, having given thanks, He broke [it] and gave [it] to them, saying, "This is My body, the [one] being given on your* behalf; be doing this in remembrance of Me." [20]And in the same manner [He took] the cup after [they] ate, saying, "This cup [is] the New Covenant in My blood, the [blood] being poured out on your* behalf (Luke 22:19f).

Thus, rather than a lamb being killed and its blood causing God to pass over our sins, the bread of the Passover would now represent Jesus' body to be given for us, and the wine would now represent Jesus' blood shed for the forgiveness of our sins. This symbolism is seen when John the Baptist declares about Jesus, "Look! The Lamb of God, the One taking away the sin of the world!" (John 1:29b). Thus, Jesus is now the Lamb, and it is by His shed blood that God will pass over our sins.

The disciples recognized this ceremony should be practiced in the churches, "[2]Now they were continuing in the teaching of the apostles and in fellowship, and in the breaking of the bread and in prayers" (Acts 2:42). And Paul indicates it was being practiced in Corinth almost 30 years later, though with some problems in the Corinthians practice of it (1Cor 11:20). In correcting their malpractice, Paul would elaborate on what the Lord's Supper represented:

[23]For I received from the Lord what I also handed down to you*, that the Lord Jesus in the night in which He was betrayed took bread, [24]and having given thanks, He broke [it] and said, "Take, eat; this is My body, the [one] being broken on behalf of you*. Be doing this in remembrance of Me." [25]And in the same manner [He took] the cup after [they] ate, saying, "This cup is the New Covenant in My blood. Be doing this, as often as you* drink [it], in remembrance of Me." [26]For as often as you* shall be eating this bread and drinking this cup, you* proclaim the death of the Lord, until He comes (1Cor 11:23-26).

Thus, Paul records Jesus as saying at the Last Supper that the bread represented His body being broken on our behalf and the wine His blood. Paul adds that Christians will engage in this ceremony "often" and that by doing so, we proclaim Jesus' death until He comes. The latter would be a reference to His Second Coming.

Putting all of this together, the Lord's Supper was participated in regularly in the Apostolic Church by all Christians. It represented the passing over of sins by God. This would be due to Jesus's body being broken for us, and His shed blood being the means of forgiveness of sins. This establishes a New Covenant. Christians are to engage in this ceremony until the Second Coming. Also, implied in Jesus' body being broken is that He had a real physical body.

The mention of the New Covenant requires a bit of explanation. The Jewish apostles would recognize this as a reference to Jeremiah 31:31-34:

> [31]"Behold, [the] days are coming," says the LORD, "and I will make a New Covenant with the house of Israel and with the house of Judah, [32]not according to the covenant which I made with their fathers in [the] day of My having taken hold of their hand to bring them out of [the] land of Egypt, for they did not remain in [or, carefully obey] My covenant, and I disregarded them," says the LORD. [33]"For this [is] the covenant which I will make with the house of Israel; after those days," says the LORD, "putting, I will put [fig., I will surely put] My laws into their mind and write them on their hearts, and I will be to them for God, and they will be to Me for a people. [34]And by no means shall they teach each his fellow-citizen and each his brother, saying, 'Know the LORD!' for all will know Me, from [the] least [one] of them and as far as [the] great [one] of them, for I will be merciful to their iniquities, and by no means shall I be reminded of their sins any longer."

The point of this passage is the Old Covenant was external. It consisted of written laws given by God to Israel, such as the Ten Commandments. A person had to read these laws to know for instance that adultery was wrong (Exod 20:17). But with the New Covenant, a person is changed from the inside out, so he or she does not need to read "You will not commit adultery" to know adultery is wrong. Their own conscious will tell them it is. Similarly, a person will not need to be taught what God is like; he or she will know God personally and come to know Him through a personal relationship with Him.

What Jesus is saying at the Last Supper is by trusting in His shed blood on the cross for forgiveness of sins, a person will experience this inner transformation and enter into a personal relationship with God through Him.

Summary of Ceremonial Tenets:

Between these two ceremonies, both of which were engaged in from the very start of the Christian movement and have continued throughout its history, the following tenets are affirmed:

1. The possibility of repentance and the forgiveness or passing over of sins.
2. The death of Jesus for our sins.

Translator's Perspective on the Canon of the NT

3. Jesus' broken body and shed blood being the means of forgiveness.
4. The reality of Jesus' physical body.
5. The burial of Jesus.
6. The resurrection of Jesus.
7. The importance of the Holy Spirit in the lives of believers.
8. The renewal of life in a convert.
9. This renewal establishes a New Covenant between God and people, transforming people from within and bringing them into a personal relationship with God.
10. Unity of believers based on essential beliefs.
11. The Second Coming.

There is overlap here, especially between numbers 7-9. The renewal of a believer comes about via the Holy Spirit, establishing the New Covenant between the believer and God. But each part is important and thus worth listing separately. And these tenets show there was a "practical" aspect to the tenets of the Apostolic Church, as an outgrowth of the doctrinal tenets.

The Essential Tenets

The tenets represented by the early Christian ceremonies parallel or elaborate on the tenets seen in the early creeds and hymns. Thus, by two lines of evidence, there were a collection of essential tenets from the very start of the Christian movement. Below is a combined list of all these essential tenets.

1. Jesus existed before His earthy life.
2. Jesus is fully human with a real physical body.
3. Jesus is the Son of God.
4. Jesus is fully God and worthy of worship.
5. The possibly of repentance and the forgiveness or passing over of sins.
6. Jesus died on the cross.
7. Jesus's death was a sacrifice for our sins.
8. Jesus redeemed and ransomed us from our sins.
9. Jesus was buried.
10. Jesus was raised bodily from the dead.
11. Jesus was seen by many after His resurrection.
12. Jesus' death, burial, and resurrection were foretold in the OT Scriptures.

13. Jesus ascended to heaven in glory.
14. Jesus is Lord.
15. Jesus is the Christ.
16. Jesus is the Mediator between people and God the Father.
17. Jesus will come again (a.k.a. the Second Coming).
18. Through Christ, we can deal with difficulties in life.
19. Through Christ, we can have renewal of life.
20. This renewal establishes a New Covenant between God and people.
21. The importance of the Holy Spirit in believer's lives.
22. God the Father, Jesus Christ, and the Holy Spirit are associated together.
23. Unity of believers based on essential beliefs.
24. The conception of God and of nature as asserted in the OT.

These two dozen tenets defined what it meant to be a first century Christian. And these tenets would have to be represented in any books to be considered for inclusion in the NT. Again, this does not mean a book had to affirm every one of these tenets, but it does mean it could not contain anything contradictory to them.

Summary on Standards

Any book to be accepted into the NT canon would have to fit the following standards:

1. Be based on the OT conception of God and of His creation.
2. Be in accordance with the doctrines of the OT in general.
3. Be written in Greek.
4. Be written by an apostle or a direct associate of an apostle.
5. Be written in the first century.
6. Be well-known throughout the churches.
7. Bear the mark of inspiration.
8. Be in accordance with the essential tenets of the early Church.

The last point would include at the bare minimum:

1. Jesus died for our sins.
2. Jesus was buried.
3. Jesus was bodily raised from the dead.

Translator's Perspective on the Canon of the NT

In the following chapters we will apply these standards to the books contained in the NT. These 27 books will be grouped differently than the traditional groupings for reasons that should be clear as we proceed.

Chapter Two
Overview of the Four Gospels and the Book of Acts

The first New Testament (NT) books to be studied are the first three books, The Gospel According to Matthew, The Gospel According to Mark, and The Gospel According to Luke. These are called the Synoptic Gospels as they, "tell the story of Jesus Christ's life and ministry from a similar point of view and are similar in structure" (*Encarta*). The Book of Acts will also be included in this chapter, as it was written by the same author as The Gospel According to Luke.

Note that the "The Gospel According to ..." is the full and proper title of these books, though "Gospel of ..." is often used. The word "Gospel" in this context means "the record of Jesus' life and teaching" (Oxford). Thus, these books are about Jesus, not about Matthew, Mark, or Luke, as the title "Gospel of ..." might seem to indicate. For short, all three books are often referred to by just their traditional authors of Matthew, Mark, and Luke. Similarly, the full title of the Book of Acts is "The Book of the Acts of the Apostles," though just "Acts" is often used. Before studying these books, we will consider a radical claim.

Historicity of Jesus

The claim is sometimes made that Jesus never existed. This claim is generally made by laypeople, but almost never by qualified historians. Part of the reason for the latter is there is evidence for the existence and many aspects of the life of Jesus from eighteen non-Christian sources which date to within a century of the life of Jesus. A century might sound like a long time to the layman, but in reality the sources for most events and persons from antiquity generally date to centuries after the fact.

In any case, following is a summary of what can be know about Jesus from Jewish, Grecian, and Roman sources, with representative source(s) in parentheses, along with the corresponding NT reference.

1) He lived during the reign of Tiberius Caesar (Tacitus; Luke 3:1,23).

2) He preached a high, ethical code of conduct (Josephus; Matt 5:21-48).

Translator's Perspective on the Canon of the NT

3) Jewish leaders said He "practiced sorcery," an indirect reference to His miracles (Talmud; Matt 12:22-24).

4) He was crucified during the Jewish Passover (Talmud; Matt 26:2).

5) He was crucified under Pontius Pilate (Tacitus, Josephus; Matt 27:1-26).

6) Darkness covered the land during His crucifixion (Thallus, Phlegon; Matt 27:45).

7) His followers worshipped Him (Lucian, Roman graffiti; Matt 28:17).

8) Shortly after His death, His disciples said He was alive (Josephus; Acts 2:22-32).

9) He was referred to as "Christ" (Tacitus, Josephus; Acts 2:36).

10) His disciples were persecuted for their preaching (Tacitus, Suetonius, Pliny the Younger; Acts 5:40-42).

11) His followers were called "Christians" (Tacitus, Josephus; Acts 11:26).

12) He had followers in Rome within 30 years of His death (Tacitus; Acts 28:16-31).

A full discussion of this issue and these sources would require an entire book in itself. In fact, it was reading just such a book that first made this writer aware of this information. The book was *Ancient Evidence for the Life of Jesus*, by Gary Habermas. That book has been issued in a new edition and is now titled, *The Verdict of History: Conclusive Evidence for the Life of Jesus*.

Habermas has several newer books that present such information: *The Case for the Resurrection of Jesus*, *The Historical Jesus: Ancient Evidence for the Life of Christ*, and *Did the Resurrection Happen?: A Conversation with Gary Habermas and Antony Flew*. The latter is a debate with an atheist. Habermas has also appeared on the John Ankerberg TV show on several occasions. Audio replays of this TV show are available on Ankerberg's website (JAShow.org) and on his smart phone app. One such appearance of Habermas was in a series titled "Evidence for the Historical Jesus."

The reader is referred to these various sources for a full discussion on this matter. But here, a few salient quotes will be presented. Unless otherwise indicated, these are taken from the first book by Habermas, but can be found in his other books as well.

Roman historian Tacitus (AD 55-117) writes, "... Christ had been executed in Tiberius' reign by the governor of Judea, Pontius Pilate."

Josephus was a Jewish historian who lived from 37-100 AD. He mentions Jesus' crucifixion in his *Antiquities of the Jews*, Book 18, Chapter 3, 3. This passage has been hotly contested, as some believe early Christians altered the passage. This belief has arisen because the passage appears "too Christian" for a Jew to have written it. However, an Arabic manuscript omits the questionable passages while retaining the phrase, "Pilate condemned him to be crucified and to die."

The Jewish Talmud (70-200 AD) records, "On the eve of the Passover, Yeshu (Hebrew for Jesus) was hanged." The word "hanged" is used in the NT to describe crucifixion, so there is no contradiction (Luke 23:39; Gal 3:13).

Lucian, a second century Greek satirist, writes about the early Christians that they, "...worship the crucified sage." This idea is reiterated in satirical Roman graffiti dating from the late first to early second century. It depicters a donkey nailed to a cross. Underneath in Latin is written, "The Christian god."

As for the darkness during Jesus' crucifixion:

> Thallus wrote a history of the eastern Mediterranean world since the Trojan War. Thallus wrote his regional history in about AD 52. Although his original writings have been lost, he is specifically quoted by Julius Africanus, a renowned third century historian. Africanus states, 'Thallus, in the third book of his histories, explains away the darkness as an eclipse of the sun—unreasonably as it seems to me.' ...

Phlegon was a Greek historian who wrote an extensive chronology around AD 137:

> In the fourth year of the 202nd Olympiad (i.e., AD 33) there was 'the greatest eclipse of the sun' and that 'it became night in the sixth hour of the day [i.e., noon] so that stars even appeared in the heavens. There was a great earthquake in Bithynia, and many things were overturned in Nicaea' (Creation.com; Darkness at the crucifixion: metaphor or real history?).

Translator's Perspective on the Canon of the NT

There was great excitement over bodies missing from tombs in Judea in the first half of the first century. This fact is known due to the discovery in Nazareth of a decree of Claudius (reigned 41-54 AD). It reads, "Ordinance of Caesar. It is my pleasure that graves and tombs remain perpetually undisturbed .... In case of violation I desire that the offender be sentenced to capital punishment on charge of violation of sepulcher." The death penalty for grave robbing? Something must have happened in Israel to cause this kind of reaction from the emperor. That "something" could have been what is recorded in the Book of Acts, namely the preaching of the apostles that Jesus had risen from the dead (Acts 2:22-36; 3:12-15; 10:34-43).

This preaching activity is confirmed by extra-biblical sources. Josephus states, (Arabic version) "They reported that he had appeared to them three days after his crucifixion and that he was alive." Tacitus records, "But in spite of this temporary setback (the crucifixion) the deadly superstition had broken out afresh, not only in Judea, where it had started, but even in Rome." The Tacitus quote is also important in that it again confirms that the resurrection was first preached in Judea, more specifically Jerusalem (Acts 2). This is near the very place where Jesus had been crucified and buried (John 19:38-42).

Finally, the disciples were so convinced Jesus had risen, they continued to preach the resurrection despite persecution and martyrdom. The Book of Acts records the slaying of James the apostle (Acts 12:2). Josephus describes the stoning of James the Just. Clement, a disciple of the apostle Paul, wrote an epistle to the Corinthians about 95 AD (see Phil 4:3). In the fifth chapter, Clement recounts the martyrdoms of Peter and Paul. This epistle and passage will be discussed in Volume Three. John the apostle left a record of his own banishment in Revelation 1:9, which will be discussed later. According to tradition, the other apostles were all also persecuted and martyred for the faith. This will be seen in the apocryphal acts that will be discussed in Volume Three. This type of fortitude in men who formally forsook and denied Christ needs to be explained (Matt 26:56,69-75).

The preaching of the apostles met with great success. The Christian movement grew rapidly despite the persecution. This growth is recorded in Acts and verified by the previous quote by Tacitus. Tacitus also adds detailed descriptions of the horrendous persecutions the early Christians suffered. These points are also mentioned by Suetonius (secretary to emperor Hadrian, 117-138 AD) and Pliny the Younger (Roman historian, 112 AD). The full quote by Tacitus will be presented in Volume Three when these persecutions are discussed in detail.

But here, these 18 non-Christian sources all verify that Jesus did in fact live, and they confirm many aspects of His life and that of the early

Church. As such, the radical claim that Jesus never existed is simply absurd. This absurdity will become even more obvious as we study the early Christian sources. But first, a look at a common objection to these sources.

The Telephone Game

You have a classroom with about 20 students in it. The teacher makes up a story and whispers it to the first student. He then whispers it to the second student; she then whispers it to the third student, and so on until it reaches the final student. The final student then stands up and recounts the story to the class. Invariably, the story the final person tells bears little relation to the story initially made up by the teacher.

The point of this little exercise is to demonstrate how rumors change as they are told in secret by one person to the next. As such, rumors should not be believed, as they are totally unreliable.

That is a good lesson, but the reason for mentioning it here is that many people try to apply this little game to the transmission of the life and teachings of Jesus. The claim is that just like the telephone game, what Jesus did and said was retold over and over again, from person to person over a period of decades, so that by the time somebody wrote it all down, it had been so distorted that nothing that was finally written down bore any resemblance to what Jesus actually said and did. As such the Gospels cannot be trusted. They are no more reliable than rumors.

This writer has heard this claim made many times, to me personally, on the internet, and even in TV shows and movies. The person who brings this up thinks they have made an unassailable point; but in fact all they have done is demonstrated they do not know what they are talking about, as the transmission of the life and teachings of Christ bears no resemblance whatsoever to this little game.

First off, Jesus did not live and speak in private. Most often, His actions and words were witnessed by multitudes of people at once, tens, hundreds, even thousands. Some of His actions and teachings were done privately, only witnessed by His apostles, but that would still be twelve people. On rare occasions only Peter, James, and John were eyewitnesses. But still, that is three people, not just one.

Second, when stories were told of what Jesus did and said, they were not whispered by one person to another one at a time. They were told out loud to groups, with many of those present being eyewitnesses of His life. Thus, if anyone tried to say Jesus did or said something He did not do or say, they would immediately be corrected by the still living eyewitnesses.

Translator's Perspective on the Canon of the NT

Third and related to the preceding, there were multiple lines of transmission, not just one as in the telephone game. In other words, multiple people would be retelling the same narratives in multiple locations. Thus, people could compare these different narratives and discern the original story behind all of these parallel lines of transmission by looking for their unity.

Fourth, people at that time were much more practiced in memorization and storytelling than we are today. We today with our widespread literacy and multitude of recording devices have little need to memorize things, as we can easily just look it up, and we transmit ideas via the written or recorded word. But in Jesus' day, memorization and oral storytelling is how traditions were passed down in a mostly illiterate, pre-tech, culture.

> Passing on oral traditions and teachings was commonplace in the Jewish culture of that day, and memorization was highly cultivated and practiced (GotQuestions?org. "When were the Gospels written?).

> Among the Jews and Arabs the memory was specially trained in the accurate repetition and perpetuation of sacred words and facts. ... The memory is strongest where it depends most on itself and least upon books (Schaff; 8566-8570).

Fifth, the one time this writer played the telephone game, the results were not at all like those assumed in the objection. When the final student stood up and related the story she had heard, it was almost identical to the original story, with one exception. There was one element in the story that was not present in the original story. When she began relating that portion of the story, half of the class started shouting, "That's not in the story!"

It only took a few seconds to determine the source of that "new" element. It was a jokester in the middle of the chain who purposely made up that element just to mess up the story. But his fabrication was quickly and soundly shouted down by all of the people who heard the story before him, and he was exposed for the fabricator that he was.

This scenario would be closer to what happened in the first century than the original assumption. If someone tried to introduce an element into the life or teachings of Jesus that were not authentic, he would be immediately exposed for the fabricator that he was and that element rejected and that person also rejected as being a reliable source for information about Jesus. And absent any such deliberate but easily exposed fabrications, the original events of the life and teachings of

Jesus would be retold in a faithful and reliable manner, with little alteration, regardless of how many times it was retold.

However, none of this really matters as one of the standards for a book to be included in the NT canon was that it had to be written by an eyewitness of the life of Christ or at least by someone who received his information directly from an eyewitness. As such, there was not a long oral tradition that had to be shifted through to find the truth in the midst of distortions. The author had heard Jesus Himself, personally, or he had received his information from a person or persons who had heard Jesus directly. As such, there was not a long line of oral transmission but at the most one transmission. This is not to say the authors did not use sources, but those sources had to be by eyewitnesses themselves, and all of that additional information would be tested against his own experiences with Jesus or with His apostles.

Only Four Gospels

It is logical for the four Gospels to be first in the canon of the NT. The Christian faith is about Jesus, and these four Gospels tell us about the life and teachings of Jesus. Moreover, it was believed very early in Church history that there were four and only four genuine Gospels:

> … there can be no doubt that by the close of the 1st century and the early part of the 2nd century, opinion was practically unanimous in recognition of the authority of the four Gospels of the canonical Scriptures. Irenaeus, Bishop of Lyons (180 AD), recognizes four, and only four Gospels, as "pillars" of the church. The Harmonies of Theophilus, bishop of Antioch (168-80 AD), and of Tatian, and the Apology of Justin Martyr carry back the tradition to a much earlier period of the century, and, as Liddon proves at considerable length (Bampton Lectures, 2nd ed., 210-19), "it is scarcely too much to assert that every decade of the 2nd century furnishes its share of proof that the four Gospels as a whole, and John's in particular, were to the church of that age what they are to the church of the present" (ISBE; "Apocryphal Gospels").

> As early as the middle of the second century, that is, fifty years after the death of the Apostle John, when yet many of his personal pupils and friends must have been living, the four Canonical Gospels, no more and no less, were recognized and read in public worship as sacred books, in the churches of Syria,

Translator's Perspective on the Canon of the NT

Asia Minor, Egypt, Italy, and Gaul; and such universal acceptance and authority in the face of Jewish and heathen hostility and heretical perversion can only be explained on the ground that they were known and used long before. Some of them, Matthew and John, were quoted and used in the first quarter of the second century by Orthodox and Gnostic writers (Schaff; 11974-11979).

Irenaeus further states:

The heretics boast that they have many more gospels than there really are. But really they don't have any gospels that aren't full of blasphemy. There actually are only four authentic gospels. And this is obviously true because there are four corners of the universe and there are four principal winds, and therefore there can be only four gospels that are authentic. These, besides, are written by Jesus' true followers" (quoted in PBS; "Emergence of the Four Gospel Canon").

Whether the science here is correct is not important. What is important is the very strong conviction there are only four authentic Gospels. In addition, many Church Fathers interpreted the four cherubs of Ezekiel's vision as symbolizing the four Gospels:

[4]And I looked, and behold, a driving wind came from [the] north and a great cloud with it and brightness round about it and fire flashing like lightning, and in [the] midst of it as an appearance of amber in [the] midst of the fire and brightness in it, [5]and in [the] midst as a likeness of four living creatures. And this [was] their appearance: [the] likeness of a person [was] upon them, [6]and four faces to one [fig., each], and four wings to one [fig., each]. [7]And their legs [were] straight, and their feet [were] feathered, and sparks as bronze flashing like lightning, and their wings [were] light in weight.

[8]And [the] hand of a person [was] under their wings on their four parts [or, sides]. [9]And the faces of them, of the four, were not turning when they are going [lit., in the to be going them]; each was going opposite their face [fig., straight forward]. [10]And [the] likeness of their faces [was] a face of a **person**, and a face of a **lion** on [the] right to the four, and a face of a calf [Heb., **ox**] on [the] left to the four, and a face of an **eagle** to the four. [11]And their wings having been stretched out above to the four; to each two having been joined to one another, and two were covering upon their bodies. [12]And each was going according to its face [fig., straight forward]; wherever the spirit was going they were going, and were not turning back (Ezek 1:4-12).

> ...the cherubim were interpreted as prophetic types of the four Gospels as early as the second century, with some difference in the application. Irenaeus (about 170) regards the faces of the cherubim (man, lion, ox, eagle) as "images of the life and work of the Son of God," and assigns the man to Matthew, and the ox to Luke, but the eagle to Mark and the lion to John (Adv. Haer., III. 11, 8, ed. Stieren I. 469 sq.). Afterwards the signs of Mark and John were properly exchanged...
>
> Augustin (De Consens. Evang., Lib. I., c. 6, in Migne's ed. of the Opera, tom. III., 1046) assigns the lion to Matthew, the man to Mark (whom he wrongly regarded as an abbreviator of Matthew), the ox to Luke, and the eagle to John, because "he soars as an eagle above the clouds of human infirmity, and gazes on the light of immutable truth with most keen and steady eyes of the heart." ...
>
> Pseudo-Athanasius (Synopsis Script.) assigns the man to Matthew, the ox to Mark, the lion to Luke. These variations in the application of the emblems reveal the defects of the analogy. The man might as well (with Lange) be assigned to Luke's Gospel of humanity as the sacrificial ox. But Jerome's distribution of the symbols prevailed (Schaff; 8326-8346).

Which cherub to identify with which Gospel is not important. What is important is that the Church Fathers universally saw the four cherubs of Ezekiel as representing the four Gospels. They could not have made this identification if there was the possibility of there being more or less than four authentic Gospels. And note that no other gospels other than the canonical four were every mentioned in this identification.

Moreover:
> The fact that by the end of the second century only four Gospels were accepted as authoritative is further borne out by the discovery of physical copies of the four works bound together in book form and dating from the late second and early third centuries (Vision).

To be clear, this quote is saying that at least by the end of the second century the four canonical Gospel had been collected together and were circulating as a unit. There were never any other Gospels associated with these four, and these four were often bound together, sometimes with Acts. Specifically, there are ten extant manuscripts containing all

Translator's Perspective on the Canon of the NT

four Gospels, with two of these also containing Acts, dating from the second to third centuries AD (Deeper Study).

These manuscripts were in the form of codexes. A codex is similar to our modern-day hardcopy book, with pages bound together on the left hand side, except it uses parchment rather than paper sheets. This format differs greatly from the scrolls that were used up until this time. Scrolls consist of rolled up papyrus leaves and were used throughout Biblical times. In fact, the Greek word *biblios*, which is usually translated "book," is better rendered "scroll," as done in the ALT (e.g. Gen 2:4; Matt 1:1).

The important point is that scrolls are limited as to the amount of material that can be recorded on them. This was seen in Volume One when it was said that the books of Samuel, Kings, and Chronicles were each originally one book. But when the Hebrew text was translated into Greek for the Septuagint, they were each broken up into two books, as Greek takes up more space than Hebrew and thus each book would no longer fit on one scroll. That is how we ended up with 1,2Samuel, 1,2Kings, and 1,2Chronicles.

The canonical Gospels would also each fit on one scroll. However, all four together would not. But the early Church was so assured all four were authentic and should be read as a unit that they began using codexes rather than scrolls just so they could bind all four of these Gospels together. In fact, it was this practice of the early Church that led to the publishing revolution of using codexes rather than scrolls (Ankerberg, "The Battle to Discredit the Bible: Part 1").

> The usual modern sense of codex, "book formed of bound leaves of paper or parchment," is due to Christianity. By the first century BC there existed at Rome notebooks made of leaves of parchment, used for rough copy, first drafts, and notes. By the first century AD such manuals were used for commercial copies of classical literature. The Christians adopted this parchment manual format for the Scriptures used in their liturgy because a codex is easier to handle than a scroll and because one can write on both sides of a parchment but on only one side of a papyrus scroll. By the early second century all Scripture was reproduced in codex form. In traditional Christian iconography, therefore, the Hebrew prophets are represented holding scrolls and the Evangelists holding codices (YourDictionary).

However, a man named Tatian (or Tatianus) found reading four Gospels too cumbersome, so in 175 AD he produced his *Diatessaron* (from Greek for "through four"). It is a harmony of the four Gospels, with the Greek texts translated into Syriac. The book received mixed reaction in the early Church, in part because later Tatian veered from orthodoxy into heretical/ Gnostic views (Johnson). But important for our discussion is Tatian did not use five gospels, nor three gospels, but four, and not just any four, but Mathew, Mark, Luke, and John. And even though his work was more convenient to read than four individual Gospels, it was unable to supplant the accepted four Gospels, as they had already been accepted as the only reliable records of Jesus' life (Ankerberg, "The Battle to Discredit the Bible: Part 1").

Finally, and moving later in Church history, Constantine had legalized Christianity in 313 AD. His nephew Julian had been raised a Christian, but he apostatized from the faith. When he ascended the throne in 363 AD, he tried to reestablish heathenism as the state religion. While doing so, he wrote a polemic against Christianity, but in his book:

> He bears witness to the genuineness and authenticity of the four gospels of Matthew, Mark, Luke, and John, and the Acts of the Apostles: and he so quotes them, as to intimate, that these were the only historical books received by Christians as of authority, and the only authentic memoirs of Jesus Christ and his apostles, and the doctrine preached by them. He allows their early date, and even argues for it. He also quotes, or plainly refers to the Acts of the Apostles, to St. Paul's Epistles to the Romans, the Corinthians, and the Galatians (Schaff; 24674-24677).

Thus, on many lines of evidence, it can be seen that very early in Church history it was believed by both those faithful to the Christian faith and those who were arguing against it that there were four and only four authentic and reliable Gospels, those of Matthew, Mark, Luke, and John.

Supposed Interdependence and Order

Matthew, Mark, and Luke are the first three of the four Gospels. They are called the Synoptic Gospels as they are very similar and thus are said to be interdependent.

> 91% of Mark is reproduced in Matthew or Luke. Likewise, Matthew and Luke are 50% and 41% consistent respectively with the other synoptics. The nature of this similarity is such as

Translator's Perspective on the Canon of the NT

to warrant the judgement that the literary relationship between these gospels could be one involving direct copying (Farmer's).

But are they really interdependent? And if so, who copied from whom? The Gospel According to Matthew is first in the canonical order for a reason—it was universally believed in the early Church that it was the first Gospel written. "According to early and practically universal tradition Mt [Matthew] wrote his Gospel before the other three, and the place assigned to it in New Testament literature favors the acceptance of this tradition" (ISBE "Matthew, the Gospel of"). However today, "It is the near-universal position of scholarship that the Gospel of Matthew is dependent upon the Gospel of Mark" (Early Christian; "Gospel of Matthew").

Thus, the early Church believed Matthew was written first. In that case, it is assumed Mark abbreviated Matthew. But today it is believed Mark was written first, then Matthew expanded upon his work. Does it matter? Not really, except for a conclusion that is drawn from this supposition:

> The ancient tradition that the author [of Matthew] was the disciple and apostle of Jesus named Matthew (see Mt 10:3) is untenable because the gospel is based, in large part, on the Gospel according to Mark (almost all the verses of that gospel have been utilized in this), and it is hardly likely that a companion of Jesus would have followed so extensively an account that came from one who admittedly never had such an association rather than rely on his own memories (Bishops; "Matthew – Introduction").

> What Matthew has done, in fact, is to produce a second and enlarged edition of Mark. Moreover, the changes which he makes in Mark's way of telling the story are not those corrections which an eyewitness might make in the account of one who was not an eyewitness. Thus, whereas in Mark's Gospel we may be only one remove from eyewitnesses, in Matthew's Gospel we are at one remove further still (Early Christian; "Gospel of Matthew").

Thus, the theory that Mark was written first and that Matthew was dependent on Mark is used to deny the Matthean authorship of the first Gospel and to assert that not only was the Gospel of Matthew not written by an apostle but that it was not even written by a direct associate of an apostle. But this really is not a logical conclusion:

> Assuming Markan priority, would an apostle use a gospel written by a non-apostle, or even any written source? This is not as weighty an argument as it appears, for "if Matthew thought Mark's account reliable and generally suited to his purposes (and he may have known that Peter stood behind it), there can be no objection to the view that an apostle depended on a nonapostolic document" (Bible.org; "Matthew: Introduction, Argument, and Outline").

We will look more in detail at the evidence for the Matthean authorship shortly, but here, why is this theory asserted? First, it would be helpful to quote a couple of statements of by Church Fathers of the second century:

> As quoted by Eusebius in *Hist. Eccl.* 3.39, Papias states: "Matthew put together the oracles [of the Lord] in the Hebrew language, and each one interpreted them as best he could." In *Adv. Haer.* 3.1.1, Irenaeus says: "Matthew also issued a written Gospel among the Hebrews in their own dialect while Peter and Paul were preaching at Rome and laying the foundations of the church" (Early Christian; "Gospel of Matthew").

The difficulty here is the earliest extant manuscripts of the Gospel of Matthew are in Greek, and there are no signs in the text that it was translated from a Hebrew original.

> The Greek Matthew, as we have it now, is not a close translation from the Hebrew and bears the marks of an original composition. This appears from genuine Greek words and phrases to which there is no parallel in Hebrew (Schaff; 8860-8861).

As such, it is theorized that these statements are referring to just a collection of the sayings of Jesus, not a full Gospel. It is said that this may or may not be the same as the hypothetical "Q" source ("from the first letter of the German word Quelle, meaning 'source'" – Bishops). Q is said to be a collection of the sayings of Jesus that all three Synoptic Gospels are dependent on.

> But it is likely that the tradition of Matthean authorship holds a kernel of truth. The Apostle Matthew may have had a hand in bringing together, in Aramaic or Hebrew, a collection

Translator's Perspective on the Canon of the NT

of sayings of Jesus. In fact, this may well have been the collection scholars call Quelle, a collection which underlies large sections of the Gospel. Is this not exactly what Papias tells us? This may have given rise to the assumption that Matthew had written the whole Gospel.

The Gospel probably came about in two major stages. It began as a collection of Aramaic sayings of Jesus, brought together by the Apostle Matthew. Then a Greek-speaking Christian scribe re-wrote it and enlarged it in its present form, probably for the Christian community at Antioch in Syria (Women; "Authorship of Matthew's Gospel").

It is also sometimes asserted that Matthew went through several different stages, with the extant Matthew being just the last in that series of redactions.

However, all of this is just theory, with no manuscript evidence whatsoever supporting it. No "Q" source has ever been discovered, nor has a Hebrew Gospel or just a collection of sayings by Jesus in either Hebrew or Greek.

Is there any evidence for a "Q" document? No, there is not. No portion or fragment of a "Q" document has ever been discovered. None of the early church fathers ever mentioned a Gospel "source" in their writings. "Q" is the invention of liberal "scholars" who deny the inspiration of the Bible (GotQuestions?org. "What is the Synoptic Problem?").

Moreover:
The theory of successive redactions of Mt, starting with an Aramaic Gospel, elaborated by Eichhorn and Marsh (1801), and the related theories of successive editions of the Gospel put forth by the Tubingen school (Baur, Hilgenfeld, Kostlin, etc.), and by Ewald (Bleek supposes a primitive Greek Gospel), lack historical foundation, and are refuted by the fact that manuscripts and versions know only the ultimate redaction. Is it credible that the churches should quietly accept redaction after redaction, and not a word be said, or a vestige remain, of any of them? (ISBE; "Matthew, the Gospel of").

As such, the Gospel According to Matthew as we now have it was most likely the original text, written by Matthew himself. In addition, despite claims, there are many who still hold to what the early Church believed—that Matthew was written first, then Mark. And, "There is no good reason to doubt that the canonical arrangement which is supported by the prevailing oldest tradition, correctly represents the order of composition" (Schaff; 8604-8606).

The arguments here can become very complex, based on external and internal evidence. But most of them are based on the idea of interdependency between the three Synoptic Gospels. But if these three Gospels are independent of each other, then all of this complex reasoning is just blowing in the wind. Still, the consensus of the early Church and today is that the Gospel According to Luke was written after Matthew and Mark, hence why it is third in the canon. Moreover, there is no doubt Luke used sources in the composition of his Gospel:

[1]Since many undertook to arrange in proper order a narrative about the events having been accomplished among us, [2]just as they were handed down to us by the ones having become eyewitnesses and attendants of the Word from the beginning, [3]it seemed good also to me, having closely followed [or, having investigated] every[thing] carefully from the beginning, to write [it out] to you in consecutive order [or, in an orderly fashion; cp. Acts 11:4], most excellent Theophilus, [4]so that you shall know the certainty [or, exact truth] about which you were instructed (Luke 1:1-4).

What were the sources Luke is referring to? His statement about "eyewitnesses" indicates these narratives were by eyewitness or at least were based on eyewitness testimony. He also indicates he utilized them in writing his Gospel. And there are many that assume these sources included Matthew and / or Mark. And there would be no difficulty in Luke utilizing them as sources for his Gospel.

However, "There is no direct evidence that any of the three Synoptists saw and used the work of the others; nor is the agreement of such a character that it may not be as easily and better explained from antecedent sources" (Schaff; 8513-8514).

If Luke had used Matthew, with Matthew being an apostle, it would be logical that he would have mentioned him. The same would be the case if Mark used Matthew. And if Matthew had used Mark, knowing his chief source was Peter, then Matthew would have mentioned that as well. But they are all silent about such sources. Moreover, if Luke knew about the Gospels by Matthew and Mark, he would not have had such a pressing need to write another Gospel, as those Gospels would already have filled the need for a complete written record of the life of Christ.

It is more likely the sources Luke refers to are the oral traditions and written down accounts of various events of the life of Christ and of

Translator's Perspective on the Canon of the NT

sermons that He preached. The oral tradition would be the preaching of the apostles.

> The chief and common source from which the Synoptists derived their Gospels was undoubtedly the living apostolic tradition or teaching which is mentioned by Luke in the first order. This teaching was nothing more or less than a faithful report of the words and deeds of Christ himself by honest and intelligent eye-witnesses....
>
> The apostolic tradition or preaching was chiefly historical, a recital of the wonderful public life of Jesus of Nazareth, and centered in the crowning facts of the crucifixion and resurrection. This is evident from the specimens of sermons in the Acts (Schaff; 8562-8564).

The written down accounts would be by various eyewitnesses of specific events or sermons of Christ who would have written down the events or sermons they witnessed.

> It is very natural that parts of the tradition were reduced to writing during the thirty years which intervened between the events and the composition of the canonical Gospels. One evangelist would record for his own use a sketch of the chief events, another the sermon on the Mount, another the parables, another the history of the crucifixion and resurrection, still another would gather from the lips of Mary the history of the infancy and the genealogies. Possibly some of the first hearers noted down certain words and events under the fresh impressions of the moment (Schaff; 8570-8572).

In this case, the Synoptics are not interdependent upon each other, but all three are dependent upon this common oral and fragmentary written tradition. This theory better explains why there are so many similarities between the three Synoptic Gospels. All three were based on the same oral and written traditions that was handed down by the apostles and other eyewitnesses of the life of Christ. There was a consistency to this tradition as it was a faithful reporting of what Jesus actually said and did. The minor differences are due to each person retelling the events in a slightly different manner. "Words can be accurately reported only in one form, as they were spoken; while events may be correctly narrated in different words" (Schaff; (8455-8456).

However, these minor differences demonstrate there was not interdependency between the Synoptics. They also demonstrate the reliability of the Gospels as they are not just copies of each other but independent witnesses. Moreover, these minor differences make the existence of these three Gospels helpful in giving us a fuller picture of the life and teachings of Christ.

> The four canonical Gospels are only variations of the same theme, a fourfold representation of one and the same gospel, animated by the same spirit. They are not full biographies, only memoirs or a selection of characteristic features of Christ's life and work as they struck each Evangelist and best suited his purpose and his class of readers. They are not photographs which give only the momentary image in a single attitude, but living pictures from repeated sittings, and reproduce the varied expressions and aspects of Christ's person....
>
> The apparent contradictions of these narratives, when closely examined, sufficiently solve themselves, in all essential points, and serve only to attest the honesty, impartiality, and credibility of the authors....
>
> The very discrepancies in minor details increase confidence and exclude the suspicion of collusion; for it is a generally acknowledged principle in legal evidence that circumstantial variation in the testimony of witnesses confirms their substantial agreement. There is no historical work of ancient times which carries on its very face such a seal of truthfulness as these Gospels (Schaff; 8241-8245; 8267-8269; 8312-8314).

This theory also best concurs with the testimony of Scripture. We know from the sermons recorded in Acts that there was in fact an oral tradition that preserved the major events of the life of Christ. Consider, for instance, Peter's sermon on the Day of Pentecost:

[22]"Men, Israelites! Pay attention to these words! Jesus the Nazarene, a Man having been attested by God among you* by miraculous works and wonders and signs which God did through Him in your* midst, just as you* yourselves also know—[23]this One, handed over by the having been designated plan and foreknowledge of God, you* having taken by lawless hands, having crucified, you* executed; [24]whom God raised up, having loosed the pangs of death, because it was not possible [for] Him to continue being held by it....

[33]"Therefore, having been exalted to the right hand of God, and having received the promise of the Holy Spirit from the Father, He poured out this which you* now see and hear (Acts 2:22-24,33).

Translator's Perspective on the Canon of the NT

Peter mention's Jesus' hometown, His miracles, His betrayal, His crucifixion, His death, His resurrection, His ascension, and Peter associates the Father, Son, and Holy Spirit together. That is five essential tenets plus other events of the life of Christ. And this is just two brief excerpts from what was probably a much longer sermon. Additional sermons with additional details are found in Acts 3:13-16; 4:8-12; 5:9-29-32; 10:34-43; 13:23-39; 17:31. In addition, we know from the prologue to Luke's Gospel that there were written records of events from Jesus' life and of His preaching (Luke 1:1).

This writer agrees with Church historian Philp Schaff:

> We conclude, then, that the Synoptists prepared their Gospels independently, during the same period (say between A.D. 60 and 69), in different places, chiefly from the living teaching of Christ and the first disciples, and partly from earlier fragmentary documents (Schaff; 8600-8601).

However, I disagree with Schaff slightly as to the dating he gives of the Synoptics. To that subject we now turn.

Date of Writing

The prologue to the Gospel According to Luke was already quoted. It states that the Gospel was written to a "most excellent Theophilus." The prologue to the Book of Acts states:

[1]The first word [or, account] indeed I made concerning all [things], O Theophilus, which Jesus began both to be doing and to be teaching, [see Luke 1:1-4] [2]until the day [in] which He was taken up [into heaven], having commanded by [the] Holy Spirit the apostles whom He chose, [3]to whom also He presented Himself living after His suffering, by many convincing proofs, appearing to them during forty days and speaking the [things] concerning the kingdom of God. [see Luke 24:36-51]

Comparing this prologue to the prologue to the Gospel of Luke, it is clear the Book of Acts is written by and to the same person as the Gospel of Luke and that Acts is a sequel to Luke. This connection is even clearer when looking at the Greek text of these books. Luke and Acts contain the most "stylistic" Greek of the NT, meaning it consists of very complex vocabulary, grammar, and sentence structure. I learned this while attending Denver seminary. Thus, when I started translating the NT, I left Luke and Acts for last. And sure enough, when I got to them, they were very difficult to translate, far more difficult than the rest of the NT.

But this difficulty was far different than the difficulty I had translating the Greek of the Apocryphal/ Deuterocanonical (A/D) books that was discussed in Volume One. Those books were difficult to translate due to the very poor nature of the Greek, while Luke and Acts are hard to translate due to the very high quality of the Greek.

To use an example from English, Facebook posts can sometimes be difficult to read due to the very poor quality of the English of many of the posts. Very often, posts contain misused words, poor grammar, and sloppy writing in general that makes it difficult to understand the point being asserted. Very often, for instance, posters confuse "your" and "you're" or "there," "their," and "they're."

Meanwhile, the *New England Journal of Medicine* (NEJM) is also difficult to read, but for completely different reasons. It contains very complex vocabulary ("big words"), complex sentence structures, and most of all complex topics, but it is usually written in accordance with proper English grammar. Thus, the A/D books are like the Facebook posts containing sloppy Greek, while Luke and Acts are like the NEJM in containing very complex Greek. This is not unexpected given that Luke was a physician, "Luke, the beloved physician, greets you*" (Col 4:14a).

In any case, the style of the Greek is so similar in Luke and Acts that there is no doubt the same author wrote both, and the prologues clearly indicate that Luke was written first, then Acts.

> The universal testimony of the ancient church traces the two books to the same author. This is confirmed by internal evidence of identity of style, continuity of narrative, and correspondence of plan. About fifty words not found elsewhere in the New Testament are common to both books (Schaff; 10110-10112).

This connection between Luke and Acts has a bearing on the dating of all three Synoptic Gospels and of Acts. Since Acts was written last of these four books, if we can accurately date it, then we can work backwards for dates of the three Synoptic Gospels.

Acts ends with the following:

And in this way we came to Rome....
[30]Now Paul remained [for] an entire two year period in his own rented quarters [ca. early 60s A.D.], and he was receiving all the ones coming in to him, [31]preaching the kingdom of God and teaching the

Translator's Perspective on the Canon of the NT

[things] concerning the Lord Jesus Christ with all confidence, without hindrance (Acts 28:14b,30-31).

First, note the use of the plural first person pronoun "we" in the first sentence. This indicates the writer was traveling with Paul on his voyage to Rome. More on that later, but here, Paul is in Rome on house arrest for two years. And the book ends right there. It reads like a cliffhanger. Many speculations have occurred as to what happened right after this, but that does not concern us. What matters is when this was.

There is strong tradition that Peter and Paul were executed under Roman Emperor Nero. Their martyrdom is recorded by the early Church historian Eusebius in his *Ecclesiastical History* (c. 320 AD).

> When the government of Nero was now firmly established, he began to plunge into unholy pursuits, and armed himself even against the religion of the God of the universe….
>
> Thus, publicly announcing himself as the first among God's chief enemies, he was led on to the slaughter of the apostles. It is, therefore, recorded that Paul was beheaded in Rome itself, and that Peter likewise was crucified under Nero. This account of Peter and Paul is substantiated by the fact that their names are preserved in the cemeteries of that place even to the present day (quoted in Bible Hub).

Moreover:

> This tradition, that Paul suffered martyrdom in Rome, is early and universal, and disputed by no counter-tradition and may be accepted as the one certain historical fact known about Paul outside of the New Testament accounts (Bible Hub).

This is important as:

> The New Testament tells a great deal about two of the most important Apostles: Peter and Paul. Contained in the book of Acts are stories of their travels, their actions, and their words. But one aspect of Peter and Paul is missing from Acts and, in fact, from the whole New Testament: how they died (Christian Timelines).

This is important as if Acts was written after the martyrdoms of Paul and Peter, it most certainly would have recorded it. Nero reigned from 54 to 68 A.D. But:

Why Are These Books in the Bible? Volume Two

The greatest threat to Nero's reign, however, was the Great Fire, which began on July 19, 64 AD and lasted for six days. ... The blame fell, of course, upon the heads of the persecuted Christians who had always viewed Nero as the anti-Christ (Ancient).

The persecutions of Christians raged until Nero's death. Thus, Peter and Paul had to have been executed between 64-68 AD. Since Acts does not mention these persecutions, let alone the martyrdoms of Peter and Paul, it is safe to say it was written before 64 AD.

The inference is that Acts was written while Paul was still alive, seeing his death is not recorded. Since there is good evidence that Paul died in the Neronian persecution about A.D. 67, the Book of Acts can be dated approximately A.D. 62 (Blue Letter).

It obviously the simplest way to understand Luke's close of the Acts to be due to the fact that Paul was still in prison. Harnack contends that the efforts to explain away this situation are not "quite satisfactory or very illuminating." He does not mention Paul's death because he was still alive. ...

The whole tone of the book [of Acts] is that which one would naturally have before 64 AD. After the burning of Rome and the destruction of Jerusalem the attitude maintained in the book toward Romans and Jews would have been very difficult unless the date was a long time afterward... The book will, I think, be finally credited to the time 63 AD in Rome (ISBE; "Acts of the Apostles").

As hinted at in the second quote, some doubt the reasoning that Acts ends with Paul still being alive as he was still alive. They base this on Paul stating to the Ephesians in Acts 20:22-25:

[22]"And now, listen! I, having been bound in my spirit [or, by the Spirit], am traveling to Jerusalem, not knowing the [things that] will be happening to me in it, [23]except that the Holy Spirit solemnly testifies in every city, saying that chains and afflictions await me. [24]But I make myself an account of nothing [or, of no account], neither do I hold my life precious to myself, so [as] to complete my course with joy and the ministry which I received from the Lord Jesus, to solemnly testify [to] the Gospel of the grace of God.

Translator's Perspective on the Canon of the NT

^{25}"And now, listen! I know that you* will no longer see my face, you* all among whom I went about preaching the kingdom of God.

The claim is this is such a clear prediction of Paul's death that it had to have been written after his death. Thus, as was often seen in Volume One, we again see the liberals' presupposition of the impossibility of predictive prophecy causing them to deny the traditional dating of a book and the clear teaching of the text. Moreover, this presupposition causes them to make the authors of Bible books into dishonest people, sticking words into people's mouths that they did not say. As a result, they are forced to say:

> It is sometimes put forward that the Gospel of Luke may be as early as 62 CE because Acts does not narrate the martyrdom of Paul. The ending of Acts is an old problem that has prompted many theories (Early Christian; "Gospel of Luke").

This article then puts forth many theories for this "problem." The discussions are quite lengthy, too lengthy to quote here, but suffice it to say, they are all solutions looking for a problem. They are put forth due to not believing that Paul actually said the preceding words through the leading of the Holy Spirit as the text asserts and to try to explain away the simplest explanation for the ending of Acts—Paul was still alive.

But taking the text at face value, Acts was written probably in about 63 AD. In that case, The Gospel of Luke would most likely have been written shortly before that.

> If Acts were written about A.D. 62, then this helps us date the gospels, since the Book of Acts is the second half of a treatise written by Luke to a man named Theophilus. Since we know that the gospel of Luke was written before the Book of Acts, we can then date the Gospel of Luke sometime around A.D. 60 or before (Blue Letter; "When Were the Four Gospels Written?").

It is almost universally agreed that Mark was written before Luke. But whether Matthew was written before Mark or vice a versa or if they are interdependent is of little matter here. What matters is both Matthew and Mark were written before Luke. Thus, if Luke was written in about 60 AD, then Matthew and Mark had to have been written in the late 50s AD. But if, as the critics claim, Mark was written first, then Matthew, then Luke, that pushes Mark even further back, into the early 50s. If

Matthew was first, then it was probably written in the early 50s, then Mark in the late 50s, then Luke in about 60 AD.

But whatever the exact dates and order, what matters is that all three Synoptic Gospels were written between 50-60 AD, with Acts being written shortly thereafter. Thus, the accounts of the life of Christ were all written within twenty to thirty years of His earthly life and thus within the lifespans of the many eyewitnesses of His life.

This is where the discussion of the telephone game becomes important. With many living eyewitnesses, if Matthew, Mark, or Luke had made things up about Jesus, had said He did or said things He did not, there would have been plenty of people willing and able to refute their assertions, but there is no record of that ever happening. The opposite in fact happened. These three Gospels were immediately and universally accepted as being reliable records of the life and teachings of Jesus.

> Also, the fact that even at that time there would have been a considerable number of eyewitnesses around to dispute and discredit any false claims, and the fact that none of the "hard sayings" of Jesus were taken from the Gospel accounts, further supports their accuracy. Had the Gospels been edited before being written down, as some liberal scholars contend, then it was a very poor job. The writers left far too many "hard sayings," and culturally unacceptable and politically incorrect accounts that would need explaining. An example of this is that the first witnesses of the resurrection were women, who were not considered reliable witnesses in the culture of that day (GotQuestions?org. "When were the Gospels written?").

Adding support to this dating, the early Church universally believed the Synoptic Gospels were written before the destruction of Jerusalem in 70 A.D.

> Irenaeus reports that it [Matthew] was written when Peter and Paul were preaching in Rome (ill.1), and Eusebius states that this was done when Matthew left Palestine and went to preach to others (*Historia Ecclesiastica*, III, 24). Clement of Alexandria is responsible for the statement that the presbyters who succeeded each other from the beginning declared that "the gospels containing the genealogies (Matthew and Luke) were written first" (Eusebius, *Historia Ecclesiastica*, VI, 14). This is, of course, fatal to the current theory of dependence on Mark, and is in consequence rejected. At any rate, there is the best

Translator's Perspective on the Canon of the NT

reason for holding that the book must have been written before the destruction of Jerusalem in 70 AD (ISBE; "Matthew, the Gospel of").

The dates for the lifetimes of Irenaeus, Clement of Alexandria, and additional Church Fathers that will be mentioned as we proceed are given on the "Church Fathers" Introductory Page. But here; this means we have early testimony to the Synoptics being written while Peter and Paul were still alive and thus before 64 AD. Note also the additional objection to Markan priority mentioned, but to continue with the dating of the Synoptics.

Date of Writing: As an apostle, Matthew wrote the Gospel of Matthew in the early period of the church, probably in A.D. 55-65. This was a time when most Christians were Jewish converts, so Matthew's focus on Jewish perspective in this Gospel is understandable (GotQuestions?org' "Gospel of Matthew).

Date of Writing: The Gospel of Mark was likely one of the first books written in the New Testament, probably in A.D. 55-59 (GotQuestions?org; "Gospel of Mark").

a. Matthew could have been written c. A.D. 50
b. Luke could have been written c. A.D. 60
c. Acts could have been written c. A.D. 64/65 (Bible.org; "An Introduction to the Gospel Of Mark")

Thus, the conservative position is rather consistent that all three Synoptic Gospels and the Book of Acts were all written between 50-65 AD. But liberals will date these books later, all after 70 A.D. The reason for this can be seen in a quote defending the conservative dates:

> The first three Gospels, and possibly also the fourth, were apparently written while the city of Jerusalem was still standing. Each of the first three Gospels contains predictions by Jesus concerning the destruction of Jerusalem and the Temple (Matthew 24; Mark 13; Luke 21), but none records the fulfillment. We know that Titus the Roman destroyed the city and Temple in A.D. 70. Hence, the composition of the first three Gospels most likely occurred sometime before this event, otherwise their destruction would have been recorded (Blue Letter; "When Were the Four Gospels Written?").

These predictions are seen in the following passages:

¹And having gone out, Jesus was departing from the temple, and His disciples approached Him to point out to Him the buildings of the temple. ²But Jesus said to them, "You* are looking at all these, are you* not? Positively, I say to you*, by no means shall [there] be left here a stone upon a stone which will not be torn down."
³Then as He is sitting on the Mount of Olives, the disciples approached Him privately, saying, "Tell us when these [things] will be? And what [is] the sign of Your Arrival [or, Coming] and of the conclusion of the age?" (Matt 24:1-3).

¹Then as He goes out from the temple, one of His disciples says to Him, "Teacher, look! What great stones! And what great buildings!" ²And Jesus having answered, said to him, "Are you looking at these great buildings? By no means shall a stone be left on a stone which by no means shall not be torn down."
³Then as He sits on the Mount of Olives, opposite the temple, Peter and James and John and Andrew began questioning Him privately. ⁴"Tell us when these [things] will be? And what [is] the sign when all these [things] shall be about to be fulfilled?" (Mark 13:1-4).

⁵And while some [were] saying about the temple, that it has been adorned with beautiful stones and dedicated offerings, He said, ⁶"These [things] which you* are looking at—days will come in which a stone will not be left on a stone, which will not be torn down." ⁷Then they questioned Him, saying, "Teacher, so when will these [things] be? And what [will be] the sign when these [things] are about to be happening?" (Luke 21:5-7).

All three of these accounts vouch the wording as if the temple is currently standing and its destruction is in the future. Thus, to conservatives, this is evidence these books were written before that date.

> The Synoptic Gospels were certainly written before A.D. 70; for they describe the destruction of Jerusalem as an event still future, though nigh at hand, and connect it immediately with the glorious appearing of our Lord, which it was thought might take place within the generation then living, although no precise date is fixed anywhere, the Lord himself declaring it to be unknown even to him. Had the Evangelists written after that terrible catastrophe, they would naturally have made some allusion to it, or so arranged the eschatological discourses of our

Translator's Perspective on the Canon of the NT

> Lord (Matt. 24; Mark 13; Luke 21) as to enable the reader clearly to discriminate between the judgment of Jerusalem and the final judgment of the world, as typically foreshadowed by the former (Schaff; 8282-8287).

However, to liberals, it is the exact opposite. "The real crux is that to accept an earlier date than 70 AD is to admit predictive prophecy" (ISBE; "Matthew, the Gospel of"). In other words, based on the presupposition that predictive prophecy is not possible, liberals consider these predictions to actually be historical references and thus the Gospels had to have been written after 70 AD.

> Because of the historical allusions found in the Gospel of Mark to the events of the First Jewish Revolt, the period of five years between 70 and 75 CE is the most plausible dating for the Gospel of Mark within the broader timeframe indicated of 65 to 80 CE. (Early Christian' "Gospel of Mark").

This liberal website Thus, dates these books anywhere from 70 to 130 AD. But note the phrase "historical allusions" not "predictive prophecies." This is despite the fact that Mark, along with Matthew and Luke, word these passages as prophecies. But the liberal scholars think they know better than the original authors what Jesus actually said and when He said it. Or more correctly, they just assume these words have been put into the mouth of Jesus, whose earthly ministry ended 40 years before these events occurred.

We saw this same reasoning in our discussion on the dating of Acts and earlier in Volume One in our discussion on the Prophetic Books. The traditional dates for those books were rejected primarily on the basis of the presupposition that predictive prophecy is not possible, Thus, the books had to be written after the time of the fulfillment of the prophecies. But if predictive prophecy is possible, then such reasoning holds no water.

> The Credibility of the Gospels would never have been denied if it were not for the philosophical and dogmatic skepticism which desires to get rid of the supernatural and miraculous at any price (Schaff; 8395-8397).

Moreover, there is universal and unquestioned early testimony that these books were written before the destruction of Jerusalem, and that dating is determined by statements in the books themselves. However, liberal scholars in their audacity think they know better and thus deny this testimony. By doing so, they are also denying that Jesus ever spoke these words. This would make the authors of the Gospels fabricators and thus not reliable witnesses to the actual words of Jesus. It is this attitude that has caused many to no longer trust the canonical Gospels. But there is no reason to so doubt them, as all of the evidence points to them being written before the destruction of Jerusalem and thus within the lifetimes of eyewitnesses of the life of Jesus. But who wrote these books? To that question we now turn.

Authors, General

Four separate works known as gospels have recorded the life of Christ for us. The traditional authorship is credited to Matthew, Mark, Luke, and John. There are three basic reasons why we believe the men bearing their names wrote the four gospels. The early church was unanimous in their testimony as to the individual authorship of each gospel. Apart from John, the writers of the various gospels were obscure figures. Why attribute these sacred writings to them if they did not compose them? There was also a tag that was glued on the outside of the scroll that would identify the individual author of the gospel. This made certain the name of the author was retained.

The evidence is clear and convincing. The traditional belief that Matthew, Mark, Luke, and John wrote the four gospels is the only view that fits the known facts (Blue Letter; "Who Wrote the Four Gospels?").

The point of this quote is that Matthew was one of the lesser known apostles, while John, Peter, and James were much better known. Thus, if you were going to forge a Gospel in the name of an apostle, it would make more sense to use one of those names rather than Matthew. And yes, John is appropriate to mention here, as it is rather universally agreed the Gospel under his name was written after the Synoptics, as we will see in Chapter Four. Thus, when the Synoptics were written, his name was still available to attach to one of them. Meanwhile, Mark and Luke were not even apostles, so why use them at all of you were forging an account of the life of Jesus?

Moreover, it was universally accepted in the early Church that these books were written by the traditional authors, with no dissents ever mentioned, and no other persons ever being proposed as the authors. This universal acceptance is best explained by the traditional authors being the actual authors. If they were not, then it is hard to explain this

Translator's Perspective on the Canon of the NT

phenomenon, as it is a far cry from the situation for some of the other books in the NT. It is simply audacious for scholars today to think they know better than those who lived at the time these books were written.

What the *International Standard Bible Encyclopedia* says in regards to Matthew would apply to the other Gospels as well:

> The Gospel ... was unanimously ascribed by the testimony of the ancient church to the apostle Matthew, though the title does not of itself necessarily imply immediate authorship. The unity and integrity of the Gospel were never in ancient times called in question (ISBE; "Matthew, the Gospel of").

Technically, the Gospels are anonymous, so even if they were not written by the traditional authors that would not be a mark of insincerity by the authors, as they made no attempts to pass themselves off as apostles. But the early Church never doubted the traditional authorships. We will look at each book in turn in the next two chapters.

Chapter Three
The Synoptic Gospels and the Book of Acts

The previous chapter overviewed the four Gospels and the Book of Acts. This chapter will study each of these books in turn, except for The Gospel According to John. It will be dealt with in the next chapter.

Matthew

The first Synoptic Gospel is The Gospel According to Matthew.

Author:

As stated in the previous chapter, it was universally believed in the early Church that Matthew was written by Matthew, a.k.a. Levi, the tax collector and one of the 12 apostles. Matthew is mentioned five times in the NT, but with some of these being parallel passages:

⁹And passing by from there, Jesus saw a man sitting at the tax-office, being called **Matthew**, and He says to him, "Be following Me!" And having stood up, he followed Him (Matt 9:9).

²Now the names of the twelve apostles are these: first Simon, the one being called Peter, and Andrew his brother, James the [son] of Zebedee and John his brother, ³Philip and Bartholomew, Thomas and **Matthew the tax collector**, James the [son] of Alpheus and Lebbeus, the one having been surnamed Thaddeus, ⁴Simon the Canaanite and Judas Iscariot, the one also having betrayed Him (Matt 10:2f).

¹³And He goes up into the mountain and summons whom He wanted, and they went to Him. ¹⁴Then He appointed twelve, so that they should be with Him, and so that He should send them out to be preaching ¹⁵and to be having power [or, authority] to be healing the diseases and to be casting out the demons.
¹⁶And He gave to Simon [the] name Peter, ¹⁷and James [son] of Zebedee and John the brother of James, and He gave them names—Boanerges, which is [fig., means], "Sons of Thunder," ¹⁸and Andrew and Philip and Bartholomew and **Matthew** and Thomas and James [son] of Alpheus and Thaddeus and Simon the Canaanite ¹⁹and Judas Iscariot, who also betrayed Him (Mark 3:13-19).

Translator's Perspective on the Canon of the NT

[27]And after these [things], He went out and saw **a tax collector by name Levi** sitting at the tax office. And He said to him, "Be following Me!" [28]And having left all behind, having gotten up, he followed Him (Luke 5:27).

[12]Now it happened in those days, He went out into the mountain to pray, and He was spending the night in the prayer of God [or, in prayer to God]. [13]And when it became day, He summoned His disciples, and having chosen from them twelve, whom also He named apostles: [14]Simon, whom also He named Peter, and Andrew his brother, James and John, Philip and Bartholomew, [15]**Matthew** and Thomas, James the [son] of Alphaeus and Simon, the one being called [the] Zealot, [16]Judas [the son; or, the brother] of James and Judas Iscariot, who also became a traitor (Luke 6:15).

[13]And when they entered [Jerusalem], they went up into the upstairs room where they were staying: both Peter and James and John and Andrew, Philip and Thomas, Bartholomew and **Matthew**, James [the son] of Alphaeus and Simon the Zealot, and Judas [the son; or, the brother] of James (Acts 1:13).

Don't get thrown by Mathew having two names. This was often the case in ancient times, as will be seen with other NT writers. But a comparison of the passages describing the calling of this man shows clearly that Levi was the same person as Matthew. Levi was probably his Hebrew name, and Matthew his Greek name.

The slight difference between these passages is interesting. Luke mentions that the tax collector "left all behind" when he followed Jesus. It was probably due to humbleness on Matthew's part that he did not mention this himself, and this is a small clue to Mathew being the author of the Gospel under his name. Note also in the list of the names of the apostles, Matthew mentions that he was a tax collector. His past probably weighed on him, and he probably felt it important to mention it, Thus, showing Christ's gracefulness in accepting and forgiving him.

But his being a tax collector is the very reason it is unlikely that his name would have been associated with this book if he was not in fact the author. This book was primarily directed towards Jews, as can be seen by the opening genealogy. But Roman tax collectors were despised by the Jews. Thus, Matthew is the least likely of the apostles to have a book accepted by Jews.

Moreover, the mention in Acts is the last mention of Matthew in the NT. This reinforces what was said before—if Matthew did not write this

Gospel, it would have made little sense for a forger to use the name of this less than prominent apostle.

Going back to Matthew being a tax collector, this fact has a couple of other important implications:

> Author: This book is known as the Gospel of Matthew because it was written by the apostle of the same name. The style of the book is exactly what would be expected of a man who was once a tax collector. Matthew has a keen interest in accounting (18:23-24; 25:14-15). The Gospel of Matthew is very orderly and concise. Rather than write in chronological order, Matthew arranges this Gospel through six discussions.
>
> As a tax collector, Matthew possessed a skill that makes his writing all the more exciting for Christians. Tax collectors were expected to be able to write in a form of shorthand, which essentially meant that Matthew could record a person's words as they spoke, word for word. This ability means that the words of Matthew are not only inspired by the Holy Spirit, but should represent an actual transcript of some of Christ's sermons. For example, the Sermon on the Mount, as recorded in chapters 5-7, is almost certainly a perfect recording of that great message (GotQuestions?org; "Gospel of Matthew").

It was stated before that there was never any suggestion of any other people as being authors of the Gospels other than the traditional authors. In addition to statements by the Church Fathers in this respect is the manuscript evidence:

> Since the times of the early church fathers, the apostle Matthew has always been accredited with the authorship of the first gospel (canonically). Even the title "According to Matthew" (*KATA MAQQAION*) is found in the earliest manuscripts, and was the most highly regarded and quoted of the gospels by the church fathers (Blue Letter; "The Gospel of Matthew").
>
> The titles of NT books were not part of the autograph, but were added later on the basis of tradition. Still, the tradition in this case is universal: every MS which contains Matthew has some sort of ascription to Matthew. Some scholars suggest that this title was added as early as 125 CE (Bible.org; "Matthew: Introduction, Argument, and Outline").

But whatever be the view we take of the precise origin of the first canonical Gospel, it was universally received in the ancient church as the work of Matthew. It was our Matthew who is often, though freely, quoted by Justin Martyr as early as A.D. 146 among the "Gospel Memoirs;" it was one of the four Gospels of which his pupil Tatian compiled a connected "Diatessaron;" and it was the only Matthew used by Irenaeus and all the fathers that follow (Schaff; 8872-8875).

Date:

This issue has already been covered, but the following quotes will add to what has already been said:

The first Gospel makes the impression of primitive antiquity. The city of Jerusalem, the temple, the priesthood and sacrifices, the entire religious and political fabric of Judaism are supposed to be still standing, but with an intimation of their speedy downfall. It alone reports the words of Christ that he came not to destroy but to fulfil the law and the prophets, and that he was only sent to the lost sheep of the house of Israel. Hence the best critics put the composition several years before the destruction of Jerusalem (Schaff; 8753-8757).

The first Gospel was well known to the author of the "Didache of the Apostles," who wrote between 80 and 100, and made large use of it, especially the Sermon on the Mount. The next clear allusion to this Gospel is made in the Epistle of Barnabas [90-135 AD], who quotes two passages from the Greek Matthew, one from 22:14: "Many are called, but few chosen," with the significant formula used only of inspired writings, "It is written." This shows clearly that early in the second century, if not before, it was an acknowledged authority in the church (Schaff; 8827-8831).

Doctrine of God:

In addition to Matthew being an apostle and thus an eyewitness of the life of Jesus, the Gospel of Matthew was highly regarded in the early Church as it presented correct theology. This can be seen in the Gospel of Matthew being grounded in the OT and all that it taught, and in its presenting the essential doctrines of the early Church as seen in the early creeds, hymns, and ceremonies of the Church presented in Chapter One.

First, in regards to the nature of God, that God is a personal being who is intimately involved with His creation is seen in the Lord's Prayer as recorded in Matthew:

> Our Father, the [One] in the heavens, let Your name be regarded as holy.
> ¹⁰Let Your kingdom come.
> Let Your will be done, as in heaven, [so] also on the earth.
> ¹¹Give us today the bread sufficient for the day.
> ¹²And forgive us our debts [fig., sins], in the same way as <u>we</u> also forgive our debtors [fig., the ones having sinned against us].
> ¹³And do not lead us into temptation [or, testing; or, trials], <u>but</u> deliver us from the Wicked [One] [or, spare us from evil].
> Because Yours is the kingdom and the power and the glory into the ages! [fig., forever!] So be it! [Gr. *Amen*] (Matt 6:9b-13).

By referring to God as "our Father," this prayer presents a very personal and intimate attitude towards God, as opposed to God being distant as seen in some other religious philosophies. This prayer also shows God is King, sovereign over His creation, the Provider of our needs, gracious in forgiving us, and worthy of praise. All of these points fit with the OT conception of God. Note that the second half of verse 13 is a textual variant, with some Greek texts not containing it. But whether genuine or not, this line fits with the tone of the rest of the prayer.

This Gospel also states there is only one God worthy of worship, "For it has been written, *'[The] LORD your God you will prostrate yourself in worship before, and Him only will you sacredly serve.'*" (Matt 4:10b). It further states this one God is the Creator, "⁴But answering, He said, 'Did you* not read that the One having made [them] from [the] beginning made them male and female?'" (Matt 19:3), and He controls nature, "He causes His sun to rise on evil [people] and good [people], and He sends rain on righteous [people] and unrighteous [people]" (Matt 5:45).

This Gospel asserts that God is almighty, "²⁶But Jesus having looked attentively [at them], said to them, 'With people this is impossible, but with God all [things are] possible!'" (Matt 19:26), and we are to love this one true God, "³⁷Then Jesus said to him, *'You will love [the] LORD your God with your whole heart and with your whole soul and with your whole understanding.'*" (Matt 22:37).

All of this is to say the God of this Gospel is the God of the OT:

Translator's Perspective on the Canon of the NT

³¹"But concerning the resurrection of the dead, you* read the [word] spoken to you* by God, saying, ³² '*I am the God of Abraham and the God of Isaac and the God of Jacob,*' did you* not? [Exod 3:6] God is not a God of dead [people], but of living [people]!" (Matt 22:31f).

This passage also shows that this Gospel conforms to the OT in other doctrinal manners, in this case with the teaching the resurrection of the dead.

Essential Tenets:

This Gospel also conforms to the essential tenets seen in the early creeds, hymns, and ceremonies. It teaches Jesus was fully human. He was conceived and born of Mary (Matt 1:18-25). He hungered (4:1), and He ate food (Matt 9:10f). But He is also divine. He can control the elements, "Then having arisen, He rebuked [or, gave orders to] the winds and the sea, and [there] became a great calm!" (8:26b). He forgives sins, which only God can do (Matt 9:1-3). He knows people's thoughts (Matt 9:4).

This Gospel asserts about Jesus, "You are the Christ, the Son of the living God!" (Matt 16:16; also Christ: 1:1,18; 16:20; 24:5; 27:62-65; Son of God: 8:29; 14:35; 27:54). He is also Lord, "For the Son of Humanity is Lord of the Sabbath" (12:8, also 7:21f; 8:2,6,8,25; 9:28; 13:51; and many others).

Being the Christ, the Son of God, and Lord, Jesus is worthy of worship, "Then the [disciples] in the boat having come, prostrated themselves in worship before Him, saying, 'Truly You are God's Son!'" (Matt 14:33). Though the word translated "worship" can also mean "reverence," given in this passage that Jesus has just controlled the forces of nature (verses 24-32), something only God can do, "worship" is the most likely meaning.

In addition, this Gospel associates God the Father, Jesus Christ, and the Holy Spirit together:

¹⁶And having been baptized, Jesus went up immediately from the water. And look! The heavens were opened to Him, and he [i.e., John the Baptist] saw the Spirit of God descending like a dove and coming upon Him. ¹⁷And listen! A voice [comes] out of the heavens, saying, "This is My Son—the Beloved—in whom I am well-pleased!" (Matt 3:16-17).

¹⁹Having gone [or, When you* have gone], make disciples of all the nations, baptizing them in the name of the Father and of the Son and of the Holy Spirit (Matt 28:19).

The baptism in the Spirit is foretold in this book:

¹¹"I indeed baptize you* in water [or, with water] to [or, because of] repentance. But the One coming after me is mightier [than] I, of whom I am not worthy to carry His sandals, He will baptize you* in [or, with] [the] Holy Spirit (Matt 3:11).

The Holy Spirit will work in the lives of believers:

¹⁹But whenever they are handing you* over, you* shall not be anxious how or what you* should speak, for it will be given to you* in that hour what you* will speak; ²⁰for you* are not the ones speaking, but the Spirit of your* Father [is] the One speaking in you* (Matt 10:19f).

It is only through Jesus that a person can come to know the Father:

²⁷All [things] were handed over to Me by My Father, and no one fully knows the Son, except the Father, nor does anyone fully know the Father, except the Son, and [the person] to whom the Son shall be desiring to reveal [Him] (Matt 11:27).

But most of all, this Gospel teaches that Jesus' blood would be "poured out on behalf of many for forgiveness of sins" (Matt 26:28b), and it records in detail the death, burial, and resurrection of Jesus and His appearances after His resurrection (Matt 27-28). It also asserts His Second Coming:

⁶⁴Jesus says to him, "You said [it]; nevertheless, I say to you*, from now on you* will see *'the Son of Humanity sitting at the right [parts]* [fig., *on the right hand*] *of the Power'* and *'coming on the clouds of heaven!* [or, *of the sky*!]'" (Matt 26:64; also 24:3).

The renewal of a believer that comes about by faith in Jesus is demonstrated by the changed lives of those who come into contact with Jesus. For instance, among Jesus' disciples is the author of this book, Matthew the tax collector. A tax collector at that time was usually dishonest, collecting more taxes than was called for and keeping the extra for himself (see Luke 3:13). But Matthew left this dishonest but lucrative profession and followed Jesus (Matt 9:9).

Moreover, in this book Jesus promises inner peace to the person who trusts in Him:

Translator's Perspective on the Canon of the NT

²⁸Come to Me, all the ones laboring and having been burdened, and I will give you* rest. ²⁹Take My yoke upon you* and learn from Me, because I am gentle and humble in heart, *'and you* will find rest for your* souls.'* [Jer 6:16, Heb.] ³⁰For My yoke [is] easy, and My burden is light" (Matt 11:28f).

As already seen, Jesus declares the Father can only be known through Him. But this leads to a personal relationship with the Father:

⁶But when you are praying, enter into your private room, and having shut your door, pray to your Father, the [One] in secret, and your Father, the [One] seeing in secret, will reward you in the open (Matt 6:6).

Finally, the already quoted "Lord's Prayer" was revolutionary when Jesus gave it, as it describes a personal relationship with God that transcended what was thought possible at the time.

Conclusion on Matthew:

Given all of this, this Gospel satisfies all of the standards for a book to be included in the NT. It Thus, is rightly a part of the canon of the NT.

Mark

Author:

Mark is another NT figure with more than one name. He is known as both John and Mark. This is mentioned in the Book of Acts, "John, the one being called Mark" (Acts 12:12,25).

Mark accompanied Paul and Silas on their first missionary journey, "²⁵Now Barnabas and Saul [Paul] returned to Jerusalem, having fulfilled the ministry [or, their mission], having taken along also John, the one being called Mark" (Acts 12:25).

But on their second journey, Mark turned back, "¹³Now having set sail from Paphos [with] the ones about [him] [fig., with his companions], Paul came to Perga of Pamphylia. But **John** [i.e., Mark], having departed from them, returned to Jerusalem" (Acts 13:13). Because of this, Paul did not want to take him along on their next trip. This led to a parting of ways of Paul and Barnabas:

³⁶Then after some days, Paul said to Barnabas, "Having returned now, we should visit our brothers [and sisters] in every city in which we have preached the word of the Lord, [to see] how they have [it] [fig.,

how they are doing]." ³⁷And Barnabas decided to take along **John, the one being called Mark**. ³⁸But Paul was not considering it good to take this [one] along with [them], the one having withdrawn from them at Pamphylia and not having gone with them to the work.

³⁹So [there] came to be a sharp disagreement, with the result that they were separated from one another, and Barnabas, having taken **Mark**, sailed away to Cyprus. ⁴⁰But Paul, having chosen Silas, went out, having been handed over [fig., committed] to the grace of God by the brothers [and sisters]. ⁴¹So he was passing through Syria and Cilicia, strengthening the assemblies. (Acts 15:36-41).

However, later, Paul and Mark reconciled, and Mark is again working with Paul, and Paul considers him to be useful:

²³Epaphras greets you (my fellow-prisoner in Christ Jesus), ²⁴[as do] **Mark**, Aristarchus, Demas, [and] Luke, my co-workers! (Phlm 1:124).

Only Luke is with me. Having picked up **Mark**, be bringing [him] with yourself, for he is useful to me for ministry [or, service] (2Tim 4:11).

Not only was Mark associated with Paul, but he was also associated with Peter, "The [woman] [i.e., Peter's wife; or, Your [sister-assembly]] in Babylon, chosen together with [you*], greets you*, and **Mark** my son [fig., disciple]" (1Peter 5:1). By "son" Peter probably means that he led Mark to faith in Jesus. Moreover, after Peter is miraculously delivered from prison, he goes to the house of Mark's mother:

¹²And having become aware of [this], he came to the house of Mary, the mother of **John, the one being called Mark**, where a considerable [number] had been gathering together and [were] praying.

Thus, Peter must have had a close relationship with Mark and his family.

This is all we know for certain about Mark. But it is enough to know that he was directly associated with the apostles. It is also possible he was an eyewitness of at least part of the life of Jesus. The following is recorded in this Gospel during the arrest of Jesus in the Garden of Gethsemane.

⁵¹And one certain young man followed Him, having put a linen cloth on [his] naked [body], and the young men seized him. ⁵²But having left behind the linen cloth, he fled from them naked (Mark 14:51f).

Translator's Perspective on the Canon of the NT

This is a rather strange thing to have recorded, and only Mark does so. As such, many believe this was Mark cryptically referring to himself. If it is, then he witnessed at least one important event in Jesus' life, His arrest in Gethsemane. But still, Mark is not a prominent figure in the early Church, and with him having withdrawn from Paul, not a very commendable one. As such, it would be strange for his name to become attached to this Gospel, unless he was in fact the author.

Author: Although the Gospel of Mark does not name its author, it is the unanimous testimony of early church fathers that Mark was the author. He was an associate of the Apostle Peter, and evidently his spiritual son (1Peter 5:13). From Peter he received first-hand information of the events and teachings of the Lord, and preserved the information in written form (GotQuestions?org; "Gospel of Mark").

There is hardly any incident related in Mark's gospel where Simon Peter was not present and the recording of minute detail shows that we have the testimony of an eyewitness (Blue Letter; "Were the Writers of the Four Gospels Qualified to Write about Jesus?").

He [Mark] was the son of a certain Mary who lived at Jerusalem and offered her house, at great risk no doubt in that critical period of persecution, to the Christian disciples for devotional meetings. Peter repaired to that house after his deliverance from prison (A.D. 44). This accounts for the close intimacy of Mark with Peter; he was probably converted through him, and hence called his spiritual "son" (1 Pet. 5: 13). He may have had a superficial acquaintance with Christ; for he is probably identical with that unnamed "young man" who, according to his own report, left his "linen cloth and fled naked" from Gethsemane in the night of betrayal (Mark 14: 51). He would hardly have mentioned such a trifling incident, unless it had a special significance for him as the turning-point in his life (Schaff; 8886-8892).

Another hint that Peter was in fact the source for the information in this Gospel can be seen by comparing an event recorded in both Matthew 16 and Mark 8. These chapters record Peter's great confession that Jesus is the Christ. Jesus follows that up with the prediction of His death. Peter tries to discourage Jesus from this, but Jesus rebukes him. In-between these events, only Matthew records the following:

> [17] And answering, Jesus said to him, "Fortunate are you, Simon Bar-Jonah ["son of Jonah"], because flesh and blood did not reveal [this] to you, but My Father, the [One] in the heavens. [18] Now I also say to you, that you are Peter ["a stone"], and on this solid rock [or, bedrock] I will build my Assembly [or, Church], and [the] gates of the realm of the dead [Gr., *hades*] will not prevail against it. [19] And I will give to you the keys of the kingdom of the heavens, and whatever you bind on the earth will have been bound in the heavens; and whatever you loose on the earth will have been loosed in the heavens" (Matt 16:17-29).

This is a grand affirmation of the authority of Peter, and some even take it as Jesus declaring that Peter is the premier apostle, the rock on which the Church is built. But Mark omitting it would reflect Peter's humbleness in not relating this part of this event, probably still not wanting accolades, knowing that he later denied Christ.

> The tradition of the church adds two important facts, that he [Mark] wrote his Gospel in Rome as the interpreter of Peter, and that afterwards he founded the church of Alexandria....
> Though not an apostle, Mark had the best opportunity in his mother's house and his personal connection with Peter, Paul, Barnabas, and other prominent disciples for gathering the most authentic information concerning the gospel history (Schaff; Kindle Location 8902--8907).

It is also clear that Mark wrote independently of Matthew and Luke given the details he provides that those writers do not. These details could only come from eyewitness testimony.

> Mark inserts many delicate tints and interesting incidents of persons and events which he must have heard from primitive witnesses. They are not the touches of fancy or the reflections of an historian, but the reminiscences of the first impressions. They occur in every chapter. He makes some little contribution to almost every narrative he has in common with Matthew and Luke (Schaff; 8991-8994).

For instance, in the account of the rich young ruler, only Mark mentions "Jesus having looked attentively at him, loved him" (Mark 10:21; cp. Matt 19:21). And only Mark includes the cry of the father of

Translator's Perspective on the Canon of the NT

the demoniac at the foot of the Mount of Transfiguration, "I do believe!" [or, I do have faith!] Lord, be helping my unbelief!" [or, my weak faith!"] (Mark 9:24, cp. Matt 19:14-16). These two statements must have left a strong impression upon Peter, who still felt guilt over his lack of faith yet took comfort in Jesus' restoration of him (Mark 15:66-72; John 21:15-17). Peter Thus, related this information to Mark.

Finally, as with the Gospel of Mathew, Mark is the only name ever associated with this Gospel in the early Church and in the manuscript evidence, and there was never any doubt about Mark being the author.

Doctrine of God:

Also like Matthew, the viewpoint of God in Mark concurs with that of the OT. God is the Creator, "But from [the] beginning of the creation, God 'made them male and female'" (Mark 10:6). God is almighty, "For all [things] are possible with God!" (Mark 10:27b).

Moreover, there is only one God, and He is to be loved fully:

[The] LORD is our God, [the] LORD is one. ³⁰And you will love [the] LORD your God with your whole heart and with your whole soul and with your whole understanding and with your whole strength' (Mark 12:29b).

Also as with Matthew, the God of Mark is clearly the God of the OT, and there is an assertion of the doctrine of resurrection.

²⁶But concerning the dead [people], that they rise: you* have read, have you* not, in the Scroll of Moses (at The Bush), how God spoke to him, saying, *'I [am] the God of Abraham and the God of Isaac and the God of Jacob?'* [Exod 3:6] ²⁷He is not the God of dead [people], <u>but</u> [the] God of living [people]! (Mark 12:26f).

Essential Tenets:

As for the early essential tenets, in this Gospel Jesus is fully human. He sleeps, "And He was in the stern, sleeping on the cushion" (Mark 4:38), and He eats and drinks, "Why is that One eating and drinking with those tax collectors and sinful [people]?" (Mark 2:16b). But He is also divine. He can control the elements, "And having woken up, He rebuked the wind and said to the sea, "Be silent! Be muzzled!" [fig., Be still!"] And the wind abated, and [there] was a great calm." (Mark 4:39). He forgives sins, which only God can do, "Child, your sins have been forgiven you" (Mark 2:5f). He knows what people are reasoning within themselves (Mark 2:8).

This Gospel also asserts that Jesus is Lord (Mark 2:28; 7:28; 9:24; and many others), Christ (Mark 1:1; 8:30; 9:41; 14:61), and the Son of God (Mark 1:1; 3:11; 5:7; 15:39). Jesus Thus, receives worship:

> "We praise You! [Gr., *Hosanna*] 'Having been blessed [is] the One coming in [the] name of [the] LORD!' [Psalm 118:26] ¹⁰Having been blessed [is] the coming kingdom in [the] name of [the] Lord of our father David! We praise You in the highest!" (Mark 11:9b-10).

Like Matthew, Mark associates the Father, Jesus, and the Holy Spirit together:

> ⁹And it happened in those days, Jesus came from Nazareth of Galilee, and He was baptized by John in the Jordan [River]. ¹⁰And immediately coming up from the water, he [i.e., John the Baptist] saw the heavens being parted and the Spirit like a dove descending upon Him. ¹¹And a voice came out of the heavens, "You are My Son—the Beloved—in whom I am well-pleased!" (Mark 1:9-11).

The baptism in the Spirit is foretold in this book:
> ⁷And he began proclaiming, saying, "He is coming after me, the [One] greater than I, of whom I am not worthy, having stooped down, to untie the strap of His sandals! ⁸I indeed baptize you* in water [or, with water], but He will baptize you* in [or, with] [the] Holy Spirit!" (Mark 1:7f).

The Holy Spirit will work in the lives of believers:

> ¹¹But when they lead you* away, handing [you*] over, stop worrying beforehand what you* shall speak, neither be thinking about [it]; but whatever shall be given to you* in that hour, this you* are to be speaking, for it is not you* speaking, but the Holy Spirit (Mark 13:11).

Mark's Gospel asserts about Jesus, "For even the Son of Humanity did not come to be served, but to serve, and to give His life [as] a ransom [or, price of release] for [or, in the place of] many" (Mark 10:45), and it teaches Jesus' blood would be "poured out for many" (Mark 14:24b). This Gospel then recounts in detail the death, burial, and resurrection of Jesus, His appearances after His resurrection and His ascension, and it predicts His Second Coming (Mark 15-16).

Conclusion on Mark:

Translator's Perspective on the Canon of the NT

Mark fulfills all of the standards for a book to be a part of the canon of the NT.

Luke/ Acts

Author:

As previous asserted, there is no doubt the same person wrote both Luke and Acts. The prologues to the books indicate this, and the singular writing style confirms it. These books will Thus, be considered together. Luke is mentioned by name three times in the letters of Paul:

[14]**Luke**, the beloved physician, greets you* (Col 4:14).

Only **Luke** is with me (2Tim 4:11).

[23]Epaphras greets you (my fellow-prisoner in Christ Jesus), [24][as do] Mark, Aristarchus, Demas, [and] **Luke**, my co-workers! (Phlm 1:124).

Paul and Luke knew each other for a long time, as Luke traveled with Paul. This can be seen from the "we" passages of the Book of Acts. They begin with Acts 16:10:

[6]Now having passed through Phrygia and the region of Galatia, having been forbidden by the Holy Spirit to speak the word in Asia, [cp. Acts 19:10] [7]having gone toward Mysia, **they** were trying to be going to Bithynia, and the Spirit did not allow them. [8]So having passed by Mysia, **they** came down to Troas. [9]And a vision appeared to Paul during the night: a certain man of Macedonia was standing, pleading with him and saying, "Having crossed over to Macedonia, help us!" [10]So when he saw the vision, immediately **we** sought to go out to Macedonia, concluding that the Lord had summoned us to preach the Gospel to them.

Note the change from third person pronoun in verses seven and eight to the first person pronoun in verse ten. The use of the first person then continues to the end of the book, except for one break (Acts 17:1- 20:5). Luke was Thus, in a unique position to write about Paul's journeys, being a witness of a large part of them. And during these journeys Paul would have related the early parts of his life to Luke, along with those of Peter and the other apostles whom he had met with. Luke was also with Paul at the end of his life, as Paul writes in his final letter, written shortly before his death, "Only Luke is with me" (2 Tim. 4: 11).

> The "we" sections begin Acts 16:10, when Paul started from Troas to Macedonia (A.D. 51); they break off when he leaves Philippi for Corinth (Acts 17: 1); they are resumed (Acts 20:5, 6) when he visits Macedonia again seven years later (A.D. 58), and then continue to the close of the narrative (A.D. 63). Luke probably remained several years at Philippi, engaged in missionary labors, until Paul's return. He was in the company of Paul, including the interruptions, at least twelve years. He was again with Paul in his last captivity, shortly before his martyrdom, his most faithful and devoted companion (2 Tim. 4: 11) (Schaff; 10138-10142).

Luke was not an eyewitness of the life of Christ, nor was he directly associated with any of the original twelve apostles. But he tells us in the prologue to his Gospel that he had "investigated everything carefully from the beginning" (Luke 1:3). Thus, his writing a Gospel would be similar to the author of the Books of Kings of the OT, as discussed in Volume One. Luke is working from eyewitness written and oral testimony, so that he can "write [it out] to you in consecutive order [or, in an orderly fashion," so that readers "shall know the certainty [or, exact truth] about which you were instructed" (Luke 1:3-4). This wording shows that Luke was very meticulous in his research. And it must be membered, he was writing at a time when many eyewitnesses to the life of Jesus were still alive; he Thus, had access to reliable firsthand sources. Moreover:

> His opportunities were the very best. He visited the principal apostolic churches between Jerusalem and Rome, and came in personal contact with the founders and leaders. He met Peter, Mark, and Barnabas at Antioch, James and his elders at Jerusalem (on Paul's last visit), Philip and his daughters at Caesarea, the early converts in Greece and Rome; and he enjoyed, besides, the benefit of all the information which Paul himself had received by revelation or collected from personal intercourse with his fellow-apostles and other primitive disciples. The sources for the history of the infancy were Jewish-Christian and Aramaean (hence the strongly Hebraizing coloring of Luke 1–2); his information of the activity of Christ in Samaria was probably derived from Philip, who labored there as an evangelist and afterwards in Caesarea. But a man of

Translator's Perspective on the Canon of the NT

>Luke's historic instinct and conscientiousness would be led to visit also in person the localities in Galilee which are immortalized by the ministry of Christ. From Jerusalem or Caesarea he could reach them all in three or four days (Schaff; 9209-9216).

To elaborate on one point mentioned here, Luke 1-2 shows signs of having been translated into Greek from a Hebrew or Aramaic original.

>The songs of Zacharias, Elizabeth, Mary, and Simeon, and the anthem of the angelic host, are the last of Hebrew psalms as well as the first of Christian hymns. They can be literally translated back into the Hebrew, without losing their beauty (Schaff; 9366-9368).

Luke possibly attained the material for these sections from Mary, the mother of Jesus, which either she or her husband Joseph had previously written down in Hebrew or Aramaic. We Thus, have every reason to believe Luke's Gospel presents an accurate history of the life and teachings of Jesus.

It should also be noted, "Luke has a great deal of original and most valuable matter, which proves his independence and the variety of his sources" (Schaff; 9222-9223). Two well-known examples of this "original and most valuable matter" are the stories of the Good Samaritan and the Prodigal Son, which only appear in Luke (10:30-36; 15:11-32). We Thus, have a third independent witness to the life and teachings of Christ.

And finally, as with Matthew and Mark, no other name was ever attached to this book other than Luke. Moreover:

>The genuineness of Luke is above reasonable doubt. The character of the Gospel agrees perfectly with what we might expect from the author as far as we know him from the Acts and the Epistles. No other writer answers the description...
>
>There are strong indications that the third Gospel was composed (not published) between 58 and 63, before the close of Paul's Roman captivity. No doubt it took several years to collect and digest the material; and the book was probably not published, i.e., copied and distributed, till after the death of Paul, at the same time with the Acts, which forms the second part and is dedicated to the same patron (Schaff; 9389-9390; 9420-9422).

Doctrine of God in Luke:
In Luke, God is almighty:

For every word will not be [fig., For nothing is] impossible with God!" (Luke 1:37b).
²⁷Then He said, "The [things] impossible with people are possible with God!" (Luke 18:27).

The God of Luke is the only God worthy of worship and of our full love:

⁸And answering, Jesus said to him, "Get behind Me, Satan! It has been written, '*You will prostrate yourself in worship before [the] LORD your God, and Him only you will sacredly serve.*'" [Deut 6:13]

²⁷Then answering, he said, "'*You will love [the] LORD your God with your whole heart* [fig., *your entire inner self*] *and with your whole soul and with your whole strength and with your whole understanding,*' and '*your neighbor as yourself.*'" [Deut 6:5; Lev 19:18] (Luke 10:27).

The God of Luke is the Provider:

²⁴Be considering the ravens, for they do not sow nor reap, to which there is no [fig., which do not have] storeroom nor barn, and God provides for them. How much more valuable you* are than the birds! (Luke 12:24).

Note also in this passage the assertion of the intrinsic distinction between human beings and animals, as was discussed in Volume One.
The God of Luke is the God of Israel:

⁶⁸"Blessed [is the] Lord, the God of Israel, for He visited and made redemption for His people (Luke 1:68).

³⁷But that the dead are raised, even Moses revealed at The Bush, when he calls [the] Lord, '*the God of Abraham and the God of Isaac and the God of Jacob.*' [Exod 3:6] ³⁸Now He is not [the] God of dead [people], but of living [people], for all are alive to Him" (Luke 20:37f).

This later passage again shows the Jewish and Christian belief in resurrection.

Essential Tenets in Luke:

Translator's Perspective on the Canon of the NT

In regards to early essential tenets, in Luke, Jesus is declared to be, "The Christ of God!" (Luke 9:20; also 2:26; 4:41; 22:67; 24:26,46). Mary is told, "the Holy One being born will be called God's Son" (Luke 1:35; also 4:4,9,41; 8:28). And He is Lord. As Peter exclaimed when he first met Jesus, "Depart from me, because I am a sinful man, O Lord!" (Luke 5:8, also 5:12; 6:5; 6:46, and many others).

In Luke, Jesus is fully human. As the angel proclaimed to Mary, "And behold, you will conceive in [your] womb, and you will give birth to a Son, and you will call His name Jesus" (Luke 1:30). Jesus slept (Luke 8:22), and He ate and drank (Luke 5:30; 7:36f; 11:37; 22:7-1). And very importantly, Jesus was still fully human after His resurrection:

[36]Now while they [were] telling these [things], Jesus Himself stood in [the] middle of them and says to them, "Peace to you*." [37]But having been startled and having become terrified, they were thinking [they were] seeing a spirit. [38]And He said to them, "Why have you* been frightened? And why do doubts arise in your* hearts? [39]See My hands and My feet, that I am I Myself. Handle Me and see, because a spirit does not have flesh and bones, just as you* see I have."

[40]And having said this, He showed His hands and His feet to them. [41]Then while they [were] refusing to believe from the joy, and marveling, He said to them, "Do you* have anything edible here?" [42]So they gave to Him a piece of a broiled fish and a honeycomb from a beehive. [43]And having taken, He ate before them (Luke 24:36-43).

Thus, after His resurrection Jesus was not a disembodied spirit but had "flesh and bones," and He ate food to demonstrate His full humanity. But Jesus was also fully divine. He forgave sins:

[20]And having seen their faith, He said to him, "Man, your sins have been forgiven you."
[21]And the scribes and the Pharisees began to reason, saying, "Who is this [Man] who speaks blasphemies? Who is able to be forgiving sins, except God alone? (Luke 5:20f).

Jesus controlled the elements, which only God can do:
[22]And it happened, on one of those days, that He stepped into a boat with His disciples, and He said to them, "Let us cross over to the other side of the lake." And they put out to sea. [23]But as they sailed, He fell asleep. And a storm of wind [fig., a windstorm] came down onto the lake, and they began being swamped and were being in danger. [24]Then having approached, they awakened Him, saying, "Master, Master, we are perishing!" And having gotten up, He rebuked the wind and the

raging of the water, and they ceased, and it became calm! ²⁵And He said to them, "Where is your* faith?" Then having been afraid, they marveled, saying to one another, "Who then is this, that He commands even the winds and the water, and they obey Him?" [cp. Job 38:25-38; Ps 135:7] (Luke 8:22-25).

Jesus knows people's thoughts:
⁴⁶Then a dispute came up among them, [as to] which of them might be the greatest. ⁴⁷But Jesus having seen the thought process of their heart [fig., having known what they were thinking within themselves], (Luke 9:46.47a).

God the Father, Jesus Christ, and the Holy Spirit are associated together in Luke:

³⁴And Mary said to the angel, "How will this be since I do not know a man?" [fig., since I am a virgin?"] ³⁵And answering, the angel said to her, "[The] Holy Spirit will come upon you, and [the] power of the Most High will overshadow you, and so the Holy One being born will be called God's Son (Luke 1:34).

²¹Now it happened, while all the people [were coming] to be baptized, Jesus also having been baptized, and praying, heaven [or, the sky] was opened, ²²and the Holy Spirit descended in bodily form like a dove upon Him, and a voice came out of heaven saying, "You are My Son—the Beloved—in You I am well-pleased!" (Luke 3:21f).

The Holy Spirit works in people's lives. It is said of John the Baptist before his birth, "For he will be great before the Lord, and he shall by no means drink wine and strong drink, and he will be filled [with the] Holy Spirit even from [the] womb of his mother" (Luke 1:15). Similarly, of John's mother it is said, "And it happened, when Elizabeth heard the greeting of Mary, the baby leapt for joy in her womb. And Elizabeth was filled with [the] Holy Spirit" (Luke 1:41). Then the same is said of his father, "And Zacharias his father was filled with [the] Holy Spirit and prophesied" (Luke 1:67).

The baptism in the Spirit is promised in this book:
¹⁶John answered, saying to all, "I indeed baptize you* in water [or, with water], but [One] mightier than I is coming, of whom I am not worthy to loose the strap of His sandals, He will baptize you* in [or, with] [the] Holy Spirit and fire (Luke 3:16).

Translator's Perspective on the Canon of the NT

The Holy Spirit is promised to all who ask:
¹¹"Now which father [among] you*, [if] his son will ask [for] a loaf of bread, he will not give to him a stone, will he? Or also [if he asks for] a fish, he will not give to him a serpent instead of a fish, will he? ¹²Or also if he asks [for] an egg, he will not give to him a scorpion, will he? ¹³If you* then being evil know [how] to be giving good gifts to your* children, how much more will the Father of heaven [fig., your* heavenly Father] give [the] Holy Spirit to the ones asking Him?" (Luke 11:11-13).

The Holy Spirit will work in the lives of believers:
¹¹"Now when they shall be bringing you* before the synagogues and the rulers and the authorities, stop being anxious how or what you* are to speak in your* defense, or what you* should say. ¹²For the Holy Spirit will teach you* in that very hour what it is necessary to say" (Luke 12:11f).

The transformation of people's lives by Jesus is seen in the lives transformed in this book. Among Jesus' disciples is "Simon, the one being called [the] Zealot" (Luke 6:15). A Zealot was seeking the violent overthrown of Roman oppression. But now this Zealot has come to follow the Prince of Peace.

This transformation is seen in the life of the sinful woman who wiped Jesus' feet (Luke 7:36-49). It is again seen in the life of Zaccheus, a rich tax collection superintendent and someone said to be a sinful man (Luke 19:1-7).

⁸Now Zaccheus having stood, said to the Lord, "Listen! The half of my possessions, Lord, I give to the poor, and if I defrauded anyone of anything, I give back four times as much." ⁹Then Jesus said to him, "Today salvation came to this house, because he also is a son of Abraham. ¹⁰For the Son of Humanity came to seek and to save the one having been lost" (Luke 19:8-10).

But most of all, Jesus proclaimed at the Last Supper, "This cup [is] the New Covenant in My blood, the [blood] being poured out on your* behalf" (Luke 22:20). The Gospel of Luke then recounts in detail the death, burial, and resurrection of Jesus, His appearances after His resurrection, and His ascension (Luke 23-24).

Conclusion on Luke:

Luke fulfills all of the standards for a book to be a part of the canon of the NT. It should be noted that many parallel passages between

Mathew, Mark, and Luke have been quoted in this chapter. That is why these three books are called the Synoptic Gospels. But upon close comparison, you will notice slight differences between these passages, indicating their independence.

Doctrine of God in Acts:

The Book of Acts follows in the same vein as Luke in regards to the nature of God. Peter declares God to be the Creator: "Master, You [are] the God, the One having *'made the heaven and the earth and the sea and all the [things] in them,'* [Exod 20:11] (Acts 4:24).

Peter declares the God of this book is the God of the OT:

¹Then the high priest said, "Do you so hold these [things]?" ²But he said, "Men, brothers and fathers, pay attention! The God of glory appeared to our father Abraham, being in Mesopotamia, before he lived in Haran ³and said to him, *'Go out from your [native] land and from your relatives, and come into a land which I shall show to you.'* [Gen 12:1] (Acts 7:1-3).

God's omniscience is declared, "Known from [the] ages [fig., from eternity] to God is all His works" (Acts 13:18).

Paul, in his sermon in Athens, proclaims several OT truths about God:

²⁴"The God, the One having made the world [or, universe; Gr., *kosmos*] and all the [things] in it, this One being Lord of heaven and of earth does not dwell in temples made with human hands, ²⁵nor is He served by [the] hands of people, [as if] needing something, [since] He is giving to all life and breath with respect to [or, in] all [things]. ²⁶And He made from one blood every nation of human beings to be living on all the face of the earth, having designated times having been appointed [for them] and the boundaries of their habitation, ²⁷[in order for them] to be seeking the Lord, if perhaps they might grope for Him and find [Him], and yet He is not far from each one of us. ²⁸'For in Him we live and move and are [fig., exist],' as also some of your* poets have said, 'For we are also His offspring' [i.e., quoting Epimendes (ca. 600 B.C.) and Aratus of Cilia (ca. 270 B.C.), respectively].

²⁹"Therefore, being offspring of God, we ought not to be thinking the Divine Nature to be similar to gold or silver or stone, an image [shaped by] humanity's skill and imagination [or, [the] craftsmanship and consideration of a person]. (Acts 17:24-29).

99

Translator's Perspective on the Canon of the NT

Thus, God is the Creator, Life-giver, Sustainer, and cannot be portrayed by an image. Note also the allusion to Adam. Then Paul declares before the high priest Ananias, that his God is the "ancestral God."

14"But I confess this to you, that according to the Way which they call a sect, in this way I sacredly serve the ancestral God, believing all the [things] according to the Law and having been written in the prophets, 15having hope [or, confident expectation] in God, which even they themselves are waiting for, [that there is] about to be a resurrection of [the] dead, both of righteous [people] and of unrighteous [people]. 16Now in this I am engaging myself, having through all [fig. always] a blameless conscience before God and people (Acts 24:14-16).

In this passage, we also seen Paul's belief in resurrection. He repeats this before Agrippa, "8Why is it judged incredible with you* if God raises [the] dead?" (Acts 26:8).

Essential Tenets in Acts:

As for early essential tenets, as we already saw, Peter preaches sermons in which he boldly proclaims many of these. On the Day of Pentecost, he proclaims:

29"Men, brothers! It is possible [for me] to speak with confidence to you* concerning the patriarch David, that he both came to the end [of his life] and was buried, and his tomb is with us until this day. 30Therefore, being a prophet and knowing that God vowed to him with an oath, from [the] fruit of his reproductive organs according to [the] flesh [fig., from one of his descendants], to raise up the Christ [or, the Messiah] to sit on his throne, 31having foreseen [this], he spoke concerning the resurrection of the Christ, that '*His soul was not left in the realm of the dead* [Gr., *hades*]*, nor did* His flesh *see decay* [or, *corruption*].' [Psalm 16:10] 32This Jesus God raised up, of which we are all witnesses! [cp. Acts 13:34-37]

33"Therefore, having been exalted to the right hand of God, and having received the promise of the Holy Spirit from the Father, He poured out this which you* now see and hear. 34For David did not ascend into the heavens, but he says himself, '*The LORD said to my Lord, "Sit at My right [parts]* [fig., *on My right side*]*, 35until I put Your enemies [as] Your footstool for Your feet."'* [Psalm 110:1] 36Therefore, let all the house of Israel know securely [fig., without a doubt] that God made Him both Lord and Christ—this Jesus whom you* crucified!" (Acts 2:29-36).

Thus, Peter preaches that Jesus was fully human, having descended from David. He was crucified and raised from the dead, according to the Scriptures. He ascended to God. He is Lord and Christ. Peter also associates Jesus with the Father and Holy Spirit, and declares the baptism by the Holy Spirit.

Shortly thereafter, Peter declares his God is the God of the Jewish forefathers and that this God raised Jesus from the dead:

¹³"The God of Abraham and Isaac and Jacob, the God of our fathers, glorified His Servant Jesus, whom you* indeed handed over and denied [or, disowned] Him to [the] face of [fig., in the presence of] Pilate, he having given judgment to be releasing [Him]. ¹⁴But you* denied [or, disowned] the Holy and Righteous One and demanded a man, a murderer, to be graciously granted to you*; ¹⁵but you* killed the Prince of Life, whom God raised from [the] dead, of which we are witnesses....
²⁵You* are sons [and daughters] of the prophets and of the covenant which God covenanted to our fathers, saying to Abraham, *'And in your Seed all the families of the earth will be blessed.'* [Gen 22:18; 26:4; 28:14; cp. Gal 3:16] ²⁶To you* first, God, having raised up His Servant Jesus, sent Him, blessing you* in the turning away [or, by turning away] each [of you*] from your* wicked ways." (Acts 3:13-15,25-26).

Then after healing a man born lame, Peter proclaims Jesus is the Christ and that He was crucified and raised from the dead:

¹⁰let it be known to you* all and to all the people of Israel that by the name of Jesus Christ the Nazarene, whom you* crucified, whom God raised from [the] dead, by Him has this [man] stood before you* healthy! (Acts 4:10).

Still Later, Peter proclaims:
³⁰The God of our fathers raised up Jesus, whom you* murdered, having hanged [Him] on a tree [or, a cross]. ³¹This One God has exalted to His right [hand as] Prince and Savior, to give repentance to Israel and forgiveness of sins. (Acts 5:30f).

Thus, his God is the God of the fathers of the Jews and this God raised up Jesus from the dead and exalted Him to His right hand, the purpose of which was to bring about forgiveness of sin. Peter reiterates these doctrines yet once again later:

Translator's Perspective on the Canon of the NT

[36]"For David indeed, having served his own generation by the counsel [or, plan] of God, fell asleep [fig., died], and he was added to [fig., buried with] his fathers and saw decay. [37]But [He] whom God raised up did not see decay. [cp. Acts 2:25-32] [38]Therefore, let it be known to you*, men, brothers, that through this One the forgiveness of sins is proclaimed to you*, [39]and from all [the things] from which you* were not able to be justified [or, declared righteous] by the Law of Moses, in this One every[one] believing is justified! (Acts 13:36-39).

Then Paul, continuing his sermon in Athens, declares Jesus was raised from the dead:

[30]Therefore indeed, the times of such ignorance having overlooked, God is now giving strict orders to all people everywhere to be repenting, [31]because He set a day in which He is about to be judging the inhabited earth in righteousness by a Man whom He designated, having given assurance to all by having raised Him from [the] dead!" (Acts 17:24-31).

The previously promised baptism in the Spirt is fulfilled in this book:

[1]And when the Day of Pentecost [had] come [ca. 30 A.D.], they were all with one mind at the same [place]. [2]And suddenly [there] came from heaven a sound like a violent rushing wind, and it filled the whole house where they were sitting! [3]And [there] appeared to them tongues as of fire distributing themselves, and [one] sat on each one of them. [4]And they were all filled of [or, with] [the] Holy Spirit, and they began to be speaking with different tongues [fig., foreign languages], just as the Spirit was giving them to be declaring boldly! (Acts 2:1-4).

This baptism in the Spirit led to those present having the boldness to proclaim Christ in the face of persecution and death, as recorded throughout this book. And during this time, the Spirit continues to work in the lives of the disciples:

[8]Then Peter, having been filled with [the] Holy Spirit, said to them (Acts 4:8).

[31]And when they had implored [God in prayer], the place was shaken in which they had been gathered together; and they were all filled with [the] Holy Spirit, and they were speaking the word of God with confidence [or, boldness] (Acts 4:31).

³Therefore, brothers [and sisters], look for seven men from [among] you*, being well spoken of, full of [the] Holy Spirit and wisdom, whom we shall appoint over this need [or, necessity]. ⁴But we will give ourselves continually to prayer and to the ministry of the word."
⁵And the word was pleasing before the whole congregation. And they chose Stephen, a man full of faith and of [the] Holy Spirit, and Philip and Prochorus and Nicanor and Timon and Parmenas and Nicolaus, a proselyte [i.e., convert to Judaism] from Antioch, ⁶whom they set before the apostles. And having prayed, they laid [their] hands on them (Acts 6:3-6).

⁸Now Stephen, full of faith and of power, was performing wonders and great signs among the people. ⁹But [there] rose up some of the [Hellenistic Jews] from the synagogue, the ones being called Freed Slaves, both of [the] Cyrenians and of [the] Alexandrians, and of the [Hellenistic Jews] from Cilicia and Asia, disputing with Stephen. ¹⁰And they were not being able to resist the wisdom and the Spirit with which he was speaking (Acts 6:8-10).

⁵⁴Now hearing these [things], they were cut through to their hearts [fig., they were infuriated], and they began gnashing their teeth at him. ⁵⁵But being full of [the] Holy Spirit, having looked intently into heaven, he [Stephen] saw [the] glory of God, and Jesus having stood at [the] right [parts] [fig., on the right side] of God. ⁵⁶And he said, "Look! I see the heavens having been opened and the Son of Humanity having stood at [the] right [parts] [fig., on the right side] of God!" ⁵⁷But they, having cried out with a loud voice, covered their ears and rushed on him with one mind.
⁵⁸And having driven [him] outside of the city, they began stoning [him]. And the witnesses laid their cloaks down at the feet of a young man being called Saul. ⁵⁹And they kept on stoning Stephen as he [was] calling on [the Lord] and saying, "Lord Jesus, receive my spirit!" ⁶⁰Then having placed the knees [fig., having knelt down], he cried out with a loud voice, "Lord, do not hold this sin against them!" And having said this, he fell asleep [fig., died]. [cp. Luke 23:34,46] (Acts 7:54-60)

Note that this passage also affirms Jesus is now our Intercessor in heaven. But to continue with the Spirit's working in the lives of the early believers, it is said:

²⁹Then the Spirit said to Philip, "Approach and be joined to this chariot" (Acts 8:29).

Translator's Perspective on the Canon of the NT

¹⁷And Ananias went away and entered into the house; and having laid his hands on him, he said, "Saul, brother, the Lord, the One appearing to you on the road in which you were coming, has sent me in order that you shall regain [your] sight and shall be filled with [the] Holy Spirit." ¹⁸And immediately [there] fell off from his eyes [something] like scales, and he regained [his] sight! And having gotten up, he was baptized. ¹⁹And having received nourishment, he was strengthened (Acts 9:17-19).

³¹Then indeed the assemblies throughout the whole of Judea and Galilee and Samaria were having peace, being edified; and going on [or, living] in the fear of the Lord and in the comfort of the Holy Spirit, they were being multiplied (Acts 9:31).

¹⁹Now as Peter [was] pondering about the vision, the Spirit said to him, "Listen! Men are seeking you (Acts 10:19).

⁴⁴While Peter [was] still speaking these words, the Holy Spirit fell upon all the ones hearing the word. ⁴⁵And the believing ones from the circumcision were astonished, as many as came with Peter, because the free gift of the Holy Spirit had been poured out on the Gentiles also. ⁴⁶For they were hearing them speaking with tongues [fig., other languages] and magnifying God. Then Peter answered, ⁴⁷"Surely no one is able to forbid the water, can he, [for] these not to be baptized who received the Holy Spirit just as we also [did]?" ⁴⁸And he commanded them to be baptized in the name of the Lord. Then they urgently asked him to stay several days (Acts 10:44-48).

²²Then the word about them was heard in the ears of the assembly, the [one] in Jerusalem, and they sent out Barnabas to pass through as far as Antioch, ²³who having arrived and having seen the grace of God, was glad, and began encouraging [them] all with purpose of [or, a resolute] heart [fig., with steadfast devotion] to be continuing with [fig., remaining loyal to] the Lord, ²⁴because he was a good man and full of [the] Holy Spirit and of faith. And a considerable crowd was added to the Lord! (Acts 11:22-24).

²⁷Now in those days prophets came from Jerusalem to Antioch. ²⁸Then one of them, by name Agabus, having stood up, signified [or, foretold] by the Spirit [of] a great famine being about to happen over all the inhabited earth [i.e., the Roman Empire]—which also [or, then] occurred during [the reign of] Claudius Caesar (Acts 11:27f).

²Now while they [were] rendering sacred service to the Lord and fasting, the Holy Spirit said, "Set apart to Me Barnabas and Saul for the work which I have called them to" (Acts 13:2).

⁹But Saul (the [one] also [called] Paul), having been filled of [or, with] [the] Holy Spirit and having looked intently on him (Acts 13:9).

⁵²Now the disciples were being filled of [or, with] joy and [the] Holy Spirit (Acts 13:52).

⁶Now having passed through Phrygia and the region of Galatia, having been forbidden by the Holy Spirit to speak the word in Asia, [cp. Acts 19:10] ⁷having gone toward Mysia, they were trying to be going to Bithynia, and the Spirit did not allow them (Acts 16:6).

⁵Now when both Silas and Timothy came down from Macedonia, Paul was held completely by the Spirit, solemnly testifying to the Jews [that] Jesus [is] the Christ (Acts 18:5).

⁶And Paul having laid [his] hands on them, the Holy Spirit came upon them, and they began speaking with tongues [fig., other languages] and prophesying. ⁷Now [there] were [in] all about twelve men (Acts 19:12).

All of this together demonstrates that the Apostolic Church operated in and through the power of the Holy Spirit. The Spirit was leading and empowering the early Christians. The apostles even bore witness not just to the life of Jesus but also to the Spirit:

²⁹But answering, Peter and the apostles said, "It is necessary to be always obedient to God rather than people! ³⁰The God of our fathers raised up Jesus, whom you* murdered, having hanged [Him] on a tree [or, a cross]. ³¹This One God has exalted to His right [hand as] Prince and Savior, to give repentance to Israel and forgiveness of sins. ³²And we are His witnesses of these matters, and also the Holy Spirit, whom God gave to the ones being obedient to Him" (Acts 5:29-32).

The transformation of lives by encountering Jesus is seen most powerfully in the life of Saul/ Paul. He was at first a persecutor of the Apostolic Church. But due to encountering the risen Jesus, he becomes the most ardent proclaimer of the new faith (Acts 9 and elsewhere).

Translator's Perspective on the Canon of the NT

Thus, this book strongly proclaims and demonstrates the essential doctrines about God from the OT and the essential tenets about Jesus and the Spirit of the Apostolic Church.

Historicity of Acts:

Does Acts report accurate history? A full discussion of this question is outside the scope of this book, but this writer hopes to address it in a future book (see Appendix Three). But here, it will be said that in almost all points in which Acts touches on secular history it concurs with secular and Jewish historians of the time, especially that of Jewish historian Josephus. There are still a few points of debate, but overall, Luke's accuracy as a historian has been verified.

> The Acts brings Christianity in contact with the surrounding world and makes many allusions to various places, secular persons and events, though only incidentally and as far as its object required it. These allusions are—with a single exception, that of Theudas—in full harmony with the history of the age as known from Josephus and heathen writers, and establish Luke's claim to be considered a well-informed, honest, and credible historian (Schaff; 10189-10192).

For instance, in Acts 17:6,8, Luke uses the Greek word *politarches* to refer to the city officials in Thessalonica. At one time, this term was unknown as a term for city officials in the Roman Empire. But an inscription was found on an arch in Thessalonica with this term on it. Thirty-five such inscriptions have now been discovered, nineteen of them in Thessalonica (Schaff; 10236-10239).

Moreover:
> The voyage and shipwreck of Paul in Acts 27. This chapter contains more information about ancient navigation than any work of Greek or Roman literature, and betrays the minute accuracy of an intelligent eye-witness, who, though not a professional seaman, was very familiar with nautical terms from close observation. He uses no less than sixteen technical terms, some of them rare, to describe the motion and management of a ship, and all of them most appropriately; and he is strictly correct in the description of the localities at Crete, Salmone, Fair Havens, Cauda, Lasea and Phoenix (two small places recently identified), and Melita (Malta), as well as the motions and effects of the tempestuous northeast wind called

Euraquilo (A. V. Euroclydon) in the Mediterranean (Schaff; 10249-10254).

In addition, "The impartiality and truthfulness of Luke is very manifest in his honest record of the imperfections of the apostolic church" (Schaff; 10276-10277). This can be seen in his recording of the neglect of the widows of the Hellenist Christians that gave rise to the office of deacons (Acts 6:1-6), the sin and condemnation of Ananias and Sapphira (Acts 5:1-11), the turning back of Mark from his first missionary journey (Acts 13:13), resulting in a split between Paul and Barnabas (Acts 15:36-40), the dispute in the Apostolic Church over circumcision (Acts 15:1ff), and Paul's temper seen in his outburst before the high-priest (Acts 23:3).

Such accuracy of details shows Luke was a conscientious historian and recorder of events that he witnessed.

Conclusion on Acts:

The Book of Acts more than satisfies all of the standards for a book to be a part of the canon of the NT.

Appeal and Mark of Inspiration

I recently heard a Jew on Christian radio show relating the story of his conversion to Christ. He said he had been raised with the belief that "The New Testament was only for Christians; it had nothing in it for Jews." But he was challenged by a Christian friend to read the NT. After much ado, he agreed and naturally began reading at the beginning, with the first chapter of Matthew. Much to his surprise, he read:

[1]A scroll of a genealogy of Jesus Christ, Son of David, Son of Abraham: [cp. Luke 3:23-38]
[2]Abraham fathered [or, begot] Isaac, and Isaac fathered Jacob, and Jacob fathered Judah and his brothers, [3]and Judah fathered Pharez and Zarah by Tamar, and Pharez fathered Hezron, and Hezron fathered Ram, [4]and Ram fathered Amminadab, and Amminadab fathered Nahshon, and Nahshon fathered Salmon, [5]and Salmon fathered Boaz by Rahab, and Boaz fathered Obed by Ruth, and Obed fathered Jesse, [6]and Jesse fathered David the king. And David the king fathered Solomon by the [wife] of Uriah (Matt 1:1-6).

There, right at the beginning of the NT was mention of Abraham, Isaac, Jacob, David, and Solomon; all prominent figures of the OT and

Translator's Perspective on the Canon of the NT

"heroes" of Judaism. As he continued to read, He realized that Jesus was the Messiah, the Redeemer promised in the OT, so he placed his faith in Jesus as his Lord and Savior.

This has been the experience of many, both Jews and non-Jews alike, in the early centuries and down through the centuries though today. Reading one or more of the Synoptic Gospels has brought them to faith in Christ. And those who are already Christians will find these Gospels to be reliable sources of information about the One in whom they have believed and will read them to their spiritual enrichment.

As such, the appeal of these books should be obvious. The Christian faith is about Jesus, and these three Gospels tell us about the life and teachings of Jesus. These Gospels record the essential aspects of Jesus' life—His birth, teachings, miracles, death for our sins, burial, resurrection, post-resurrection appearances, and ascension. And people coming to faith in Christ and being spiritual enriched is what is meant by a book bearing the marks of inspiration. As such, these books easily meet that criteria.

The Book of Acts then tells the story of the growth of the early Church, and the early Christians' faithfulness in preaching the Gospel, including proclaiming the essential aspects of the life of Christ. Their boldness in doing so in the face of adversities is an example for Christians today to follow. It also tells us much about two principle figures in the spreading of the Christian faith—Peter and Paul. These two will then write many of the books to be discussed which are found in the NT. Thus, their backstories are good for Christians to know and their examples good to follow. And many people have been inspired in their Christian walks by this book, Thus, Acts also bears the marks of inspiration.

9/11 and Remembrance

Before concluding this chapter, it would be good to look at an important issue from a different angle. It was established in the previous chapter that Jesus's death and resurrection occurred in 30 AD. It is generally agreed that His ministry lasted about three and half years. This is based on the number of Jewish feasts Jesus attended, as indicated in the Synoptic Gospels. This would mean His ministry lasted from about 26-30 AD. This date range is verified by Jesus being born before the death of Herod the Great in 4 BC and Luke telling us Jesus "was about thirty years old when He began [His public ministry]" (Luke 3:23). Allotting for parts of years and rounding off, that gives the start date of 26 AD.

Why Are These Books in the Bible? Volume Two

With the date range of 26-30 AD for Jesus' ministry and with the Synoptic Gospels being written 50-60 AD, that means these Gospels were written 20-34 years after the recorded events. But is that too long for eyewitnesses to remember clearly the events they witnessed?

Consider this: if the reader lived in the United States and was over five years old on September 11, 2001, I am sure you can tell me exactly what happened on that fateful day. Not only that, but you could tell me where you were when you first heard what was happening, what you did throughout that day, and even how you felt. And to this day the thought of that day is probably still very emotional. I know as I still have to fight back tears every time I think of that day and even as I am writing this section.

As I finish the 2023 update of this book, it is September 11th, the 22nd anniversary of that fateful day. That is within that 20-34 years after period. Maybe by now some who were alive then have forgotten that day, but I seriously doubt it. I would bet the remembrance of that day will still be crystal clear until the day we die. It was simply a too earth-shaking, life-altering, and emotion-producing day to ever be forgotten.

If someone during this time period wanted to write a book detailing the events of that day and its effects on Americans, he would not need to depend on second-hand testimony, or third-hand or fourth-hand as the telephone game discussed in Chapter Two would have it. He could easily find plenty of still living eyewitnesses of that momentous day to interview. And these would not be just people who witnessed the events on TV but who were there in New York City and saw the planes fly into the World Trade Center and saw the aftermath. He could also interview people who fled from the Twin Towers before they collapsed.

He could also go to Washington D.C. and interview people who saw the plane crash into the Pentagon and who witnessed the aftermath of that event. He could even interview the loved ones who were talking on cell phones with the heroes of Flight 93 before they rushed the hijackers.

He could also read the many articles that were written by these eyewitnesses that have appeared in newspapers, magazines, and on the Internet since that day. He might even be able to get his hands on diaries or journals of these people and other Americans describing their lives and feelings on that day. With all of this first-hand testimony, he could easily write a reliable history of 9/11 and its aftermath. And the many living eyewitnesses could verify that his book was reliable.

But if he were to screw up and say things happened that did not happen, or if he were to say things didn't happen that did happen, then this multitude of eyewitnesses would rise up and shout, "You're wrong! I was there! I saw those events! I know what happened!" And such was the case in the first century.

Translator's Perspective on the Canon of the NT

When Mathew, Mark, and Luke wrote their Gospels, there were still multitudes of living eyewitnesses who had witnessed the life of Jesus and who could be interviewed. Luke tells us specifically that he did just that, along with reading their written testimonies. Mark interviewed the eyewitness Peter and was possibly an eyewitness of at least one event of Jesus' life himself, while Matthew was an eyewitness. And even Mark and Mathew probably interviewed others as well and read their testimonies.

Among these eyewitnesses would be the multitudes of people who had been healed by Jesus and who could never forget what He did for them. There would also be the multitudes who had their lives transformed by encountering Him and who could never forget that. And there would be those who witnessed Jesus raising people from the dead who could never forget what they witnessed. And there would be the over 500 still living eyewitnesses to whom Jesus appeared after His death and resurrection who would still get emotional whenever they thought about it.

These are not ordinary daily events that are easily forgotten. They are monumental events that simply cannot be forgotten. People do not forget life-altering and strong emotion-producing events. As such, their testimonies were reliable, and these reliable testimonies were incorporated into the Gospels.

Moreover, if the authors of these Gospels screwed up and said Jesus did and said things He did not, or if they denied He said and did things He did say and do, there would be multitudes of eyewitness who would shout, "You're wrong! I was there! I saw those events! I know what happened!" But such was never the case when the Synoptic Gospels were penned and began to circulate well within the lifetimes of those eyewitnesses who had experienced these life-altering events.

This is why a discussion of the dating and authors of these books is so important. It puts the Synoptics within this time-period of when eyewitnesses were still alive and who could verify or falsify the contents of these books. And it means the authors were eyewitnesses themselves and/ or could easily attain information from eyewitnesses. And it was those very eyewitnesses who accepted these books as being reliable records of the life of Jesus and as having been written by the traditional authors.

Conclusion to the Synoptic Gospels and Acts

The evidence is very strong that Matthew wrote The Gospel According to Mathew, that Mark wrote The Gospel According to Mark, that Luke wrote The Gospel According to Luke and The Book of the Acts of the Apostles and that all four of these books were written in the first century, in fact, before 65 AD. They were all based on eyewitness testimony and thus record reliable histories. They also contain theological sound doctrines on the nature of God and present the essential tenets of early Christian Church. Thus, these four books rightly were included in the canon of the New Testament.

> The first and fourth Gospels were composed by apostles and eye-witnesses, Matthew and John; the second and third under the influence of Peter and Paul and by their disciples Mark and Luke, so as to be indirectly likewise of apostolic origin and canonical authority. Hence Mark is often called the Gospel of Peter, and Luke the Gospel of Paul....
> The gospel story, being constantly repeated in public preaching and in private circles, assumed a fixed, stereotyped form; the more readily, on account of the reverence of the first disciples for every word of their divine Master. Hence the striking agreement of the first three, or synoptical Gospels, which, in matter and form, are only variations of the same theme. Luke used, according to his own statement, besides the oral tradition, written documents on certain parts of the life of Jesus, which doubtless appeared early among the first disciples. The Gospel of Mark, the confidant of Peter, is a faithful copy of the gospel preached and otherwise communicated by this apostle; with the use, perhaps, of Hebrew records which Peter may have made from time to time under the fresh impression of the events themselves (Schaff; 8249-8251; 8257-8262).

Translator's Perspective on the Canon of the NT

Chapter Four
The Gospel According to John

There are five books in the New Testament that are traditionally ascribed to the apostle John: The Gospel According to John, the three epistles of John (1John, 2John, 3John), and The Revelation. Before looking at these books, it will be good to take a look at what we know about the apostle John from elsewhere in the New Testament (NT):

The Apostle John in the NT

There is more than one person named John in the NT, including the apostle John, John the Baptist, and John Mark, and there is possibly more than one John of importance in the early Church, as we will see later. This book will Thus, refer to the John under discussion as "John the apostle" or "the apostle John." His calling is mentioned in the Synoptic Gospels:

²¹And having gone on from there, He saw two other brothers, James the [son] of Zebedee and **John** his brother, in the boat with Zebedee their father mending their nets, and He called them. ²²Then immediately, having left the boat and their father, they followed Him (Matthew 4:21f).

¹⁹And having gone on from there a little [further], he saw James, the [son] of Zebedee, and **John** his brother, and they [were] in the boat mending the nets. ²⁰And immediately He called them. Then having left their father Zebedee in the boat with the hired workers, they went away after Him (Mark 1:19f).

¹And it happened, while the crowd [was] pressing upon Him to be hearing the word of God, that He had stood beside the lake of Gennesaret. ²And He saw two boats standing beside the lake, but the fishermen, having disembarked from them, were washing their nets. ³Then having stepped into one of the boats, which was Simon's, He asked him to put out a little from the land. And having sat down, He began teaching the crowds from the boat. ⁴Then when He ceased speaking, He said to Simon, "Put out into the deep [water] and let down your* nets for a catch."
⁵And answering, Simon said to Him, "Master, having labored through the whole night we caught nothing, but at Your word I will let

Translator's Perspective on the Canon of the NT

down the net." ⁶And having done this, they caught a great number of fish, but their net began breaking. ⁷And they signaled to their partners, the ones having come in the other boat, to help them. And they came and filled both the boats, with the result that they were being sunk.

⁸But Simon Peter having seen, fell down at the knees of Jesus, saying, "Depart from me, because I am a sinful man, O Lord!" ⁹For astonishment seized him, and all the [fishermen] with him, at the catch of the fish which they caught, ¹⁰and likewise also James and **John**, [the] sons of Zebedee, the ones [who] were partners with Simon. And Jesus said to Simon, "Stop being afraid! From now [on] you will be catching people." ¹¹And having brought the boats to the land, having left all, they followed Him (Luke 5:9-11).

Thus, the calling of John the apostle is recorded consistently in the Synoptics, indicating that he was fisherman before being called by Jesus. His brother James was also called with him. They both followed Jesus very quickly, with only Luke mentioning the miraculous catch of fish that probably helped them in their decision to follow Jesus.

The apostle John is then included among the lists of the twelve apostles in the Synoptic Gospels:

²Now the names of the twelve apostles are these: first Simon, the one being called Peter, and Andrew his brother, James the [son] of Zebedee and **John** his brother, ³Philip and Bartholomew, Thomas and Matthew the tax collector, James the [son] of Alpheus and Lebbeus, the one having been surnamed Thaddeus, ⁴Simon the Canaanite and Judas Iscariot, the one also having betrayed Him (Matthew 10:2-4).

¹⁶And He gave to Simon [the] name Peter, ¹⁷and James [son] of Zebedee and **John** the brother of James, and He gave them names— Boanerges, which is [fig., means], "Sons of Thunder," ¹⁸and Andrew and Philip and Bartholomew and Matthew and Thomas and James [son] of Alpheus and Thaddeus and Simon the Canaanite ¹⁹and Judas Iscariot, who also betrayed Him (Mark 6:16-19).

¹²Now it happened in those days, He went out into the mountain to pray, and He was spending the night in the prayer of God [or, in prayer to God]. ¹³And when it became day, He summoned His disciples, and having chosen from them twelve, whom also He named apostles: ¹⁴Simon, whom also He named Peter, and Andrew his brother, James and **John**, Philip and Bartholomew, ¹⁵Matthew and Thomas, James the [son] of Alphaeus and Simon, the one being called [the] Zealot, ¹⁶Judas

[the son; or, the brother] of James and Judas Iscariot, who also became a traitor (Luke 6:12-16).

Thus, all three Synoptics list the apostle John fourth, after Peter and his brother Andrew and after John's brother James. John being mentioned after his brother James was probably due to him being the younger of the two, just as Andrew was probably younger than his brother Peter. And Church tradition has it that John was the youngest of the apostles overall, while Peter was one of if not the oldest.

But whatever their ages, these four always being mentioned first shows the apostle John's prominent place among the apostles. This prominence is further demonstrated by just these four, or sometime only three of them, Andrew excepted, being included in some important scenes in the life of Jesus:

²⁹Then immediately, having come out from the synagogue, they went into the house of **Simon and Andrew, with James and John**. ³⁰Now the mother-in-law of Simon was lying down, being sick with a fever. And immediately they tell Him about her. ³¹And having come near, He raised her up, having taken hold of her hand. And the fever immediately left her! Then she began serving them (Mark 1:29-31).

³⁷And He did not allow anyone to follow with Him, except **Peter and James and John**, the brother of James.
³⁸Then He comes into the house of the synagogue leader and sees a commotion, weeping, and loud wailing. ³⁹And having gone in, He says to them, "Why are you* so upset and weeping? The young child did not die, <u>but</u> is sleeping!" ⁴⁰And they began laughing at Him. But having sent [them] all out, He takes the father of the young child and the mother and those with Him, and He goes in where the child was lying. ⁴¹And having taken hold of the hand of the young child, He says to her [in Aramaic], *"Talitha koumi!"* which is, being translated, "Girl (I say to you), get up!" ⁴²And immediately the girl rose up and was walking about! (for she was twelve years [old]). And they were amazed [with] great amazement. ⁴³And He gave strict orders to them that no one should know [about] this. Then He said [for something] to be given to her to eat (Mark 5:37-43).

²Then after six days Jesus takes **Peter and James and John**, and He leads them up privately into a high mountain alone. And He was transfigured [or, His appearance was changed, Gr., *metamorphoomai*] before them. ³And His garments became radiant, extremely white like snow, such as a bleacher [or, launderer] on the earth is not able to whiten

Translator's Perspective on the Canon of the NT

[them]. ⁴Then Elijah with Moses appeared to them, and they were conversing with Jesus (Mark 9:2-4).

³²And they come to a place, the name of which [is] Gethsemane. And He says to His disciples, "Sit here until I pray." ³³Then He takes **Peter and James and John** with Him, and He began to be greatly disturbed and to be suffering from distress. ³⁴And He says to them, "My soul is deeply grieved, even to death; stay here, and be keeping watch" (Mark 14:32-34).

⁷Then the day of the [Feast of] Unleavened Bread came, in which it was necessary [for] the Passover [or, Paschal Lamb] to be sacrificed. ⁸And He sent **Peter and John**, saying, "Having gone, prepare the Passover for us, so that we shall eat" (Luke 22:7).

Thus, John the apostle was one of the privileged three or four of the apostles to witness the healing of Simon's mother-in-law, the raising of the synagogue leader's daughter, the transfiguration of Jesus, and Jesus praying in Gethsemane before His arrest. It was also John, along with Peter, whom Jesus sent to prepare the Passover, which would be Jesus' Last Supper.

This information is why it was said in the last chapter that if the Synoptic Gospels were forgeries, it makes little sense they would have been written in the names of Matthew, Mark, and Luke. It would have made more sense to forge them in the names of Peter, Andrew, James, or John. But this means the Synoptic writers had to get their information for the afore-listed events from one of these three or four men.

That said; we get some idea of the character of the apostle John from the name Jesus gives to him and his brother, "Sons of Thunder." This indicates they were passionate men. This is confirmed by the few times John is recorded as speaking in the Synoptics:

³⁸Then **John** answered Him, saying, "Teacher, we saw someone casting out demons in Your name, who does not follow us, and we tried to prevent him, because he does not follow us." ³⁹But Jesus said, "Stop preventing him, for [there] is no one who will perform a miraculous work in [or, on the basis of] My name and will soon [afterwards] be able to speak evil of Me. ⁴⁰For [the one] who is not against you* is for you*. ⁴¹For whoever gives you* a cup of water to drink in My name because you* are Christ's [or, are [followers] of Christ], positively I say to you*, he shall by no means lose his reward" (Mark 9:38-41).

Here John the apostle seems to express his desire for exclusiveness, to have Jesus all for his and the apostles' own.

^{35}And **James and John**, the sons of Zebedee, approached Him, saying, "Teacher, we desire that whatever we ask, You shall do for us." ^{36}So He said to them, "What do you* want Me to do for you*?" ^{37}Then they said to Him, "Grant to us that we shall sit, one at Your right [parts] [fig., on Your right side] and one at Your left [parts] [fig., on Your left side], in Your glory" (Mark 10:35-37).

After this, Jesus rebukes James and John, and the other apostles are indignant (Mark 10:38-45). This shows that James and John were rather brash. This is why many think they were the youngest of the apostles, with John being the younger brother and only in his teens during Jesus' earthly ministry.

^{1}Then as He goes out from the temple, one of His disciples says to Him, "Teacher, look! What great stones! And what great buildings!" ^{2}And Jesus having answered, said to him, "Are you looking at these great buildings? By no means shall a stone be left on a stone which by no means shall not be torn down."
^{3}Then as He sits on the Mount of Olives, opposite the temple, **Peter and James and John and Andrew** began questioning Him privately. ^{4}"Tell us when these [things] will be? And what [is] the sign when all these [things] shall be about to be fulfilled?" (Mark 13:1-4).

We Thus, see it was the "Big Four" who prompted Jesus to give His discourse on the destruction of Jerusalem that was discussed in the previous chapter.

And having gone, they went into a village of Samaritans in order to prepare for Him. ^{53}And they did not receive Him, because His face was [fig., He had resolved to be] going to Jerusalem. ^{54}So His disciples **James and John** having seen [this], they said, "Lord, do You want [that] we should tell [fig., command] fire to come down from heaven and to consume them, as also Elijah did?" [see 2Kings 1:9-14] ^{55}But having turned, He rebuked them and said, "You* do not know of what sort of spirit you* are! ^{56}For the Son of Humanity did not come to destroy [the] lives of people, but to save!" And they went on to another village (Luke 9:52b-56).

Translator's Perspective on the Canon of the NT

Here again we see the brashness of James and John and even their seemingly lack of concern for outsiders, in this case Samaritans, whom Jews had a long standing animosity with.

But in the Book of Acts, the apostle John's character seems to have mellowed. The brashness and lack of concern are gone. This could be because of just getting older, but more likely it is due to the influence of being with Jesus for three years and then of being filled with the Holy Spirit on the Day of Pentecost. For the latter, John is mentioned as being in the upstairs room before the arrival of the Holy Spirit.

¹³And when they entered [Jerusalem], they went up into the upstairs room where they were staying: both **Peter and James and John and Andrew**, Philip and Thomas, Bartholomew and Matthew, James [the son] of Alphaeus and Simon the Zealot, and Judas [the son; or, the brother] of James. [cp. John 14:22; Jude 1:1] ¹⁴These all were continuing with one mind in prayer and petition, together with [the] women [cp. Luke 8:2-3; 23:55-24:10] and Mary the mother of Jesus, and with His brothers (Acts 1:13-14).

Here we see once again that the Big Four are mentioned first among the apostles and other disciples, but in a different order. Andrew is now last, possibly because his position among the apostles is now lower than that of the other three. But it should be noted that "the women" are with the apostles. Thus, we get a first hint that John the apostle's exclusivity is not so strong anymore.

After Pentecost is the following scene:

¹Now **Peter and John** were going up at the same [time] to the temple at the hour of prayer, the ninth [hour] [i.e., 3:00 p.m.]. ²And a certain man being lame from [the] womb of his mother was being carried, whom they were laying every day at the gate of the temple, the [gate] being called Beautiful, [in order for him] to be asking [for] a charitable gift from the ones entering into the temple, ³who having seen Peter and John about to be entering into the temple, began asking [for] a charitable gift. ⁴But Peter, having looked intently toward him, along with John, said, "Look at us!" ⁵So he began fixing his attention on them, expecting to receive something from them. ⁶But Peter said, "Silver and gold do not belong to me [fig., I do not have silver and gold], but what I do have, this I give to you: in the name of Jesus Christ the Nazarene, get up and be walking about!" (Acts 3:1-6).

Why Are These Books in the Bible? Volume Two

This healing causes much stir among the Jewish leaders. They Thus, call Peter and John the apostle before them. Acts then states:

>[13]And observing the confidence of **Peter and John**, and having perceived that they are uneducated and untrained men, they began marveling, and they were recognizing them that they were [or, had been] with Jesus. [14]Then seeing the man having stood with them, the one having been healed, they had nothing to say against [them] (Acts 4:13).

Peter and John being called "uneducated and untrained men" will be important shortly. But here, note that even the Jewish leaders noticed their confidence. This was because "they had been with Jesus."

>[18]And having summoned them, they gave strict orders to them not to be speaking at all nor to be teaching in the name of Jesus. [19]But answering, **Peter and John** said to them, "Whether it is righteous before God to listen to you* rather than God, you* judge. [20]For we are not able not to [or, we cannot but] be speaking [about] what we saw and heard."

Peter and John together proclaim their boldness to preach about Jesus. Thus, John's brashness is now being put to a good use.

>[14]Now the apostles in Jerusalem having heard that Samaria had received the word of God sent **Peter and John** to them, [15]who, having come down, prayed concerning them in order that they shall receive [the] Holy Spirit—[16]for He had not yet fallen upon any of them, but they had only been baptized in the name of Christ Jesus. [17]Then they began laying hands on them, and they were receiving [the] Holy Spirit (Acts 8:14-17).

We see here that that the apostle John's discriminatory attitude towards Samarians has softened, and he now prays for Samaritan believers to receive the Holy Spirit. Thus, the Holy Spirit working in John was able to overcome the animosity between Jews and Samaritans.

>[1]Now about that time [ca. 44 AD] Herod the king [i.e., Herod Agrippa I, grandson of Herod the Great] put his hands to mistreat [or, persecute] some of the [believers] from the assembly. [2]Then he executed **James the brother of John** with [the] sword (Acts 12:1f).

This is the last time John the apostle is mentioned in the Book of Acts, and it is by way of recording his brother's death. It should be noted

Translator's Perspective on the Canon of the NT

that the "James" that is mentioned later in Acts is James, the oldest of Jesus' brothers. That will be important in a moment and much later. But here, the apostle John fades from view, while Paul becomes the prominent figure in Acts. But then Paul mentions John in one of his epistles:

⁹and having known the grace, the one having been given to me, **James and Cephas [i.e., Peter] and John**, the ones highly regarded to be pillars, gave to me and to Barnabas [the] right [hand] of fellowship, so that we indeed [should go] to the Gentiles, but they to the circumcision [i.e., Jews] (Gal 2:9).

The James here is the aforementioned brother of Jesus. Thus, James the brother of Jesus has replaced James the brother of John in being a pillar of the early Church, with Peter and John still being the other two.

And that is all we know outside of the writings of John about John the apostle. But the following quotes summarize his life afterwards:

At the end of the 2nd century, Polycrates, bishop of Ephesus, claims that John's tomb is at Ephesus, identifies him with the beloved disciple, and adds that he "was a priest, wearing the sacerdotal plate, both martyr and teacher." That John died in Ephesus is also stated by Irenaeus, bishop of Lyon c. 180 CE, who says John wrote his Gospel and letters at Ephesus and Revelation at Patmos (Encyclopedia Britannica; "Saint John the Apostle").

But the Apocalypse implies that he stood at the head of the churches of Asia Minor. This is confirmed by the unanimous testimony of antiquity which is above all reasonable doubt, and assigns Ephesus to him as the residence of his later years. He died there in extreme old age during the reign of Trajan, which began in 98. His grave also was shown there in the second century. We do not know when he removed to Asia Minor, but he cannot have done so before the year 63. For in his valedictory address to the Ephesian elders, and in his Epistles to the Ephesians and Colossians and the second to Timothy, Paul makes no allusion to John, and speaks with the authority of a superintendent of the churches of Asia Minor. It was probably the martyrdom of Peter and Paul that induced John to take charge of the orphan churches, exposed to serious dangers and trials (Schaff, 6099-6105).

Thus, the apostle John spent his later years in Ephesus, overseeing the churches in that area. Before looking at the writings of John for information about John, we need to establish if John the apostle did in fact write them and other important information in regards to them. We will do so by looking at each book in turn.

The Gospel According to John

We will start with the Gospel According to John.

Author:

In my first year of studying Greek at Denver Seminary, we were taught that the Gospel of John and 1John contained the easiest Greek in the NT. During that first year, we were assigned to translate many passages from the Gospel of John. Then the final assignment was to translate all of 1John. Thus, when I decided to translate the entire NT, I started with the Gospel of John. And it was in fact very easy to translate, with simple vocabulary and grammar. That is exactly what you would expect from a fisherman who was "uneducated and untrained" and for whom Greek was possibly a second language, with Aramaic being his first language. Thus, the style of Greek of the fourth Gospel fits with John the apostle being the author of the book.

John does not name himself in this book, but there is internal evidence that this Gospel was written by an eyewitness. It begins by stating:

[14]And the Word [fig., the Expression of [Divine] Logic] became flesh and tabernacled among us, and we beheld His glory, glory as of an only-begotten [or, uniquely-begotten] from [the] Father, full of grace and truth (John 1:14).

Notice the "us" and "we." The writer seems to be saying he saw Jesus during His earthly life. The next possible hint the writer makes to himself is at the Last Supper:

[23]Now there was reclining [at the table] one of His disciples on the bosom of Jesus, whom Jesus was loving. [24]So Simon Peter motioned to this one to inquire who it might be, concerning whom He speaks. [25]Then that one, having leaned back Thus, on the breast of Jesus, says to Him, "Lord, who is it?" [26]Jesus answers, "That one it is to whom I, having dipped the piece of bread, will give [it]." And having dipped the piece

Translator's Perspective on the Canon of the NT

of bread, He gives [it] to Judas Iscariot, [son] of Simon. ²⁷And after the piece of bread, then Satan entered into that one (John 13:23).

Now some think it would be too arrogant for the author to refer to himself as the disciple "whom Jesus was loving." But it really is a sign of how much he appreciated the love of Jesus. This same phrase also appears in a scene while Jesus is on the cross:

²⁵Now [there] stood by the cross of Jesus His mother and the sister of His mother, Mary [the wife] of Cleopas and Mary the Magdalene [i.e., four women are mentioned]. ²⁶Then Jesus, having seen His mother and the disciple having stood by whom He was loving, He says to His mother, "Woman, look!, your son." ²⁷Next He says to the disciple, "Look! Your mother." And from that hour the disciple took her into his own [home] (John 19:25-.27).

The next possible hint of the writer to himself is after the arrest of Jesus:

¹⁵And Simon Peter was following Jesus, and the other disciple. Now that disciple was known to the high priest and entered with Jesus into the courtyard of the high priest. ¹⁶But Peter had stood at the gate outside. Therefore, the other disciple who was known to the high priest went out and spoke to the female doorkeeper, and he brought in Peter (John 18:15f).

By saying "the other disciple" without naming him, the writer seems to assume his readers will know he is referring to himself. In a similar vein, when the apostles are told about the empty tomb of Jesus, the writer records the following:

³So Peter went out, and the other disciple, and they began going to the tomb. ⁴Now the two were running together, and the other disciple ran ahead more quickly than Peter and came first to the tomb. ⁵And having stooped down, he sees the linen strips lying, although he did not enter. ⁶Then Simon Peter comes, following him, and he entered into the tomb. And he looks upon the linen strips lying [there], ⁷and the facecloth which was on His head not lying with the linen strips, <u>but</u> apart, having been rolled up in one place (John 20:3-7).

Some see in this footrace to the tomb an indication of Peter and John's respective ages, with the apostle John winning the race due to being younger. But age really is not a reliable indicator of speed. I am sure when Usain Bolt turns fifty he will still be able to beat many 20-somethings in a footrace. But this footrace probably does at least show John was not an old man at this time, c. 30 AD.

For those who don't know, Usain Bolt won gold medals in the 100 and 200 meter dashes and 4 x 100 relays at the 2008, 2012, and 2016 Olympics, making him the first track athlete to win nine gold medals.

In any case, the closest the writer comes to mentioning his name is near the end of the book:

¹After these things Jesus revealed Himself again to the disciples on the sea of Tiberias. Now He revealed Himself in this manner: ²[There] were together Simon Peter and Thomas, the one being called Didymus, and Nathanael from Cana of Galilee and the [sons] of Zebedee and two others of His disciples (John 21:1f).

By only referring to himself and his brother as "the [sons] of Zebedee" and listing them last rather first as in the Synoptic Gospels is probably a sign of humility on John's part.

In addition, throughout this Gospel, it bears the marks of being written by an eyewitness in the details it gives of the geography and culture of first century Israel.

> The author was a Jew of Palestine. He gives, incidentally and without effort, unmistakable evidence of minute familiarity with the Holy Land and its inhabitants before the destruction of Jerusalem. He is at home in the localities of the holy city and the neighborhood [see John 1:28; 2:19; 5:2; 9:7; 10:23; 11:18; 18:1,28; 19:13,17]....
>
> He is equally familiar with other parts of Palestine and makes no mistakes such as are so often made by foreigners [see John 1:44,46; 2:1; 3:23; 4:5; 6:19]. ...
>
> He is well acquainted with the confused politico-ecclesiastical Messianic ideas and expectations of the Jews (1:19-28,45-49; 4:25; 6:14,15; 7:26; 12:34, and other passages); with the hostility between Jews and Samaritans (4:9,20,22; 8:48); with Jewish usages and observances, as baptism (1:25; 3:22,23; 4:2), purification (2:6; 3:25, etc.), ceremonial pollution (18:28), feasts (2:13,23; 5:1; 7:37, etc.), circumcision, and the Sabbath (7:22,23) (Schaff; 9904-9909; 9915-9916).

This Gospel also bears the mark of being written by someone who knew both Hebrew and Greek. This can be seen in that though written

Translator's Perspective on the Canon of the NT

in Greek, it has many Hebrew parallelisms and antagonism in it, such as seen in the prologue:

³All [things] came to be through Him, and without Him not even one thing came to be which has come to be. ⁴In Him was life, and the life was the Light of the people. ⁵And the Light shines in the darkness, and the darkness did not overpower [or, comprehend] it (John 1:2-5).

Note the repetition of thought in verses three and four and the antagonism in verse five. This format is seen in OT poetry, such in the first Psalm.

²<u>But</u> his desire [is] in the Law of the LORD; and in His Law he will study day and night....
⁶For the LORD knows [the] way of righteous [people], but [the] way of ungodly [people] will perish (Psalm 1:2,6).

This Gospel ends with the following:

²⁰And Peter, having been turned around, sees the disciple whom Jesus was loving following, who also reclined in the dinner on His breast and said, "Lord, who is the one betraying You?" [John 13:23-25] ²¹Peter having seen this one, says to Jesus, "Lord, but what [about] this one?" ²²Jesus says to him, "If I want him to be remaining until I come, what [is that] to you? <u>You</u> be following Me!" ²³Therefore, this word went out among the brothers [and sisters], "That disciple does not die." Yet Jesus did not say to him, "He does not die," <u>but</u> "If I want him to be remaining until I come, what [is that] to you?" [i.e., by tradition, John died of old age in Ephesus, ca. 98 AD]
²⁴This is that disciple, the one testifying concerning these things and having written these things, and we know that his testimony is true. ²⁵But there are also many other things—as many as Jesus did—which, if they should be written one by one, not even the world itself I suppose would have room for the scrolls being written. So be it! (John 21:20-25).

Some claim about this passage, "21:24 is part of the appendix of the gospel and should not be assumed to have come from the same hand as that responsible for the body of the gospel" (Early Christian). This is because the Gospel seems to end with chapter 20:

³⁰Now indeed many other signs Jesus also did in the presence of His disciples which have not been written in this scroll. ³¹But these have

been written so that you* shall believe [or, be convinced] that Jesus is the Christ, the Son of God, and so that believing you* shall be having life in His name (John 20:30f).

That much is true, and maybe the final chapter was an afterthought by John. But there are no manuscripts of this Gospel that include chapters 1-20 without chapter 21, and there is no significant change in the style of Greek going from the first 20 chapters to the last chapter that would require a different author.

> The last two verses of the twentieth chapter indicate clearly indeed that the Evangelist intended to terminate his work here: … But the sole conclusion that can be deduced from this is that the twenty-first chapter was afterwards added and is therefore to be regarded as an appendix to the Gospel. Evidence has yet to be produced to show that it was not the Evangelist, but another, who wrote this appendix. The opinion is at present fairly general, even among critics, that the vocabulary, style, and the mode of presentation as a whole, together with the subject-matter of the passage reveal the common authorship of this chapter and the preceding portions of the Fourth Gospel (New Advent; "Gospel of St. John").

Moreover, throughout this Gospel, the author writes as if he is an eyewitness of the events. As such, "Here we are driven to the alternative: either the writer was a true witness of what he relates, or he was a false witness who wrote down a deliberate lie" (Schaff; 9944-9945). But this is where the ending becomes important due to the line, "we know that his testimony is true." The "we" here could very well be the people who encouraged John to write his Gospel, as attested to in the Muratorian fragment that was discussed previously:

> The fourth Gospel is that of John, one of the disciples. When his fellow-disciples and bishops entreated him, he said, "Fast ye now with me for the space of three days, and let us recount to each other whatever may be revealed to each of us." On the same night it was revealed to Andrew, one of the apostles, that John should narrate all things in his own name as they called them to mind (quoted in New World Encyclopedia; "Muratorian fragment").

Translator's Perspective on the Canon of the NT

Moreover,

> ... the concluding verse of the appendix, John 21:24, is a still older testimony of a number of personal friends and pupils of John, perhaps the very persons who, according to ancient tradition, urged him to write the Gospel. The book probably closed with the sentence: "This is the disciple who beareth witness of these things, and wrote these things." To this the elders add their attestation in the plural: "And we know that his witness is true." A literary fiction would not have been benefited by an anonymous postscript. The words as they stand are either a false testimony of the pseudo-John, or the true testimony of the friends of the real John who first received his book and published it before or after his death (Schaff; 9850-9855).

In addition, taking the final chapter as a genuine part of the original Gospel of John, we see a reference back to the scene at the Last Supper, and this passage led to the idea that John would not die until Jesus' Second Coming. But John corrects that misconception. However, as the note in the ALT indicates, John did live a long life, until near the end of the first century. But this is where there is some disagreement. In the Gospel of Mark, after the earlier quoted request of James and John to sit at Jesus' side in His glory, the following conversation occurs:

> [38]But Jesus said to them, "You do not know what you* ask. Are you* able to drink the cup which I am drinking and to be baptized [with] the baptism which I am being baptized?" [39]So they said to Him, "We are able." Then Jesus said to them, "Indeed, the cup which I am drinking, you* will drink, and the baptism which I am being baptized [with], you* will be baptized [with]. [40]But to sit at My right [parts] [fig., on My right side] and at My left [parts] [fig., on My left side] is not mine to give, but [it is for those] for whom it has been prepared" (Mark 10:38-40).

Since Jesus was crucified and James was executed, there are some in Church history who believed that John the apostle was executed as well. If he had been executed around the same time as James, then he would not have lived long enough to have written this Gospel. This is the case given that there is almost universal agreement both in the early Church and today that John's Gospel was the last of the canonical Gospels to be written, as will be discussed shortly.

However, no such martyrdom is mentioned in the Book of Acts. Since James' martyrdom is mentioned, you would think his brother's would be too, if he was executed during the time period of Acts. In fact, there is no mention of John being martyred in the early Church.

> ... the earliest patristic evidence for this supposition is from the fifth century (Philip of Side and the Syrian martyrology of 411 CE), from sources which show themselves to be unreliable as historical guides in other matters. (Bible.org; "The Gospel of John: Introduction, Argument, Outline").

But what we have from more reliable testimony is, "The consentient testimony of the church of the 2nd century is that the later years of John were spent at Ephesus, where he wrote his Gospel and gathered round him many disciples" (ISBE).

Thus, the idea that John was martyred has little basis. As for Jesus' statement, tradition has it that John the apostle was persecuted and exiled, and that would fulfill His words about John "drinking the cup" that He would drink. What this means is John would have lived long enough to write this Gospel. There is other evidence for Johannine authorship:

> As with the other gospels, no MSS [manuscripts] which contain John's Gospel affirm authorship by anyone other than John. Once again, as with the others, this is short of proof of Johannine authorship, but the unbroken stream suggests recognition (or at least acknowledgment) of Johannine authorship as early as the first quarter of the second century. Indeed, John's Gospel is unique among the evangelists for two early papyri (P66 and P75, dated c. 200) attest to Johannine authorship. Since these two MSS were not closely related to each other, this common tradition must precede them by at least three or four generations of copying (Bible.org' "The Gospel of John: Introduction, Argument, Outline").

At the end of the 2nd century, the Christian church was in possession of four Gospels, which were used as sacred books, read in churches in public worship, held in honor as authoritative, and treated as part of a Canon of Scripture. One of these was the Fourth Gospel, universally ascribed to the apostle John as its author. We have the evidence on this point of Irenaeus, of Tertullian, of Clement of Alexandria, a little later of Origen. Clement is witness for the belief and practice of the church in Egypt and its neighborhood; Tertullian for the church in Africa; and Irenaeus, who was brought up in Asia Minor, was

Translator's Perspective on the Canon of the NT

a teacher at Rome, and was bishop of Lyons in Gaul, for the churches in these lands. ... For there is evidence of the belief in the apostolic authorship of two Gospels by apostles, and of two by companions of the apostles, as an existing fact in the churches long before the end of the 2nd century (ISBE).

Irenaeus, who, as a native of Asia Minor and a spiritual grand-pupil of John, is entitled to special consideration, says: "Afterward" [i.e., after Matthew, Mark, and Luke] "John, the disciple of the Lord, who also had leaned upon his breast, did himself publish a Gospel during his residence at Ephesus in Asia." ...

For nearly eighteen centuries the Christian church of all denominations has enjoyed the fourth Gospel without a shadow of doubt that it was the work of John the Apostle....

The External Proof of the Johannean authorship is as strong, yea stronger than that of the genuineness of any classical writer of antiquity, and goes up to the very beginning of the second century, within hailing distance of the living John. It includes catholic writers, heretics, and heathen enemies. There is but one dissenting voice, hardly audible, that of the insignificant sect of the Alogi who opposed the Johannean doctrine of the Logos (hence their name, with the double meaning of unreasonable, and anti-Logos heretics) and absurdly ascribed both the Gospel of John and the Apocalypse to his enemy, the Gnostic CerinThus, (Schaff; 9516-9518; 9804-9806; 9811-9816).

If we except the heretics mentioned by Irenaeus (*Against Heresies* III.11.9) and Epiphanius (*Haer.*, li, 3), the authenticity of the Fourth Gospel was scarcely ever seriously questioned until the end of the eighteenth century (New Advent; "Gospel of St. John").

The heretics mentioned were Gnostics, the philosophy of which will be discussed in Volume Three. But here, their testimony is hardly trustworthy, as they did not believe basic Christian doctrines and thus had every reason to try to discredit this Gospel and its teaching about the *Logos*, (Greek for "Word," from John 1:1).

But putting that unreliable testimony aside, the style of writing, the testimony of the book itself, the manuscript evidence, the testimony of Apostolic and Church Fathers, and the universal testimony of the

Church in general throughout most of its history all attest to John the apostle as having written this Gospel.

However, despite this strong internal and external evidence there are many today who doubt John's authorship. But other than the points already mentioned, the only reason that can be given for this denial is:

> If the author of the Gospel of John were an eyewitness, presumably the author would have known that Jesus and his compatriots were permitted to enter the synagogues. But at several points it is stated that those who acknowledged Jesus as the Christ during the life of Jesus were put out of the synagogue. This anachronism is inconceivable as the product of an eyewitness (Early Christian; "Gospel of John").

What this quote is referring to is the following passages:

²²These things his parents said because they were afraid of the Jews, for the Jews had already agreed together that if anyone shall confess Him [as the] Christ, he should be expelled from the synagogue. ²³Because of this, his parents said, "He is of age, ask him" (John 9:22-23).

⁴²Nevertheless, still also out of the rulers many believed [or, trusted] in Him, but because of the Pharisees they were not confessing [Him publicly], so that they should not be expelled from the synagogue (John 9:42).

¹"These things I have spoken to you*, so that you* shall not be caused to stumble [fig., fall away; or, abandon your* faith]. ²They will make you* be expelled from the synagogue, but an hour is coming that every[one] having killed you* shall think [they are] offering sacred service to God (John 16:1f).

I will have to admit that these verses have confused me somewhat. In reading the Synoptics and Acts, it does not appear like there was animosity between the Jewish leadership and the followers of Jesus during Jesus' lifetime. It was only after His death and resurrection that such occurred. But it is possible these verses are not referring to a widespread attitude and action by the central Jewish authorities, but just local animosities and actions by select synagogue leaders.

This is possible given the following scene. After Jesus preached in a synagogue in Capernaum and angered the Jews, the following happens:

Translator's Perspective on the Canon of the NT

> [28] And all [the people] in the synagogue were filled with rage, hearing these things. [29] And having risen, they forced Him outside the city and brought Him as far as [the] brow of the hill on which their city had been built, in order to throw Him down from the cliff. [30] But He, having passed through [the] middle of them, went away (Luke 4:28-30).

This would Thus, be one synagogue that the early Jewish Christians would not be welcome in, and there easily could have been others. And note that John says "synagogue" not "synagogues." Thus, John would not be wrong in his statements. Such a possibility is even mentioned by this same critical source, but in a different context.

> Those who relate the expulsion to a formal effort on the part of Judaism to purge itself of Christian believers link the composition of the gospel with a date soon after the Council of Jamnia, which is supposed to have promulgated such an action. Hence, these scholars would date John after 90. Those inclined to see the expulsion more in terms of an informal action on the part of a local synagogue are free to propose an earlier date (Early Christian; "Gospel of John")

This quote is in reference to the dating of this Gospel, which we will get to in a moment, but first to finish up with the author, none of the arguments against Johannine authorship are very compelling, while there is much evidence, both internal and external, that upholds the traditional view that John the apostle is the author of this Gospel.

> A review of this array of testimonies, external and internal, drives us to the irresistible conclusion that the fourth Gospel is the work of John, the apostle. This view is clear, self-consistent, and in full harmony with the character of the book and the whole history of the apostolic age; while the hypothesis of a literary fiction and pious fraud is contradictory, absurd, and self-condemned. No writer in the second century could have produced such a marvelous book, which towers high above all the books of Justin Martyr and Irenaeus and Tertullian and Clement and Origen, or any other father or schoolman or reformer (Schaff; 9965-9969).

Date of Writing:

"The Gospel of John is usually assumed to have been the last of the four gospels composed" (Blue Letter; "When Were the Four Gospels

Written?"). This assumption is true for both the early Church and today. The former is evidenced by it being the last Gospel in the canonical order. Also, given its many differences from the Synoptics, many assume John had copies of those Gospels before him. He Thus, purposely chose to record events, miracles, and sayings of Jesus that Matthew, Mark, and Luke did not record. Given this, if Luke was written about 60 AD, then John would have to have been written sometime after that. But how much afterwards?

There are two basic opinions, and both are due to the Gospel of John not mentioning the Jewish revolt that began in 66 AD and the resulting destruction of Jerusalem and of the temple in 70 AD. This omission can be accounted for by John either writing before these events or so long afterwards they were not still central in the minds of Jews.

To use an example from our day, if someone living in New York City were to write a story about someone else who also lived in NYC, it would be inconceivable that it would not mentioned 9/11 if he was writing in the fall of 2001. Anyone living in NYC, or anywhere in the USA for that matter, was greatly affected by that fateful day. But if the story was being written before September 11, 2001, then it would be impossible for it to mention 9/11.

Similarly, if that person were to write such a story at the same time as I am updating this book in 2023, it would be conceivable that it would not mention 9/11. Enough time has passed that someone living in NYC would not feel compelled to mention it.

For example, I have been binge-watching the TV series *Blue Bloods*. It is the story of a family of police officers and a lawyer living in New York City. I started watching it with the pilot made 2010. In the first few seasons, 9/11 was mentioned several times. The series is still running in 2023. I have not gotten to the newer episodes, but I would bet they are less likely to mention 9/11, with 9/11 now being 22 years in the past.

The point is, if the apostle John was writing in the 90s, as many suppose, almost 30 years after the destruction of Jerusalem, it is understandable why he did not mention it. Thus, either the pre-66 date or the 90s date for the Gospel According to John are possibilities.

But going back to an earlier discussion, if John had been martyred, then the earlier date might be possible, but not the later. But it was shown that he almost certainly was not martyred. Instead, "According to the tradition universally accepted in the church, John survived till the time of Trajan (98 AD)" (ISBE).

If John the apostle was a teenager when Jesus called him in 26 AD, and if this tradition is correct, he would have lived into his 80s, dying in the late 90s AD. And Thus, he would have been alive to write his Gospel

Translator's Perspective on the Canon of the NT

in the 90s AD, and that is the time period traditionally assigned to this book. "According to the general opinion, the Gospel is to be referred to the last decade of the first century, or to be still more precise, to 96 or one of the succeeding years" (New Advent).

One line of internal evidence for the later date is John's method of giving time. In the Synoptic Gospels, the Jewish method is used. That is, the day begins at sunset, or 6:00 pm, with the hour count restarting at sunrise, or at 6:00 am. This is clearly seen in the following parable.

[1]"For the kingdom of the heavens is like a person, a landowner, who went out early in the morning [i.e., probably about 6:00 a.m.] to hire laborers for his vineyard. [2]And having agreed with the laborers for a denarius [for] the day [i.e., a normal day's wage], he sent them into his vineyard. [3]And having gone out about [the] third hour [i.e., 9:00 a.m.], he saw others having stood in the marketplace idle. [4]And he said to those [ones], 'You* also be going into the vineyard, and whatever is just I will give to you.*' [5]And they went off. Again, having gone out about [the] sixth and [the] ninth hour [i.e., 12:00 noon and 3:00 p.m., respectively], he did in the same manner. [6]Then about the eleventh hour [i.e., 5:00 p.m.], having gone out, he found others having stood idle, and he says to them, 'Why have you* stood here idle the whole day?' [7]They say to him, 'Because no one hired us.' He says to them, 'You* also be going into the vineyard, and whatever is just you* will receive.' (Matt 20:1-7).

The timetable of this parable only makes sense if the bracketed time conversions are correct. In other words, the "third hour" makes sense if it is three hours after 6:00 am, but it makes no sense if Matthew is using our time method and thus it is 3:00 am or 3:00 pm. The same goes for the sixth, ninth, eleventh hours. Now let's apply this reasoning to the crucifixion of Jesus as recorded by Mark.

[24]And having crucified Him, they divide His garments, casting a lot on them [to determine] who should take what. [25]Now it was the third hour [i.e., 9:00 a.m.] when they crucified Him. [26]And the inscription of the accusation against Him had been inscribed ...

[33]Now the sixth hour [i.e., 12:00 noon] having come, darkness came over the whole land until the ninth hour [i.e., 3:00 p.m.]. [34]And at the ninth hour, Jesus shouted with a loud voice, saying [in Aramaic], *"Eloi, Eloi, lima sabachthani?"*—which is, having been translated, *"My God, My God, for what* [or, *why*] *did You abandon Me?"* [Psalm 22:1] [35]And some of the ones having stood by, having heard, said, "Listen! He is calling Elijah!" [36]So one [of them] having ran and having filled a sponge

Why Are These Books in the Bible? Volume Two

with wine vinegar [i.e., an inexpensive, sour wine effective for quenching thirst], and having put [it] around a reed, began giving [it] to Him to drink, saying, "Leave [Him] alone! Let us see if Elijah comes to take Him down."

³⁷But Jesus having released [fig., uttered] a loud cry, breathed His last. (Mark 15:24-37).

Thus, Jesus was first nailed to the cross at 9:00 am. Darkness came over the land from noon until 3:00 pm, at which point, Jesus died. Matthew and Luke agree with this timetable, except they do not give the time when Jesus was nailed to the cross:

⁴⁴Now it was about the sixth hour [i.e., 12:00 noon], and darkness came over the whole land until the ninth hour [i.e., 3:00 p.m.]. ⁴⁵And the sun was darkened, and the veil [or, curtain] of the sanctuary was torn in the middle! ⁴⁶And having called out with a loud voice, Jesus said, "Father, *into Your hands I will commit [or, will entrust] My spirit!*" [Psalm 31:5, LXX] And having said these [things], He breathed His last (Luke 23:44-46, also, Matt 27:45-50).

Now compare this timetable to the following from the Gospel of John:

¹³So Pilate, having heard this word, brought Jesus outside and sat down on the judgment seat at a place being called Pavement, but in Hebrew, *Gabbatha*. ¹⁴Now it was [the] preparation [day] of the Passover, and [it was] about the sixth hour [i.e., 12:00 noon Jewish time or 6:00 a.m. Roman time]. And he says to the Jews, "Look! Your* king!" ¹⁵But they cried out [or, shouted], "Take [Him] away! Take [Him] away! Crucify Him!" Pilate says to them, "Shall I crucify your* king?" The chief priests answered, "We have no king except Caesar." ¹⁶Therefore, he then handed Him over to them so that He should be crucified.

And they took Jesus and led [Him] away. ¹⁷And carrying His cross, He went out to a place being called Place of a Skull, which is called in Hebrew, *Golgotha*, ¹⁸where they crucified Him, and with Him two others, [one] on this side and [one] on that side, and Jesus in the middle (John 19:13).

John does not give us a time for when Jesus was nailed to the cross, but he does give us the time of His trial beforehand, the sixth hour. As the bracketed information notes, this would be 12:00 noon if John was following Jewish time. But that would make no sense. Jesus could not

133

Translator's Perspective on the Canon of the NT

have been tried three hours after He was crucified. But if John was following Roman time, then it makes perfect sense. Roman time is the same as ours, with the hour count starting at midnight and noon. Thus, the sixth hour is 6:00 am. This would allot three hours between the time Jesus appeared before Pilate and the time He was nailed to the cross. That fits the timetable just fine.

But why is John using Roman time while Matthew, Mark and Luke, are using Jewish time? The best supposition is that the three Synoptic authors are writing at a much earlier time, before the destruction of Jerusalem, when Jewish time was still being used. But after that event, Jewish time fell into disfavor even among Jews, Thus, John uses Roman time.

On a side note; this time usage by John is important when interpreting other passages in John, such as the story of the woman at the well, recorded in John 4:5-42. It begins:

> ⁵Then He comes to a city of Samaria, being called Sychar, near the place which Jacob gave to Joseph his son. ⁶Now a well of Jacob was there. So Jesus, having grown weary from the journey, was sitting Thus, by the well. It was about the sixth hour [i.e., 12:00 noon Jewish time or 6:00 p.m. Roman time]. ⁷A woman comes from Samaria to draw water.

I have heard many sermons preached on this passage that assume Jewish time. The preacher would Thus, make a big deal about the woman coming at high noon, when it was hot and when water was not normally drawn. But in fact, the woman came at 6:00 pm, not an abnormal time. I will leave it to the reader to decide how that affects the interpretation.

In any case, along with this internal evidence, there is much external evidence for John having written in his Gospel in the 90s:

> … we have direct evidence concerning the date of composition. The so-called "Monarchian Prologue" to the Fourth Gospel, which was probably written about the year 200 or a little later, says concerning the date of the appearance of the Gospel: "He [sc. the Apostle John] wrote this Gospel in the Province of Asia, after he had composed the Apocalypse on the Island of Patmos". The banishment of John to Patmos occurred in the last year of Domitian's reign (i.e. about 95). A few months before his death (18 September, 96), the emperor had discontinued the persecution of the Christians and recalled the exiles (Eusebius, Church History III.20.5-7). This evidence

would therefore refer the composition of the Gospel to A.D. 96 or one of the years immediately following.

The place of composition was, according to the above-mentioned prologue, the province of Asia. Still more precise is the statement of St. Irenaeus, who tells us that John wrote his Gospel "at Ephesus in Asia" (Against Heresies III.1.2). All the other early references are in agreement with these statements (New Advent).

There is thus testimony by the Church Fathers that John the apostle wrote his Gospel c. 96 AD in Ephesus.

Another point is the purpose of John's Gospel. Early testimony states it was written to combat Gnosticism. That movement will be discussed in Volume Three, but here it will be said the movement did not start in earnest until the late first century, Thus, the earlier date for John's Gospel would not work, but the 90s date does.

Now there are some who try to date this book even later, after 100 AD to as late as 200 AD. That claim is tied in with the claim that John the apostle did not write this Gospel, as even if John was a teenager in 26 AD, he could hardly have lived much past 100 AD. But, "Discovery of certain papyrus fragments dated around A.D. 135 require the book to have been written, copied, and circulated before then" (GotQuestions?org; "Gospel of John"). Most specifically is the Rylands fragment:

> This small papyrus fragment is the oldest known copy of any part of the New Testament.
>
> The fragment, found in Egypt in 1920, is just 9 cm x 6 cm, and is written on both sides. It has been identified as part of John's Gospel – John chapter 18 verses 31-33 on the front, and verses 37-38 on the back. The whole page would have been about 21 cm high by 20 cm wide, and the entire Gospel would have taken about 130 pages.
>
> Experts have dated this fragment to between AD 125 and AD 150. ... The papyrus, called the 'Rylands fragment', technical name P52, is now in the John Rylands Library at Manchester (Facing).

Moreover:

> The importance of this fragment is quite out of proportion to its size, since it may with some confidence be dated in the first half of the second century A.D., and thus ranks as the earliest known fragment of the New Testament in any language.

Translator's Perspective on the Canon of the NT

It provides us with invaluable evidence of the spread of Christianity in areas distant from the land of its origin; it is particularly interesting to know that among the books read by the early Christians in Upper Egypt was St. John's Gospel, commonly regarded as one of the latest of the books of the New Testament. Like other early Christian works which have been found in Egypt, this Gospel was written in the form of a codex, i.e. book, not of a roll, the common vehicle for pagan literature of that time (Bible Researcher; "Papyrus 52: A Fragment of John's Gospel").

John Rylands Papyrus or Rylands Fragment – earliest known N.T. manuscript, dated about 125 CE. John Rylands Library, Mancester, England (Deeper Study).

The date I learned for this fragment at Denver Seminary was 125 AD, which fits with the time period indicated in these quotes. It would have taken some time for a copy of John's Gospel to have been made, then for that copy to have traveled all the way from Ephesus to Egypt, then for a copy to be made as a codex and to be distributed. Given all of this, this little papyrus easily pushes the date of the writing of the original document into the first century and thus into the lifetime of the apostle John. Moreover:

The style of the fourth Gospel differs widely from the ecclesiastical writers of the second century, and belongs to the apostolic age. It has none of the technical theological terms of post-apostolic controversies, no allusions to the state of the church, its government and worship, but moves in the atmosphere of the first Christian generation (Schaff; 9771-9774).

And in regards to the much later dating of the critics, Schaff writes:

Nor are the negative critics agreed as to the time of composition. Under the increasing pressure of argument and evidence they have been forced to retreat, step by step, from the last quarter of the second century to the first, even within a few years of John's death, and within the lifetime of hundreds of his hearers, when it was impossible for a pseudo-Johannean book to pass into general currency without the discovery of the fraud… These vacillations of criticism reveal the impossibility of locating the Gospel in the second century (Schaff; 10065-10072).

To emphasize an important point in this quote, being forced by the Rylands Fragment and other reasons to date this book to at least by the early second century puts the critics in the untenable position of claiming the early Church was fooled by a forgery at a time when friends and disciples of the apostle John were still alive and could testify as to whether he wrote this book or not. These would include Ignatius and Polycarp, whose writings are extant and will be discussed in Volume Three. Yet no such objections were ever raised against this book.

> Literary fictions were not uncommon in the ancient church, but men had common sense and moral sense then as well is now to distinguish between fact and fiction, truth and lie. It is simply incredible that the ancient church should have been duped into a unanimous acceptance of such an important book as the work of the beloved disciple almost from the very date of his death, and that the whole Christian church, Greek, Latin, Protestant, including an innumerable army of scholars, should have been under a radical delusion for eighteen hundred years, mistaking a Gnostic dream for the genuine history of the Saviour of mankind, and drinking the water of life from the muddy source of fraud (Schaff; 10083-10088).

Thus, all of the evidence, both internal and external, points to this Gospel having been written by John the apostle in the 90s AD.

Doctrine of God:

John's Gospel begins with a dramatic prologue:

¹In [the] beginning was the Word [fig., the Expression of [Divine] Logic], and the Word was with [fig., in communion with] God, and the Word was God [fig., was as to His essence Deity]. ²This One was in the beginning with God. ³All [things] came to be through Him, and without Him not even one thing came to be which has come to be. ⁴In Him was life, and the life was the Light of the people. ⁵And the Light shines in the darkness, and the darkness did not overpower [or, comprehend] it (John 1:1-4).

The opening phrase "In [the] beginning" is identical to the opening phrase of the Book of Genesis, which of course continues, "made the

Translator's Perspective on the Canon of the NT

heaven and the earth." Thus, the Word and God already existed before the universe was created. Then God through the Word creates all things, and in the Word is life and light.

This conception of God is in accordance with the Jewish conception of God, except that it makes Jesus equal to and one with God. That would be blasphemy to a Jew, and throughout this book it is Jesus' claim to deity that gets Him in trouble with the Jewish authorities and which eventually leads to His arrest and crucifixion. But still, John's conception of God begins with the Jewish conception of God.

This personal nature of the one true God as seen in the OT is seen this book by God being called Father numerous times (e.g., John 1:14,18; 2:17;3 3:35; 4:21; 5:17-23, and many more), and in prayers offered to God (John 11:41f; 17:1-26). It is also strongly affirmed that there is only one true God, "Now this is eternal life: that they shall be knowing You, the only true God" (John 17:3a). The OT conception of the incorporeality of God is also asserted:

"God [is] Spirit [fig., [is] as to His essence Spirit], and it is necessary [for] the ones prostrating themselves in worship before Him to be prostrating in worship in spirit and truth" (John 4:24).

Essential Tenets:

This Gospel is filled with statements that uphold the essential tenets of the early Church. John 1:1,14 were already quoted which assert the pre-existence of Jesus ("In [the] beginning was the Word), and the humanity of Jesus ("And the Word became flesh"). The latter is further demonstrated by recording Jesus as "having grown weary from the journey" (4:6) and as saying "I am thirsty" (19:28). And in the shortest verse in the Bible, "Jesus wept" (John 11:35).

This Gospel also strongly asserts that Jesus is fully God and worthy of the same honor as the Father. This is seen not only in the Prologue but also in the following passages:

[13]"And no one has ascended into heaven, except the One having descended from heaven—the Son of Humanity, the One being in heaven (John 3:13).

[19]So Jesus answered and said to them, "Most positively, I say to you*, the Son is not able to be doing anything of Himself unless He sees the Father doing [it], for whatever He is doing, these also the Son likewise does. [20]For the Father affectionately loves the Son and shows to Him all which He Himself does, and greater works than these He will show to Him, so that you* shall be marveling. [21]For even as the Father

raises the dead [people] and makes alive, so also the Son makes alive whom He wills. ²²For neither does the Father judge anyone, but He has given all judgment to the Son, ²³so that all shall be honoring the Son just as they honor the Father. The one not honoring the Son does not honor the Father who sent Him. ²⁴Most positively, I say to you*, the one hearing My word and believing [or, trusting] the One having sent Me has eternal life and does not come into judgment, but has passed from death into life!

²⁵"Most positively, I say to you*, an hour is coming and now is when the dead [people] will hear the voice of the Son of God, and those having heard will live. ²⁶For even as the Father has life in Himself, so He gave also to the Son to be having life in Himself. ²⁷And He gave also to Him authority to be making judgment, because He is [the] Son of Humanity (John 5:19-27).

Note also the teaching of resurrection in this passage.

²⁸Then Jesus said to them, "When you* lift up the Son of Humanity then you* will know that I Am, and from Myself I do nothing, but just as My Father taught Me, these things I speak. ²⁹And the One having sent Me is with Me; the Father did not leave Me alone, because I always do the things pleasing to Him." ³⁰While speaking these things, many believed [or, trusted] in Him (John 8:28-30).

⁵⁸Jesus said to them, "Most positively, I say to you*, before Abraham came to be, I Am!" [cp. Exod 3:14] (John 8:58).

³⁰I and the Father are one!"
³¹Therefore, the Jews again took up stones so that they should stone Him. ³²Jesus answered to them, "Many good works I showed to you* from my Father. On account of which work of them do you* stone Me?" ³³The Jews answered Him, saying, "Concerning a good work we do not stone You, but for blasphemy, and because You, being a human being, are making Yourself God."

³⁴Jesus answered them, "Has it not been written in your* Law, *'I said, "You* are gods?"'* [Psalm 82:6] ³⁵If He called those ones "gods" to whom the word of God came (and the Scripture is not able to be broken), ³⁶[why of] whom the Father sanctified and sent into the world, do you* say, 'You blaspheme,' because I said, 'I am God's Son?' ³⁷If I am not doing the works of My Father, do not believe Me. ³⁸But if I am doing [them], even if you* do not believe Me, be believing the works, so that you* shall know and believe that the Father [is] in Me, and I [am]

Translator's Perspective on the Canon of the NT

in Him." ³⁹Therefore, they were seeking again to seize Him, and He went out from their hand (John 10:30-39).

⁸Philip says to Him, "Lord, show to us the Father, and it is sufficient for us." ⁹Jesus says to him, "[For] so long a time I am [or, have I been] with you*, and you have not known Me, Philip? The one having seen Me has seen the Father, and how do you say, 'Show to us the Father?' ¹⁰Do you not believe [or, Are you not convinced] that I [am] in the Father and the Father is in Me? The sayings which I speak to you*, I do not speak from Myself, but the Father abiding in Me, Himself does the works. ¹¹Be believing Me that I [am] in the Father and the Father [is] in Me, but if not [fig., or else] be believing Me because of the works themselves (John 14:8-11).

³Now this is eternal life: that they shall be knowing You, the only true God, and Jesus Christ whom You sent (John 17:3).

This Gospel associates the Father, Jesus, and the Holy Spirit together:

³²And John testified, saying, "I have seen the Spirit coming down like a dove out of heaven, and He remained upon Him. ³³And I did not know Him; but the One having sent me to baptize in water, that [One] said to me, 'Upon whomever you see the Spirit coming down and remaining upon Him, this is the One baptizing in [or, with] [the] Holy Spirit.' ³⁴And I have seen and have testified that this is the Son of God!" (John 1:32-34).

³⁴For [He] whom God sent speaks the sayings of God, for God does not give the Spirit by measure (John 3:34).

³⁸The one believing [or, trusting] in Me, just as the Scripture said, 'Out of his belly [or, innermost being] will flow rivers of living water." [no specific OT reference, but for general idea see Isaiah 55:1; 58:11; Ezek 47:1; Joel 3:18; Zech 13:1; 14:8] ³⁹But this He said concerning the Spirit, whom the ones believing in Him were about to be receiving, for [the] Holy Spirit was not yet [given], because Jesus was not yet glorified (John 7:38f).

¹⁵"If you* are loving Me, keep My commandments. ¹⁶And I will ask the Father, and another Counselor [or, Helper; cp. 1Jn 2:1] He will give to you*, so that He shall dwell with you* into the age [fig., forever]— ¹⁷the Spirit of the truth, whom the world is not able to receive, because

it does not look upon [or, watch [for]] Him, nor knows Him. But you* know Him, because He dwells with you* and will be in you* (John 14:15-17).

²⁶But the Counselor [or, Helper], the Holy Spirit, whom the Father will send in My name, that One will teach you* all [things] and will cause you* to remember all [things] which I said to you* (John 14:26).

¹²"I still have many things to be saying to you*, but you* are not able to be bearing [them] now. ¹³But when that One shall come—the Spirit of the truth—He will guide you* into all the truth. For He will not speak from Himself, but as many things as He hears He will speak, and He will announce to you* the coming [things]. ¹⁴That One will glorify Me, because He will take from [what is] Mine and will announce [it] to you*. ¹⁵All [things], as many as the Father has, are Mine, for this reason I said, 'He takes from [what is] Mine and will announce [it] to you*' (John 16:12-15).

This book teaches very clearly the renewal of the believer by the Holy Spirit, but by using a term more familiar than renewal:

⁵Jesus answered, "Most positively, I say to you, unless someone is born from water and Spirit, he is not able to enter into the kingdom of God. ⁶The [thing] having been born from the flesh is flesh, and the [thing] having been born from the Spirit is spirit. ⁷Stop marveling that I said to you, 'It is necessary [for] you* to be born from above [or, born again].' ⁸The Spirit breathes where He desires, and you hear His voice, but you do not know from where He comes and where He goes. [or, The wind blows where it wishes, and you hear its sound, but you do not know from where it comes and where it goes. – cp. John 20:22; Acts 2:2-4] In this manner [or, Like this] is every[one] having been born from the Spirit" (John 3:5-8).

Being born again is the most popular way to describe the renewal by the Spirit. But this is not the only way the new life is described in this book:

¹³Jesus answered and said to her, "Every[one] drinking of this water will thirst again. ¹⁴But whoever drinks of the water which I will give to him will by no means thirst into the age! [fig., will never thirst again!] But the water which I will give to him will become in him a well of water springing up to eternal life!" (John 4:13f).

Translator's Perspective on the Canon of the NT

⁶³The Spirit is the One giving life; the flesh does not accomplish [or, benefit] anything. The words which I have spoken to you* are spirit and are life! (John 6:63).

¹⁰The thief does not come except so that he should steal and kill and destroy. I came so that they shall have life, and they shall have [it] abundantly! (John 10:10).

²¹So Jesus said to them again, "Peace to you*. Just as the Father has sent Me, I also send you*." ²²And having said this, He breathed on [them] and says to them, "Receive [the] Holy Spirit" (John 20:21).

This renewal is also seen in the people who encounter Jesus in this book: Nicodemus (John 3:1ff), the woman at the well (John 4:1ff), and the woman caught in adultery (John 7:53-8:11).

In this Gospel, Jesus first describes the purpose of His death:

¹⁴"I am the good shepherd, and I know My [own], and I am known by My [own]. ¹⁵Just as the Father knows Me, and I know the Father, and I lay down My life on behalf of the sheep (John 10:14f).

³¹"Now is [the] judgment of this world; now the ruler of this world will be cast out. ³²And I, if I am lifted up from the earth, I will draw [or, drag] all [people; or, peoples] to Myself." ³³But this He was saying signifying by what sort of death He was about to die (John 12:31-33).

This Gospel then records in detail the death, burial, resurrection, and post-resurrection appearances of Jesus in chapters 18-21. It teaches that Jesus is Lord (4:1,11,49; 5:7; 6:23; and many others), Christ (1:17,40; 4:42; 6:69; 11:27), and the Son of God (John 1:34,49; 3:18; 5:25; 9:35-37; 11:4,27. In fact, the stated purpose for this book is to convince people that Jesus is the Christ, the Son of God:

³⁰Now indeed many other signs Jesus also did in the presence of His disciples which have not been written in this scroll. ³¹But these have been written so that you* shall believe [or, be convinced] that Jesus is the Christ, the Son of God, and so that believing you* shall be having life in His name (John 20:30f).

Appeal and Mark of Inspiration:

The appeal of this Gospel would be similar to that of the Synoptic Gospels. It records the life, miracles, teachings, and actions of Jesus.

And probably even more so than the Synoptics, multitudes of people have come to faith in Christ by reading this Gospel, and many more have been spiritually enriched by reading this book. This Gospel Thus, clearly bears the mark of inspiration. It even contains the best know verse of the Bible, which summarizes very nicely many of the creedal tenets:

[16]For God so loved the world that He gave His only-begotten [or, unique] Son, so that every[one] believing [or, trusting] in Him shall not perish, <u>but</u> shall be having eternal life! (John 3:16).

Conclusion on the Gospel According to John:

The Gospel According to John was written by an apostle in the first century. It was universally accepted as such in the early Church and had widespread appeal back then that continues to this day. It presents correct doctrine in regards the nature of God and early essential tenets. It is thus rightly included in the canon of the NT. In the next chapter we will look at other Johannine writings.

Translator's Perspective on the Canon of the NT

Chapter Five
The Epistles of John and The Revelation

Having studied the Gospel According to John, it is now time to consider other books traditionally ascribed to the apostle John.

First Epistle of John

The next Johannine book to be discussed is the First Epistle of John.

Author:

It was stated in the previous chapter that the Gospel of John and 1John contain the easiest Greek in the NT. In fact, after translating portions of the Gospel of John throughout their first year, a standard assignment for Greek students at the end of their first year of study is to translate all of 1John. And having translated both books, there is little doubt in this writer's mind that the same person wrote both books, as the style of the Greek is very similar.

However, like the Gospel of John, strictly speaking, 1John is anonymous. But it does emphatically claim to have been written by an eyewitness of the life of Jesus, as seen in the prologue:

[1]What was from [the] beginning, what we have heard, what we have seen with our eyes, what we looked upon and our hands handled, concerning the Word of the life—[2]and the life was revealed, and we have seen and testify and declare to you* the eternal life, which was with the Father and was revealed to us—[3]what we have seen and have heard we declare to you*, so that you* also shall be having fellowship with us, and indeed our fellowship [is] with the Father and with His Son Jesus Christ. [4]And these things we write to you*, so that our joy shall have been made full (1John 1:1-3).

The author of this epistle never identified himself by name, but Christians since the beginning of the church have considered this letter authoritative, believing it was written by John the apostle. That group of witnesses includes Polycarp, an early second-century bishop who as a young man knew John personally. In addition, the author clearly places himself as part of a group of apostolic eyewitnesses to the life and ministry of

Translator's Perspective on the Canon of the NT

Jesus, noting that "what we have seen and heard we proclaim to you also" (1John 1:3) (Insight).

Moreover, "there are significant similarities in style, vocabulary, theological emphases, and perhaps even structure between the two works" (Bible.org; "The Authorship of 1 John"). Compare the preceding prologue with the following verses from the Gospel of John:

¹In [the] beginning was the Word (John 1:1).
¹⁴And the Word [fig., the Expression of [Divine] Logic] became flesh and tabernacled among us, and we beheld His glory, glory as of an only-begotten [or, uniquely-begotten] from [the] Father, full of grace and truth (John 1:14).
¹⁵so that every[one] believing [or, trusting] in Him shall not perish, but shall be having eternal life" (John 3:15).
¹¹These things I have spoken to you* so that My joy shall abide in you*, and your* joy shall be made full (John 15:11).
³Now this is eternal life: that they shall be knowing You, the only true God, and Jesus Christ whom You sent (John 17:3).

And compare the famous John 3:16 verse with the following from 1John:

⁹By this was the love of God revealed in us, because God has sent His only-begotten [or, unique] Son into the world, so that we should live through Him. ¹⁰In this is love, not that we loved God, but that He loved us and sent His Son [as] a propitiation [or, appeasing sacrifice] concerning our sins! ¹¹Beloved, if God so loved us, we also ought to be loving one another (1John 4:9-11).

Now compare the following pairs of passages:

---

²³The one hating Me, also hates My Father (John 15:23).

²³Everyone denying the Son neither has the Father (1John 2:23).

---

¹⁸"If the world hates you*, you* know that it has hated Me before you* (John 15:18).

¹³Stop marveling, my brothers [and sisters], if the world hates you* (1John 3:13).

¹³Greater love has no one than this, that someone lays down his life on behalf of his friends (John 15:13).

¹⁶By this we have come to know love, because that One laid down His life on our behalf, and we ought to be laying down our lives on behalf of the brothers [and sisters] (1John 3:16).

---

¹⁶For God so loved the world that He gave His only-begotten [or, unique] Son, so that every[one] believing [or, trusting] in Him shall not perish, but shall be having eternal life! (John 3:16).

¹⁴And we have seen and testify that the Father has sent the Son [as] Savior of the world! (1John 4:14).

---

³⁶The one believing [or, trusting] in the Son has eternal life, but the one refusing to believe the Son will not see life, but the wrath of God abides on him (John 3:36).

¹²The one having the Son has the life; the one not having the Son of God does not have the life (1John 5:12).

---

¹³And whatever you* ask in My name, this I will do, so that the Father is glorified in the Son. ¹⁴If you* ask Me anything in My name, I will do [it] (John 14:13f).

¹⁴And this is the confidence which we have before Him, that if we shall be asking anything according to His will, He hears us. ¹⁵And if we know that He hears us, whatever we ask, we know that we have the requests which we have requested from Him (1John 5:14f).

It can be seen there is slightly different language but very similar concepts. There was Thus, no doubt in the early Church that John the apostle wrote this book. But despite this similarity and the early and universal testimony, there ae some today who make things much more complicated:

Translator's Perspective on the Canon of the NT

> There are similarities of language and thought [between the Gospel of John and 1John], yet there are small subtle differences. We simply do not know; the most we can say is that probably at least two authors are involved in the gospels and letters of John, and perhaps three. What is important is that the similarities of style, tone, and thought point to the existence of a Johannine "school." Whether the final form of these texts is the work of one author, or two, or three, their ideas, theology, contents, tone, and style have taken shape not in the mind of one man, but in a group, probably formed of one strong leader and a few intimate followers" (Early Christian; "1John").

This is high-sounding reasoning, but there is not a scrape of historical evidence that such a "school" existed and contributed to the writing of the books attributed to the apostle John. It is just scholars today trying to make themselves sound smarter than the early Church. Having translated these books, I did not see any warrant for saying they were put together by more than one author, as the writing style is similar throughout. Moreover, the "small subtle differences" between the two books is easily explained by them being different types of literature—a Gospel versus a letter.

> Arguments for a dual authorship are based chiefly on certain theological emphasis and developments in the Epistle, which are absent from the Gospel; and invariably these arguments have been pressed with complete disregard of the fact that the one writing purports, at least, to be a Gospel, the other, an utterance of the writer *in propria persona*. If, for example, it is urged that the words "He is faithful and righteous to forgive us our sins" have a more Pauline ring than any utterance of the Fourth Gospel, or that the conceptions in the Epistle of propitiation, intercession, and cleansing are presented in a more explicit and technical form than in the Gospel, it is a fair reply to ask, Why not? Is it to be accepted as a canon of criticism that the writer of that Gospel must necessarily have put all his own theological expressions into the mouth of Him whose teaching he proposed to report? (ISBE; John, the Epistles of").

The point is, any difference between these two books are due to the author faithfully reporting the words of Jesus in his Gospel about Jesus but then interpreting Jesus' words in his own words in his epistle. But both books are in substantial agreement as to their meanings, with 1John strongly asserting many important Christian tenets, as will be seen shortly. Thus, 1John was universally accepted as canonical in the early Church.

> As to the reception of the Epistle in the church, it is needless to cite any later witness than Eusebius (circa 325), who classes it among the books (*homologoumena*) whose canonical rank was undisputed. It is quoted by Dionysius, bishop of Alexandria (247-265), by the Muratorian Canon, Cyprian, Origen, Tertullian, Clement of Alexandria, and Irenaeus. Papias (who is described by Irenaeus as a "hearer of John and a companion of Polycarp") is stated by Eusebius to have "used some testimonies from John's former epistle"; and Polycarp's Epistle to the Philippians (circa 115) contains an almost verbal reproduction of 1 Jn 4:3 (ISBE; John, the Epistles of").

To remind the reader, the word *homologoumena* means "spoken the same" meaning the Church as a whole had the same opinion on this book. This is opposite of *antilegomena*, which indicates differences of opinion.

Date of Writing:

The date of this book would be similar as to that for the Gospel of John, though most would agree that the Gospel came first then the epistle. "Although some have proposed a reverse sequence, most contemporary commentators assume that I John was written after the fourth gospel" (Early Christian; "1John).

This idea is based on the epistle presupposing the readers know information in the Gospel. Consider the following pairs of passages:

---

[12]"This is My commandment, that you* shall be loving one another just as I loved you* (John 15:13).

[11]Because this is the message which you* heard from [the] beginning, that we should be loving one another (1John 3:11).

---

[30]Now indeed many other signs Jesus also did in the presence of His disciples which have not been written in this scroll. [31]But these have been written so that you* shall believe [or, be convinced] that Jesus is the Christ, the Son of God, and so that believing you* shall be having life in His name (John 20:30f).

[13]These things I wrote to you*, the ones believing [or, trusting] in the name of the Son of God, so that you* shall know that you* have eternal life, and so that you* shall be believing [or, shall continue believing] in the name of the Son of God (1John 5:13).

Note also how these passage show additional similarity of thought between these two books.

That said; if the Gospel is dated in the early 60s, then 1John would be in the early to mid-60s. Similarly, if the Gospel is dated in the mid-90s, then 1John would be in the mid to late-90s. The only reason to date it any later would be if one denies the Johannine authorship.

Doctrine of God:

The doctrine of God in 1John is similar to that in the Gospel and in the rest of the canonical books.

[5]And this is the message which we have heard from Him and announce to you*, that God is light [fig., is as to His essence light], and in Him [there] is no darkness at all (1John 1:5).

[19]And by this we know that we are of the truth, and we will assure our hearts [fig., consciences] before Him, [20]because if our heart [fig., conscience] shall be condemning [us], that God is greater than our heart, and He knows all things (1John 3:19f).

[7]Beloved, let us be loving one another, because love is from God, and every one loving has been begotten from God and knows God. [8]The one not loving did not know [or, come to know] God, because God is love [fig., is as to His essence love] (1John 4:7).

[12]No one has seen God at any time (1John 4:12a).

[19]We know that we are from God, and the whole world lies in evil [or, in the evil [one]] (1John 5:19).

[21]Little children [or, [My] dear children], guard yourselves from the idols! So be it! 1John 5:21).

Thus, God in 1John is light, indicating His goodness, He is all-knowing, He is love, and He is incorporeal and thus cannot be expressed by idols. Also, the world being said to be "in evil" fits with the OT concept of a fallen world.

Essential Tenets:

That Jesus is fully human is an important point of 1John. This is possibly because 1John was written to combat Gnosticism, which denied Jesus was fully human. That belief will be explained in Volume Three, but here, in addition to the prologue, consider the following strongly worded passage:

[2]By this is known the Spirit of God: every spirit which confesses Jesus Christ [as] having come in [the] flesh is of God. [3]And every spirit which does not confess Jesus Christ [as] having come in [the] flesh is not from God, and this is the [spirit] of the Antichrist which you* heard that it is coming and now is already in the world (1John 4:2f).

Jesus is also God:

[20]Now we know that the Son of God [has] come, and He has given to us understanding, so that we shall know the true [One]. And we are in the true [One], in His Son, Jesus Christ. This One is the true God and eternal life! (1John 5:20).

1John asserts that Jesus died for our sins and is our Mediator before the Father:

[7]But if we shall be walking about in the light [i.e., in truth and righteousness], as He is in the light, we have fellowship with one another, and the blood of Jesus Christ His Son cleanses [or, purges] us from all sin (1John 1:7).

[1]My little children [or, My dear children], I am writing these things to you* so that you* do not sin. And if anyone should sin, we have a Counselor [or, an Advocate; cp. John 14:16] with the Father, Jesus Christ, [the] righteous. [2]And <u>He</u> is [the] propitiation [or, appeasing sacrifice] concerning our sins, but not concerning ours only, <u>but</u> also concerning [those] of the whole world! (1John 2:1f).

[6]This is the One having come through water and blood—Jesus Christ; not by the water only, <u>but</u> by the water and the blood (1John 5:6a).

Translator's Perspective on the Canon of the NT

Jesus' resurrection and ascension are not specifically mentioned, but the following clearly implies Jesus is still alive:

[12]The one having the Son has the life; the one not having the Son of God does not have the life (1John 5:12).

In 1John, Jesus is the Christ and the Son of God, and faith in Jesus is essential for salvation:

[22]Who is the liar, except the one denying that Jesus is the Christ [or, the Messiah]? This one is the antichrist, the one denying the Father and the Son (1John 2:22).

[15]Whoever shall confess that Jesus is the Son of God, God abides in him, and he in God (1John 4:15).

[1]Every one believing [or, who is convinced] that Jesus is the Christ [or, the Messiah] has been begotten from God, and every one loving the One having begotten loves also the one having been begotten from [or, by] Him (1John 5:1).

[5]Who is the one overcoming the world, if not the one believing [or, who is convinced] that Jesus is the Son of God? (1John 5:5).

[10]The one believing [or, trusting] in the Son of God has that testimony in him; the one not believing God, has made Him a liar, because he has not believed in the testimony which God has testified concerning His Son. [11]And this is the testimony, that God gave eternal life to us, and this life is in His Son. [12]The one having the Son has the life; the one not having the Son of God does not have the life (1John 5:10).

The Father, Son, and Spirit are associated together:

[23]And this is His commandment, that we should believe in the name of His Son Jesus Christ, and we should be loving one another, just as He gave commandment. [24]And the one keeping His commandments abides in Him, and He in him; and by this we know that He abides in us, from the Spirit whom He gave to us (1John 3:23f).

[12]No one has seen God at any time. If we shall be loving one another, God abides in us, and His love has been perfected in us. [13]By this we know that we abide in Him, and He in us, because He has given

to us of His Spirit. ¹⁴And we have seen and testify that the Father has sent the Son [as] Savior of the world! (John 4:12-14).

⁶This is the One having come through water and blood—Jesus Christ; not by the water only, but by the water and the blood. And the Spirit is the One testifying, because the Spirit is the truth. ⁷Because three are the ones testifying: ⁸the Spirit and the water and the blood, and the three are into the one [or, are for the one [thing]; fig., agree as one] (1John 5:6-8).

These passages also refer to the Spirit indwelling the believer, which is another way of describing the baptism in the Spirit.
Thus, 1John fit the doctrinal standards for a book to be included in the canon of the NT.

Appeal and Mark of Inspiration:
With 1John having so many similarities to the Gospel of John, its appeal is similar to that book. It tells us much about the Person and Work of Jesus, and people have come to faith in Christ from reading this little book and have been encouraged in their Christian walk. It Thus, also bears the mark of being inspired.

Conclusion on 1John:
1John was written in the first century by John the apostle. It contains much doctrinal information that is in accordance with the basic doctrines of the Church, and it has widespread appeal. It was Thus, rightly included in the canon.

Second and Third Epistles of John

The next books to be discussed are the second and third epistles of John. These books will be discussed together as they are very similar. One thing they have in common is they are the first books among the *antilegomena* to be discussed.

Length:
2John consists of just 13 verses and 3John of 14 verses. They are thus the shortest books in the Bible. And this short length is one reason these books were disputed.

Being so short, they were not very well known. This should be easy to understand. If the reader is a longtime church goer, how many times have heard a sermon preached from one of these little books? Chances

Translator's Perspective on the Canon of the NT

are you answered "Never." But how many times have you heard a sermon preached from the Gospel of John. Chances are you answered, "Many." It would have been the same situation in the early Church. The average church goer probably never heard these books read or preached on in their meetings, and the average Christian leader never used material from them to prepare a sermon. Thus, few Christians even knew they existed.

In addition, with being so short, there is simply not much doctrine in them to decide if they fit with doctrinal standards.

Moreover, with such little material to work with, it is hard to compare the writing style of these books with other books to help to determine their author. And that leads the next point.

Author:

These books begin with the following superscriptions:

[1]The Elder, To [the] chosen Kyria [or, elect lady] and to her children, whom I love in truth (2John 1:1).

[1]The Elder, To Gaius, the beloved [fig., my dear friend], whom I love in truth (3John 1:1).

These letters end with the following subscriptions:

[12]Having many [things] to be writing to you*, I did not intend [to do so] through a sheet of papyrus and ink, but I hope [or, expect] to come to you* and to speak mouth to mouth [fig., face to face], so that our joy shall have been filled. [13]The children of your chosen [or, elect] sister [fig., The members of your sister assembly] greet you. So be it! (2John 1:12f).

[13]I had many [things] to be writing, but I do not want to write to you through ink and pen. [14]But I hope [or, expect] soon to see you, and we will speak mouth to mouth [fig., face to face]. Peace to you! Our friends greet you. Be greeting our friends by name (3John 1:13f).

Notice how similar these superscriptions and subscriptions are. This is evidence these two letters were written by the same person.

Written in response to similar problems, the Second and Third Letters of John are of the same length, perhaps determined by the practical consideration of the writing space on one piece of papyrus. In each letter the writer calls himself "the Presbyter [Elder]," and their common authorship is further evidenced by internal similarities in style and wording, especially in the introductions and conclusions (Bishops; "The Second Letter of John").

But who is this person? The writer does not give his name, but only identifies himself as "The Elder" (or "Presbyter," from the Greek word *presbuteros*). If this were John the apostle writing, it seemed strange to some in the early Church that he would identify himself as an elder. As will be discussed later, Paul will identify himself as "an apostle" throughout his writings, and an apostle is a much higher rank in the Church than an elder. However, Peter calls himself an "elder" near the end of his first epistle (1Peter 5:1). But that is after identifying himself as "an apostle" at the beginning of it (1Peter 1:1). But here, the writer only calls himself an elder.

However:
The tradition from the earliest days of the church states that the author was the apostle John. There have been various conjectures over the years that another disciple of Christ named John may have been responsible for this letter (Got?Questions.org; Book of 2 John).

Moreover:
Although traditionally attributed to John the apostle, these letters were probably written by a disciple or scribe of an apostle. The traditional place and date of composition, Ephesus at the end of the first century, are plausible for both letters (Bishops; "The Second Letter of John").

These considerations led to the theory that there were two people named John living at Ephesus during the time period in which the Johannine letters were written.

Were there two Johns at Ephesus? Or was there only one? Or, if there was only one, was he John the Evangelist, or only John the Presbyter? Here there is every possible variety of opinion. Many hold that there were two, and many that there was only one. Many who hold that there was only one, hold that the one was John the son of Zebedee; others hold, with equal assurance, that he was a distinct person (ISBE; "John, Gospel of").

Translator's Perspective on the Canon of the NT

Lending credence to the possibility there were two men of prominence named John in the early Church living in Ephesus at the same time is the following:

> During the 3rd century two rival sites at Ephesus claimed the honour of being the apostle's grave. One eventually achieved official recognition, becoming a shrine in the 4th century (Encyclopedia Britannica; "Saint John the Apostle").

If there were two men, John the apostle, and his disciple, John the elder, this then could cause some such confusion in their graves. It could also cause confusion as to who wrote which books associated with the name John. It is this situation that gave rise to earlier mentioned notion of a "Johannine school," although that is to go far beyond the actual evidence. But what is rather sure is if there were two men named John, then the elder would have been a disciple of the apostle, Thus, any books written by the elder could still warrant canonical status. Thus, if any of the five books traditionally ascribed to the apostle John were in fact written by the elder John, that would not negate their canonical status. It would just make those books similar to the Gospels of Mark and Luke in being written by a direct associate of an apostle.

Despite the lack of material to work with, in translating these books, they did appear to have a similar writing style as the fourth Gospel and 1John, but it was not identical. 2,3John seemed a little more stilted and less easy flowing than the Gospel and 1John. In other words, the Greek is not quite as simple as the Gospel and 1John. But that difference could be attributed to these books being more focused in their audience.

3John is clearly written to one person, but there is some dispute about the first superscription. "This could either have been a lady of important standing in the church or a code which refers to the local church and its congregation (Got?Questions.org; "Book of 2 John"). Either way, this is more focused than the intended general audiences of the Gospel of John and 1John. And this difference could be why the writing style is somewhat different. People write differently when they are writing to one person than when they are writing for a wide audience.

As a writer, I know this to be true for myself. I try to keep things as simple as possible for my books and for articles for my newsletters and websites, not knowing the knowledge level of potential readers. But when I write an email to a person I know, I know what their knowledge level is, so I do not write below that level.

On the other hand, this similarity yet difference could be explained by the writer of 2,3John being a student of the writer of the Gospel and 1John and thus picking up some of his writing style, while retaining some of this own style.

Moreover, even with little material to work with, some similarity of thought can be discerned between these two epistles and the Gospel and 1John. Compare the following sets of verses.

---

[11]Because this is the message which you* heard from [the] beginning, that we should be loving one another (1John 3:11).

[5]And now I urgently ask you, Kyria, not as writing to you a new commandment, but [the one] which we were having from the beginning, that we should be loving one another (2John 1:5).

---

[15]"If you* are loving Me, keep My commandments (John 14:15).

[6]And this is love, that we are walking about [fig, conducting ourselves] according to His commandments. This is the commandment, just as you heard from the beginning that you should be walking about in it (2John 1:6).

---

[3]And every spirit which does not confess Jesus Christ [as] having come in [the] flesh is not from God, and this is the [spirit] of the Antichrist which you* heard that it is coming and now is already in the world (1John 4:3).

[7]Because many deceivers [have] entered into the world, the ones not confessing Jesus Christ [as] coming in [the] flesh; this is the Deceiver and the Antichrist (2John 1:7).

---

[4]And these things we write to you*, so that our joy shall have been made full (1John 1:4).

[12]Having many [things] to be writing to you*, I did not intend [to do so] through a sheet of papyrus and ink, but I hope [or, expect] to come to you* and to speak mouth to mouth [fig., face to face], so that our joy shall have been filled (2John 1:12).

Translator's Perspective on the Canon of the NT

⁷Little children [or, [My] dear children], let no one be leading you* astray [fig., be deceiving you*]. The one practicing righteousness is righteous, just as He is righteous. ⁸The one practicing sin is from the Devil, because the Devil [has been] sinning from [the] beginning. For this [reason] the Son of God was revealed, so that He should destroy the works of the Devil. ⁹Everyone having been begotten from God is not practicing sin, because His seed abides in him, and he is not able to be sinning, because he has been begotten from God. ¹⁰By this are revealed [who are] the children of God and the children of the Devil. Everyone not practicing righteousness is not from God, and the one not loving his brother (1John 3:7-10).

¹¹Beloved, stop imitating the evil, <u>but</u> [be imitating] the good. The one doing good is from God; the one doing evil has not seen God (3John 1:11).

Given all of these similarities, it is most likely the same person wrote all four of these books. At the very least, the Gospel and 1John were written by the apostle John, while 2 and 3John were written by the elder John, who was directly influenced by the apostle John. Thus, at the most you have two different authors, with each writing the whole of his particular document. But there is no indication of a "school" writing these books collectively or via one redaction after another as liberals claim. The following quote summarizes the most important points:

> They [2, 3John] belong to the seven *Antilegomena*, and have been ascribed by some to the "Presbyter John," a contemporary of the apostle, though of disputed existence. But the second Epistle resembles the first, almost to verbal repetition, and such repetition well agrees with the familiar tradition of Jerome concerning the apostle of love, ever exhorting the congregation, in his advanced age, to love one another. The difference of opinion in the ancient church respecting them may have risen partly from their private nature and their brevity, and partly from the fact that the author styles himself, somewhat remarkably, the "elder," the "presbyter." This term, however, is probably to be taken, not in the official sense, but in the original, signifying age and dignity; for at that time John was in fact a venerable father in Christ, and must have been revered and loved as a patriarch among his "little children" (Schaff; 10410-10416).

Date of Writing:

There is not sufficient internal or external evidence to give a firm date for the writing of these books. But given their connection to 1John, they were probably written about the same time as it, or in the 90s AD. "The Book of 2 John would most likely have been written at about the same time as John's other letters, 1 and 3 John, between A.D. 85-95" (GotQuestions?org; "Book of 2John").

Doctrine of God:

Given their short nature, neither of these books mention anything about the nature of God. But that is probably due their personal nature. The writer knew the intended reader(s) had a correct conception of God and thus did not need to articulate it. That again is a difference between writing a letter to one person versus something intended for a wider audience, where such could not be assumed.

Essential Tenets:

The main essential tenet mentioned in 2John is the full humanity of Jesus. This is probably because like 1John, 2John was intended to combat Gnosticism:

[7]Because many deceivers [have] entered into the world, the ones not confessing Jesus Christ [as] coming in [the] flesh; this is the Deceiver and the Antichrist (2John 1:7).

2John refers to Jesus as "Christ" four times (1:3,7,8,9) and as the Son of the Father twice (1:3,7). It also asserts the equality of the Son with the Father:

[9]Every one transgressing and not abiding in the teaching [or, doctrine] of Christ does not have God. The one abiding in the teaching [or, doctrine] of Christ, this one has both the Father and the Son (2John 1:9).

The renewal by the Spirit is implied in the preceding verse, as it is in the following verse:

[4]I greatly rejoiced that I have found [some] of your children walking about [fig., conducting themselves] in truth, just as we received a commandment from the Father (2John 1:4).

Translator's Perspective on the Canon of the NT

3John was primarily written to encourage Gaius to support true teachers and to rebuke a false one. It assumes Gaius knows the difference between the two. It Thus, does not teach doctrine, but it does imply the new birth in the following verses:

³For I rejoiced greatly when [some] of [the] brothers [and sisters] came and testified of the truth in you, just as you are walking about [fig., conducting yourself] in truth (3John 1:3).

⁹Every one transgressing and not abiding in the teaching [or, doctrine] of Christ does not have God. The one abiding in the teaching [or, doctrine] of Christ, this one has both the Father and the Son (3John 1:9).

Appeal and Mark of Inspiration:

Given their short nature, there is not much widespread appeal to these books. That is the primary reason for them being among the *antilegomena*. But they do give us a look into the personal nature of early Church correspondences and some of the issues they dealt with. And the encouragements to love one another, to keep Christ's commandments, to walk in the truth, while testing teachers to be sure they are teaching the truth, are good injunctions for us today. Thus, even with the lack of material, these epistles bear be the mark of inspiration.

Conclusion on 2, 3John:

These are short books that do not have much to offer, but what they do provide is useful. And there is every reason to believe they were written by an apostle or at least a direct association of an apostle in the first century. And what little doctrine they assert is sound. For these reasons it was correct, despite some objections, for the early Church to have eventually accepted these little books into the canon of the NT.

The Revelation of Jesus Christ

Before beginning our discussion on the final Johannine writing, I need to express a pet peeve of mine. The title of this book is not "Revelations" (plural) as many refer to this book. It is "The Revelation" (singular), or more fully, "The Revelation of Jesus Christ" as seen in the first four words of the book in just about any English translation. This book is a singular continuous revelation or disclosure of progressive or concurrent events from Jesus to John, not a bunch of unrelated revelations/ disclosures as the plural would have it.

But there are other names for this book, "Revelation to John, also called Book of Revelation or Apocalypse of John" (Encyclopedia Britannica; "Revelation to John"). Note that "apocalypse" comes from the Greek word for "revelation" (*apokalupis*).

That said, this book was also among the *antilegomena*. It was in fact one of the last books of the NT to be fully accepted as canonical. One of the reasons for it being "spoken against" was uncertainty about its author.

Author:

The name "John" appears four times in this book:

¹[The] revelation of [or, disclosure from] Jesus Christ, which God gave to Him to show to His bondservants what [things are] necessary to occur with quickness. And He made [it] known, having sent through His angel [or, messenger] to His bondservant **John**, ²who testified to the word of God and to the testimony of Jesus Christ, as many [things] as he also saw (Rev 1:1f).

⁴**John**, To the seven assemblies [or, churches], the [ones] in Asia: Grace to you* and peace from God, the One being and the One [who] was and the One [who is] coming, and from the seven spirits which [are] [fig., the seven-fold Spirit who is] before His throne, ⁵and from Jesus Christ, the faithful witness, the firstborn of [fig., the first to be raised from] the dead and the ruler of the kings of the earth (Rev 1:4f).

⁹I, **John**, the [one being] your* brother and partner in the affliction and kingdom and patient endurance in Jesus Christ, came to be in the island, the one being called Patmos, because of the word of God and because of the testimony of Jesus Christ (Rev 1:9).

⁸And I, **John**, [am] the one hearing and seeing these [things]. And when I heard and saw, I fell down to prostrate myself in worship [or, reverence] before the feet of the angel, the one showing these [things] to me. ⁹And he says to me, "See [that you do] not! I am a fellow-bondservant of you and of your brothers the prophets and of the ones keeping the words of this scroll. Prostrate yourself in worship before God!" (Rev 22:8).

The traditional view is that John the apostle wrote this book while exiled to Patmos for preaching the Gospel during a time of Roman persecution of Christians. This is based on Revelation 1:9, which was just quoted.

Translator's Perspective on the Canon of the NT

The fact of his banishment to Patmos is confirmed by the unanimous testimony of antiquity. It is perpetuated in the traditions of the island, which has no other significance. "John—that is the thought of Patmos; the island belongs to him; it is his sanctuary. Its stones preach of him, and in every heart, he lives" (Schaff, 6123-6126).

But is this the apostle John, the elder John, or some other person named John? Or is this an attempt to forge this book under the name of an apostle? These and even more complex theories have been proposed:

Revelation to John appears to be a collection of separate units composed by unknown authors who lived during the last quarter of the 1st century, though it purports to have been written by an individual named John—who calls himself "the servant" of Jesus—at Patmos, in the Aegean Sea. The text includes no indication that John of Patmos and John the Apostle are the same person (Encyclopedia Britannica; "Revelation to John").

Despite the claim here that there is "no indication that John of Patmos and John the Apostle are the same person" there is some such indication:

... in his inspired character, position of authority in the Asian churches, and selection as the medium of these revelations, can hardly be thought of as other than the well-known John of the Gospels and of consentient church tradition (ISBE; "Revelation of John").

One of the reasons for debates about the author is:

Traditionally it has been claimed that he is the John, son of Zebedee, known to us from the gospel stories, but this is most unlikely. It has also been claimed that he is the "John" of the fourth gospel, but the difference in language and style alone makes this identification quite impossible (Early Christian; "The Book of Revelation").

This quote reflects this liberal websites' belief that John the apostle did not write the Gospel of John. That issue was addressed in the preceding chapter. But here, the important point is the claim that the

Gospel and the Revelation could not be written by the same person due to the greatly different writing style and language used.

There is no doubt the writing style is different between this book and the Gospel. As stated, the Gospel contains the simplest Greek in the NT, while the Revelation uses considerably more stylistic Greek. It is for this reason that some propose John the elder as the author, with him also being the author of 2,3John, as all three books contain more stylistic Greek that the Gospel and 1John. Thus, a possible conservative theory is that the Gospel of John and 1John were written by the apostle John, while 2 and 3John and The Revelation were written by the elder John, but some conservatives hold to all five books being written by the apostle John.

Either of these theories would be in accordance with the standards for books to be included in the canon of the NT. But the theories of the liberals about schools, multiple authors with multiple redactions, or forgeries for all five of these books would call their place in the canon into question. That is why these issues are so important.

But in favor of one of the conservative views is that despite many differences, there are many parallels of thought between The Revelation and the other four Johannine books. Compare the following sets of passages:

---

[13]Jesus answered and said to her, "Every[one] drinking of this water will thirst again. [14]But whoever drinks of the water which I will give to him will by no means thirst into the age! [fig., will never thirst again!] But the water which I will give to him will become in him a well of water springing up to eternal life!" (John 4:13f).

[38]The one believing [or, trusting] in Me, just as the Scripture said, 'Out of his belly [or, innermost being] will flow rivers of living water." [no specific OT reference, but for general idea see Isaiah 55:1; 58:11; Ezek 47:1; Joel 3:18; Zech 13:1; 14:8] [39]But this He said concerning the Spirit, whom the ones believing in Him were about to be receiving, for [the] Holy Spirit was not yet [given], because Jesus was not yet glorified (John 7:38f).

[17]Because the Lamb, the [One] in [the] center of the throne, shepherds them. And He leads them to living fountains of waters [or, springs of waters of life], and God will wipe away every tear from their eyes" (Rev 7:17).

Translator's Perspective on the Canon of the NT

⁶And He said to me, "I have become the Alpha and the Omega, the Beginning and the End! [or, the Origin and the Fulfillment!] I will give to the one thirsting from the spring of the water of life without cost (Rev 21:6).

¹And he showed to me a pure river of water of life, bright as crystal, coming out [fig., flowing] from the throne of God and of the Lamb, [cp. Zech 14:8] ²in the middle of its open street. And the river from here and from there [fig., And on each side of the river] [was] a tree of life, producing twelve fruits, according to each month [fig., monthly] yielding its fruits. And the leaves of the tree [are] for [the] healing of the nations. [cp. Ezek 47:7,12] (Rev 22:1f).

¹⁷And the Spirit and the bride say, "Be coming!" And the one hearing, let him say, "Be coming!" And the one thirsting, let him come. The one desiring, let him take [the] water of life without cost (Rev 22:17).

---

¹⁵I do not ask that You take them out of the world, but that You keep them out of evil [or, from the evil [one]] (John 17:15).

¹⁰Because you kept the word of My patient endurance, I also will keep you from the hour of the trial, the one about to be coming upon the whole inhabited earth, to test the ones dwelling on the earth (Rev 3:10).

In [the] beginning was the Word [fig., the Expression of [Divine] Logic], and the Word was with [fig., in communion with] God, and the Word was God [fig., was as to His essence Deity].... ¹⁴And the Word [fig., the Expression of [Divine] Logic] became flesh and tabernacled among us, and we beheld His glory, glory as of an only-begotten [or, uniquely-begotten] from [the] Father, full of grace and truth (John 1:1,14).

¹¹And I saw heaven having been opened. And look! A white horse, and the One sitting on it, being called Faithful and True, and He judges and wages war in righteousness. ¹²Now His eyes [are] a flame of fire, and on His head [are] many royal bands [or, diadems] having names having been written [on them], and a name having been written [on them] which no one knows, except Himself, ¹³and having been clothed with a robe having been covered with [or, dipped in] blood, and His

name is called, The Word of God [fig., the Expression of Divine Logic] (Rev 19:12-13).

---

²⁹The next day he sees Jesus coming towards him and says, "Look! The Lamb of God, the One taking away the sin of the world! (John 1:29).

⁶And I saw in [the] middle of the throne and of the four living creatures, and in [the] middle of the elders, a Lamb having stood as if having been slain [i.e., Jesus (Rev 5:6a).

Note that it is only in the Gospel of John and in The Revelation in the NT that water and life are associated, that Jesus says He will "keep" someone "from" trial or evil, and that Jesus is called "the Word" and a "Lamb."

As for the many differences in language and writing style between The Revelation and the Gospel and epistles, they are considerably different types of literature, with apocalyptic literature like The Revelation having its own unique writing style.

> Symbolic language, however, is one of the chief characteristics of apocalyptic literature, of which this book is an outstanding example. Such literature enjoyed wide popularity in both Jewish and Christian circles from ca. 200 B.C. to A.D. 200 (Bishops; "The Book of Revelation).

> Because of intricate and unusual symbolic language, the Book of Revelation is hard for modern people to read. They are not used to this kind of literature. Not so for people in the ancient world who would have been more accustomed to the complex nature of apocalyptic literature (PBS; Understanding the Book of Revelation")

Thus, the type of literature of The Revelation involves a particular style of writings that would have been familiar to people at that time. And if John were to write such literature, he would need to change his normal way of writing to fit with that style.

By way of example, I am used to writing non-fiction, but if I were to write a fictional novel, then I would need to use a completely different writing style. To do so would mean I would need to familiarize myself with the writing style of novels, not being much of a novel reader

Translator's Perspective on the Canon of the NT

myself. However, John would have been familiar with apocalyptic literature. He would have Thus, known how to change from his normal writing style he used for his Gospel and three letters to the writing style of apocalyptic literature when writing The Revelation. Thus, differences of language and writing style is to be expected between these works, but there are enough similarities so as not to preclude the same author writing all five books. However, the following expresses a different conservative opinion:

> Indeed, vocabulary, grammar, and style make it doubtful that the book could have been put into its present form by the same person(s) responsible for the fourth gospel. Nevertheless, there are definite linguistic and theological affinities between the two books. The tone of the letters to the seven churches (Rev 1:4–3:22) is indicative of the great authority the author enjoyed over the Christian communities in Asia. It is possible, therefore, that he was a disciple of John the apostle, who is traditionally associated with that part of the world (Bishops; "The Book of Revelation).

Thus, again, it is possible John the apostle wrote the Gospel, while his disciple, John the elder, wrote The Revelation. Meanwhile, the testimony of the early Church supports Johannine authorship, though not without some dispute.

> The author of the book calls himself John (Rev 1:1, 4, 9; 22:8), who because of his Christian faith has been exiled to the rocky island of Patmos, a Roman penal colony. Although he never claims to be John the apostle, whose name is attached to the fourth gospel, he was so identified by several of the early church Fathers, including Justin, Irenaeus, Clement of Alexandria, Tertullian, Cyprian, and Hippolytus. This identification, however, was denied by other Fathers, including Denis of Alexandria, Eusebius of Caesarea, Cyril of Jerusalem, Gregory Nazianzen, and John Chrysostom (Bishops; "The Book of Revelation).

See the Introductory Page "Church Fathers" for the dates for these men. But here, examining this list, for the most part the earlier Church Fathers accepted the Johannine authorship, while later ones denied it.

Overall, the evidence favors either John the apostle or John the elder having written this book. But whichever of these two wrote The

Revelation, it would still fulfill the standard of authorship for a book to be included in the canon of the NT.

Date of Writing:

Dating The Revelation requires taking a look at its interpretation.

> Many scholars, however, agree that Revelation is not simply an abstract spiritual allegory divorced from historical events, nor merely a prophecy concerning the final upheaval at the end of the world, couched in obscure language. Rather, it deals with a contemporary crisis of faith, probably brought on by Roman persecutions. Christians are consequently exhorted to remain steadfast in their faith and to hold firmly to the hope that God will ultimately be victorious over his (and their) enemies. Because such a view presents current problems in an eschatological context, the message of Revelation also becomes relevant to future generations of Christians who, Christ forewarned, would likewise suffer persecution. The victory of God over Satan (in this case, the perseverance of Christians in the face of Roman persecution) typifies similar victories over evil in ages still to come and God's final victory at the end of time (Encyclopedia Britannica; "Revelation to John").

Mentioned in this quote are three possible interpretations of this book. The first is that it is a symbolic history of Roman persecution of Christians in the first century. This is known as the preterist viewpoint. The second is that it is an end-time prophecy, which will include persecutions of Christians. This is known as the eschatological or futurist viewpoint. The third is that it is both. The persecutions and upheavals of a current historical situation typify ones that will occur in the last days. This could be a called a double-fulfillment view.

The first viewpoint was the most common view throughout most of Church history, while the second is the most common in evangelical circles since the early 1900s. The third was seen in our discussion of some prophetic books in the Old Testament in Volume One in regards to the two re-gatherings of Jews to Israel, first in the 6th century BC then again starting in 1948.

Where this becomes important to our discussion of the date of this book is if one subscribes to the first or third views, then this book must either be dated to the time of the persecutions of Christians under Nero or under Domitian, since those are the only two Roman emperors in the first century who persecuted Christians.

Translator's Perspective on the Canon of the NT

Nero was emperor from 54–68 AD, while Domitian was emperor from 81–96 AD (Encyclopedia Britannica). In both cases, it was near the end of their reigns that the persecutions occurred. But which of these two time periods is most likely involves trying to interpret the various imagery in The Revelation as to which emperor best fits it, most especially the identification of "the number of the beast."

> [18]Here is the wisdom—the one having understanding, let him calculate the number of the beast, for it is the number of a person [or, of humanity]. And its number is six hundred sixty-six (Rev 13:18).

> The problem is that no clear identification can be made linking 666 with any particular ancient historical name. Attempts have been made to alter spellings and incorporate titles to try to make a multitude of names fit, but nothing conclusive has emerged....
> The repetition of six three times seems to indicate what might be called the "completeness of sinful incompleteness" found in the beast. The beast epitomizes imperfection, while appearing to achieve divine perfection. Three sixes parody the divine Trinity of three sevens (Gospel Coalition).

The point of the first paragraph is that in ancient times letters were used to indicate numbers. People would Thus, try to find a name of a person or historical power whose letters added up to 666, but none of the likely possibilities fit, unless they were creatively misspelled or combined with possible titles, such as spelling "Nero Caesar" as Neron Kaesar" or using "Lateinos" for the Roman (Latin) Empire. Adding to the difficulty is it is debated if the numbers should be associated with Hebrew or Greek letters, and the number associations are a bit confusing:

> The Hebrew Aleph [first letter of the Hebrew alphabet] counts 1, Beth 2, etc., Yodh 10; but Kaph (the eleventh letter) counts 20, Resh (the twentieth letter) 200, etc. The Greek letters, with the addition of an acute accent (as a', b'), have the same numerical value in their order down to Sigma, which counts 200; except that "' (st) is used for 6, and F' (an antiquated letter Koppa between p and r) for 90. The Hebrew alphabet ends with Tau = 400, the Greek with Omega = 800. To express thousands an accent is put beneath the letter, as, ,a, = 1,000; ,b, = 2,000; ,i, = 10,000 (Schaff; 11646-11650).

Given this uncertainty, it is difficult to decide between these two time periods. It is also possible the number does not refer to a name but is purely symbolic:

> The number 666 (three sixes) must, in itself, be a significant number, if we keep in view the symbolism of numbers which runs through the whole Apocalypse. It is remarkable that the numerical value of the name Jesus is 888 (three eights), and exceeds the trinity of the sacred number (777) as much as the number of the beast falls below it (Schaff; 11657-11660).

Favoring the earlier date is it would further explain how the apostle John could write both The Revelation and the Gospel According to John. "This helps us at the same time more easily to explain the difference between the fiery energy of the Apocalypse and the calm repose of the fourth Gospel, which was composed in extreme old age" (Schaff; 11536-11537).

In other words, if The Revelation was written in the 60s and the Gospel in the 90s AD, those interviewing 30 years would help to explain why John's writing style has changed. He had matured and calmed down in his old age and thus so did his writing style.

Now if one takes the purely futuristic viewpoint, then the date could be anytime in the second half of the first century. However:

> Almost all New Testament scholars now take the view that Revelation was written during the reign of Domitian, sometime around 95-96 CE. He is the "beast from the sea" beyond doubt (PBS; Understanding the Book of Revelation").

The reason for this is "Nero's persecution was local and short-lived" (Religion Facts), while those under Domitian were more wide-spread and long-lasting.

> "In 93 Domitian executed some Christians for refusing to offer sacrifices before his image; according to tradition these included his nephew Flavius Clemens." [Will Durant, *Caesar and Christ*, p. 292]. In his last few years, he became exceedingly paranoid. "After Saturninus' revolt, indictments and convictions rapidly increased; aristocrats were exiled or killed, suspected men were tortured, even by having 'fire inserted into their private parts.'" [Will Durant, *Caesar and Christ*, p. 292].

Translator's Perspective on the Canon of the NT

"Domitian has also been accused of mass executions of Christians, which is true, but it wasn't necessarily a purge targeted at that single group. Domitian ruled in an almost tyrannical reign of terror in which many perished, not just Christians" (UNRV History, "Christian Persecution")

Did Domitian persecute Christians? The evidence is "yes," though he did not specifically target this one group. Rather, he made life difficult for those he termed as "atheists," that is those who refused to worship the Roman gods. In his later years he made himself out to be a god and persecuted just about anyone of whom he had the least suspicion (La Vista).

Domitian's demands to be worshipped and the persecutions under him Thus, better fit the situation portrayed in The Revelation than the reign of Nero.

By portraying the Emperor and his provincial authorities as "beasts" and henchmen of the dragon, Satan, the author was calling on Christians to refuse to take part in the imperial cult, even at the risk of martyrdom (PBS; "Understanding the Book of Revelation").

What is important for our study is there are some conservatives who interpret The Revelation using the historical approach, some who use a purely futuristic approach, and some, like this writer, who use the double-fulfillment approach, while liberals generally follow the historical approach. But both conservatives and liberals agree this book should be dated to the reign of Domitian and thus in the first century, and that is all that matters for this book to be considered for inclusion in the canon.

The reason even liberals limit the date to first century persecutions is the next persecuting emperor was Trajan, and persecutions under him did not occur until 112-117 AD. But at that time, "Christianity is outlawed but Christians are not sought out." It was not until Marcus Aurelius in 161-180 that persecutions again became more widespread (Religion Facts; "Persecution in the Early Church"). The late second century is way too late for this book, as even liberals will concede and the previous quotes from Church Fathers attest.

The following quotes are taken from a conservative and a liberal source, respectively.

Date of Writing: The Book of Revelation was likely written between A.D. 90 and 95 (Got?Questions.org; "Book of Revelation").

The Book of Revelation was written sometime around 96 CE in Asia Minor (PBS; "Understanding the Book of Revelation").

But it must be noted:
This mysterious book—whether written between 68 and 69, or under Domitian in 95—was undoubtedly intended for the church of that age as well as for future ages, and must have been sufficiently adapted to the actual condition and surroundings of its first readers to give them substantial aid and comfort in their fiery trials. Owing to the nearness of events alluded to, they must have understood it even better, for practical purposes, than readers of later generations (Schaff, 5564-5568).

The Old Testament prophets were not clearly understood until the fulfilment cast its light upon them, and yet they served a most useful purpose as books of warning, comfort, and hope for the coming Messiah. The Revelation will be fully revealed when the new heavens and the new earth appear— not before (Schaff; 11443-11445).

Doctrine of God:

The Revelation has much to say about God:

[8]"I am the Alpha and the Omega [i.e., the first and last letters of the Greek alphabet]," says [the] Lord God, "The One being and the One [who] was and the One [who is] coming—the Almighty!" (Rev 1:8).

[8]And the four living creatures, each one having six wings apiece covered with eyes around and within, and they do not have rest day and night, saying:

"Holy, holy, holy [is] [the] Lord God, the Almighty, the One [who] was and the One being and the One [who is] coming!"

[9]And whenever the living creatures ascribe glory and honor and thanksgiving to the One sitting on the throne, the One living into the ages of the ages [fig., forever and ever], [10]the twenty-four elders will fall down before the One sitting on the throne and will prostrate

Translator's Perspective on the Canon of the NT

themselves in worship before the One living into the ages of the ages [fig., forever and ever], and they will cast their victor's wreaths before the throne, saying:

> [11]"You are worthy, our Lord and God, the Holy [One], to receive the glory and the honor and the power, because <u>You</u> created all [things], and because of Your will they were [fig., existed] and were created!" (Rev 4:9-11).

[11]And all the angels had stood around the throne, and the elders and the four living creatures, and they fell down on their face[s] before the throne and prostrated themselves in worship before God, [12]saying:

> "Amen! The blessing and the glory and the wisdom and the thanksgiving and the honor and the power and the strength [belong] to our God into the ages of the ages! [fig., forever and ever!] So be it!" (Rev 7:11f).

[16]And the twenty-four elders, the ones sitting on their thrones before the throne of God, fell on their faces and prostrated themselves in worship before God, [17]saying:

> "We give thanks to You, O Lord God, the Almighty, the One being and the One [who] was, because You have taken Your great power and reigned [or, began to reign] as King! [18]And the nations were enraged, and Your wrath came, and the time of the dead to be judged [came], and [the time] to give the reward to Your bondservants the prophets and to the holy ones and the ones fearing Your name, to the small and to the great, and to destroy the ones utterly destroying the earth."

[19]And the temple of God was opened in heaven, and the ark of the covenant of the Lord was seen in His temple, and [there] occurred lightning flashes and voices and peals of thunder and great hail (Rev 11:16-19).

[7]And I heard [an angel] of the altar saying, "Yes, Lord God, the Almighty, true and righteous [are] Your judgments!" (Rev 16:7).

[1]After these [things] I heard [something] like a loud voice of a large crowd in heaven, saying:

"Praise the Lord! [Gr., *Allelouia*] The salvation and the power and the glory [are] of our God! ²Because His judgments [are] true and righteous; because He judged the great prostitute who was utterly destroying the earth with her fornication, and He avenged the blood of His bondservants [shed] by her hand" (Rev 19:1f).

¹⁰And I fell before his [an angel's] feet to prostrate myself in worship [or, reverence] before him, and he says to me, "See [that you do] not! [cp. Dan 8:17,18] I am your fellow bondservant and of your brothers [and sisters], the ones having the testimony of Jesus. Prostrate yourself in worship before God! For the testimony of Jesus is the spirit of prophecy" (Rev 19:10).

Thus, God in The Revelation is Eternal, Almighty, the Creator, Judge, Holy, King, Righteous, and the only One worthy of worship. All of this agrees with the OT conception of God.

Essential Tenets:

The Revelation also is filled with assertions of the early essential tenets of the Church.

¹[The] revelation of [or, disclosure from] Jesus Christ, which God gave to Him to show to His bondservants what [things are] necessary to occur with quickness. And He made [it] known, having sent through His angel [or, messenger] to His bondservant John, ²who testified to the word of God and to the testimony of Jesus Christ, as many [things] as he also saw (Rev 1:1f).

⁵and from Jesus Christ, the faithful witness, the firstborn of [fig., the first to be raised from] the dead and the ruler of the kings of the earth. To the One loving us and having bathed us from our sins in His blood. ⁶And He made us a kingdom, priests to His God and Father—to Him [be] the glory and the power into the ages of the ages! [fig., forever and ever!] So be it!

⁷*"Look! He is coming with the clouds,"* [Dan 7:13] and *"every eye will see Him, even [the ones] who pierced Him, and all the tribes of the earth will beat their breasts [fig., mourn] because of Him."* [Zech 12:10, Heb.] (Rev 1:5-7).

⁹I, John, the [one being] your* brother and partner in the affliction and kingdom and patient endurance in Jesus Christ, came to be in the

Translator's Perspective on the Canon of the NT

island, the one being called Patmos, because of the word of God and because of the testimony of Jesus Christ (Rev 1:9).

¹⁷And when I saw Him, I fell at His feet as dead. And He placed His right [hand] on me, saying, "Stop being afraid! I am the First and the Last, ¹⁸and the living One. And I became dead. And look! I am living into the ages of the ages [fig., forever and ever]. So be it! [or, Amen!] And I have the keys of death and of the realm of the dead [Gr., *hades*] (Rev 1:17f).

⁸"And to the angel of the assembly in Smyrna write: 'These [things] says the First and the Last, who became dead and lived [or, came to life] (Rev 2:9).

¹⁸"And to the angel of the assembly in Thyatira write: 'These [things] says the Son of God, the One having His eyes like a flame of fire and His feet like fine brass [or, burnished bronze] (Rev 2:19).

⁶And I saw in [the] middle of the throne and of the four living creatures, and in [the] middle of the elders, a Lamb having stood as if having been slain (Rev 4:6a).

¹⁰And they cry out with a loud voice, saying, "The salvation [belongs] to our God, the One sitting on the throne, and to the Lamb!" (Rev 7:10).

¹⁴And I said to him, "My Lord, you know." And he said to me, "These are the ones coming out of the great tribulation, and they washed their long robes and made [them] white in the blood of the Lamb (Rev 7:14).

¹⁴These will wage war with the Lamb, and the Lamb will conquer them, because He is Lord of lords and King of kings, and the [ones] with him [are] called and chosen and faithful" (Rev 17:14).

¹⁶And He has on the robe and on His thigh a name having been written:

KING OF KINGS
AND LORD OF LORDS
(Rev 19:16).

[20]The One testifying to these things says, "Yes, I am coming quickly!" So be it! Yes, be coming, Lord Jesus! (Rev 21:20).

[21]The grace of the Lord Jesus Christ [be] with all the holy ones. So be it! (Rev 21:21).

Thus, in this book, Jesus is the Christ, the Son of God, Lord, King, and eternal. He died for our sins, but He is now alive, and He is coming again. The Revelation also proclaims Jesus is worthy of worship:

[11]And I looked, and I heard as [it were the] voice of many angels around the throne and of the living creatures and of the elders; and the number of them was ten thousand [times] ten thousand, and thousands of thousands, [12]saying with a loud voice:

"Worthy is the Lamb, the One having been slain, to receive the power and the wealth and wisdom and strength and honor and glory and blessing!"

[13]And every creature which is in heaven and in the earth and under the earth and on the sea, and the [things] in them, I heard all saying:

"To the One sitting on the throne and to the Lamb, [be] the blessing and the honor and the glory and the might [or, dominion] into the ages of the ages! [fig., forever and ever!] So be it!"

[14]And the four living creatures saying the "So be it" and the elders fell down and prostrated themselves in worship (Rev 5:11-14).

Notice that God is said to be sitting on the throne here, but later it is said, "Because the Lamb, the [One] in [the] center of the throne, shepherds them" (Rev 7:17). Thus, Jesus is equal with the Father. The Spirit is also associated with the throne:

[5]And from the throne proceed lightning flashes and voices and peals of thunder. And seven lamps of fire [were] burning before His throne, which are seven spirits [fig., which is [the] seven-fold Spirit] of God (Rev 4:5).

God the Father, Jesus Christ, and the Holy Spirit are associated together:

Translator's Perspective on the Canon of the NT

⁴John, To the seven assemblies [or, churches], the [ones] in Asia: Grace to you* and peace from God, the One being and the One [who] was and the One [who is] coming, and from the seven spirits which [are] [fig., the seven-fold Spirit who is] before His throne, ⁵and from Jesus Christ, the faithful witness, the firstborn of [fig., the first to be raised from] the dead and the ruler of the kings of the earth (Rev 1:4f).

⁷'The one having an ear, let him hear [or, pay attention to] what the Spirit says to the assemblies. To the one overcoming, I will give to him to eat from the tree of the life which is in the Paradise of My God' (Rev 1:7).

¹²Here is [the] patient endurance of the holy ones, the ones keeping the commandments of God and the faith of Jesus. ¹³And I heard a voice out of heaven saying, "Write: 'Fortunate [or, Blessed] [are] the dead, the ones dying in [the] Lord from now [on]!'" "Yes," says the Spirit, "so that they shall rest from their labors, but their works follow with them" (Rev 14:12f).

¹⁷And the Spirit and the bride say, "Be coming!" And the one hearing, let him say, "Be coming!" And the one thirsting, let him come. The one desiring, let him take [the] water of life without cost (Rev 22:17).

The renewal of the Spirit is also implied in the preceding verse. The general resurrection is described in the following passage:

¹¹And I saw a great white throne and the One sitting on it, from whose face the earth and heaven fled away, and a place was not found for them. ¹²And I saw the dead, the great and the small, having stood before the throne, and scrolls were opened, and another scroll was opened, which is [the Scroll] of Life. [cp. Dan 7:9,10] And the dead were judged by the [things] having been written in the scrolls, according to their works. ¹³And the sea gave up the dead, the [ones] in it, and death and the realm of the dead [Gr. *hades*] gave up the dead, the [ones] in them. And they were judged, each one according to their works (Rev 20:11-13).

All of these assertions are in line with the early essential tenets of the Church.

Appeal:
To Christians who are being persecuted, this book is a great comfort. It boldly declares the persecutors will be judged and the righteous vindicated, and the faith of Christians will be rewarded. It Thus, provides great encouragement for Christians to hold to their faith and to confess Christ in the face of persecution.

For those who hold to a futuristic or double-fulfillment, this book prepares Christians for what lies ahead. But ultimately, The Revelation provides encouragement for all peoples in proclaiming that in the end good will triumph over evil.

The praises of God and of the Lamb in this book are spiritually uplifting, leading us to also praise the Father and Son. This book Thus, bears the mark of inspiration.

> The theme of the Apocalypse is: "I come quickly," and the proper attitude of the church toward it is the holy longing of a bride for her spouse, as expressed in the response (Rev. 22: 20): "Amen: come, Lord Jesus." It gives us the assurance that Christ is coming in every great event, and rules and overrules all things for the ultimate triumph of his kingdom; that the state of the church on earth is one of continual conflict with hostile powers, but that she is continually gaining victories and will at last completely and finally triumph over all her foes and enjoy unspeakable bliss in communion with her Lord (Schaff; 11482-11486).

Conclusion on the Revelation:
The Revelation most certainly was written in the first century by either an apostle or a direct associate of an apostle. It presents an orthodox viewpoint of God and of many early essential tenets of the Church. It has widespread appeal for those suffering persecution and for all people looking for relief from suffering.

The fact that there were some disputes initially about this book shows the early Christians did not accept books into the canon without first critically analyzing them. The Revelation was the least disputed of the *antilegomena*, and these minor disputes were eventually resolved, and thus The Revelation was rightly included in the canon of the NT.

Conclusion on the Writings of John

The theology and phraseology running through these five books argues strongly for one author for all five books, or at the very least, one

Translator's Perspective on the Canon of the NT

teacher and his student as the authors. Either way, these books present Jesus in all of His glory as the only-begotten from the Father, full of grace and truth (John 1:14).

> His [John's] theology marks the culminating height of divine knowledge in the apostolic age. It is impossible to soar higher than the eagle, which is his proper symbol. His views are so much identified with the words of his Lord, to whom he stood more closely related than any other disciple, that it is difficult to separate them; but the prologue to his Gospel contains his leading ideas, and his first Epistle the practical application. The theology of the Apocalypse is also essentially the same, and this goes far to confirm the identity of authorship (Schaff; 7823-7827).

Chapter Six
The Pauline Epistles
Part One

We now come to the thirteen epistles traditionally ascribed to the apostle Paul. The traditional order of these epistles is by their perceived importance. But we will study them in four groups in the order in which they were most likely written.

Early Epistles (52-53 AD):
1Thessalonians
2Thessalonians

Major Epistles (55-58 AD):
Galatians
1Corinthians
2Corinthians
Romans

Prison Epistles (61-63):
Ephesians
Philippians
Colossians
Philemon

Pastoral Epistles (64 AD):
1Timothy
Titus
2Timothy

Background to the Pauline Epistles

It would be good to first cover some background material before getting to the epistles themselves. Paul is another person who went by two names. Along with Paul (his Greek name), he was also known as Saul (his Hebrew name; Acts 13:9). He was not one of the original twelve apostles. But he is accepted as an apostle due to his dramatic conversion from being a persecutor of the Christian faith to proclaiming it by Jesus having appeared to him personally and having commissioned him to preach the Gospel to the Gentiles (Acts 8:1-3.; 9:1-22; 26:12-17;

Translator's Perspective on the Canon of the NT

1Cor 9:1f). He also performed miracles (Acts 14:1-10, 16:16-18; 19:11f; 28:3-6; Rom 14:18f). Such are the signs of an apostle (2Cor 12:12; Heb 2:4). He was also commissioned directly by the Holy Spirit (Acts 13:1-4). His authority and commission were confirmed by the original apostles (Acts 9:26-30; 15:22; Gal 2:9). For all of these reasons, his authority was never questioned in the early Church.

His thirteen epistles are all among the *homologoumena*, meaning there was never any doubt in the early Church that all 13 were written by Paul and that they were authoritative. This is seen in all 13 being listed in early canon lists, as was discussed in Chapter One. It is also confirmed by all 13 having circulated as a unit very early in Church history. There are 20 Greek manuscripts from the second through fourth centuries which contain all 13 of these epistles. Seven of these contain just these 13 epistles, ten also contain the Four Gospels, and two also contain Acts (Deeper Study).

However, despite this evidence for universal acceptance of the Pauline authorship of all 13 of these epistles in the early Church, there are many today who deny that Paul wrote at least some of these epistles. But first, an important question.

Did Paul the Apostle Really Exist?

Out of curiosity, I Googled the above question and found many webpages that denied Paul the apostle ever even existed. But none of these pages were found on reputable websites. Instead, even liberal reputable websites acknowledge Paul's existence, even if they do not fully accept the NT assertions about him and what he wrote.

For instance, the website for *Encyclopedia Britannica* has a lengthy, eleven-page article on "Saint Paul, the Apostle." Not once in the article does it ever question Paul's existence, even though it does deny that Paul wrote six of the 13 letters ascribed to him.

In the article for "First Epistle to Timothy" on the website for the *New World Encyclopedia*, while denying Paul wrote this epistle, the article states, "Whoever the real author of the letter is, Paul and Timothy were historical people in the relationship of mentor and student."

Similarly, an article on PBS' website titled "The Real Paul" denies Paul wrote the same six epistles as the *Encyclopedia Britannica* and denies that Acts is fully reliable in its portrayal of Paul. It even asserts there were three or four different "Pauls" meaning three or four different men wrote the Pauline epistles, and these men are different from the Paul of Acts. But amidst all of these radical assertions, not once does it deny there ever was a historical Paul. It just asserts that we cannot fully trust the NT picture of him. And even this very liberal article admits:

> Some recent commentators do not mark differences between the Paul of the seven undisputed letters, the Paul of Ephesians and Colossians, the Paul of the Pastoral Epistles, and the Paul of Acts, differences explained with characteristic clarity and elegance by Garry Wills in his *What Paul Meant* (Viking, 2006).

In other words, radical liberal assertions are now being backed off from by repeatable liberal scholars.

However, the webpages that make the radical claim that Paul never existed and even deny the existence of the twelve original apostles and of Jesus Himself are all personal websites or forums, where many other ludicrous claims are made as well, and/ or, they are filled with hate and vitriolic bashing of Christians.

For instance, a thread on Yahoo! Answers is titled "Did Jesus, Paul and St. Peter really exist?" The following is one of the responses:

> Historically, most of the New Testament of the Bible was written about 300 years after the events described. (Most sensible Christians know it is written by holy men - and unlike the Koran does not purport to be written - or 'revealed' by God. Good luck with not being plagued by fanatics btw).
>
> Realistically, if you wanted to find evidence of what happened in the 17th century you would struggle, even with the advances in documentation we have now. Trying to establish whether a person in the first century was invented or not would be improbable if not impossible.

A true historian would probably shudder at the comments in the second paragraph. The forum responder is basically saying we cannot know anything about anything before 400 years ago. And this is how radical you have to be in order to deny the existence of Jesus, Peter, and Paul, as there is as much evidence for their existence as there is for just about any other notable figure from antiquity.

I'm including the first paragraph as I actually heard the first idea from the husband of a close friend a while ago, "The New Testament was not written until 325 AD." The claim was so absurd that I initially stumbled on how to respond. But once I gathered myself, I tried to explain to him what the reader of this book should know by this point. There are dozens of manuscripts of various NT books that date from the

Translator's Perspective on the Canon of the NT

second and third centuries, with many of these containing all four Gospels, Acts, and/ or all 13 Pauline epistles. Moreover, there are a multitude of references to and quotations from the NT books in the writings of the Church Fathers from the second and third centuries. As such, there is no doubt the NT was written long before the fourth century.

What my friend's husband and the forum responder might be thinking of is the earliest *complete* manuscripts of the NT (*Codex Sinaiticus* and *Codex Vaticanus*) date from the fourth century (Bible Research), but that is a far cry from saying the NT books were not written until that time. The exact date of 325 is when the Council of Nicaea was held, but its primary issue was refuting the teachings of Arius, who denied the deity of Christ. It also issued 20 canons that dealt with various Church issues. But it most certainly was not involved in writing the NT or even deciding what books should be in the NT (Christian History for Everyman; "The Council of Nicea").

As for this apparent Muslim's assertion that the Bible does not claim to have been revealed by God, I address that in the first Scripture Study in my *Scripture Workbook*, where I cite hundreds of Scripture verses that show otherwise. I will expand on that section in one of my proposed books (see Appendix Three). Such claims simply expose the person as someone who has never actually studied the relevant issues. But in regards to the main issue at hand:

> As far as I know, no reputable scholar denies the reality of the person Paul. He is credited by historians for being the chief architect of the spread of Christianity to the Greeks in the Roman Empire. Even hard line skeptics such as Robert Price and Bart Ehrman agree that Paul was a real person and that he wrote at least some of the books of the New Testament....
>
> If you have come across chat on the internet from people saying there is no real evidence that Paul ever existed, you can assume that these people have absolutely no idea what they are talking about (Evidence for Christianity; "Is there historical evidence that the apostle Paul was a real person?").

Relationship of Acts and the Paulines

One last point worth investigating before discussing each epistle is that of the relationship of the Pauline epistles to the Book of Acts. Each epistle can easily be placed in their historical context within Acts, except for the Pastorals, as will be discussed in the next chapter. And within the Pauline epistles are reiterations of events of Paul's life reported in Acts.

> The Acts gives us the external history of the apostolic church; the Epistles present the internal life of the same. Both mutually supplement and confirm each other by a series of coincidences in all essential points. These coincidences are all the more conclusive as they are undesigned and accompanied by slight discrepancies in minor details (Schaff; 10160-10163).

As discussed previously, "slight discrepancies in minor details" is exactly what to expect when two eyewitnesses report independently about the same event. The points of parallel are the following:

Conversion: Acts 9:1ff; 22:1ff; 26:1ff / Gal 1:15-17; 1Cor 15:8; 1Tim 1:13-16.
Escape in a basket. Acts 9:23– 25/ 2Cor 11: 32f.
Visits to Jerusalem: Acts 9: 26f; 15: 2/ Gal 1:18; 2:1.
Being stoned: Acts 14:19f/ 1Cor 11:29.
Left at Athens alone: Acts 17:16/ 1Thes 3:1,7.
Working with his hands: Acts 18:3; 20: 34/ 1Thes. 2:9; 1Cor. 4:11f.
Visits to Corinth: Acts 18:1; 20:2/ 1Cor. 2:1; 4: 19; 16: 5.
Apollos at Corinth: Acts 18: 27f/ 1Cor. 1:12; 3:6.
Becoming a Jew to the Jews: Acts 16:3; 18:18; 21:23-26/ 1Cor 9:20.
Baptizes Crispus and Gaius: Acts 18: 8/ 1Cor. 1:14-17.
Collection for the poor brethren: Acts 28:23/ 1Cor 16:1.
Last journey to Jerusalem: Acts 20:6; 24:17/ Rom 15:25f.
Desire to visit Rome: Acts 19:21/ Rom 1:13; 15:23.
In bonds. Acts 28:16-20/ Eph 6:19f.

With that background, we will now investigate each group of the Pauline epistles.

The Early Epistles

The two epistles to the Thessalonians are thought to be the earliest books of the NT to be written. The initial preaching of the Gospel to the Thessalonians by Paul is recorded in Acts 17:1-15:

[1]Now having traveled through Amphipolis and Apollonia, they came to Thessalonica, where the synagogue of the Jews was. [2]Then according to the custom with Paul, he went in to them, and for three

Translator's Perspective on the Canon of the NT

Sabbaths he reasoned with them from the Scriptures, ³opening up and placing before [them] [fig., explaining and demonstrating] that it was necessary [for] the Christ to suffer and to rise again from [the] dead, and [saying], "This [One] is the Christ—Jesus, whom I am proclaiming to you*." ⁴And some of them believed and were joined with Paul and Silas, both a large number of the God-worshiping Greeks and not a few [fig., a large number] of the first [fig., prominent] women (Acts 17:1-4).

Paul Thus, had a fruitful ministry in Thessalonica initially, but then "the Jews, the ones refusing to believe" (Acts 17:5) ran him out of town (Acts 17:10,14f). He later wrote these epistles to them.

Thessalonica, a large and wealthy commercial city of Macedonia, the capital of "Macedonia secunda," the seat of a Roman proconsul and quaestor, and inhabited by many Jews, was visited by Paul on his second missionary tour, A.D. 52 or 53, and in a few weeks he succeeded, amid much persecution, in founding a flourishing church composed chiefly of Gentiles (Schaff; 10504-10506).

Author:

Paul identifies himself as the author in the salutations of both of these epistles:

¹Paul and Silvanus and Timothy, To the assembly [or, church] of [the] Thessalonians in God [the] Father and [the] Lord Jesus Christ: Grace to you* and peace from God our Father and [the] Lord Jesus Christ! (1Th 1:1).

¹Paul and Silvanus and Timothy, To the assembly [or, church] of [the] Thessalonians in God our Father and [the] Lord Jesus Christ: ²Grace to you* and peace from God our Father and [the] Lord Jesus Christ! (2Th).

Notice how similar these two salutations are. Silvanus is probably the same as Silas. He and Timothy accompanied Paul to Thessalonica and remained there after Paul was chased out, but they joined up with him later (Acts 17:14f; 18:5). It was Thus, appropriate for Paul to include them in the salutation, but it is doubtful they actually contributed to the contents of these short letters.

Paul then mentions himself once more in each of these letters:

¹⁸For this reason, we wanted to come to you* (indeed I, Paul), both once and twice [fig., time and again], and [yet] Satan hindered us (1Th 2:17).

¹⁷The greeting by my hand, Paul, which is a sign in every letter; in this way I write (2Th 3:17).

The second verse is interesting. While the terminology often used is that Paul "wrote" this and other letters, more correctly Paul generally dictated his letters to a scribe, but then Paul penned just his signature at the end himself. But Paul is still the author, even if he did not do the actual writing. This is also possibly the case for Bible books by other authors. Thus, this book generally uses the term "author" rather than "writer" when referring to who is ultimately responsible for the contents of Bible books.

> The handwriting was not Paul's since he wrote just the final greeting and prayer (2 Thessalonians 3:17). It seems that Paul dictated the letter, maybe to Timothy or Silas (Easy English Bible; "The Lord has not come yet").

That Paul is the author of both of these letters can also be seen in how he refers to the Thessalonians:

²We give thanks to God always concerning you* all, making mention of you* in our prayers, ³constantly remembering your* work of faith and labor of love and patient endurance in the hope [or, confident expectation] of our Lord Jesus Christ, in [the] presence of our God and Father, ⁴knowing brothers [and sisters], having been loved by God, your* election [or, [God's] choosing of you*] (1Th 1:2-4).

¹¹Now [may] our God and Father Himself and our Lord Jesus Christ direct our way to you*. ¹²And [may] the Lord cause you* to increase and to abound in love to one another and to all [people], even as we also [do] for you*, ¹³in order to establish your* hearts [as being] blameless in holiness before our God and Father at the Arrival of our Lord Jesus Christ with all His holy ones [or, saints] (1Th 3:11-13).

³We ought to be giving thanks to God always for you*, brothers [and sisters], just as it is fitting, because your* faith grows abundantly, and the love of each one of you* all for one another increases, ⁴with the result that we ourselves are boasting of you* in the assemblies [or,

Translator's Perspective on the Canon of the NT

churches] of God about your* perseverance and faith in all your* persecutions and afflictions which you* endure (2Th 1:3-4).

Notice that in the first epistle Paul prays that the Thessalonians' love would increase, and in the second epistles he thanks God that it has. Additional parallels between these two epistles will be seen when we present doctrines and essential tenets from these epistles.

The similarity of writing style also confirms that the same person is the author of both of these epistles.

> The literary dependence of II Thessalonians on I Thessalonians cannot be gainsaid. The writer of the former must have written the latter, and that too not very long thereafter. 2 Thessalonians 2:15 and 3:6 are to be explained by 1 Thessalonians 4:1-8 and 11. The style of the two letters is admittedly identical; the prayers (I, iii 11, v, 23; II, ii, 16, iii, 16), greetings (I, i, 1; II, i, 1, 2) thanks (I, i, 2; II, i, 3), and transitions (I, iv, 1; II, iii, 1) are remarkably alike in form. Two-thirds of II Thess. is like to I Thess. in vocabulary and style. Moreover, the structure of the Epistle, its subject-matter, and its affectionate outbursts of prayer for the recipients and of exhortation are all decidedly Pauline characteristics (New Advent; "Epistles to the Thessalonians").

The Pauline authorship of both epistles is strongly confirmed by the Church Fathers:

Authenticity [of 1Th]. Ignatius, ad Polycarp 1, Ephes. 10, says "pray without ceasing" (1 Thes. 5:17); so Polycarp, ad Philipp. 4. This epistle is in the Muratorian Canon, that of Marcion, and Laodicea, A.D. 364. Irenaeus (*adv. Haer.* 5:6, section 1) quotes 1 Thes. 5:23; Clement of Alexandria (*Paed.* 1:88) quotes 1 Thes. 2:7; Tertullian (*de Resurr.* Carnis 24) quotes 1:9,10; 5:1; Caius in Eusebius (Eccl. Hist.) vi. 20, Origen (*contra Celsus* 3), also confirm it. Tertullian quotes this epistle 20 times.

Genuineness [of 2Th]. Polycarp (Ep. ad Philipp. 11) alludes to 1 Thes. 1:4; 3:15, and so attests it. Justin Martyr (*Dial.Trypho*, 193, sec. 32) alludes to 2 Thes. 2:3. Irenaeus (iii. 7, section 2) quotes 2 Thes. 2:8. Clement of Alexandria quotes 2 Thes. 3:2 as Paul's words (*Strom.* i. 5, section 554; Paedag. i. 17). Tertullian (*de Resurr.* Carnis, chap. 24) quotes 2 Thes. 2:1,2 as part of Paul's epistles (Fausset's; Thessalonians, Epistles of).

As such, these epistles were never doubted as genuine writings of Paul in the early Church. And conservative scholars today also universally accept the Pauline authorship.

> Almost all conservative scholars believe that Paul wrote 2 Thessalonians from Corinth. The basis for this conclusion is that Paul, Silas, and Timothy were present together in Corinth (Acts 18:5). The New Testament does not refer to them being together from then on, though they may have been. Paul evidently wrote 1 Thessalonians from Corinth, too. The topics he treated in the second epistle seem to grow out of situations he alluded to in the first epistle. They reflect a very similar situation in the Thessalonian church. Corinth, therefore, seems the probable site of composition of 2 Thessalonians (Thomas L. Constable. "Notes on 2 Thessalonians." Posted on Sonic Light).

But despite this strong internal and external evidence, there are some liberal scholars today who doubt the Pauline authorship of at least the second epistle. A liberal website says the following about 1Thessalonians:

> The epistle to the Thessalonians is certainly one of the most ancient Christian documents in existence. It is typically dated c. 50/51 CE. It is universally assented to be an authentic letter of Paul (Early Christian; "1Thessalonians").

But it then says about 2Thessalonians:

> Second Thessalonians is widely regarded as pseudonymous. The reference in 2:2 suggests that the letter belongs to the deutero-Pauline period, and the letter may have been intended to replace 1Thessalonians entirely. The time of composition is likely to have been in the last two decades of the first century when hopes in the imminent *parousia* were faltering (Early Christian; "2Thessalonians").

The word *Parousia* means "coming" or "Arrival" as it is rendered in the ALT. The term refers to the Second Coming of Christ. This issue and 2Thessalonians 2:2 will be addressed shortly, but here, despite the claim that "Second Thessalonians is widely regarded as pseudonymous" this is the only webpage I could find that denied the Pauline authorship of this letter. I am sure there are others that I didn't find, and some books as well, but such a belief is hardly "widespread."

Translator's Perspective on the Canon of the NT

The issue of the *Parousia* is one reason for this denial, but another is explained and refuted as follows:

> Its very similarity to I Thess. in vocabulary and style is made to militate against the authenticity of II Thess.; the letter is too Pauline; the author was a clever forger, who, some sixty years later, took up I Thess. and worked it over. There has been no motive assigned for such a forgery; no proof given that any post-Apostolic writer was so cunning as to palm off this letter as a Pauline imitation (New Advent; "Epistles to the Thessalonians").

Thus, once again some scholars today think they are smarter than the early Church. "The Church Fathers fell for a forgery, but we know better." But the liberals do not give any proof for this claim, except to say the two books are "too similar." As we will see, liberal will use both the idea of two books being "too similar" and being "too dissimilar" to deny they were written by the same person. Thus, liberals will find "proof" of their ideas no matter what the relationship is. But in regards to 2Thessalonians, there is also the issue of the *Parousia* that will be addressed later. But here, it will be said the internal and external evidence argues strongly for the Pauline authorship of both of these letters.

Date of Writing:

Paul visited Thessalonica about 50 AD. 1Thessalonians would have been written shortly after that, and then 2 Thessalonians shortly thereafter.

> For the above reasons, it appears that Paul composed 2 Thessalonians quite soon after 1 Thessalonians, perhaps within 12 months. This would place the date of composition in the early A.D. 50s, perhaps A.D. 51, and would make this the third of Paul's canonical writings, assuming Galatians was his first (Thomas L. Constable. "Notes on 2 Thessalonians." Posted on Sonic Light).

The only reason to doubt this dating is if one doubts the Pauline authorship of 2Thessalonians. But as we have seen, there is little reason to do so. These books are thus rightly considered to be among the earliest NT books to have been written.

Doctrine of God:

These letters speak of God as "the Father" (1Th 1:1,3; 2:13; 3:9,11,13; 2Th 1:1; 2:16). Prayers and thanksgiving are offered to this God (1Th 1:2; 3:9f; 5:16,25; 2Th 1:11; 3:1). Thus, God is seen as personal and close, not impersonal and distant.

God is said to be "the One examining our hearts" (1Th 2:4) and thus is seen as being omniscient. God is Judge (2Th 1:5-7), but He is also love (2Th 3:5).

That is not much about the nature of God. But it must be membered that Paul had been in Thessalonica, and while there Paul would have taught the Thessalonians the basics of the Christian faith, which would have included the nature of God. This can be seen in that the Thessalonians are said to have "turned to God from the idols" (1Th 1:9). As such, Paul did not need to repeat information about the nature of God in his letters to them. This is again a difference between writing a letter to people you know as opposed to a document for a general audience. You can assume the readers know things when writing the former but not the latter.

Essential Tenets:

Jesus is referred to as "Lord Jesus Christ" eight times in 1Thessalonians (1:1 {2x}; 1:3; 3:11,13; 5:9,23,28) and nine times in 2Thessalonians (1:1,2,12; 2:1,14,16; 3:6,12,17). Thus, these epistles assert that Jesus is both Lord and Christ.

Paul says he taught the Thessalonians, "to be waiting expectantly for His Son from the heavens, whom He raised from the dead—Jesus—the One rescuing us from the coming wrath" (1Th 1:10). In this sentence Paul is affirming Jesus is the Son of God, was raised from the dead, and is coming again.

The Second Coming is again confirmed in 1Th 3:13, "in order to establish your* hearts [as being] blameless in holiness before our God and Father at the Arrival of our Lord Jesus Christ with all His holy ones [or, saints]." Then again in 2Th 2:8, "And then the lawless [one] will be revealed, whom the Lord will consume with the spirit [or, breath] of His mouth and will destroy by the appearance of His Arrival [or, Coming]."

Both epistles also group God and Jesus together in such a manner that Jesus is seen as equal to the Father:

Grace to you* and peace from God our Father and [the] Lord Jesus Christ! (1Th 1:1b).

[11]Now [may] our God and Father Himself and our Lord Jesus Christ direct our way to you* (1Th 3:11).

Translator's Perspective on the Canon of the NT

For this [is the] will of God in Christ Jesus for you* (1Th 5:17b).

[13]in order to establish your* hearts [as being] blameless in holiness before our God and Father at the Arrival of our Lord Jesus Christ with all His holy ones [or, saints] (1Th 3:13).

[1]Paul and Silvanus and Timothy, To the assembly [or, church] of [the] Thessalonians in God our Father and [the] Lord Jesus Christ: [2]Grace to you* and peace from God our Father and [the] Lord Jesus Christ! (2Th 1:1).

[12]in order that the name of our Lord Jesus is glorified in you*, and you* in Him, according to the grace of our God and of [the] Lord Jesus Christ [or, of our God and Lord, Jesus Christ] (2Th 1:12).

[14]For since we believe that Jesus died and rose again, so also God will bring the ones having fallen asleep through [fig., having died in] Jesus with Him (2Th 2:14).

[16]Now may our Lord Jesus Christ Himself, and our God and Father, the One having loved us and having given eternal comfort and good hope [or, confident expectation] by grace, [17]comfort your* hearts and establish you* in every good word and work (2Th 2:15f).

[5]Now may the Lord direct your* hearts into the love of God and into the patient endurance of Christ (2Th 3:5).

The Father, Son, and Holy Spirit are also associated together:

[13]But <u>we</u> ought to be giving thanks to God always concerning you*, brothers [and sisters], having been loved by [the] Lord, that God chose you* from [the] beginning for salvation, by sanctification of [the] Spirit and faith [in] the truth, [14]to which He called you* through our Gospel [or, Good News] to [the] obtaining of [the] glory of our Lord Jesus Christ (2Th 2:13f).

The Holy Spirit works in the lives of believers and is given to them:

[5]Because our Gospel [or, Good News] did not come to you* in word only, <u>but</u> also in power and in [the] Holy Spirit and in much assurance [or, with full conviction], even as you* know of what sort we became among you* for your* sake. [6]And <u>you*</u> became imitators of us and of

the Lord, having received the word in much affliction [or, during a great trial], with [the] joy of [the] Holy Spirit, ⁷with the result that you* became examples to all the ones believing in Macedonia and Achaia (1Th 1:5-7).

⁸Therefore, the one rejecting [this] [or, regarding [this] as nothing] does not reject a person, but God, the One having also given His Holy Spirit to you* (1Th 4:8).

The Thessalonians' lives were transformed by Christ:

⁹For they themselves report about us what kind of entrance we had to you*, and how you* turned to God from the idols, to be serving as a bondservant to [the] living and true God, ¹⁰and to be waiting expectantly for His Son from the heavens, whom He raised from the dead—Jesus— the One rescuing us from the coming wrath (1Th 1:9f).

That is not a lot of essential doctrinal assertions, but again, Paul is writing to people whom he visited personally and had already taught them the essentials of the Christian faith.

The Parousia:

Mention was made that supposed contradictions between 1 and 2Thessalonians in regards to the *Parousia* or Second Coming of Christ are proof Paul did not write the latter. The passages in question are the following:

¹³But we do not want you* to continue being unaware, brothers [and sisters], concerning the ones having fallen asleep [fig., who have died], so that you* shall not be sorrowing just as also the rest, the ones not having hope [or, confident expectation]. ¹⁴For since we believe that Jesus died and rose again, so also God will bring the ones having fallen asleep through [fig., having died in] Jesus with Him.
¹⁵For this we say to you* by [the] word of [the] Lord, that we, the ones living, the ones being left to the Arrival of the Lord, by no means shall precede the ones having fallen asleep [fig., who have died]. ¹⁶Because the Lord Himself with a shout of command, with a voice of an archangel [or, a chief messenger [of the Lord]] and with [the] trumpet of God, will descend from heaven, and the dead in Christ will rise first, ¹⁷then we, the ones living, the ones being left, will be caught up together with them in [the] clouds to a meeting of the Lord in [the] air, and so we will always be with [the] Lord! ¹⁸Therefore, be comforting one another with these words.

Translator's Perspective on the Canon of the NT

¹Now concerning the times and the seasons, brothers [and sisters], you* have no need [of] my writing to you*. [cp. Acts 1:7] ²For you* yourselves accurately know that the Day of [the] Lord comes in this manner: as a thief in [the] night. [cp. Matt 24:40-44; 2Peter 3:10] ³For when they say, "Peace and safety!" then destruction comes upon them suddenly, even as the birth-pains [come upon] the one having in [the] womb [fig., who is pregnant], and by no means shall they escape (1Th 4:13-5:3).

¹Now we request of you*, brothers [and sisters], in regard to the Arrival [or, Coming] of our Lord Jesus Christ and of our gathering together to Him, ²for you* not to be quickly shaken in mind nor to be disturbed, neither by spirit nor by word nor by letters as [written] by us, as [if] that Day of Christ has arrived. ³Let no one deceive you* by any means, because [that Day will not come] unless the apostasy comes first, and the man of lawlessness is revealed, the son of destruction [or, the one destined to be lost], ⁴the one being in opposition [or, being hostile] and puffing himself up with pride over every[thing] being called god or [every] object of worship, with the result that he sits down in the sanctuary of God as God, displaying himself that he is God. ⁵You* do remember that, being yet with you*, I said these things to you*, do you* not? ⁶And now, you* know the [thing] restraining, for him to be revealed in his own time. ⁷For the secret [or, mystery] of lawlessness is already supernaturally working, only the one [or, the One] now restraining [will continue to do so] until he [or, He] comes [or, appears] out of [the] midst. ⁸And then the lawless [one] will be revealed, whom the Lord will consume with the spirit [or, breath] of His mouth and will destroy by the appearance of His Arrival [or, Coming], ⁹of whom is his [i.e., the lawless one's] arrival according to [the] supernatural working of Satan, in all power and signs and wonders of deceit [fig., counterfeit miracles], ¹⁰and in all deception of the unrighteousness among the ones perishing, because they did not receive the love of the truth for them to be saved. ¹¹And because of this, God will send to them a supernatural working of deception, for them to believe the lie, ¹²so that they shall be judged, all the ones not having believed the truth, but the ones having delighted in unrighteousness (2Th 2:6-12).

The argument is as follows:
In 1 Thessalonians the *parousia*, the coming of Jesus from heaven as apocalyptic judge and redeemer, is imminent. When Paul speaks of "we who are alive, who are left until the coming of the Lord" (1 Thes 4:15), he clearly expects the event in his

own lifetime. But 2 Thes 2:3-12 sets out an elaborate program of what must first happen before that event can occur" (Early Christian; "2 Thessalonians").

This whole argument hinges on Paul's use of "we." Because he used that pronoun in 1Thessalonians rather than "those," it is said Paul believed the Parousia was imminent. But then sixty years later when Jesus had not returned, some unknown writer forged 2Thessalonians to quiet down the disgruntled Christians.
But the use of that pronoun in 1Thessalonians does not imply any such thing. In the first letter, Paul specifically says, "you* yourselves accurately know that the Day of [the] Lord comes in this manner: as a thief in [the] night." That statement clearly echoes the words of Jesus when He said:

⁴⁰"Then two [people] will be in the field, one is taken, and one is left behind. ⁴¹Two women [will be] grinding in the mill, one is taken, and one is left behind. ⁴²Therefore, keep watching! Because you* do not know in what hour your* Lord is coming. ⁴³But know this, if the homeowner had known in what watch [of the night] the thief is coming, he would have kept watch and would not have allowed his house to be broken into. ⁴⁴Because of this, you* also become ready, because in what hour you* do not think, the Son of Humanity is coming (Matt 24:40-44).

The Gospel According to Matthew was probably not yet written when 1Thessalonians was written, as all sides would agree. This is thus evidence that the words of Jesus were accurately circulating before the Gospels were written, with Paul probably learning this when he met with the apostles. But the import here is, Paul knew that no one knew when Jesus was returning. It could be soon, or it could be much later. It is that uncertainty that is reflected in his use of "we." It simply indicates his hope that it would be soon. But then some Thessalonians misunderstood him, just as some do today, that Paul meant it would definitely be soon. Thus, Paul wrote his second letter to correct that misunderstanding. But rather than being corrected, today's liberal scholars come up with their elaborate unsubstantiated theories.

The purpose of Bible prophecy is not for us to make a calendar, but to build character. Paul emphasized this fact in both of his Thessalonian letters, and our Lord warned us not to set dates for His coming (Mt 24:36, 42). Date-setters are usually upsetters, and that is exactly what happened in the

Translator's Perspective on the Canon of the NT

Thessalonican assembly (Dr. Warren Wiersbe, quoted in Precept Austin; "2 Thessalonians Resources").

Other "Unpauline" Elements:

Another argument of liberals is that the second letter reflects a time of Roman persecution, which did not happen until much later. This is based on the following passage:

> [6]since [it is] a righteous [thing] with God to repay with affliction the ones afflicting you* [7]and [to repay] with relief to you*, the ones being afflicted, along with us in the revelation of the Lord Jesus from heaven, with [the] angels of His power [or, His powerful messengers], [8]in a fire of flame [or, a flaming fire], giving [fig., inflicting] vengeance on the ones not knowing God and to the ones not obeying the Gospel [or, Good News] of our Lord Jesus, [9]who will suffer divine justice, eternal ruin, from [the] face [fig., presence] of the Lord and from the glory of His strength, [10]when He comes to be glorified in [or, among] His holy ones [or, saints] in that Day and to be marveled at among all the ones having believed, because our testimony to you* was believed (2Th 1:6-10).

It is true Roman persecutions did not occur until Nero and Domitian, as discussed previously. But Jewish persecutions of Christians were occurring in the 50s, as seen in the Book of Acts, with Paul himself having been persecuted in Thessalonica. As such, this passage perfectly reflects the situation in Thessalonica in the 50s.

It is further claimed the eschatology (doctrine of future things) of Paul reflects that of The Revelation and thus it had to be written after that book and thus not until after the mid-90s. However:

> As for the further objection that the apocalyptic character of ii, 2-12, is post-Pauline and dependent upon so late a composition as the Apocalypse of John (A.D. 93-96) or, worse still upon the Nero redivivus story (Tacitus "Hist.", II, viii), we answer that this assertion is entirely gratuitous. St. Paul got his apocalyptic ideas from the very same source as John, that is either from revelation to himself or from the Old Testament or from tradition (New Advent; "Epistles to the Thessalonians").

In other words, that 2Thessalonians reflects The Revelation is because both Paul and John were basing their books on OT apocalyptic books like Ezekiel. They are thus independent works but with a common source. But it is also possible that John had access to 2Thessalonians when he wrote The Revelation; Thus, The Revelation is based on 2Thessalonians rather than vice-a-versa.

The other point in this quote is that both John and Paul were writing under the inspiration of the Holy Spirit. Liberals will not accept this idea as they generally deny the whole idea of divine revelation, but it accounts for the unique nature of the Bible, as has been mentioned at various points in this volume and in Volume One.

It is also claimed the Christology (doctrine of Christ) is more advanced in 2Thessalonians than in 1Thessalonians. But go back and compare the quoted passages about God and Jesus. You will see they paralleled each other very nicely, with the latter not being noticeably "more advanced" than the former. This is just a made up notion in the minds of the critics.

Finally, it is said there are words that are unique to 2Thessalonians, which are not found in 1Thessalonians or in other Pauline writings. That is true, but that is because Paul is addressing a topic in 2Thessalonians that he does not address elsewhere, that of the events at the Second Coming, so of course he uses different words.

By way of example, I have a two-part article on the S.A.I.D. principle on my fitness website. That is the only place where I directly address the issue of Specific Adaptation to Imposed Demands. Except for the first term, I do not use these or related words much or at all elsewhere, but I wrote that article, as I did most of the other articles on my three websites. In the same way, this letter is the only place Paul addresses the "the lawless [one]" and related issues. It is thus no surprise he uses terms in it that he does not use elsewhere.

Appeal and Mark of Inspiration:

The issue of the end-times is of great fascination to many. Personally, I think many Christians get too wrapped in such speculations and that leads them to be less than profitable in other areas of their Christian life, such as using their belief that lawlessness will increase in the End Times to excuse their lack of social action. And in a way Paul is addressing that mindset in these letters. Apparently, there were some in Thessalonica who were using the idea that Jesus was coming soon as an excuse not to work. Thus, Paul writes, "if anyone is not willing to be working neither let him be eating!" (2Th 3:10b). As such, these letters are of great importance to counteract such false notions. At the same time, the fact of the Second Coming is a great comfort for Christians in the face of persecutions and of a sinful and suffering world. But we cannot let that comfort lead us to not try to improve this world while it still exists.

<u>Translator's Perspective on the Canon of the NT</u>

Moreover, these letters encourage love for one another, prayer and thanksgiving to God, and other Christian virtues. And many have been encouraged to improve their lives as a result. As such, there is much appeal in these letters, and they Thus, bear the mark inspiration.

Conclusion on the Early Epistles:

1 and 2Thessalonians were written by Paul the Apostle in the mid-first century. They contain sound doctrine and are a source of great comfort and inspiration to many. They are thus rightly included in the canon of the NT.

The Major Epistles

"If a man known as Paul the Apostle ever lived and wrote anything, he wrote Romans, 1, 2Corinthians, Galatians."

The above words were spoken by my New Testament professor at Denver Seminary. He was responding to claims like we have already seen by liberals that Paul did not author some of the letters traditionally ascribed to him. But in the case of these four epistles, there is little doubt even among liberals that Paul is the author of these letters. In fact, it is the writing style and theology of these books that are used to compare other Pauline letters to in order to determine if Paul actually authored them. The following passage from the *Encyclopedia Britannica* expresses well the liberal mindset:

> The seven undoubted letters constitute the best source of information on Paul's life and especially his thought; in the order in which they appear in the New Testament, they are Romans, 1Corinthians, 2Corinthians, Galatians, Philippians, 1Thessalonians, and Philemon. The probable chronological order (leaving aside Philemon, which cannot be dated) is 1Thessalonians, 1Corinthians, 2Corinthians, Galatians, Philippians, and Romans. Letters considered "Deutero-Pauline" (probably written by Paul's followers after his death) are Ephesians, Colossians, and 2Thessalonians; 1 and 2Timothy and Titus are "Trito-Pauline" (probably written by members of the Pauline school a generation after his death) ("Saint Paul, the Apostle").

A similar sentiment is presented by a liberal scholar on PBS' website:

For Borg and Crossan there is more than one Paul in the New Testament and no less than three Pauls. The first is "the radical Paul," author of the seven genuine letters that go under his name: Romans, 1 and 2Corinthians, Galatians, 1Thessalonians, Philippians, and Philemon. Then there is "the conservative Paul" of 2Thessalonians, Ephesians, and Colossians ("the disputed letters") and "the reactionary Paul" of the Pastoral Epistles (PBS; "The Real Paul").

A liberal would have to be so radical as to deny that Paul ever existed to deny the Pauline authorship of the four major epistles. But as we already saw, no reputable historian does so.

We have from him [Paul] thirteen Epistles; how many more were lost, we cannot even conjecture. The four most important of them are admitted to be genuine even by the most exacting and skeptical critics. They are so stamped with the individuality of Paul, and so replete with tokens of his age and surroundings, that no sane man can mistake the authorship. We might as well doubt the genuineness of Luther's work on the Babylonian captivity, or his Small catechism (Schaff; 10420-10423).

That said; these four epistles are the longest and most doctrinally filled epistles in the Pauline corpus. They were Thus, deemed to be the most important of his epistles and placed first among his epistles in the canonical order, with Romans being the most important of all and thus placed first, but we will deal with them in chronological order.

Galatians

"Galatians is one of the four letters of Paul known as the *Hauptbriefe*, which are universally accepted as authentic. It is typically dated c. 54 CE" (Early Christian; "Galatians"). There is not much debate on the author and date as even this liberal site affirms the traditional view, but we will take a quick look at both.

Author:
The salutation to this epistle is as follows:

[1]Paul, an apostle (not from people [or, human [authority]] nor by a person, but by Jesus Christ, and God [the] Father, the One having raised

Translator's Perspective on the Canon of the NT

Him from [the] dead) ²and all the brothers [and sisters] with me, to the assemblies [or, churches] of Galatia (Gal 1:1).

Paul immediately names himself and established his authority as being an apostle due to the direct call of Jesus on his life. This is a reference to his conversion on the road to Damascus (Act 9). But he also includes those with him in the greeting. Paul then refers to himself by name once more in this epistle, "Listen! I, Paul, say to you* that if you* are circumcised, Christ will not benefit you* at all" (Gal 5:2).

This epistle also includes some personal information about Paul, such as his meeting with the "pillars" of the Church that was mentioned previously.

Near the end of this epistle, Paul writes, "¹¹See with what large letters I wrote to you* with my own hand!" (Gal 6:11). Most likely Paul was dictating this epistle, but he wrote this one sentence himself. We saw this previously and will see it again. But here, some see in this a clue as to Paul's "weakness in the flesh" that he mentions in this letter (4:13). Some believe it was eye problems, and thus we have an explanation as to why Paul usually dictated his letters, but when he wrote his one sentence at the end he needed to use large letters due to not being able to see very well.

That said; there is much evidence that Paul is the author of this letter.

> Attempts to dismember this writing, and to appropriate it for other hands and later times than those of the apostle Paul, are idle in view of its vital coherence and the passionate force with which the author's personality has stamped itself upon his work; the *Paulinum pectus* speaks in every line. The two contentions on which the letter turns—concerning Paul's apostleship, and the circumcision of Gentile Christians—belonged to the apostle's lifetime: in the fifth and sixth decades these were burning questions; by the 2nd century the church had left them far behind (ISBE; "Galatians, Epistle to the").

> Written by Paul, as the style proves. The heading and allusions to the apostle of the Gentiles in the first person throughout confirm his authorship (Gal. 1:1,13-24; 2:1-14). Irenaeus (*Adv. Haer.*, 3:7, sec. 2, referring to Gal. 3:19), Polycarp (Phil. 3, , quoting Gal. 4:26; 6:7), Justin Martyr (*Orat. ad Graecos*, alluding to Gal. 4:12; 5:20), Tertullian (*De Praescr.*, 60), uphold his authorship (Fausset's; "Galatians, Epistle to").

Date of Writing:

The opening quote to this section stated that Galatians was written circa 54 AD. But there is some debate on this, as some date it in 49 AD, making it the earliest of Paul's epistles. The difference is a debate about whether this epistle was addressed to northern or southern Galatia. If it is the former, then this book would have been written in 54 AD; if the latter, then in 49 AD. The debate hinges on the two times Galatia is mentioned in Acts:

⁶Now having passed through Phrygia and **the region of Galatia**, having been forbidden by the Holy Spirit to speak the word in Asia (Acts 16:6),

²³And having spent some time [there], he went out, passing through in order **the Galatian region** and Phrygia, strengthening all the disciples (Acts 18:3).

The question is if Paul wrote this epistle after the first visit to Galatia or the second. Settling this issue is rather complicated and even confuses this writer, so I will not take a position on it. But I will say that most commentators seem to favor the 54 AD date, so that is the date I will go with. And it really does not matter, as either way all sides agree Paul wrote this epistle very early. And a difference of five years and the exact destination makes no difference in the genuineness or interpretation of this letter.

Doctrine of God:

Given that Paul had personally visited Galatia and most likely founded the church there, he would have taught them the OT conception of God. This can be seen in the following passage:

⁸But at that time indeed, not having known God, you* were serving as bondservants to the [idols] not being by nature gods. [cp. 1Cor 8:5,6; Acts 17:29] ⁹But now, having known God, but rather having been known by God, how is it that you* are turning back again to the weak and poor [fig., worthless], rudimentary elements [or, basic teachings] to which once more you* desire again to be serving as bondservants? (Gal 4:8-9).

Paul's preaching was probably the reason why the Galatians turned from idols to serve the one true God. He Thus, knows they know the correct conception of God, but apparently they have veered from it. Paul

Translator's Perspective on the Canon of the NT

Thus, did not need to rehash what he had personally taught them but simply to encourage them to abide by it. This epistle Thus, says little more than this about the nature of God.

Essential Tenets:

This epistle contains much in the way of affirming essential tenets. Maybe Paul wasn't in Galatian long enough to fully explain all of these essential points, having spent most of his time teaching about the nature of God, which the Galatians clearly needed to hear. But whatever the case, Paul begins this epistle by declaring:

¹Paul, an apostle (not from people [or, human [authority]] nor by a person, but by Jesus Christ and God [the] Father, the One having raised Him from [the] dead) (Gal 1:1).

In this opening verse, Paul affirms Jesus was raised from the dead, while ascribing his apostleship to both Jesus and the Father, Thus, linking the two together. This thought leads Paul to break out in praise:

³Grace to you* and peace from God [the] Father and our Lord Jesus Christ, ⁴the One having given Himself for our sins, in order that He should deliver us out of the present evil age, according to the will of our God and Father, ⁵to whom [be] the glory into the ages of the ages! [fig., forever and ever!] So be it! (Gal 1:3)

In this praise, Paul affirms that Jesus died for our sins, while again linking the Father and Jesus together. He also calls Jesus "our Lord Jesus Christ." Jesus is called "Lord" at least four more times (1:18; 6:14,17,18) and Christ 40 more times (e.g., 1:1,6f,10,12). Jesus is called God's Son in 1:16; 2:20; 4:4,6. Pauls' affirmation in 2:20 is powerful:

²⁰I have been crucified with Christ, but no longer do I live, but Christ lives in me! But [that] which I now live in [the] flesh, I live by faith in the Son of God, the One having loved me and having given Himself [or, having handed Himself over] for me.

Paul then expands on this idea by teaching that salvation comes by faith in Christ's death:

¹¹Now that no one is justified [or, declared righteous] before God by [the] Law is evident, because *"The [person] righteous by faith will live* [or, *"The righteous [person] will live by faith*]." [Hab 2:4]

¹²But the Law is not by faith, but *"The person having done them [i.e., all the commandments of the Law] will live by them."* [Lev 18:5] ¹³Christ redeemed us [or, set us free] from the curse of the Law, having become a curse on our behalf—for it has been written, *"Under a curse* [fig., *Condemned by God] [is] every[one] hanging upon a tree"*— [Deut 21:23] ¹⁴so that the blessing of Abraham shall come to the Gentiles in Christ Jesus, so that we shall receive the promise of the Spirit through faith (Gal 3:11-14).

Here Paul affirms Jesus was "hanged on a tree" Thus, again affirming His crucifixion. But he now affirms that the reason for His death was so that we could be declared righteous by faith in Him. This was all "according to the Scriptures." Paul also affirms Jesus's death on the cross by way of a metaphor. Jesus was literally crucified, but we die to self when we trust in Him. As a result, we are able to live a righteous life by the strength He gives us. Paul also says Jesus gave Himself for us. This affirms Jesus's death was for our sins.

Jesus' humanity is affirmed in 4:4, "But when the fullness [or, completion] of the time came, God sent forth His Son, having been born of a woman, having been born under [the] Law."

The Father, Son, and Holy Spirit are associated together, "Now because you* are sons [and daughters], God sent forth the Spirit of His Son into your* hearts, crying out, 'Dad [Gr. *Abba*], Father!'" (Gal 4:6).

The Holy Spirit was working in the lives of the Galatians, though they had turned from a dependence on Him. But then Paul reminds them of all the Spirit does for believers:

²This only I want to learn from you*: did you* receive the Spirit by works of [the] Law or by hearing with faith? ³Are you* so foolish? Having begun in [or, by] [the] Spirit, are you* now being completed [or, perfected] in [or, by] [the] flesh? ⁴Did you* endure so many things for nothing—if indeed [it was] really for nothing? ⁵Therefore, the One supplying the Spirit to you* and supernaturally working miraculous powers [or, miracles] among you*, [is He doing so] by works of [the] Law or by hearing with faith? (Gal 3:2-5).

¹³Christ redeemed us [or, set us free] from the curse of the Law, having become a curse on our behalf—for it has been written, *"Under a curse* [fig., *Condemned by God] [is] every[one] hanging upon a tree"*— [Deut 21:23] ¹⁴so that the blessing of Abraham shall come to the Gentiles in Christ Jesus, so that we shall receive the promise of the Spirit through faith (Gal 3:13f).

Translator's Perspective on the Canon of the NT

⁶Now because you* are sons [and daughters], God sent forth the Spirit of His Son into your* hearts crying out, "Dad [Gr. *Abba*], Father!" ⁷Therefore, you are no longer a bondservant, but a son, and if a son, also an heir of God through Christ! (Gal 4:6f).

⁴You* were cut off from Christ, you* who are justified [or, declared righteous] by [the] Law! You* fell away from His grace! ⁵For we, by [the] Spirit, by faith, eagerly wait for [the] hope [or, confident expectation] of righteousness. ⁶For in Christ Jesus neither circumcision has any power [or, avails anything] nor uncircumcision, but faith working through love (Gal 5:4-6).

¹⁶But I say, be walking about [fig., conducting yourselves] in [or, by] [the] Spirit, and you* shall by no means fulfill [or, carry out] the lust of [the] flesh. ¹⁷For the flesh lusts contrary to the Spirit, and the Spirit contrary to the flesh. Now these are hostile to one another, so that what you* should be desiring, these [things] you* are not doing. ¹⁸But since you* are led by [the] Spirit, you* are not under [the] Law (Gal 5:16-18).

The renewal by the Sprit is described in a very detailed manner:

²²But the fruit of the Spirit is: love, joy, peace [or, freedom from anxiety], patience, goodness [or, kindness], moral excellence [or, generosity], faith, ²³gentleness [or, considerateness], [and] self-control. Against such there is no law. ²⁴Now the [ones] of Christ [fig., those who belong to Christ] [have] crucified the flesh with its passions and its desires [or, lusts]. ²⁵Since we live in [or, by] [the] Spirit, let us also be keeping in line with [fig., be living in conformity with] the Spirit (Gal 5:22-25).

Before ending this epistle, Paul once more affirms Jesus' death on the cross for us and that we metaphorically can be crucified with him, "But for me, [I will] absolutely not boast except in the cross of our Lord Jesus Christ, by means of whom to me [the] world has been crucified and I to the world" (Gal 6:14).

Appeal and Mark of Inspiration:

There is much appeal in this book to both Christians and non-Christians. For the latter, it teaches the way of salvation is by faith in Jesus' death on the cross for our sins. To those of us who have already believed, it teaches we are to live the Christian life not by our own efforts by the power of the Spirit now living in us. This righteous life can be lived not by following a set of rules but by being led by the Spirit:

> [16] But I say, be walking about [fig., conducting yourselves] in [or, by] [the] Spirit, and you* shall by no means fulfill [or, carry out] the lust of [the] flesh. [17] For the flesh lusts contrary to the Spirit, and the Spirit contrary to the flesh. Now these are hostile to one another, so that what you* should be desiring, these [things] you* are not doing. [18] But since you* are led by [the] Spirit, you* are not under [the] Law (Gal 5:16-18).

And in an earth-shaking passage, Paul declares this new life is available to all people, regardless of who they are:

> [28] There is not Jew nor Greek, there is not bondservant nor free, there is not male and female, for you* are all one in Christ Jesus (Gal 3:28).

Many people have come to faith in Christ by reading this epistle and have been encouraged in their Christian walk by it. This book Thus, bears the mark of inspiration.

Conclusion on Galatians:

Galatians was without any doubt authored by Paul in the mid-first century. It contains many essential doctrinal affirmations and a wealth of encouragement for putting one's faith in Christ and for living a righteous life. This book was Thus, rightly included in the canon of the NT without any doubts.

1Corinthians

Corinth was the metropolis of Achaia, on the bridge of two seas, an emporium of trade between the East and the West—wealthy, luxurious, art-loving, devoted to the worship of Aphrodite. Here Paul established the most important church in Greece, and labored, first eighteen months, then three months, with, perhaps, a short visit between (2Cor 12:14; 13: 1) (Schaff; 10532-10535).

1Corinthians is the next of the four major works of Paul about which there is no doubt as to its authenticity. "This is one of the epistles the authenticity of which has never been called in question by critics of any school, so many and so conclusive are the evidences of its Pauline origin" (Easton's; "Corinthians, First Epistle To the"). But we will take a quick look at the relevant issues.

Author:

The salutation to this epistle is, "Paul, a called apostle [or, called [to be] an apostle] of Jesus Christ by [the] will of God, and Sosthenes the brother" (1Cor 1:1).

Thus, once again Paul declares he is the author and that he is an apostle, and he again includes another person with him as sending the letter. He later also again indicates that he dictated this letter but added a subscription by his own hand, "The greeting of [me] Paul with my hand" (1Cor 16:21).

The evidence for Pauline authorship is overwhelming:

> 1 and 2Corinthians, Galatians and Romans, all belong to the period of Paul's third missionary journey. They are the most remarkable of his writings, and are usually distinguished as the four great or principal epistles; a distinction which not only is a tribute to their high originality and intrinsic worth, but also indicates the extremely favorable opinion which critics of almost all schools have held regarding their authenticity. Throughout the centuries the tradition has remained practically unbroken, that they contain the very *pectus Paulinum*, the mind and heart of the great apostle of the Gentiles, and preserve to the church an impregnable defense of historical Christianity. What has to be said of their genuineness applies almost equally to both [1 and 2Corinthians] (ISBE; "Corinthians, First Epistle To the").

> The historical and internal evidence that they [1 and 2Corinthians] were written by St. Paul is so overwhelmingly strong that their authenticity has been frankly admitted by every distinguished writer of the most advanced critical schools. They were contained in the first collections of St. Paul's Epistles, and were quoted as Scripture by early Christian writers. They were referred to as authorities by the early heretics and translated into many languages in the middle of the second century. The unique personality of St. Paul is impressed upon their every page (New Advent; "Epistles to the Corinthians").

> Its [1Corinthians'] authenticity is attested by Clement of Rome (Ep., c. 47), Polycarp (Ep. to Philipp., c. 11), Ignatius (ad

Eph., 2), and Irenaeus (*Adv. Haer.*, 4:27, section 3) (Fausset's; "Corinthians, First Epistle To the").

The first Church Father mentioned here is Clement. We will discuss his epistle to the Corinthians in Volume Three. But here, it was written in the 90s AD and includes the following passage:

¹Take up the epistle of the blessed Paul the Apostle. ²What did he first write to you* at [the] beginning of the Gospel? ³Upon a truth, spiritually [or, Truly, with the aid of the Spirit], he wrote to you* concerning himself and also Cephas and also Apollos, because even at that time you* to have made partialities (1Clement 47:1-3).

This is an obvious reference to the following passage from 1Corinthians:

¹²Now I say this, that each of you* are saying, "I indeed am of Paul," "But I of Apollos," "But I of Cephas [i.e., Peter]," "But I of Christ."
¹³Has Christ been divided? Paul was not crucified for you*, was he? Or were you* baptized into the name of Paul? (1Cor 1:12f).

Despite this universal acceptance of the Pauline authorship of this this letter, I recently say a webpage in which the writer referred to this epistle as "supposedly written by Paul." Anytime you read such, know that the person is simply displaying his or her lack of knowledge of the background of the NT and thus their comments about the Bible in general should be disregarded.

Date of Writing:
Paul had an extended ministry in Corinth, despite some opposition:

¹Then after these [things], Paul having departed out of Athens, came to Corinth. ²And having found a certain Jew by name Aquila, of Pontus by race [or, a native of Pontus], recently having come from Italy, and Priscilla his wife (because of Claudius ordering all the Jews to depart out of Rome [ca. 49 A.D.]), he came to them. ³And because of being of the same trade, he stayed with them and was working, for they were tent-makers [by] trade. [cp. 2Thes 3:8] ⁴Now he was reasoning in the synagogue every Sabbath, and he was persuading Jews and Greeks.
⁵Now when both Silas and Timothy came down from Macedonia, Paul was held completely by the Spirit, solemnly testifying to the Jews [that] Jesus [is] the Christ. ⁶But when they set themselves in opposition against [him] and [were] blaspheming, having shaken [the dust] off [of

Translator's Perspective on the Canon of the NT

his] clothes, he said to them, "Your* blood [be] on your* head! I am clean. From now [on] I will go to the Gentiles!"
⁷And having departed from there, he went to [the] house of a certain [man] by name Justus, worshiping God, whose house was being next door to the synagogue. ⁸Then Crispus the synagogue leader believed in the Lord together with his whole house, and many of the Corinthians, hearing, were believing and were being baptized. ⁹Then the Lord said to Paul by means of a vision in the night, "Stop being afraid, but be speaking and do not be silent; ¹⁰because I am with you, and no one will set on [fig., attack] you to harm you, because [there] are many people [belonging] to Me in this city." ¹¹And he settled [there] a year and six months teaching the word of God among them (Acts 18:1-11).

After this time, Paul sets off for Ephesus (Acts 18:19). He then travels around some more, then returns to Ephesus and stays there for three years (Acts 19:1). It is during this second stay at Ephesus that most commentators believe this epistle was written due to its proximity to Corinth.

> During the years that St. Paul was at Ephesus he must have frequently heard from Corinth, as it was distant only 250 miles, and people were constantly passing to and fro. A ship sailing at the rate of four miles an hour would cover the distance in three days (New Advent; "Epistles to the Corinthians).

In 2Corinthians 12:14, Paul writes, "Listen! A third time I am ready to come to you*." Acts only records the one visit of Paul to Corinth, Thus, some have speculated that prior to writing 1Corinthians, Paul made a quick trip to Corinth from Ephesus. But others think this "visit" is a reference to the letter Paul mentions in 1Cor 5:9 that has been lost to us, "I wrote to you* in the epistle not to be associating with fornicators." Either way, Paul learned about what was happening in Corinth and thus wrote this letter, then shortly thereafter he wrote 2Corinthians. This was all probably occurring in 57 AD.

> The First Epistle to the Corinthians was composed in Ephesus shortly before Paul's departure for Greece, in the spring of A.D. 57. It had been preceded by another one, now lost (1Cor 5:9). It was an answer to perplexing questions concerning various disputes and evils which disturbed the peace and spotted the purity of the congregation….
> The Second Epistle to the Corinthians was written in the summer or autumn of the same year, 57, from some place in

Macedonia, shortly before the author's intended personal visit to the metropolis of Achaia (Schaff; 10547-10549; 10580-10582).

Doctrine of God:

Since Paul had founded the Corinthian church himself, he knows what he taught them about the nature of God. Thus, in this letter, he assumes they remember these teachings while articulating additional ideas. This is seen in the following passages.

[20]For you* were bought [or, redeemed] with a price. Therefore, glorify God in your* body and in your* spirit, which are God's (1Cor 6:20).

In saying the body and spirit belong to God, Paul is assuming that God created both, perfectly in line with OT teaching (Gen 1:1; Zech 12:1).

[4]So concerning the eating of the meats sacrificed to idols, we know that an idol [is] nothing in the world, and that [there is] no other God except for one.
[5]For even if they are called "gods," whether in heaven or on earth (just as there are gods many and lords many), [6]<u>but</u> to us [there is] one God, the Father, of whom [are] all [things], and we [exist] for Him; and one Lord Jesus Christ, through whom [are] all [things], and we [exist] through Him (1Cor 5:4-6).

Here, Paul strongly affirms there is only one true God, while the gods which idols represent are all false and "nothing."

[1]Now I do not want you* to be unaware, brothers [and sisters], that all our fathers were under the cloud, and all passed through the sea, [2]and all were baptized into Moses in the cloud and in the sea, [3]and all ate the same spiritual food, [4]and all drank the same spiritual drink, for they were drinking of a spiritual rock following [them]; but that rock was Christ. [5]<u>But</u> God was not well pleased with the majority of them, for they were struck down in the wilderness (1Cor 10:1-4).

Here, Paul is assuming the God who led the Israelites out of Egypt and during the wilderness wanderings is the same God he proclaims.

[12]For even as the woman [is] from the man, so also the man [is] by the woman, but all such [things are] from God (1Cor 11:12).

207

Translator's Perspective on the Canon of the NT

Here Paul is asserting that God created both men and women, just as the OT teaches.

³⁷And what you sow, you do not sow what the body is going to be, but bare grain; it may be of wheat or of some of the remaining [grains]. ³⁸But God gives to it a body just as He willed, and to each of the seeds its own body (1Cor 15:37f).

Here Paul is asserting that God makes the plants and their seeds, just as the OT asserts. He sums it all up as:

²⁶"For the earth [is] the LORD's and its fullness" (1Cor 10:26).

Thus, Paul's God is the Creator of people and nature, the only true God, and the same God as in the OT.

Essential Tenets:

Like Galatians, 1Corinthians is filled with essential tenets. In fact, the most certain early creed imbedded in the NT is found in this epistle, in 15:1-3. That passage was covered in detail in Chapter One, so comments thereupon will not be repeated here. But Paul's many more statements in line with essential tenets will be quoted.

First, the phrase "Lord Jesus Christ" occurs 11 times in this epistle (e.g. 1:1,2,3,7,8,10). Paul calls Jesus "Lord" and "Christ" each dozens of more times. He says Jesus is God's Son in 1:9, 15:28. Then Paul unites Jesus with God in 1:3, "Grace to you* and peace from God our Father and [the] Lord Jesus Christ!" Paul then affirms many more essential tenets:

⁷with the result that you* are not falling short [or, lacking] in any spiritual gift, eagerly waiting for the revelation of our Lord Jesus Christ, ⁸who also will confirm [or, sustain] you* to the end, blameless in the day of our Lord Jesus Christ. ⁹God [is] faithful, by whom you* were called into [the] fellowship of His Son, Jesus Christ our Lord (1Cor 1:7-9).

The phrases "the revelation of our Lord Jesus Christ" and "day of our Lord Jesus Christ" are almost certainly references to the Second Coming.

¹⁸For the word [or, message] of the cross indeed is silliness to the ones perishing, but to us, the ones being saved, it is [the] power of God! (1Cor 1:18).

²For I decided [or, determined] not to know any[thing] among you*, except Jesus Christ, and this One having been crucified! (1Cor 2:2).

Here are references to the death of Jesus, by way of mentioning the cross He died on and Him being crucified.

¹⁴Now God both raised up the Lord and will raise us up through His power (1Cor 6:14).

Here is reference to the resurrection of Jesus and the general resurrection.

²⁰For you* were bought [or, redeemed] with a price. Therefore, glorify God in your* body and in your* spirit, which are God's (1Cor 6:20).

¹¹And the brother being weak will perish because of your knowledge, for the sake of whom Christ died (1Cor 8:11).

Here are references to why Jesus died, it was for us, to redeem us.

²³For I received from the Lord what I also handed down to you*, that the Lord Jesus in the night in which He was betrayed took bread, ²⁴and having given thanks, He broke [it] and said, "Take, eat; this is My body, the [one] being broken on behalf of you*. Be doing this in remembrance of Me." ²⁵And in the same manner [He took] the cup after [they] ate, saying, "This cup is the New Covenant in My blood. Be doing this, as often as you* drink [it], in remembrance of Me." ²⁶For as often as you* shall be eating this bread and drinking this cup, you* proclaim the death of the Lord, until He comes (1Cor 11:23-26).

This is a description of the Last Supper. Interestingly, this description parallels the one found in the Gospel of Luke. Neither were actually at the Last Supper, so one of them must have heard this from one of the original twelve apostles then told it to the other during their travels together, but it is hard to say who told who. But the important point here is in this description is an affirmation of the death of Jesus and His Second Coming, along with the New Covenant God makes with believers that was discussed in Chapter One.

Translator's Perspective on the Canon of the NT

³For this reason, I make known to you* that no one speaking by [the] Spirit of God, says "Accursed Jesus" [or, "Jesus [is] accursed" – Gr., *anathema*], and no one is able to say "Lord Jesus" [or, "Jesus [is] Lord"], except by [the] Holy Spirit (1Cor 12:3).

This is a strong affirmation that Jesus is Lord.

¹²But if Christ is preached that He has been raised from [the] dead, how are some among you* saying that [there] is no resurrection of [the] dead? ¹³But if [there] is no resurrection of [the] dead, neither has Christ been raised. ¹⁴But if Christ has not been raised, in that case, our proclamation [is] empty [fig. without purpose], and your* faith also [is] empty. ¹⁵And we also are found [to be] false witnesses of God, because we testified of God that He raised up Christ, whom He did not raise if indeed [the] dead are not raised. ¹⁶For if [the] dead are not raised, neither has Christ been raised. ¹⁷But if Christ has not been raised, your* faith is futile [or, worthless]; you* are still in your* sins. ¹⁸In that case, also, the ones having fallen asleep [fig., having died] in Christ perished. ¹⁹If in this life only we have been hoping [or, have been having confident expectation] in Christ, we are of all people most pitiful.
²⁰But now Christ has been raised from [the] dead! He became the first-fruits of the ones having fallen asleep [fig., having died]. ²¹For since by means of a man death [came], also by means of a Man [is] [the] resurrection of [the] dead (1Cor 15:12-20).

This is the chapter that begins with the embedded creed that was quoted in Chapter One. But here we began after that quote. The reason Paul quoted that creed was to introduce a discussion of the resurrection of Jesus and how that prefigures the resurrection of all people at the end of time. It should be noted how Paul states in no uncertain terms that the resurrection of Christ and the future resurrection of all people are essential doctrines of the Christian faith.

⁴⁷The first man [is] out of the earth, earthy [or, made of dust]; the second Man [is the] Lord from heaven (1Cor 15:47).

Here Paul affirms the full humanity and deity of Jesus.

The Holy Spirit was working in the lives of the Corinthians, starting with how Paul preached the Gospel to them:

Why Are These Books in the Bible? Volume Two

⁴And my word [or, message] and my proclamation [were] not in persuasive words of human wisdom, <u>but</u> in demonstration of [the] Spirit and of power, ⁵so that your* faith shall not be in [the] wisdom of people, <u>but</u> in the power of God (1Cor 2:4).

¹⁰But God revealed [them] to us through His Spirit. For the Spirit searches all [things], even the depths of God.
¹¹For who among people knows the [things] of the person, except the spirit of the person, the [one] in him? In the same way also no one knows the [things] of God, except the Spirit of God. ¹²But <u>we</u> did not receive the spirit of the world, <u>but</u> the Spirit, the [One] from God, so that we should know the [things] having been graciously given to us by God; ¹³which [things] also we speak, not in words taught by human wisdom, <u>but</u> in [words] taught by [the] Holy Spirit, interpreting spiritual [things] by spiritual [words] [or, combining spiritual [ideas] with spiritual [words]].
¹⁴But a natural [or, unspiritual] person does not receive the [things] of the Spirit of God, for they are silliness to him, and he is not able to know [them], because they are spiritually [or, with the aid of the Spirit] examined. ¹⁵But the spiritual [person] indeed examines all [things], but he himself is examined by no one. ¹⁶*"For who knew [the] mind of [the] LORD? Who will instruct Him?"* [Isaiah 40:13, LXX; Jer 23:18] But <u>we</u> have the mind of Christ (2Cor 2:10-16).

Here, the personality and Deity of the Sprit are affirmed. The Spirit also indwells believers:

"You* know that you* are a temple of God, and the Spirit of God dwells in you*, do you* not? (1Cor 3:16).

¹⁹You* know, do you* not, that your* body is a temple of the Holy Spirit in you*, which you* have from God, and [that] you* are not your* own? ²⁰For you* were bought [or, redeemed] with a price. Therefore, glorify God in your* body and in your* spirit, which are God's (1Cor 6:19f).

The renewal by the Spirit is described by Paul:

⁹You* know that unrighteous [persons] will not inherit [the] kingdom of God, do you* not? Stop being led astray [fig., being deceived]; neither fornicators, nor idolaters, nor adulterers, nor passive partners in male-male sex, nor active partners in male-male sex, ¹⁰nor

211

Translator's Perspective on the Canon of the NT

covetous [persons], nor thieves, nor drunkards, nor slanderers [or, abusive persons], nor swindlers will inherit [the] kingdom of God.

¹¹And these some [of] you* were! [or, And such were some of you*!] But you* yourselves were washed [fig., purified], but you* were sanctified, but you* were justified [or, declared righteous] in the name of the Lord Jesus and in [or, by] the Spirit of our God! (1Cor 6:9-11).

In this passage we see the outworking of the New Covenant. There were Corinthians who *were* for instance adulterers. But they turned from that sin not because of reading the Ten Commandments but due to the Spirit of God having renewed them from the inside out.

Then in 1Cor 12-14 is an extended discussion about spiritual gifts. These are given to believers by the Spirit. A discussion of these gifts are outside of the scope of this book, but I address them in "Scripture Studies #27, 28 in my *Scripture Workbook* (see Appendix Two), and hope to do so in more depth in a forthcoming book (see Appendix Three). But the import here is these gifts are the Holy Spirit working in and through believers for the benefit of all believers, "But to each [one] has been given the manifestation of the Spirit for the advantage [of all] [or, for the common good] (1Cor 12:7).

Paul ends his epistle with a phrase that is somewhat hard to translate. It could be a reference to either the first or second coming of Christ.

²²If anyone does not affectionately love the Lord Jesus Christ, let him be accursed! [Gr., *anathema*] The Lord has come! [or, O Lord come! – Gr., *maranatha*] (1Cor 16:22).

Appeal and Mark of Inspiration:

This epistle would have been of great interest to the original recipients, as the Corinthians had apparently sent a letter to Paul asking many questions, and Paul responds to those questions here (see 7:1a, "Now concerning [the things] of which you* wrote to me"). But Paul's answers are important for us today as many today have the same questions that the Corinthians asked.

Besides the answers to these questions, Paul also affirms many essential doctrinal tenets. This book is thus a treasure trove of doctrinal truths that are vital for all Christians and those investigating the Christian faith to know. There is thus wide appeal to this book.

In this letter, Paul speaks with an air of authority, even alluding to him writing by way of inspiration, "And I think I also to be having [the] Spirit of God" (7:40b). And Paul's authority and inspiration in this epistle was accepted by the original recipients and without any doubts by the early Church at large, as this letter bears the mark of inspiration.

Conclusion on 1Corinthians:

This epistle is one of the four major epistles about which there has never been any doubt as to the Pauline authorship. It was clearly written in the first century and circulated beyond the original recipients shortly after being read by them. It is filled with vital doctrinal teachings and practical advice. This books Thus, has wide appeal and bears the mark of inspiration. As such, it was rightly included without question in the canon of the NT.

2Corinthians

2Corinthians is the third book of the four major works of Paul about which there is no doubt as to its authenticity. But we will take a quick look at the relevant issues.

Author:

Paul opens this letter by writing:

Paul, an apostle of Jesus Christ by [the] will of God, and Timothy the brother, to the assembly [or, church] of God, the one being in Corinth, with all the holy ones [or, saints], the ones being in all Achaia (2Cor 1:1).

Paul Thus, once again includes Timothy with him and even mentions all of the Christians with him as greeting the Corinthians. Paul refers to himself by name once more in this epistle:

Now I, Paul, myself plead with you* by the gentleness and kindness of Christ; [I] who according to face [fig., in presence] indeed [am] humble [or, servile] among you*, but being absent, act boldly toward you* (2Cor 10:1).

It is because of such passages that the following is said about this letter:

This epistle, it has been well said, shows the individuality of the apostle more than any other. "Human weakness, spiritual strength, the deepest tenderness of affection, wounded feeling, sternness, irony, rebuke, impassioned self-vindication,

Translator's Perspective on the Canon of the NT

> humility, a just self-respect, zeal for the welfare of the weak and suffering, as well as for the progress of the church of Christ and for the spiritual advancement of its members, are all displayed in turn in the course of his appeal."--Lias, *Second Corinthians* (Easton's; "Corinthians, Second Epistle To the").

And finally, that this letter was authored by Paul was affirmed by the Church Fathers:

> 871.15 Its genuineness is attested by Irenaeus (*Haer.*, 3:7, section 1), Athenagoras (*De Res. Mort.*), Clement of Alexandria (*Strom.*, 3:94, 4:101), and Tertullian (*Pudic.*, 13) (Fausset's; "Corinth").

> The Second Epistle was known from the very earliest times. There is a trace of it in that portion of "The Ascension of Isaiah" which dates back to the first century (Knowling, "The Testimony of St. Paul to Christ", p. 58; Charles, "The Ascension of Isaiah", pp. 34, 150). It was known to St. Polycarp, to the writer of the Epistle to Diognetus, to Athenagoras, Theophilus, the heretics Basilides and Marcion. In the second half of the second century it was so widely used that it is unnecessary to give quotations (New Advent; (Epistles to the Corinthians").

Polycarp and the Epistle to Diognetus are among the Apostolic Fathers whose writings will be addressed in Volume Three. But here, these books are dated to the early second century, showing the early acceptance of 2Corinthians.

Date of Writing:

"The Second Epistle was written a few months after the First" (New Advent; (Epistles to the Corinthians").

"Time of writing. After Pentecost A.D. 57, when Paul left Ephesus for Troas" (Fausset's; "Corinth").

There is little doubt about this timetable. There were very specific reasons Paul wrote this letter that are clear from its contents:

> Reasons for writing. To explain why he deferred his promised visit to Corinth on his way to Macedonia (1 Cor. 4:19; 16:5; 2 Cor. 1:15,16), and so to explain his apostolic walk, and vindicate his apostleship against gainsayers (2 Cor. 1:12,24;

Why Are These Books in the Bible? Volume Two

6:3-18; 7:2; 10; 11 ; 12). Also to praise them for obeying his first epistle, and to charge them to pardon the transgressor, as already punished sufficiently (2 Cor. 2:1-11; 7:6-16). Also to urge them to contributions for the poor brethren at Jerusalem (2 Cor. 8) (Fausset's; "Corinth").

Doctrine of God:

Paul opens this epistle by declaring:

³Blessed [be] the God and Father of our Lord Jesus Christ, the Father of compassions and God of all comfort, ⁴the One comforting us in all our affliction, for our being able to be comforting the ones in every affliction by means of the comfort with which we are comforted ourselves by God. ⁵Because just as the sufferings of Christ abound to us, in the same manner our comfort also abounds through Christ (2Cor 1:3).

In this exclamation, Paul demonstrates that God is personal and intimately involved with His creation, especially with people.

⁹But we ourselves have had in ourselves the sentence of death, so that we shall not be relying on ourselves, but on God, the One raising the dead (2Cor 1:9).

Here Paul affirms the idea of resurrection that we saw in the OT and previous NT books and attributes it to the power of God.

⁶Because God [is] the One having said [for] light to shine out of darkness, who shined in our hearts to [give] the illumination of the knowledge of the glory of God in [the] face of Jesus Christ (2Cor 4:6).

Paul is alluding to Genesis 1:3 and affirming God is the Creator.

¹⁶And what harmony [is there for the] temple of God with idols? (2Cor 6:16).

Here Paul express the clear distinction between the one true God and the false gods represented by idols.

⁶But God, the One comforting the downcast [or, the ones of humble circumstances], comforted us by the arrival of Titus (2Cor 7:6).

Translator's Perspective on the Canon of the NT

Here again Paul affirms the personal caring nature of God, along with His providence working in people's lives.

Be living at peace, and the God of love and peace will be with you* (2Cor 13:11b).

Here Paul affirms that God is love and thus the good Creator God of the OT. Thus, the God of Paul in 2Corinthians is clearly the same God as the God of the OT.

Essential Tenets:

Paul affirms many essential tenets in this epistle. First, the phrase "Lord Jesus Christ" appears five times in the epistle (1:2,3; 8:9; 11:30; 13:14). Jesus is clearly called Lord three more times (1:4; 4:5,10,14), while there are many more references that most likely are referring to Jesus, though they could be referring to the Father (e.g. 2:12; 3:16-18). Jesus is called Christ 45 more times (e.g. 1:1,5,19,21). Jesus is called the Son of God in 1:19:

For the Son of God, Jesus Christ, the One having been preached among you* by us—by me and Silvanus and Timothy—did not become "Yes" and "No," but in Him it has become "Yes."

In this epistle, Paul sees a unity between God and Jesus:

³Blessed [be] the God and Father of our Lord Jesus Christ (2Cor 1:3a).

⁴And such confidence [or, trust] we have by means of Christ toward God (2Cor 3:4).

³But even if our Gospel has been hidden, it has been hidden among the ones perishing, ⁴among whom the god of this age [i.e., Satan] blinded the minds of the unbelieving, in order for the illumination of the Gospel of the glory of Christ not to shine on them, who is the image of God (2Cor 4:3f).

In the third passage is a clear teaching of the deity of Jesus. Paul then refers to the sufferings, death, and resurrection of Christ on our behalf:

⁵Because just as the sufferings of Christ abound to us, in the same manner our comfort also abounds through Christ (2Cor 1:5).

¹⁴For the love of Christ compels us, having judged [or, concluded] this: that since One died on behalf of all, consequently, these all died. ¹⁵And He died on behalf of all, so that the ones living should no longer be living to themselves, but to the One having died and having been raised on behalf of them (2Cor 5:14f).

Paul explains that Christ's death was for our sins, to reconcile us with God:

¹⁸And all these [things are] of God, the One having reconciled us to Himself through Jesus Christ and having given to us the ministry of that reconciliation, ¹⁹how that God was in Christ reconciling [the] world to Himself, not imputing their transgressions to them and having put in [or, having committed to] us the word of that reconciliation. ²⁰Therefore, we serve as ambassadors on behalf of Christ, as though God [were] appealing through us: we implore [you*] on behalf of Christ, be reconciled to God! ²¹For the One not having known sin, He made sin on our behalf, so that we shall become [the] righteousness of God in Him (2Cor 5:18-21).

The reception of the Spirit is worded as:

²¹Now the One inwardly strengthening you* with us into Christ and having anointed us [is] God, ²²the One also having sealed us and having given the down payment [or, guarantee] of the Spirit in our hearts (2Cor 1:21).

⁵Now the One having prepared us for this same [thing is] God, the One having given to us the down payment [or, guarantee] of the Spirit (2Cor 5:5).

The New Covenant of an inner change versus the Old Covenant of the Law is indicated in the following passages:

²You* are our letter, having been written in our hearts, being known and being read by all people; ³being made known that you* are [the] letter of Christ having been ministered [or, cared for] by us, having been written not with ink, but with [the] Spirit of [the] living God, not in tablets [made of] stone, but in fleshy tablets of hearts (2Cor 3:2).

⁷Now if the ministry of death, having been engraved in letters in stones, came in glory, with the result that the sons [and daughters] of Israel were not able to look intently upon the face of Moses because of

Translator's Perspective on the Canon of the NT

the glory of his face, the [glory which was] passing away, [8]how will the ministry of the Spirit not be more in glory? [or, be more glorious?] [9]For if the ministry of condemnation [had] glory, by much more the ministry of righteousness abounds [or, excels] in glory. [10]For even the [thing] having been glorified has not been glorified, in this respect, because of the surpassing glory [fig., the glory which is superior to it]. [11]For if the [thing] passing away [was] with glory, by much more the [thing] remaining [is] in glory [or, [is] glorious] (2Cor 3:7-11).

The unity of the Father and Spirit is indicated by Paul writing, "Now the Lord is the Spirit; and where the Spirit of [the] Lord [is], there [is] liberty" (2Cor 4:16). Paul ends this epistle by associating the Father, Son, and Holy Spirit together, "The grace of the Lord Jesus Christ and the love of God and the fellowship of the Holy Spirit [be] with you* all! So be it!" (2Cor 13:14).

Thus, many essential tenets are affirmed in this epistle.

Appeal and Mark of Inspiration:

The personal nature of this epistle makes it appealing to many, as it gives a look into the character of Paul. But it also provides practical advice for dealing with church problems, while teaching essential Christian doctrines. It also puts forth the following glorious promise:

[17]Therefore, if anyone [is] in Christ, [he is] a new creation; the old [things] passed away; behold, all [things] have become new! (2Cor 5:17).

The authority of Paul is reaffirmed in this letter, and that authority has always been accepted in the Church. For all of these reasons, this epistle bears the mark of inspiration.

Conclusion on 2Corinthains:

There are many doctrinal affirmations and practical advice in this epistle. It was clearly written by Paul in the first century, with many personal details about Paul, whose authority is unquestioned. As such, this letter was rightly included in the canon of the NT without question.

Romans

Romans is unique among Paul's epistles in that Paul had yet to visit Rome at the time of its writing, while his other letters were addressed to churches he had founded or at least visited. This affected its content, as we will see shortly. But first, a quick look at authorship would be helpful.

Author:

The salutation to this epistle is as follows, "¹Paul, a bondservant of Jesus Christ, a called apostle, having been separated [or, appointed] to the Gospel [or, Good News] of God" (Rom 1:1).

But then at the end of this epistle is the following, "²²I Tertius (the one having written this epistle) greet you* in [the] Lord" (Rom 16:22).

This apparent contradiction is easily resolved. Paul dictated this epistle to Tertius. We saw this before, and it is most often the case with NT letters. The author dictated his words to a scribe. In this case, the scribe is named, but that is not always the case.

It was already stated that there is no doubt Paul is the author of this letter. As such, little more needs to be said here, except to acknowledge that point. "No suspicion on the head of the genuineness of the Epistle exists which needs serious consideration" (ISBE; "Romans, The Epistle to").

> The epistles of Clement (Cor. 35) and Polycarp (ad Philippians 6) quote respectively Rom. 1:29-32 and Rom. 14:10-12. Irenaeus (iv. 27, section 2) quotes it as Paul's (Rom. 4:10,11). Melito's "Hearing of Faith" is entitled from Rom. 10 or Gal. 3:2,3. The Muratorian Canon, Syriac and Old Latin versions, have it. Heretics admitted its canonicity; so the Ophites (*Hippol. Haer.* 99; Rom. 1:20-26); Basilides (238, Rom. 8:19-22; 5:13,14); Valentinus (195, Rom. 8:11); the Valentinians Heracleon and Ptolemaeus; Tatian (*Orat.* 4, Rom. 1:20), and Marcion's canon. The epistle of the churches of Vienne and Lyons (Eusebius, *H. E.* v. 1; Rom. 8:18); Athenagoras (13, Rom. 12:1; 37, Rom. 1:24); Theophilus of Antioch (*Autol.* 79, Rom. 2:6; 126, Rom. 13:7,8). Irenaeus, Tertullian, and Clement of Alexandria often quote it (Fausset's; "Romans, Epistle to the").

Date of Writing:

"… like all Paul's letters, Romans too arose out of a specific situation, when the apostle wrote from Greece, likely Corinth, between A.D. 56 and 58 (cf. Acts 20:2–3)" (Bishops; "The Letter to the Romans"). As with the author, there is little debate on this date. The only question is if it is closer to 56 or 58 AD. The reason for this certainty is the information contained in the letter itself:

Translator's Perspective on the Canon of the NT

Date and place of writing. Paul wrote while at Corinth, for he commends to the Romans Phoebe, deaconess of Cenchreae, the port of Corinth (Rom. 16:1,2). He was lodging at Gaius' house (Rom. 16:23), a chief member of the Corinthian church (1 Cor. 1:14). Erastus, "treasurer" (chamberlain, KJV), belonged to Corinth (2 Tim. 4:20; Acts 19:22). The time was during his visit in the winter and spring following his long stay at Ephesus (Rom. 20:3); for he was just about to carry the contributions of Macedonia and Achaia to Jerusalem (Rom. 15:25-27; compare Acts 20:22), just after his stay at Corinth at this time (Acts 24:17; 1 Cor. 16:4; 2 Cor. 8:1,2; 9:1 ff). His design of visiting Rome after Jerusalem (Rom. 15:23-25) at this particular time appears incidentally from Acts 19:21.

Thus, Paul wrote it in his third missionary journey, at the second of the two visas to Corinth recorded in Acts. He remained then three months in Greece. He was on the point of sailing to Jerusalem when obliged to alter his purpose; the sea therefore was by this time navigable. It was not late in the spring, for, after passing through Macedon and visiting the coast of Asia Minor, he still expected to reach Jerusalem by Pentecost (Acts 20:16). He must therefore have written the epistle to the Romans early in spring, A.D. 58 (Fausset's; "Romans, Epistle to the").

The reason why this dating is important is the following:

The reader's attention is invited to this date. Broadly speaking, it was about 30 years at the most after the Crucifixion. Let anyone in middle life reflect on the freshness in memory of events, whether public or private, which 30 years ago made any marked impression on his mind. Let him consider how concrete and vivid still are the prominent personages of 30 years ago, many of whom of course are still with us. And let him transfer this thought to the 1st century, and to the time of our Epistle. Let him remember that we have at least this one great Christian writing composed, for certain, within such easy reach of the very lifetime of Jesus Christ when His contemporary friends were still, in numbers, alive and active.

Then let him open the Epistle afresh, and read, as if for the first time, its estimate of Jesus Christ—a Figure then of no legendary past, with its halo, but of the all but present day. Let him note that this transcendent estimate comes to us conveyed in the vehicle not of poetry and rhetoric, but of a treatise pregnant with masterly argument and admirable practical wisdom, tolerant and comprehensive. And we think that the reader will feel that the result of his meditations on date and circumstances is reassuring as to the solidity of the historic basis of the Christian faith (ISBE; "Romans, The Epistle to").

This point was elaborated on at length in Chapters One and Two but bears repeating. This epistle, as with the Synoptic Gospels, was without any doubt written within the lifetimes of those who had heard Jesus preach. Furthermore, it was written to a church Paul had not founded. Thus, the original readers already had knowledge of the Christian faith independent of Paul. As such, if in this doctrinally filled epistle Paul taught things contrary to Jesus and what other Christians were teaching, this epistle would have been rejected as teaching heresy. But it was immediately and universally accepted as an authoritative writing in the early Church. We Thus, have in this epistle a correct articulation of early Christian doctrine. As such, Christian doctrines did not slowly develop over many decades or even centuries as many claim. They were right there at the beginning of the proclamation of the Christian message.

Doctrine of God and of Nature:

Paul opens this epistle by writing:

[8]First indeed I thank my God through Jesus Christ for all of you*, that your* faith is being proclaimed in the whole world. [9]For God is my witness, whom I sacredly serve in my spirit in the Gospel of His Son, how I constantly make mention of you*, [10]always imploring in my prayers, if in some way now at last I will succeed, by the will of God, to come to you* (Rom 1:8-10).

Thus, Paul's God is a personal God who can be invoked in prayer and should be thanked for all good in life, as He is in control of what happens. This is in line with OT ideas about God.

Then later in the first chapter, Paul echoes the OT prophets:

[18]For the wrath of God is revealed from heaven upon all ungodliness and unrighteousness of people, [upon] the ones suppressing the truth in unrighteousness. [19]For this reason, the [thing] known of God is revealed among [or, within] them, for God revealed [it] to them. [20]For from [the] creation of [the] world His invisible [attributes] are plainly seen, being understood by the [things] made, both His eternal power and divinity, so that they are without excuse.

[21]For this reason, having known God, they did not glorify [Him] as God nor did they give thanks, <u>but</u> they were given over to deception in

Translator's Perspective on the Canon of the NT

their thought processes [or, they became futile in their speculations], and their senseless heart was darkened. ²²Professing to be wise, they were made silly; ²³and they exchanged the glory of the incorruptible God for a likeness of an image of corruptible people and of birds and of four-footed animals and of reptiles.

²⁴And so God also gave them over in the lusts of their hearts to impurity [or, immorality], to the dishonoring of their bodies among themselves; ²⁵who exchanged the truth of God for the lie [or, changed the truth of God into a lie], and worshipped and sacredly served the creation rather than the One having created, who is blessed into the ages [fig., forever]. So be it! (Rom 1:18-25).

In this passage, Paul proclaims God is the Creator of all things, is worthy of worship, cannot be represented by images, is eternal, and His wrath is upon all who worship false gods or images instead of Him. This is perfectly in line with the OT teaching of the nature of God and the sinfulness of trying to represent His being by images. In chapter three Paul teaches the universal sinfulness of people:

> *"[There] is not a righteous [person], not even one. ¹¹[There] is not [a person] understanding; there is not [a person] diligently seeking after God. ¹²All turned aside, together they became unprofitable; [there] is not [a person] doing goodness* [or, *what is right*]*, [there] is not so much as one.* [Psalm 14:1-3; 53:1-3; Eccl 7:20]

> ¹³*"Their throat [is] a grave having been opened; with their tongues they were deceiving; [the] venom of poisonous snakes [is] under their lips.* [Psalm 5:9, LXX; 140:3]

> ¹⁴*"Whose mouth is full of cursing and bitterness.* [Psalm 10:7, LXX]

> ¹⁵*"Their feet [are] swift to shed blood. ¹⁶Ruin and misery [are] in their ways. ¹⁷And [the] way of peace they did not know.* [Isaiah 59:7,8]

> ¹⁸*"[There] is no fear of God before their eyes."* [Psalm 36:1]

Not only is this all quoted from the OT, but this proclamation is perfectly in line with the OT teaching of the fallen nature of human beings, as is Paul writing, "For all sinned and fall short of the glory of God" (Rom 3:23).

On a side note, rather than these verses stringing together several different OT passages, it is possible all of this comes from Psalm 14:1-3 in the Septuagint (LXX), which includes all of this text as part of an "extra" passage found in the LXX. This was explained in Volume One.

In any case, later Paul asks rhetorically, "[Is He] the God of Jews only, but not also of Gentiles? Yes, also of Gentiles" (Rom 3:29). This is in line with the OT teaching that the LORD God of the Jews is the Creator of all and the God of all.

Paul recognizes nature is fallen, but also that it will be redeemed as taught in the OT:

[20]For the creation was subjected to futility, not of its will, but because of the One having subjected [it] in hope [or, confident expectation], [21]because even the creation itself will be set free from the servitude of the corruption into the liberty of the glory of the children of God. [22]For we know that all the creation groans together and labors together in birth-pains until now (Rom 8:20-22).

God is so personal and near that believers can even refer to Him as "Dad [Gr. *Abba*], Father!" (Rom 8:15). Finally, Paul proclaims the omniscience of God and how very much greater He is than us. This is again perfectly in line with the OT conception of God:

[33]O [the] depth of [the] riches of both [the] wisdom and knowledge of God! How inscrutable [are] His judgments and unfathomable His ways! (Rom 11:33).

Essential Tenets:

This epistle is so filled with affirmations of early essential tenets it will be difficult to quote all of the relevant passages; but they are so important, it is worth a try. But we will save time by not repeating the three times Paul quotes early Christian creeds in this letter. The creeds are found in 1:3-4, 4:25, 10:9. For the discussion on those passages, see Chapter One.

But here, it will be noted Jesus is called "Christ" 68 times in this epistle and "Lord" at least 18 times. It could be many more, but there are many times when it is hard to determine if "Lord" is referring to the Father or the Son. The phrase "Jesus Christ our Lord" appears four times (1:4; 5:21; 6;11; 7:25), and Jesus is called God's "Son" seven times (1:3,4,9; 5;10; 8:3,29,32).

Paul opens this epistle by associating the Father, Son, and Spirit together, while affirming the Sonship and resurrection of Jesus:

Translator's Perspective on the Canon of the NT

¹Paul, a bondservant of Jesus Christ, a called apostle, having been separated [or, appointed] to the Gospel [or, Good News] of God, ²which He promised beforehand through His prophets in [the] Holy Scriptures, ³concerning His Son, the One having come from [the] seed of David according to [the] flesh, ⁴the [One] having been designated Son of God with power according to [the] Spirit of holiness, by [the] resurrection from [the] dead, Jesus Christ our Lord, ⁵through whom we received grace and apostleship for obedience of faith among all the nations on behalf of His name, ⁶among whom you* also are called of Jesus Christ (Rom 1:1-6).

Paul then boldly declares, "For I am not ashamed of the Gospel of Christ, for it is [the] power of God to salvation to every[one] believing, both to [the] Jew first and to [the] Greek!' (Rom 1:16). Thus, Paul teaches the Gospel of salvation by faith in Christ. He elaborates on this idea as follows:

²³For all sinned and fall short of the glory of God, ²⁴being justified [or, declared righteous] freely by His grace through the redemption [or, setting free], the [one] in Christ Jesus, ²⁵whom God Himself put forward publicly [as] a mercy seat [or, propitiation] through faith in His blood, for a demonstration of His righteousness, because of the passing over of the sins having previously occurred in the tolerance of God, ²⁶for a demonstration of His righteousness in the present time, for Him to be righteous and justifying the [person] [or, declaring the [person] righteous] [who has] faith in Jesus (Rom 3:23-26).

Thus, Paul upholds the righteousness of God as taught in the OT, but he then tells us we can be redeemed by the blood of Christ. That is a central tenet of the early Church. Paul continues in this vein:

⁸But God demonstrates His own love to [or, for] us, [in] that us still being sinful [people] [fig., while we were still sinners], Christ died on our behalf!
⁹Much more then, having been justified [or, declared righteous] now by His blood, we will be saved from the wrath through Him. ¹⁰For if, being enemies, we were reconciled to God through the death of His Son, much more, having been reconciled, we will be saved by His life. ¹¹But not only [this], but we also boast [or, rejoice] in God, through our Lord Jesus Christ, through whom we now received the reconciliation (Rom 5:8-11).

Thus, Paul asserts that Christ died for our sins and that He is alive. The latter is a reference to His resurrection, which Paul declarers more clearly in the passages in which he quotes the aforementioned creeds and in the following passage:

[8]But if we died with Christ, we believe that we will also live together with Him, [9]knowing that Christ, having been raised up from [the] dead, no longer dies; death no longer exercises lordship over Him (Rom 6:8).

Paul gets very excited in proclaiming our salvation in Christ, "For the wages of sin [is] death, but the gracious gift of God [is] eternal life in Christ Jesus our Lord!" (Rom 6:23).

The reception of the Holy Spirit by believers is declared:

[5]and hope [or, confident expectation] does not disappoint [us], because the love of God has been poured out in our hearts by [the] Holy Spirit, the One having been given to us! (Rom 5:5).

Paul then describes the New Covenant:

[4]Accordingly, brothers [and sisters], you* also were made dead to the Law through the body of Christ, for you* to become [joined] to another, to the One having been raised up from [the] dead, so that we should bear fruit to God. [5]For when we were in the flesh, the passions of the sins, the ones [aroused] through the Law, were working in our body parts [in order] to bear fruit to death. [6]But now we were released from the Law, having died in [that] by which we were held, with the result that we serve as bondservants in newness of spirit [or, of [the] Spirit] and not in oldness of letter (Rom 7:4-6).

Then in a favorite passage of many Christians and one that was instrumental in this writer's conversion, Paul expands on the idea of the New Covenant, while again affirming the resurrection of Christ and explaining its importance to us, while associating the Father, Son, and Spirit together and mentioning the reception of the Spirit:

[1]Consequently, [there is] now no condemnation to the [ones] in Christ Jesus, [who] do not walk about [fig., conduct themselves] according to [the] flesh, but according to [the] Spirit [or, to spirit, and possibly elsewhere in 8:2-15]. [2]For the law of the Spirit of the life in Christ Jesus set me free from the law of sin and of death! [3]For the [thing] impossible [for] the Law [to do] in that it was weak through the flesh,

Translator's Perspective on the Canon of the NT

God [did], having sent His own Son in the likeness of sinful flesh, and concerning sin, condemned sin in the flesh, ⁴so that the righteous requirement of the Law should be fulfilled in us, the ones not walking about [fig., conducting ourselves] according to [the] flesh, but according to [the] Spirit.

⁵For the ones being according to [the] flesh set their minds on the [things] of the flesh, but the [ones] according to [the] Spirit [on] the [things] of the Spirit. ⁶For the mind-set [or, the way of thinking] of the flesh [is] death, but the mind-set of the Spirit [is] life and peace. ⁷Because the mind-set of the flesh [is] hostile towards God, for it is not subject to the law of God, nor indeed is it able [to be]. ⁸Now the ones being in [the] flesh are not able to please God.

⁹But you* are not in [the] flesh but in [the] Spirit, since [the] Spirit of God dwells in you*; but if anyone does not have [the] Spirit of Christ, this one is not His. ¹⁰But if Christ [is] in you*, on the one hand the body [is] dead because of sin, on the other hand the Spirit [is] life because of righteousness. ¹¹But if the Spirit of the One having raised up Jesus from [the] dead dwells in you*, the One having raised up Christ from [the] dead will also give life to your* mortal bodies through His Spirit indwelling in you*.

¹²So consequently, brothers [and sisters], we are debtors [fig., under obligation], not to the flesh to be living according to the flesh. ¹³For if you* live according to [the] flesh, you* are about to die; but if by [the] Spirit you* put to death the activities of the body, you* will live.

¹⁴For as many as are led by [the] Spirit of God, these are the sons [and daughters] of God. ¹⁵For you* did not receive a spirit of servitude again for fear, but you* received [the] Spirit of adoption [fig., the Spirit that legally and formally makes you sons and daughters] by whom we cry out, "Dad [Gr. *Abba*], Father!" ¹⁶That very Spirit testifies with our spirit that we are children of God! ¹⁷Now if children, also heirs—heirs on the one hand of God, joint-heirs on the other hand with Christ, since we suffer together, so that we shall also be glorified together (Rom 8:1-17).

The indwelling of the Spirit and His importance to us is indicated by the following passages:

²⁶So in the same manner also, the Spirit helps our weaknesses; for what we will pray for, according as it is necessary [for us], we do not know, but that very Spirit makes intercession on our behalf with inexpressible groanings. ²⁷Now the One searching the hearts knows what [is] the mind-set of the Spirit, because according to God He pleads on behalf of [the] holy ones (Rom 8:26f).

¹⁷For the kingdom of God is not eating and drinking, <u>but</u> righteousness and peace and joy in [the] Holy Spirit (Rom 14:17).

In another favorite passage of many Christians, Paul declares Christ died, rose again, is now in heaven (Thus, implying His ascension), and is now our Intercessor:

³¹What then will we say about these [things]? Since God [is] for us [or, on our side], who [is] against us? ³²The [One] who indeed did not spare His own Son, <u>but</u> [who] handed Him over on behalf of us all, how will He not also with Him graciously give to us all [things]? ³³Who will bring a charge against [the] chosen ones of God? God [is] the One justifying [or, declaring righteous]. ³⁴Who [is] the one condemning? Christ [is] the One having died, but rather also, having been raised up, who is also at [the] right hand of God, who also intercedes on our behalf (Rom 8:31-34).

Then Paul declares both the humanity and deity of Christ:

⁵of whom [are] the fathers and out of whom [is] the Christ [or, the Messiah] (the [ancestral descent] according to [the] flesh), the One being over all God blessed into the ages! [fig., forever!] So be it! (Rom 9:5).

Finally, the Father, Son, and Spirit are associated together, while again affirming the resurrection of Jesus:

¹¹But if the Spirit of the One having raised up Jesus from [the] dead dwells in you*, the One having raised up Christ from [the] dead will also give life to your* mortal bodies through His Spirit indwelling in you* (Rom 8:25).

³⁰Now I call on [or, plead with] you*, brothers [and sisters], through our Lord Jesus Christ, and through the love of the Spirit, to strive together with me in prayers on behalf of me to God (Rom 15:30).

Thus, this epistle strongly affirms almost all of the essential early tenets of the Christian Church.

Appeal and Mark of Inspiration:

This letter is the closest we have to a complete systematic theology in the Bible. It lays out all of the most vital Jewish and Christians

Translator's Perspective on the Canon of the NT

teachings about God and Jesus Christ. That is what we would expect given that Paul was writing to a church he had not founded or even visited. As such, he Thus, could not assume they knew all of this doctrine. This epistle Thus, has great appeal to anyone wishing to know what the Bible teaches on these matters, both Christians and non-Christians alike. It even contains one of the most beloved verses in the Bible:

[28]But we know that to the ones loving God all things work together for good, to the ones being called according to [His] purpose (Rom 8:28).

Many have come to faith in Christ by reading this epistle, including this writer. It is also filled with sound practical advice for Christian living. This book Thus, clearly bears the marks of inspiration.

Conclusion on Romans:

Like Galatians and 1,2Cornithins, Paul's Epistle to the Romans without any doubt was written by Paul the Apostle in the first century. It is filled with sound doctrinal statements and practical advice. As such, it was rightly included without question in the canon of the NT.

Chapter Seven
The Pauline Epistles
Part Two

The previous chapter studied the Early and Major Epistles of Paul. This chapter will look at the Prison and Pastoral Epistles.

The Prison Epistles

The next four epistles are called the prison epistles because Paul was mostly likely in prison at the time of their compositions.

> Like the Epistles to the Colossians, to the Philippians, and to Philemon, that to the Ephesians was written during the leisure hours of one of the Apostle's imprisonments (Ephesians 3:1; 4:1; 6:20)" (New Advent; "Epistle to the Ephesians").

> During his confinement in Rome, from A.D. 61 to 63, while waiting the issue of his trial on the charge of being "a mover of insurrections among all the Jews throughout the world, and a ringleader of the sect of the Nazarenes" (Acts 24:5), the aged apostle composed four Epistles, to the Colossians, Ephesians, Philemon, and Philippians. He Thus, turned the prison into a pulpit, sent inspiration and comfort to his distant congregations, and rendered a greater service to future ages than he could have done by active labor (Schaff; 10682-10686).

The debate on when and where this imprisonment was will be discussed shortly. But here it will just be said these four epistles are grouped together by this background.

Ephesians

> None of the epistles which are ascribed to Paul have a stronger chain of evidence to their early and continued use than that which we know as the Epistle to the Ephesians. Leaving for the moment the question of the relation of Eph to other New Testament writings, we find that it not only colors the phraseology of the Apostolic Fathers, but is actually quoted (ISBE; "Ephesians, Epistle to the").

Translator's Perspective on the Canon of the NT

The *International Standard Bible Encyclopedia* goes on to state this epistle is quoted in 1Clement, 2Clement, Ignatius to the Ephesians, Ignatius to Polycarp, Polycarp to the Philippians, the Shepherd of Hermas, the Epistle of Barnabas, and The Didache. We will look at all of these writings of the Apostolic Fathers in Volume Three, but here it will be said these are all late first to mid-second century documents. As such. we have very early attestation to this epistle.

Destination:

Before looking at the author, it will be helpful to look at the intended audience for this letter. It is addressed "to the [ones] being in Ephesus and faithful in Christ Jesus" (1:1). But there is some question as to this ascription:

> [In Ephesus]: the phrase is lacking in important early witnesses such as P46 (3rd cent.), and *Sinaiticus* and *Vaticanus* (4th cent.), appearing in the latter two as a fifth-century addition. Basil and Origen mention its absence from manuscripts. ... Without the phrase, the Greek can be rendered, as in Col 1:2, "to the holy ones and faithful brothers in Christ" (NAB footnote).

However, the words "in Ephesus" are found in all other Greek manuscripts. Moreover:

> ... the opening line of this epistle makes little sense without the phrase ("to the saints who are and are faithful..."? or perhaps "to the saints who are also faithful," though with this sense the *ousin* is redundant and the *kai* is treated somewhat unnaturally). What is interesting is Marcion's canon list which speaks of the letter to the Laodiceans among Paul's authentic epistles. This, coupled with some internal evidence that the writer did not know his audience personally (cf. 1:15; 3:2; absence of personal names throughout), suggests that Ephesians was an encyclical letter, intended for more than one audience.
>
> Does this mean that the shorter reading is to be preferred? Yes and no. A plausible scenario is as follows, assuming Pauline authorship ... Paul sent the letter from Rome, intending it first to go to Ephesus. At the same time, Colossians was dispatched. Going counterclockwise through Asia Minor, this letter would first come to Ephesus, the port of entry, then to Laodicea, then Colossae. Tychicus' instructions may well have

been for each church to "fill in the blank" on the address line (NET Bible footnote).

The reference to Tychuis is due to him being the carrier of this letter:

[21]Now so that you* shall also know the [things] with reference to me [fig., my circumstances], what I am doing, Tychicus will disclose to you* all things, the beloved brother and faithful minister [or, deacon] in [the] Lord, [22]whom I sent to you* for this very [purpose], so that you* shall know the things concerning us, and that he shall comfort [or, encourage] your* hearts (Eph 6:21f).

The related verse from Colossians reads:

[16]And when this epistle is read aloud before you*, cause that it shall also be read aloud in the assembly of the Laodiceans, and you* should also read aloud the [epistle] from Laodicea (Col 4:16).

Thus, whether the words "in Ephesus" is original with Paul or added shortly thereafter, it is clear this letter did go to the church at Ephesus. And since Paul founded the church at Ephesus and spent three years, there, he would have been very familiar to its inhabitants. But this also most likely was a circular letter, intended for a wider audience than just the Ephesians. It probably went first to Ephesus, next to Laodicea, then to Colossae.

With going to Ephesus first and it being the largest of these cities and the one most familiar with Paul, they would have made the most copies with the name of their church inserted at the beginning; that is why it shows up in most manuscripts. But Paul had not founded or visited the latter two cities. Why all of this is important will be seen shortly.

Author:

This epistle opens with the following salutation:

[1]Paul, an apostle of Jesus Christ by [the] will of God, to the holy ones [or, saints], the [ones] being in Ephesus and faithful in Christ Jesus: [2]Grace to you* and peace from God our Father and [the] Lord Jesus Christ! (Eph 1:1f).

Paul then mentions himself once more, "For this reason, I, Paul, the prisoner of Christ Jesus on behalf of the Gentiles" (Eph 1:1). This verse also indicates why this is called a prison epistle.

Translator's Perspective on the Canon of the NT

However, some today doubt the Pauline authorship. This was seen in the quote from the *Encyclopedia Britannica* cited in the previous chapter which placed Ephesians among the "Deutero-Pauline" writings. It is to be admitted that the earlier mentioned quotes from Ephesians in the Apostolic Fathers do not specifically mention Paul (or anyone else) as the author. However, they would not have quoted it as authoritative if it had not been written by an apostle. Moreover, it is specifically indicated as being by Paul by later Church Fathers:

> By Paul, as Eph. 1:1; 3:1 prove. So Irenaeus, *Haer.* 5:2,3; 1:8,5; Clemens *Alex., Strom.* 4:65, Paed. 1:8; Origen, *Celsus* 4:211. Quoted by Valentinus A.D. 120, Eph. 3:14-18, as we know from Hippolytus, *Refut. Haeres.*, p. 193. Polycarp, Epistle to Phil., 12, witnesses to its canonicity. So Tertullian, *Adv. Marcion*, 5:17, Ignatius, Eph. 12, refers to Paul's affectionate mention of the Christian privileges of the Ephesians in his epistle (Fausset's; Ephesians, Epistle to the").

The verse from Ignatius to the Ephesians reads:

> ²You* are a passage for the ones being put to death into God. Fellow-initiates of Paul, of the one having been sanctified, of the one having born witness [or, having been martyred], worthy to be deemed blessed, whom may it be to me to be found his footsteps, when I shall attain of God; who in all his epistles makes mention of you* in Christ Jesus (IEp 1:2).

The only epistle in which Paul mentions the Ephesians by name is this one, Thus, showing the "in Ephesus" was included in the earliest copies of Ephesians and that the early Church believed Paul wrote this epistle.

But despite this early evidence, there are three reasons liberals deny of Pauline authorship of this epistle. First is supposed differences in writing style from the undoubted Pauline letters. Second is the use of words only found in this epistle. Third is a supposed more advanced theology in this epistle as compared to the undoubted Pauline letters and to Colossians, which was written about the same time as this one.

But on the first point, as just indicated, this letter was most likely a circular letter, intended for a wide audience, including churches Paul had not visited. As such, Paul would have used a slightly different writing style than if he was only writing to people he knew personally.

On the use of unique words:
The number of unique words in the book of Ephesians is exactly the same as the number of unique words (*hapax legomena*) in the book of Romans. The purpose, subject matter, recipients and occasion explain the use of new words (Bible.org; "Introduction to Ephesians").

Note that *hapax legomena* means spoke once, meaning words that only occur once in the NT or at least only once in the Pauline corpus.

On the last reason, this letter is somewhat later than other Pauline epistles, and he had more time to write it with being in prison; Thus, it is logical that it shows a more advanced and detailed theology. Moreover, being a circular letter, Paul probably wanted to articulate Christian doctrines as precisely as possible for the benefit of those whom he had not taught personally.

As for its relationship to Colossians:
Apparently, soon after writing Colossians, with time on his hands in prison, he developed these same themes. Ephesians is characterized by long sentences and developed theological concepts (1:3-14, 15-23; 2:1-10, 14-18, 19-22; 3:1-12, 14-19; 4:11-16; 6:13-20). It takes Colossians as a starting point and draws out its theological implications. Ephesians' central theme is the unity of all things in Christ, which was a contrast to the incipient Gnostic concept (Bible.org; "Introduction to Ephesians").

The reference to "long sentences" is mainly due to Ephesians 1:3-14 being just one sentence in the Greek. Most versions break it up into two or more sentences. But it is actually one long sentence and is translated as such in my ALT. Knowing this is important as possibly Paul was so outraged at the Gnostic heresies that he just couldn't speak fast enough in proclaiming the truth as he dictated this letter.

As for Gnosticism, that aberrant theology will be discussed in detail in Volume Three. But here, it will be said it is clear Paul is combating an early form of it in this letter and in Colossians, just as John did in his writings. That would be another reason why there is "advanced theology" in this letter. As is often the case in Christian history, heretical aberrations have forced Christian theologians to articulate more precisely long-standing Christian doctrines.

Finally, another objection to this letter is that it is "too similar" to Colossians. The idea is, a forger expanded upon Colossians in forging

Translator's Perspective on the Canon of the NT

this letter. But an even better explanation is that Paul wrote both letters about the same time, styling each letter to its intended audience.

Date of Writing:

The time and place of his writing Ephesians turn on the larger question of the chronology of Paul's life and the relation of the Captivity Epistles to each other; and the second question whether they were written from Caesarea or Rome. Suffice it here to say that the place was undoubtedly Rome, and that they were written during the latter part of the two years' captivity which we find recorded in Acts 28:30. The date will then be, following the later chronology, 63 or 64 AD; following the earlier, which is, in many ways, to be preferred, about 58 AD (ISBE; "Ephesians, Epistle to the").

Paul was held in prison in Caesarea after being arrested in Jerusalem when a riot almost broke out over his preaching. This scenario is recorded in Acts 21-23. Paul remained in prison in Caesarea for over two years (Acts 24:27). He was then sent by ship to Rome, the journey being recorded in Acts 27-28. Paul then remained in Rome in house arrest for two years (Acts 28:30). Thus, Paul had two extended prison stays during which he could have written the prison epistles. There is much debate on which is to be preferred, with even this quote being somewhat confused as to as which is being advocated. But the evidence favors the Roman captivity.

The traditional view dates the four Epistles from the Roman captivity, and there is no good reason to depart from it. Several modern critics assign one or more to Caesarea, where he cannot be supposed to have been idle, and where he was nearer to his congregations in Asia Minor. But in Caesarea Paul looked forward to Rome and to Spain; while in the Epistles of the captivity he expresses the hope of soon visiting Colossae and Philippi. In Rome he had the best opportunity of correspondence with his distant friends, and enjoyed a degree of freedom which may have been denied him in Caesarea. In Philippians he sends greetings from converts in "Caesar's household" (Phil. 4:22), which naturally points to Rome; and the circumstances and surroundings of the other Epistles are very much alike (Schaff; 10693-10698).

However, a difference of five or six years is not really that important. A date of the late 50s to early 60s AD would be close enough.

What is important is that Paul was in prison, and this is reflected in comments in the letters. And being in prison gave Paul time to think through his theology, and this letter is filled with it.

Doctrine of God:

In the long sentence at the beginning of this letter, Paul articulates his belief in the sovereignty of God working in divine election. That doctrinal issue is addressed in my *Scripture Workbook* and will be dealt with more fully in a future book (see Appendixes Two and Three). But here, Paul states, "He chose us in Him before [the] laying of the foundation of [the] world" (Eph 1:4). This shows Paul's belief that God existed before the world was created.

Paul then calls God, "the Father of glory" (1:17). Calling God Father shows God is personal and reachable, despite being glorious. This is emphasized by declaring, "God, being rich [fig., abundant] in mercy, because of His great love [with] which He loved us" (2:4). Thus, God is full of both mercy and love.

Later Paul refers to "one God and Father of all, who [is] over all and through all and in us all" (4:6). Thus, there is one God, who is Lord of all of that exists. Then a second time Paul refers to God as "Father" (5:21).

Thus, the God of Ephesians is the only God, personal, reachable, full of love and mercy. This all fits with the conception of God seen in the OT and previous NT books.

Essential Tenets:

This letter is filled with affirmations of early Christian essential tenets. The phrase "Lord Jesus Christ" appears seven times (1:2,3,17; 3:14; 5:20; 6:23,24). Jesus is called Lord at least twice more (1:15; 3:11), though possibly many more times (e.g., 4:1,5,17). Jesus is called Christ 40 additional times (e.g. 1:1,3,5). Jesus is called the Son of God in 4:13. It is through Jesus, "we have the redemption by means of His blood, the forgiveness of transgressions" (1:7). Paul then elaborates on this theme at length:

¹And you* being dead in transgressions and sins, ²in which at one time you* walked about [fig., conducted yourselves] according to the age [fig., the practices] of this world, according to the ruler of the authority of the air [i.e., Satan; cp. 2Cor 4:4], of the spirit of the one now supernaturally working in the sons [and daughters] of disobedience; ³among whom also we at one time lived in the lusts of our flesh, doing the desires of the flesh and of the thoughts, and we were by nature children of wrath, as also the others.

Translator's Perspective on the Canon of the NT

⁴But God, being rich [fig., abundant] in mercy, because of His great love [with] which He loved us, ⁵even while we were dead in transgressions, made us to live together with Christ (by grace you* have been saved), ⁶and He raised [us] up together and seated [us] together in the heavenlies in Christ Jesus, ⁷so that He should show in the ages, the ones coming, the surpassing riches [fig., abundance] of His grace in goodness [or, kindness] toward us in Christ Jesus!
⁸For by grace you* have been saved, through faith, and this [is] not from you*; [it is] the gift of God, ⁹not by works, so that no one shall boast. ¹⁰For we are His workmanship, having been created in Christ Jesus for good works, which God prepared beforehand so that we should walk about [fig., conduct ourselves] in them (Eph 2:1-10).

In this passage, Paul proclaims all the essentials of the Christian Gospel. We are all sinners, dead in sin before God. But God by His love provided a means of forgiveness, which is by faith in Christ, not by anything we might do. Paul then specifies the means of that salvation, "But now, in Christ Jesus, you*, the ones at one time being far away, became near by the blood of Christ" (Eph 2:13). Thus, as we have seen many times, it is by the shed blood of Christ that we can be saved.
Then in another long sentence, Paul proclaims some unique Christian doctrines, probably the "advanced theology" the critics are talking about:

⁸To me, the very least of all [the] holy ones, was given this grace, to proclaim the Gospel among the Gentiles, the unfathomable riches of Christ, ⁹and to enlighten all [as to] what [is] the administration of the secret, the one having been hidden from the ages in God, the One having created all things through Jesus Christ, ¹⁰so that the many-sided [or, manifold] wisdom of God should be revealed now through the Assembly [or, Church] to the principalities and the authorities in the heavenlies, ¹¹according to [the] purpose [or, plan] of the ages, which He made in Christ Jesus our Lord, ¹²in whom we have the boldness [or, joyful sense of freedom] and the access [or, privilege to enter] in assurance by means of faith in Him (Eph 3:8-12).

Thus, Paul declares God "created all things through Jesus Christ." This seems to conflict with Genesis 1:1, which has God creating the heaven and the earth directly. But it is in line with John writing about "the Word" (Jesus), "All [things] came to be through Him, and without Him not even one thing came to be which has come to be" (John 1:3).

Why Are These Books in the Bible? Volume Two

Thus, both John and Paul see Jesus as being the means by which God created the universe. What makes this difficult is God had declared through Isaiah, "I [am] the LORD, the One completing all [things]; I stretched out the heaven **alone** and established the earth" (Isa 44:24b). And Job says about God, "⁸The One having stretched out the heaven **alone** and walking on [the] sea as on ground" (Job 9:8).

Thus, if God created the universe "alone," how could Jesus have been involved? The only plausible answer is in some way Jesus is one with God yet distinct from God. This theology is one basis for the doctrine of the Trinity. That doctrine is addressed in my *Scripture Workbook* and will be dealt with more fully in a future book (see Appendixes Two and Three). But here, it is clear that Paul like John taught the deity of Jesus.

But also here, Paul declares that is through Jesus we have full access to the Father. Thus, Jesus is the Mediator and the means by which we can have a personal relationship with God.

Paul elaborates further on this theme when he associates the Father, Son, and Spirit together:

¹⁸Because by means of Him we both have the access [or, privilege to enter] by one Spirit to the Father. So, consequently, you* are no longer strangers and foreigners, but fellow-citizens with the holy ones and [members] of the household of God, ²⁰having been built on the foundation of the apostles and prophets, Jesus Christ Himself being [the] cornerstone, ²¹in whom [the] entire building having been joined together is growing into a holy temple in [the] Lord, ²²in whom also you* are being built together into a habitation for God in the Spirit (Eph 2:18-22).

The reception of the Spirit and its importance is indicated by the following passages, while again associating the Father, Son, and Spirit together:

¹³in whom you* also, having heard the word of the truth, the Gospel [or, Good News] of your* salvation, in whom also having believed [or, having trusted], you* were sealed with the Holy Spirit of the promise, ¹⁴who is [the] down payment [or, guarantee] of our inheritance, with respect to the redemption of His acquired possession, to the praise of His glory! (Eph 1:13f).

¹⁴Because of this, I bow my knees towards the Father of our Lord Jesus Christ, ¹⁵from whom every family in [the] heavens and on earth is named, ¹⁶so that He shall grant to you*, according to the riches [fig.,

Translator's Perspective on the Canon of the NT

abundance] of His glory, to be strengthened with power by means of His Spirit in the inner person, [17][in order for] Christ to dwell in your* hearts by means of faith, having been firmly established and having been founded [or, having your* foundations laid] in love, [18]so that you* shall be fully able to comprehend with all the holy ones what [is] the width and length and depth and height [19]and to know the love of Christ [which] surpasses knowledge, so that you* shall be filled to all the fullness of God (Eph 3:14-19).

[30]And stop grieving the Holy Spirit of God, by whom you* were sealed [or, secured] for [the] day of redemption (Eph 4:30).

The unity of believers by the Spirit centered around essential tenets of the faith is declared:

[3]making every effort to be keeping the unity of the Spirit in the bond of peace: [4]one body and one Spirit, just as also you* were called in one hope [or, confident expectation] of your* calling; [5]one Lord, one faith, one baptism [or, immersion], [cp. 1Cor 12:13] [6]one God and Father of all, who [is] over all and through all and in us all (Eph 4:3-6).

The renewal by the Spirit is described:

[8]For you* were at one time darkness, but now [you* are] light in [the] Lord; as children of light be walking about [fig., conducting yourselves] [9](for the fruit of the Spirit [is] in all moral excellence [or, generosity] and righteousness and truth), [10]proving [or, discovering] what is acceptable to the Lord (5:8-10).

All of these points are in line with the early essential tenets of the Church.

Appeal and Mark of Inspiration:

Being a circular letter, Paul included much in this letter that would be of interest to a wide range of Christians. It has detailed theology, practical advice, and personal information about Paul. It even contains one of the most memorized passages of Scripture:

[8]For by grace you* have been saved, through faith, and this [is] not from you*; [it is] the gift of God, [9]not by works, so that no one shall boast (Eph 2:8f).

Many have come to understand the Gospel due to this passage. There is thus widespread appeal to this epistle, which why it was quoted so often by the Apostolic and Church Fathers. And all of this theology is in line with OT and essential tenets. This book Thus, bears the mark of inspiration.

Conclusion on Ephesians:

Liberals might doubt the Pauline authorship of this epistle, but no such doubts were articulated in the early Church. Instead, this book had widespread appeal due to it being filled with sound theology and practical advice. It was Thus, rightly included in the canon of Scripture.

Colossians

Colossians is a companion letter to Ephesians, so it will be dealt with next. Much of what was just said about Ephesians would apply to this letter.

Recipients:

Before looking at the author and theology of this book, it would be good to take a quick look at the recipients.

> The cities of Colossae, Laodicea, and Hierapolis are mentioned together as seats of Christian churches in the closing chapter of Colossians, and the Epistle may be considered as being addressed to all, for the apostle directs that it be read also in the churches of the Laodiceans (Col. 4: 13– 16). They were situated within a few miles of each other in the valley of the Lycus (a tributary of the Maeander) in Phrygia on the borders of Lydia, and belonged, under the Roman rule, to the proconsular province of Asia Minor (Schaff; 10712-10716).

> Three cities are mentioned in Colossians, Colossæ (i, 2), Laodicea, and Hierapolis (iv, 13.) These were situated about 120 miles east from Ephesus in Phrygia, in Western Asia Minor, Colossæ and Laodicea being on the banks of the Lycus, a tributary of the Mæander. All three were within two or three hours' walk from one another. Sir William Ramsay has shown that these towns lay altogether outside the routes followed by St. Paul in his missionary journeys; and it is inferred from Coloss., i, 4, 6, 7, 8 and ii, 1, that they were never visited by the Apostle himself. The great majority of the Colossian Christians

Translator's Perspective on the Canon of the NT

appear to have been Gentile converts of Greek and Phrygian extraction (i, 26, 27; ii, 13) (New Advent; "Epistle to the Colossians").

Thus, Paul never visited Colossae, and the church there was composed of mostly Gentile (non-Jewish) converts. This background will affect Paul's style of writing and what doctrines he presents to the Colossians.

Author:

The salutation to this letter reads, "Paul, an apostle of Jesus Christ by [the] will of God, and Timothy the brother" (Col 1:1). Paul then mentions himself twice more:

²³since indeed you* are continuing in the faith, having been firmly established and steadfast, and are not being shifted away from the hope [or, confident expectation] of the Gospel [or, Good News] which you* heard, the one having been preached in all the creation under heaven, of which I, Paul, became a servant (Col 1:23).

¹⁸The greeting by the hand of me, Paul; be remembering my bonds [fig., imprisonment]. Grace [be] with you*. So be it! (Col 4:18).

The last verse indicates something we have seen before. After dictating this letter, Paul always ends it with a subscription in his own handwriting. This last verse of the epistle also tells us Paul authored this letter while in prison. He mentions this one time previous to this:

²Be continuing earnestly in prayer; be staying alert in it with thanksgiving, ³praying at the same time also concerning us, that God opens to us a door for the word, to speak the secret of Christ (on account of which I have also been bound), ⁴that I shall reveal it [or, make it clear], as it is necessary [for] me to speak (Col 4:2-4).

The writing style of this letter is similar to Ephesians and the other Pauline writings, at least in this translator's opinion. It even includes a long sentence in 1:9-17. This is not quite as long as Ephesus 1:3-14, but it is similar in its pattern.

Some would object to this assessment, saying this letter has a higher quality of style, more involved sentences, and many unique words as compared to other Pauline letters. But this letter was written in prison, when Paul had more time on his hand. Thus, he would have had time to think through what he wanted to say and express it as carefully as possible. This is especially true given he had not visited this church. He would Thus, want to be as clear as possible. As for unique words, as has been asserted before, different topics require different terminology.

The theology of this letter is similar to other Pauline letters, especially Ephesians, except in it he is combatting an incipit form of Gnosticism, which apparently was affecting the Colossians. This would Thus, affect his writing style and the theology he presents. This would also explain differences in what theological points he mentions in this letter as compared to his other letters. Moreover:

> The Epistles to the Colossians and Ephesians were written about the same time and transmitted through the same messenger, Tychicus. They are as closely related to each other as the Epistles to the Galatians and to the Romans. They handle the same theme, Christ and his church; as Galatians and Romans discuss the same doctrines of salvation by free grace and justification by faith…
>
> They must stand or fall together. But they will stand. They represent, indeed, an advanced state of christological and ecclesiological knowledge in the apostolic age, but they have their roots in the older Epistles of Paul, and are brimful of his spirit. They were called forth by a new phase of error, and brought out new statements of truth with new words and phrases adapted to the case. They contain nothing that Paul could not have written consistently with his older Epistles, and there is no known pupil of Paul who could have forged such highly intellectual and spiritual letters in his name and equaled, if not out-Pauled Paul. The external testimonies are unanimous in favor of the Pauline authorship, and go as far back as Justin Martyr, Polycarp, Ignatius, and the heretical Marcion (about 140), who included both Epistles in his mutilated canon (Schaff; 10874-10877; 10895-10901).

Thus, the internal evidence points to Paul as being the author. However, despite Schaff's claim, the external evidence for Pauline authorship is not as strong as for previous letters:

> The external evidence for the Epistle to the Colossians, prior to the middle of the 2nd century, is rather indeterminate. In Ignatius and in Polycarp we have here and there phrases and terminology that suggest an acquaintance with Colossians but not much more (Ignat., Ephes., x.3, and Polyc. x.1; compare with Col 1:23). The phrase in Ep Barnabas, xii, "in him are all

Translator's Perspective on the Canon of the NT

things and unto him are all things," may be due to Col 1:16, but it is quite as possibly a liturgical formula. The references in Justin Martyr's Dialogue to Christ as the firstborn (Grk: *prototokos*) are very probably suggested by Col 1:15, "the firstborn of all creation" (Dial., 84, 85, 138). The first definite witness is Marcion, who included this epistle in his collection of those written by Paul (Tert., Adv. Marc., v. 19). A little later the Muratorian Fragment mentions Colossians among the Epistles of Paul (10b, l. 21, Colosensis). Irenaeus quotes it frequently and by name (Adv. haer., iii.14, 1). It is familiar to the writers of the following centuries (e.g. Tert., *De praescrip.*, 7; Clement of Alexandria, *Strom.*, I, 1; Orig., *Contra Celsum*, v. 8) (ISBN; "Colossians, Epistle to the").

However, "The authenticity was not questioned until the second quarter of the 19th century when Mayerhoff claimed on the ground of style, vocabulary, and thought that it was not by the apostle" (ISBN; "Colossians, Epistle to the"). Thus, despite the early evidence not being as strong in affirming the Pauline authorship as for other letters, it was never denied either. But liberal scholars are apt to deny everything, no matter how little evidence they have for their doubts.

Date of Writing:

The date for the writing of Colossians would be similar to that of Ephesians, the late 50s or early 60s AD, depending on which imprisonment they were written during.

> Once Rome is assumed to be the place of imprisonment, the question arises—which time? Acts records that Paul was imprisoned in the early 60's. However, he was released and wrote the Pastoral letters (I & II Timothy and Titus) and was then rearrested and killed before June 9, A.D. 68 (the date of Nero's suicide), probably in A.D. 67.
>
> The best educated guess for the writing of Colossians (Ephesians and Philemon) is Paul's first imprisonment, in the early 60's. (Philippians was the last of the prison letters, probably written toward the mid 60's.) (Bible.org. "Introduction to Colossians").

This quote includes information that will be investigated when we get to the next two Prison Epistles and the Pastoral Epistles.

Doctrine of God:

The first verse of this epistle has already been quoted in regards to the author, but it is also important in regards to Paul's conception of God, "Paul, an apostle of Jesus Christ by [the] will of God, and Timothy the brother (Col 1:1)." So Paul views God as being in control of his life.

Paul then refers to "the invisible God" (Col 1:15b), "God the Father" (2:9b), and "the supernatural working of God" (Col 2:12b). Thus, for Paul, God is an incorporeal Being, He is personal and reachable, and He works miracles.

Paul then writes, "because of which [things] the wrath of God is coming upon the sons and daughters] of disobedience" (Col 3:6). Thus, God shows wrath towards sinners. But this is balanced with the following, "And let the peace of God be exercising control in your* hearts, to which also you* were called in one body, and become thankful" (Col 3:15). Thus, God can also be the source of inner peace for those who trust and obey Him.

God is also the One to thank for whatever abilities we have in life:

And every[thing], whatever you* shall be doing in word or in deed, [be doing] all [things] in [the] name of [the] Lord Jesus, giving thanks to the God and Father through Him (Col 3:17).

God can also be prayed to, and He answers prayer by sovereignly working in our lives:

²Be continuing earnestly in prayer; be staying alert in it with thanksgiving, ³praying at the same time also concerning us, that God opens to us a door for the word, to speak the secret of Christ (on account of which I have also been bound), ⁴that I shall reveal it [or, make it clear], as it is necessary [for] me to speak (Col 4:2).

Paul closes this epistle the same way he opens it, with a reference to God being in control:

¹²Epaphras greets you*, the [one] from you* [or, [who is one] of you*], a bondservant of Christ, always striving earnestly on your* behalf in his prayers, so that you* shall stand perfect and having been fulfilled [or, completed] in all [the] will of God (Col 4:12).

That is not a lot of information about God, but it is all in line with the OT conception of God.

Translator's Perspective on the Canon of the NT
Essential Tenets:

Like Ephesians, this letter is filled with affirmations of essential tenets. Paul refers to Jesus as "the Lord Jesus Christ" twice in this epistle, both in the opening (Col 1:2,3). He calls Jesus "Lord" at least three more times (Col 2:6,17; 3:24) and Christ 24 more times (e.g., Col 1:3,4,7,24,27,28). Jesus is called the Son of God's love (Col 1:13).

Then in the second half of the aforementioned long sentence, Paul writes:

[12]giving thanks to the Father, the One having qualified us for the portion of [or, to share in] the inheritance of the holy ones in the light, [13]who rescued us out of the dominion of the darkness and transferred [us] into the kingdom of the Son of His love, [14]in whom we have redemption, the forgiveness of sins, [15]who is [the] image of the invisible God, firstborn of [fig., existing before] all creation; [16]because by Him all [things] were created, the [things] in the heavens and the [things] on the earth, the visible [things] and the invisible [things], whether thrones or dominions or rulers or authorities; all such [things] have been created through Him and for Him, [17]and He is before all [things] and all [things] are held together by Him (Col 1:12-17).

Here Paul asserts that Jesus is the source of redemption and forgiveness of sins. He is the image of God. He existed before all of creation, and it was by Jesus that God created (a concept we have seen before). He is the upholder of all of creation.

[18]And He is the head of the body, the Assembly [or, Church]; who is [the] beginning, [the] firstborn [fig., the first to be raised] from the dead, so that He shall be having preeminence in all [things]; [19]because in Him all the fullness [of the Godhead] was pleased to dwell [cp. Col 2:9], [20]and through Him to reconcile all [things] to Himself, having made peace through the blood of His cross, through Him, whether the [things] on the earth or the [things] in the heavens (Col 1:18-20).

Here, Jesus was the first to be raised from the dead, implying that others will be later. The fullness of God dwells in Jesus. And it is by His death on the cross that we are reconciled to God.

[21]And you* at one time having been alienated and enemies in the mind by your* evil works, yet now He reconciled [you*] [22]in the body of His flesh through His death, to present you* holy and unblemished [fig., without fault] and free from reproach before Him, [23]since indeed you* are continuing in the faith, having been firmly established and

steadfast, and are not being shifted away from the hope [or, confident expectation] of the Gospel [or, Good News] which you* heard, the one having been preached in all the creation under heaven, of which I, Paul, became a servant (Col 1:21-23).

Here Paul refers to "the body of His flesh through His death." Thus, Paul affirms the full humanity of Jesus, and His death in His body was the source of our reconciliation to God.

⁹Because in Him dwells all the fullness of the Godhead [or, Deity] bodily, ¹⁰and you* have been made full [or, have been completed] in Him, who is the Head of every rule and authority, ¹¹in whom you* also were circumcised with a circumcision done without human hands, by the putting off of the body of the sins of the flesh by the circumcision of Christ, ¹²having been buried together with Him in baptism [or, immersion], in which you* also were raised together [with Him] through faith in the supernatural working of God, the One having raised Him from the dead (Col 2:9-12).

In verse nine, Paul declares in no uncertain terms the full deity and full humanity of Jesus. Then in verse twelve he affirms that Jesus was raised from the dead, and in verses 10-12 he refers to the New Covenant of the inner change brought about in the believer.

¹³And you*, being [spiritually] dead in [or, because of] the [or, your*] transgressions and the uncircumcision of your* flesh, He made you* alive together with Him, having forgiven us all these [or, our] transgressions, ¹⁴having blotted out [or, canceled] the handwritten record of debts in the ordinances against us, which was contrary to us, and He has taken it out of the way, having nailed it to the cross; ¹⁵having disarmed the rulers and the authorities, He publicly disgraced them, having triumphed over them by it [i.e., the cross] (Col 2:13-15).

Christ's death on the cross is the means by which we can be forgiven and are no longer bound by legalistic attempts to make ourselves right with God. By "the rulers and the authorities" is probably meant evil spiritual forces. These were disarmed by Christ's death as well.

¹⁷And every[thing], whatever you* shall be doing in word or in deed, [be doing] all [things] in [the] name of [the] Lord Jesus, giving thanks to the God and Father through Him (Col 3:17).

Translator's Perspective on the Canon of the NT

Here Paul asserts that Jesus is our Mediator before the Father. And finally, he indicates it is by the Spirit that believers love one another:

⁷just as you* also learned from Epaphras, our beloved fellow-bondservant, who is a faithful [or, trustworthy] servant [or, minister] of Christ on your* behalf, ⁸the one having also declared [or, made clear] to us your* love in [the] Spirit (Col 1:7).

Thus, Paul affirms many early essential tenets in this short epistle.

Appeal and Mark of Inspiration:

This epistle had great appeal at the time as it directly confronted the incipit Gnostic heresy that was then growing.

> The Colossian heresy was an Essenic and ascetic type of Gnosticism; it derived its ritualistic and practical elements from Judaism, its speculative elements from heathenism …
>
> It taught an antagonism between God and matter and interposed between them a series of angelic mediators as objects of worship. It Thus, contained the essential features of Gnosticism, but in its incipient and rudimental form, or a Christian Essenism in its transition to Gnosticism. In its ascetic tendency it resembles that of the weak brethren in the Roman congregation (Rom. 14: 5, 6, 21). Cerinthus, in the age of John, represents a more developed stage and forms the link between the Colossian heresy and the post-apostolic Gnosticism (Schaff; 10748-10755).

Gnosticism was a very dangerous heresy that confronted the early Church, and some today still believe some of its teachings. As such, this epistle is still relevant today. This epistle also contains much practical advice and even an earthshaking pronouncement:

⁹Stop lying to one another, having put off the old [or, former] person with his practices, ¹⁰and having put on the new [person], the [one] being renewed in full [or, true] knowledge according to [the] image of the One having created him, ¹¹where there is not Greek and Jew, circumcision and uncircumcision, foreigner, Scythian, bondservant, [or] free person, but Christ [is] all [things] and in all [things]. [cp. Gal :28] (Col 3:9-11).

This sense of equality was unknown in the ancient world, but Paul asserts it here and in the cross-referenced verse in Galatians. This would be one more evidence that Paul is the author of both letters. But here it shows the universal appeal of this letter. And the wealth of sound doctrinal information and practical advice means it bears the mark of inspiration.

Conclusion on Colossians:

Some today might doubt the Pauline authorship of this letter, but none did in the early Church. It was clearly written in the first century, and it is filled with sound doctrinal and practical assertions, has widespread appeal, and was universally accepted as authoritative in the early Church. It was Thus, rightly included without question in the canon of the NT.

Philippians

Paul's epistle to the Philippians is the next prison epistle to be studied. Before getting to the discussion, some information about Philippi would be interesting:

> Philippi was a city of Macedonia, founded by and called after Philip, the father of Alexander the Great, in a fertile region, with contiguous gold and silver mines, on the banks of a small river and the highway between Asia and Europe, ten miles from the seacoast. It acquired immortal fame by the battle between Brutus and Mark Antony (b.c. 42), in which the Roman republic died and the empire was born. After that event it had the rank of a Roman military colony, with the high-sounding title, "Colonia Augusta Julia Philippensis." Hence its mixed population, the Greeks, of course, prevailing, next the Roman colonists and magistrates, and last a limited number of Jews, who had a place of prayer on the riverside. It was visited by Paul, in company with Silas, Timothy, and Luke, on his second missionary tour, in the year 52, and became the seat of the first Christian congregation on the classical soil of Greece (Schaff; 10936-10942).

Author:

The salutation to this letter reads:

[1]Paul and Timothy, bondservants of Jesus Christ, To all the holy ones [or, saints] in Christ Jesus, the ones being in Philippi, with [the] overseers and ministers [or, deacons] (1:1).

Translator's Perspective on the Canon of the NT

This is the only time Paul mentions his name in this epistle. But Philippians is among the seven letters that *Encyclopedia Britannica* and PBS calls "undoubted letters" as to their Pauline authorship, and there is little doubt that Paul wrote it.

> The genuineness of the epistle is very generally admitted today. It was in the Canon of Marcion. Its name occurs in the list on the Muratorian Fragment. It is found in both the Peshitta and the Old Latin versions. It is mentioned by Polycarp and quoted in the letter of the churches of Lyons and Vienne, in the Epistle of Diognetus, and in the writings of Irenaeus and Clement of Alexandria (ISBN; Philippians, Epistle to the").

Polycarp also wrote a letter to the Philippians in 98-117 AD. His epistle states:

> [2]For neither I, nor any another like to me, is able to follow after the wisdom of the blessed and glorious Paul, who having been among you* according to the face [fig., in the presence] of the people at that time, accurately and steadfastly taught the word concerning truth, who also absent from you*, wrote an epistle, into which if you look closely into, you will be able to be built up in the faith having been given to you* (Pol 3:2).

The only issue in regards to Paul's letter is some think it was not originally just one letter but pieced together from fragments of three letters. This is due to the way it seems to jump from topic to topic, with little logical progression. This is seen, for instance, in the third chapter beginning with "Finally" in most versions, but the letter is only halfway through. But a look at the background to this letter explains this style of the letter. Paul's ministry in Philippi is recorded in Acts 16. It begins:

> [11]Therefore, having set sail from Troas, we sailed a straight course to Samothrace, and on the next [day] to Neapolis, [12]and from there to Philippi, which is a first [fig., prominent] city of the district of Macedonia, a [Roman] colony. Then we were staying in that very city [for] several days. [13]And on the Sabbath day we went forth outside of the city, by a river, where prayer was customarily to be [fig., made]; and having sat down, we began speaking to the women having assembled.

Apparently, there was not sufficient Jewish men in the city for a synagogue, but Paul found some Jewish women and preached Christ to them, and they believed in the Lord. But then Paul cast a spirit of divination out of a slave girl, which outraged her owners. They incited the townspeople against them, which led to Paul and Silas being beaten then imprisoned. But God caused an earthquake, which could have allowed Paul, Silas, and the other prisoners to escape. But they did not flee, which led to the conversion of the jailer and his family. Paul then left Philippi, but he visited it three times afterwards. But there never were very many Christian converts in the city, just as there were not very many Jews. That is why this letter is addressed to "the ones being in Philippi" rather than "the church at Philippi." Compare, for instance, Paul's salutation in 1Corinthians, "To the assembly [or, church] of God, the one being in Corinth" (1:2).

Paul's later visits show he was affectionate towards this small group of believers, and this shows in the letter. It is informal in style, and this explains why it jumps at times. When writing to friends, people do not usually think through their letter before composing it but simply write down thoughts as they come to them.

> It is a simple letter to personal friends. It has no theological discussions and no rigid outline and no formal development. It rambles along just as any real letter would with personal news and personal feelings and outbursts of personal affection between tried friends. It is the most spontaneous and unaffected of the Pauline Epistles (ISBN; Philippians, Epistle to the").

> The Epistle reflects, in familiar ease, his relations to this beloved flock, which rested on the love of Christ. It is not systematic, not polemic, nor apologetic, but personal and autobiographic, resembling in this respect the First Epistle to the Thessalonians, and to some extent, also, the Second Epistle to the Corinthians. It is the free outflow of tender love and gratitude, and full of joy and cheerfulness in the face of life and death (Schaff; 10957-10960).

As for Philippians 3:1 beginning with "Finally," the Greek is literally "the rest" and thus it is rendered as "[As to] the rest" in the ALT. Again, Paul is dictating ideas as they come to him, without thinking through how much more he has to say.

Date of Writing:

This epistle was clearly written from prison, as Paul refers to his "bonds" four times, all in the first chapter:

Translator's Perspective on the Canon of the NT

⁷just as it is right for me to be thinking this about all of you*, because I hold you* in my heart, both in my bonds [fig., imprisonment] and in the defense and confirmation of the Gospel, all of you* being fellow-partakers with me of grace (Phil 1:7).

¹²Now I want you* to be knowing, brothers [and sisters], that the [things] with reference to me [fig., my circumstances] have come rather for [the] progress of the Gospel, ¹³with the result that my bonds have become known [as being] in Christ in the entire Fortified Palace [or, among the whole palace guard] and to all the rest, ¹⁴and the majority of the brothers [and sisters] in [the] Lord, having gained confidence by my bonds [fig., imprisonment], are all the more bold to be fearlessly speaking the word. ¹⁵Some indeed even because of envy and strife [or, rivalry], but some also because of goodwill [or, good motives] are preaching Christ. ¹⁶The [former ones] indeed proclaim Christ out of selfish ambition [or, self-interest], not sincerely [or, with a pure motive], supposing to be causing me to be experiencing distress in my bonds, ¹⁷but the [latter ones] out of love, knowing that I stand [or, am appointed] for [the] defense of the Gospel (Phil 1:12-17).

There is again debate if this was Paul's imprisonment in Caesarea or in Rome. If the former, this letter would have been written in the late 50s AD, if the latter, about 63-64 AD. But either way, it would have been near the end of the imprisonment, as there was time for the Philippians to hear about Paul's situation and to send him support, "⁴Nevertheless, you* did well, having shared with [me] in my affliction [or, hardship]" (Phil 4:14).

Doctrine of God:

Most of the converts in Philippi were Jews, so they would have already had a correct conception of God. And having visited Philippi on several occasions, Paul would have had much time to teach the converts more in this regard. He Thus, assumes they understand the true nature of God in this letter. With that assumption, Paul mostly focuses on the personal and caring nature of God in this letter. Paul opens this letter by praying:

²Grace to you* and peace from God our Father and [the] Lord Jesus Christ. ³I give thanks to my God upon every remembrance of you*, ⁴always, in my every petition on behalf of all of you*, making petition with joy, ⁵because of your* fellowship in [or, contribution to] the Gospel [or, Good News] from [the] first day until now, ⁶having been confident [or, persuaded] of this very [thing], that the One having begun

Why Are These Books in the Bible? Volume Two

a good work in you* will complete [or, perfect] [it] until [the] day of Christ Jesus (Phil 1:2-6).

Thus, Paul sees God as the source of grace and peace, and God can be prayed to; He is thus personal and reachable. He works a good work in us. Paul continues this prayer for five more verses, showing his affection for the Philippians. He ends the prayer by writing, "to [the] glory and praise of God" (1:11b). Thus, Paul sees God as One worthy of glory and praise.

He then writes, "³for God is the One supernaturally working in you* both to be desiring and to be supernaturally working for the sake of His good pleasure" (Phil 2:13). Paul Thus, teaches that God can do supernatural works and works within us to bring about His will for us. Thus, Paul clearly believes in a sovereign God.

²⁵And I considered [it] necessary to send to you* Epaphroditus, my brother and fellow-worker and fellow-soldier, but your* apostle [or, messenger] and public servant to my need, ²⁶since he was longing for you* all, and being distressed, because you* heard that he was sick. ²⁷For indeed he was sick nearly to death, but God showed him mercy, but not him only, but also me, so that I would not have sorrow upon sorrow (Phil 3:25-27).

Here Paul sees God as the source of health and healing. Notice also again Paul's affection toward the Philippians.

⁷And the peace of God, the [peace] surpassing all understanding, will guard [or, protect] your* hearts and your* thoughts in Christ Jesus (Phil 4:2).

the God of peace will be with you* (Phil 4:9b).

Paul again declares that God is the source of inner peace.

¹⁹Now my God will fully supply all your* need [or, your* every need] according to His riches [fig., abundance] in glory in Christ Jesus! ²⁰Now to our God and Father [be] the glory into the ages of the ages! [fig., forever and ever!] So be it! (Phil 4:19f).

Paul closes this epistle by declaring God is the One who supplies our needs and by calling God "Father" Thus, showing again He is personal and cares for us.

Translator's Perspective on the Canon of the NT

This is not a lot of information about God, but it all fits with the OT conceptions of a personal, caring, reachable God.

Essential Tenets:

Since Paul had visited this city, he would have taught the Philippians the essentials of the Christian faith. But despite this and despite this letter being only four chapters, this letter contains much information in line with the early essential tenets. Paul uses the phrase "Lord Jesus Christ" three times (1:2; 3:20; 4:23). He clearly calls Jesus "Lord" at least three more times (2:11,19; 3:8) and possibly many more times (e.g. 4:1-5). He calls Jesus "Christ" 35 more times (e.g. 1:1,6,8).

Paul refers to "the day of Christ" (1:10b), which is probably a reference to the Second Coming, which he surely would have taught them about and thus they would have understood this reference.

Paul then presents one of the most powerful passages in the NT in regards to the nature of Jesus:

⁵Indeed, be letting the frame of mind [or, attitude] be in you* which [was] also in Christ Jesus, ⁶who existing in the nature of God, did not consider being equal to God something to be held onto, ⁷but He emptied Himself, having taken the nature of a bondservant, having come to be in the likeness of people, ⁸and having been found in appearance as a person, He humbled Himself, having become obedient to the point of death—even of death of a cross. ⁹And so God highly exalted Him [or, put Him in the most important position] and gave to Him a Name, the [Name] above every name, ¹⁰so that at the Name of Jesus every knee shall bow, of heavenly [ones] and of earthly [ones] and of [ones] under the earth, ¹¹and every tongue [fig., person] shall confess that Jesus Christ [is] Lord to [the] glory of God [the] Father! [cp. Isaiah 45:23; Rom 10:9] (Phil 2:5-11).

In this passage, Paul without any doubt declares the full humanity and the full deity of Jesus. He also affirms the death of Jesus on the cross. Then in the following passage Paul again affirms the death of Christ, and His resurrection. He also affirms that salvation is by faith in Christ and the future resurrection of people in general:

⁷But whatever [things] were gains to me, these I have considered loss for the sake of Christ. ⁸But indeed, therefore, I also consider all [things] to be loss for the sake of the surpassing excellency of the knowledge of Christ Jesus my Lord, for the sake of whom I suffered loss of all [things], and I consider them to be garbage, so that I shall gain Christ ⁹and be found in Him, not having my righteousness, the

[righteousness] from [the] Law [fig., legalistic, outward righteousness], but the [righteousness] by means of faith in Christ, [which is] the righteousness from God on the basis of faith; [10][so as] to know Him and the power of His resurrection and the fellowship of His sufferings, being conformed to His death, [11]if in some way I shall arrive [fig., attain] to the resurrection of the dead (Phil 3:7-11).

Next, Paul again refers to the cross of Christ and declares Jesus is the Savior and is coming again. He also again alludes to the general resurrection:

[18]For many walk about [fig., conduct themselves] of whom frequently I was speaking to you*, but now also weeping I speak [of] the enemies of the cross of Christ, [19]whose end [is] destruction, whose god [is] the belly [fig., their appetites; cp. Rom 16:18] and [whose] glory [is] in their shame, who set their minds on the [things] of the earth. [20]For our citizenship exists in [the] heavens, from where also we eagerly await a Savior, [the] Lord Jesus Christ, [21]who will transform the body of our humble state for it to become similar in nature [or, conformed] to the body of His glory, according to the supernatural working [or, energy] [by which] He also is able to subject all [things] to Himself (Phil 3:18-21).

Paul also affirms the working of the Spirit in his life and that of all believers:

For I know that this will lead to deliverance for me, through your* petition and [the] provision of the Spirit of Christ Jesus (Phil 1:19).

[3]For we are the [true] circumcision, the [ones] sacredly serving in [or, by] the Spirit of God and boasting in Christ Jesus and not having placed trust [or, not having confidence] in [the] flesh, [4]although I have trust [or, confidence] also in [the] flesh (Phil 3:3f).

Note the use of "Spirit of Christ" then "Spirit of God," showing the unity of the Son and the Father. There is then yet another reference to the Second Coming, "Let your* gentleness [or, considerateness] be known to all people. The Lord [is] near!" (Phil 4:5).

Paul ends this letter by ascribing grace to Jesus, just as he did to God at the beginning of the letter. Thus, Paul again equates God and Christ, "The grace of the Lord Jesus Christ [be] with you* all. So be it!" (Phil 4:23).

Translator's Perspective on the Canon of the NT
Appeal and Mark of Inspiration:
The personal, affectionate nature of this letter gives us an insight into the person of Paul. He was bold and tough when he needed to be, but he could also be tender and compassionate. This is a good example for all of us. Along with these personal insights, this letter presents God as being compassionate towards us and provides insightful passages about Jesus, His nature, work on the cross, and Second Coming. This letter even contains one of the better known and beloved verses of the Bible:

[13]I am capable of all [things] in Christ, the One strengthening me! (Phil 4:13).

This letter Thus, has widespread appeal. All of this information is also in line with early essential tenets and is vital for Christian belief and living the Christian life. This epistle Thus, bears the mark of inspiration.

Conclusion on Philippians:
This letter was written by Paul the apostle in the first century. With its personal nature, sound doctrine, and practical advice, it has great appeal and bears the mark of inspiration. It was Thus, rightly included in the canon of the NT with no question as to its genuineness.

Philemon

We now come to the shortest of Paul's epistles. With being so short, you would think it would be little known and thus have its authenticity questioned, but that was not the case in the early Church or even today.

Author:
The salutation to this letter, is, "[1]Paul, a prisoner of Christ Jesus, and Timothy the brother, To Philemon our beloved [brother] and co-worker (Phlm 1:1)." Paul then refers to himself twice more:

[8]For this reason, having much boldness [or, confidence] in Christ to be commanding you [to be doing] the proper [thing], [9][yet] on account of love I rather appeal, being such a one as Paul, an old man, but now also a prisoner of Jesus Christ (Phlm 1:8).

[19]I, Paul, wrote [this] with my [own] hand (Phlm 1:19a).

Why Are These Books in the Bible? Volume Two

In the first verse, Paul tells us he is in prison. The last reference is interesting as it asserts Paul wrote this entire letter himself, rather than dictating it and just adding his signature at the end as is his usual practice. This letter was universally attested in the early Church as being written by Paul.

> Authenticity of. Origen (*Hom.* 19, Jer. 1:185) quotes it as Paul's. Tertullian (*Marcion* 5:21), "the brevity of this epistle is the cause of its escaping Marcion's falsifying hands." Eusebius (E. H. 3:25) ranks it among "the universally acknowledged (*homologoumena*) epistles of the canon." Jerome (*Prooem.* Philem. iv. 442) argues against those who thought its subject beneath an apostle. Ignatius (Eph. 2, Magnes. 12) alludes to Philem. 1:20. Compare Polycarp 1 and 6. The catalogues, the Muratori Fragment, the list of Athanasius (Ep. 39), Jerome (Ep. 2 ad Paulin.), the council of Laodicea (A.D. 364), and the third of Carthage (A.D. 397) support it. Its brevity accounts for the few quotations from it in the fathers. Paley (*Hor. Paul.*) shows its authenticity from the undersigned coincidences between it and the epistle to the Colossians (ISBE; "Philemon, Epistle to").

Philemon 1:20 referred to in this quote reads, "Yes, brother, may I have profit of you [or, let me benefit from you] in [the] Lord. Refresh my bowels [fig., heart] in [the] Lord." The passages from Ignatius are as follows:

[1]Now concerning my fellow-bondservant Burrhus, your* minister [or, deacon] according to God, being blessed in all [things], I pray [for] him to continue, for your* honor and of the overseer. And Crocus also, worthy of God and you*, whom I received [as] an example of love from you*; he refreshed me according to all things, as also him may the Father of our Lord Jesus Christ refresh; together with Onesimus and Burrhus and Euplus and Fronto, through whom I saw all of you* according to love (IEp 2:1).

[1]May I have joy of you* according to all [or, in all respects], if indeed I shall be worthy! For though I also have been bound, I am not compared to one of you* having been released. I know that you* were not puffed up, for you* have Jesus Christ in yourselves (IMg 12:1a).

In the first mentioned passage, Ignatius refers to being "refreshed" by Crocus. That is an allusion at best. But the verse does show Onesimus was still around and thus could be asked about this letter, as he was the

Translator's Perspective on the Canon of the NT

carrier, along with of Colossians (4:9). This quote Thus, gives support to both of these epistles. But I cannot figure out where the allusion is in the second passage.

But still, the various early canonical lists all include this letter. Moreover, there was never any denial this letter was not written by Paul in the early Church, nor is there today.

The reason for this is universal acceptance is rather simple—why forge such a meaningless letter? It also bears many similarities of style to Paul's other letters, especially Philippians, which was written soon afterwards and is unquestioned, as we just saw. Thus, this letter is accepted on its coattails so to speak.

Date of Writing:

This letter was written at the same time as Colossians. This can be known by what we just saw, Onesimus was the carrier for both.

> Place and time of writing. The same bearer Onesimus bore it and epistle to Colossians; in the latter (Col. 4:7-9) Tychicus is joined with Onesimus. Both address Archippus (Philem. 1:2; Col. 4:17). Paul and Timothy stand in both headings. In both Paul writes as a prisoner (Philem. 1:9; Col. 4:18). Both were written at Rome during the early and freer portion of Paul's first imprisonment, A.D. 62; in Philem. 1:22 he anticipates a speedy release (Fausset's; Philemon, Epistle to").

Doctrine of God:

Being so short and personal, there are only two mentions of God in this letter:

> ³Grace to you* and peace from God our Father and [the] Lord Jesus Christ! ⁴I give thanks to my God, always making mention of you in my prayers (Phlm 1:3f).

But these two references are important. They show Paul's belief God is Father and thus is personal and reachable, so He can be thanked for good things in life and prayed to.

Essential Tenets:

In the preceding quoted passage, Jesus is called "Lord Jesus Christ." He is so called in 1:15 as well. He is called Lord at least one more time (1:5) and Christ five more times (1:1,6,8,9,23). But that is it as far as essential tenets go.

But such a lack of theology is what we would expect in such a short and personal letter. Paul knew Philemon personally, and the purpose of this letter was not to teach but to encourage Philemon to do the right thing, as we will see next.

Appeal and Mark of Inspiration:

You would think there would not be much widespread appeal to this letter given that it is a personal letter written to encourage Philemon to do one thing. But the thing Paul was encouraging him to do was to set his runaway slave Onesimus free.

[15]For perhaps because of this, he departed for an hour [fig, for a while], so that you shall be having him eternally, [16]no longer as a bondservant [or, slave], but above a bondservant, a beloved brother, especially to me, but how much more to you, both in [the] flesh and in [the] Lord. [17]Therefore, since you have fellowship with me, receive him as me. [18]But since he wronged you or owes [something], be charging this to me [or, to my account] (Phlm 1:15-18).

Paul has often been criticized for his comments about slavery in his other letters. And a full discussion of that subject is out of the scope of this book, but I address it in my *Scripture Workbook* and hope to do so in more detail it in a future book. But it will be said here; this passage shows Paul really did not approve of slavery, and it is one reason the early Church was opposed to slavery. Thus, despite its brevity, this letter is very important.

But an interesting question is why this letter was even preserved. For the other Pauline letters, the answer is rather obvious. The letters were written to churches or groups of people. They were Thus, initially read to many people at once. With the contents having widespread appeal, they were then copied and distributed to other churches. But this letter was written to one person and addressed one issue relevant to that person alone. Why then was it copied and distrusted?

A possible answer is who carried it to Philemon, Onesimus and Tychicus, who also carried Colossians (Col 4:7,9). Thus, copies of this letter were probably made when Colossians was copied.

Conclusion on Philemon:

This letter was certainly written by Paul in the first century. The letter-carrier Onesimus was still around at the beginning of the next century to verify this. It has little to commend it as a canonical book due to its brevity, but given its unquestioned Pauline authorship, it was included in the canon on the coattails of Paul's other letters.

Translator's Perspective on the Canon of the NT
Pastoral Epistles

The Pastoral Epistles are 1Timothy, Titus, and 2Timothy. The two Timothys are generally grouped together for logical reasons, but we will separate them as Titus was written between them. They are called "Pastoral" as they deal with local church issues.

> The First and Second Epistles to Timothy, and the Epistle to Titus form a distinct group among the letters written by Paul, and are now known as the Pastoral Epistles because they were addressed to two Christian ministers (ISBE; "Pastoral Epistles").

These three letters are generally grouped together as they were written about the same time, deal with the same issues, and contain similar language and teachings. They were Thus, were most certainly written by the same person. But there is much question as to who this person was. Since the question of the one author is tied up with the date of writing, these two issues will be addressed together for all three epistles, as will the teachings or doctrines found in them.

Author and Date of Writing:
The salutations of these letters are as follows:

Paul, an apostle of Jesus Christ according to [the] command of God our Savior and of [the] Lord Jesus Christ our hope [or, confident expectation] (1Tim 1:1).

Paul, an apostle of Jesus Christ by [the] will of God, according to [the] promise of life, the [one] in Christ Jesus (2Tim 1:1).

Paul, a bondservant of God and an apostle of Jesus Christ, according to [the] faith of [the] chosen ones of God and [the] full [or, true] knowledge of [the] truth, the [one] according to godliness (Tit 1:1).

Thus, the author claims to be Paul, as in all of the previous epistles we have looked at. The early Church accepted this ascription.

On 1 and 2Timothy:
FIRST EPISTLE. Its authenticity as Paul's writing, and its canonical authority as inspired, were universally recognized by the early church with the solitary exception of the Gnostic

Marcion. 1 Timothy and 2 Timothy are in the Peshito Syriac of the second century. The Muratorian Fragment on the canon in the same century acknowledges them.

On Titus:
Genuineness. Ignatius (Tralles, 3) uses "behavior" (*katasteema*), in the New Testament found only in Titus 2:3. Clement of Rome quotes it, Ep. ad Cor. 2 Irenaeus, i. 16, section 3, calls it Paul's epistle. Theophilus (*ad Autol*. iii. 14) quotes it as Scripture. Justin Martyr in the second century alludes to Titus 3:4 (*Dial. contra Tryph*. 47). Compare Clem. Alex. *Strom*. 1:350, and Tertullian *Praescr. Haer*. 6 (Fausset's; "Timothy; Epistles to" and Titus, Epistle to").

On all epistles:
In regard to the genuineness of the epistles there is abundant external attestation. Allusions to them are found in the writings of Clement and Polycarp. In the middle of the 2nd century the epistles were recognized as Pauline in authorship, and were freely quoted.

Marcion indeed rejected them, and Tatian is supposed to have rejected those to Timothy. But, as Jerome states in the preface to his Commentary on Titus, these heretics rejected the epistles, not on critical grounds, but merely because they disliked their teaching. He says they used no argument, but merely asserted, "This is Paul's; This is not Paul." It is obvious that men holding such opinions as Marcion and Tatian held, would not willingly ascribe authority to epistles which condemned asceticism. So far, then, as the early Church can guarantee to us the authenticity of writings ascribed to Paul, the Pastoral Epistles are guaranteed (Marcus Dods, *Introduction to the New Testament*, 167; quoted in ISBE; "Pastoral Epistles").

There never was a serious doubt as to the Pauline authorship of these Epistles until the nineteenth century, except among a few Gnostics in the second century. They were always reckoned among the *Homologumena*, as distinct from the seven *Antilegomena*, or disputed books of the New Testament. As far as external evidence is concerned, they stand on as firm a foundation as any other Epistle. They are quoted as canonical by Eusebius, Tertullian, Clement of Alexandria, and Irenaeus.

Translator's Perspective on the Canon of the NT

Reminiscences from them, in some cases with verbal agreement, are found in several of the Apostolic Fathers. They are included in the ancient MSS [manuscripts] and Versions, and in the list of the Muratorian canon. Marcion (about 140), it is true, excluded them from his canon of ten Pauline Epistles, but he excluded also the Gospels (except a mutilated Luke), the Catholic Epistles, and the Apocalypse (Bible Hub; "Pastoral Episltes").

Thus, there were some at the time of the early Church that rejected the Pauline authorship, but they were heretics who did not like the teachings of these letters. That was their only reason for rejection. But those within the Church always accepted these books without question. But today there are many who deny the Pauline authorship of these books. They do so for several reasons.

The first is that the travels of Paul mentioned in these epistles do not fit into the timeline of Paul's travels as recorded in the Book of Acts.

[3]Just as I urged you to remain in Ephesus while I traveled to Macedonia, so that you should give strict orders to certain [ones] to stop teaching a different [or, heretical] doctrine (1Tim 1:3).

[5]On account of this I left you in Crete, so that you should set in order the things lacking and appoint [or, set up] elders [Gr. *presbuteros*] in every city [cp. Acts 14:23], as I commanded you (Tit 1:5).

[13]When you come, bring the cloak which I left in Troas with Carpus, and the scrolls, especially the parchments (2Tim 4:13).

[20]Erastus stayed in Corinth, but I left Trophimus sick in Miletus (2Tim 4:20).

Acts does record visits of Paul to all of these cities, but they are at different times or orders. In Acts, Paul visits Macedonia then Ephesus, not the other way around (Acts 16:6-13; 18:19). The only time in Acts he was in Crete was when he was traveling by ship as a prisoner to Rome (Acts 27), but Titus was not with him, and Paul was in no position to be appointing anyone to do anything as he was a prisoner. He was in Troas in Acts 16:8-11 and again in Acts 20:4-6 and in Miletus in Acts 20:15, but these were earlier in his life, while 2Timothy was clearly written shortly before his death (4:6-8). And with Acts ending with Paul in prison in Rome, if he was executed at that time, then there is no place for these visits to these cities. However:

To my mind the historical difficulties of the Pastoral Epistles are an argument for rather than against their Pauline origin. For why should a forger invent difficulties when he might so easily have fitted his fictions in the frame of the situation known from the Acts and the other Pauline Epistles? (Schaff, 4963-4965).

Moreover, there is strong tradition that Paul was released from that Roman imprisonment, made a fourth missionary journey, and then was re-arrested, jailed, and executed in Rome under Nero. Indications of this are seen in Romans, when Paul indicates his desire to travel to Spain (15:24,29). No such visit is recorded in Acts. In fact, the farthest west Paul gets is Rome. However, the following appears in First Clement:

> [1]But that we shall cease from ancient examples, let us come upon the having become near competitors. Let us take the noble examples of own generation. [2]Through jealousy and envy, the greatest and righteous pillars {of the Assembly} were persecuted and competed as far as death.
> [3]Let us take before our eyes the good Apostles. [4]Peter, who through unjust jealousy, endured not one or two, but many toils, and in this way having born witness [or, martyrdom; Gr., *martureo*], he went into the being owed place of glory.
> [5]On account of jealously and strife, Paul made known [the] prize of patient endurance, [6]having seven times worn bonds [or, chains], having been exiled, having been stoned, having become a preacher both in the east and in the west, he took [or, obtained] the suitable credit [or, fame] of his faith, [7]having taught the whole world righteousness and having come upon the terminus [Gr., *terma*] of the west and having borne witness under the ones ruling. In this way he was released from the world and was taken up into the holy place, having become a great [Gr. *megas*] example of patient endurance (1Clement 5:1-7).

Spain would be the "terminus of the west" to someone in Rome as Clement was when he wrote his epistle, "{The assembly [or, church] of God sojourning [at] Rome, to the assembly of God sojourning [at] Corinth" (1Clement 1:1). Thus, Clement indicates Paul did travel to Spain. But this would have had to have been after his first Roman imprisonment. This would be in line with Pauls' expectation that he would be released at that time, as he indicates in the last written of the Prison Epistles:

Translator's Perspective on the Canon of the NT

²¹For to me to be living [is] Christ and to die gain! ²²But if [I am] to be living in [the] flesh, this [will mean] to me fruit from labor [or, fruitful labor]. And what will I choose [or, prefer]? I do not know. ²³But I am hard-pressed by the two, having the desire to depart and to be with Christ, [which is] far better, ²⁴but to be remaining in the flesh is more necessary for your* sake. ²⁵And having become convinced of this, I know that I will remain and will continue with you* all, for your* progress and joy in the faith, ²⁶so that your* boasting shall be abounding in Christ Jesus in [or, because of] me by means of my arrival again to you (Phil 1:21-26).

> Moreover:
> It should also be observed that there is the direct and corroborative evidence of Paul's release, afforded by such writers as Cyril of Jerusalem, *Ephrem Syriac.*, Chrysostom and Theodoret, all of whom speak of Paul's going to Spain. Jerome (Vir. Ill., 5) gives it as a matter of personal knowledge that Paul traveled as far as Spain. But there is more important evidence still. In the Muratorian Canon, 1,37, there are the words, *profectionem Pauli ab urbe ad Spaniam proficiscentis* ("the journey of Paul as he journeyed from Rome to Spain" – quoted in ISBE; "Pastoral Epistles").

If all of this is true, then 1Timothy and Titus would have been written during this fourth missionary journey, or between 63-68 AD. Then 2Timothy would have been written shortly before Paul's death in 68 AD during a second imprisonment in Rome, as in it Paul expects to die:

⁶For I am already being poured out as a drink offering, and the time of my departure has arrived. ⁷I have fought the good fight; I have finished the course [or, race]; I have kept the faith. ⁸Finally, [there] is laid up for me the victor's wreath [or, crown] of righteousness which the Lord, the Righteous Judge, will give to me in that Day, but not only to me, <u>but</u> also to all the ones having loved His appearing (2Tim 4:6-8).

The date of 68 AD is due to the tradition that Paul was executed under Nero, shortly before his suicide in 68 AD.

> Later Christian tradition favours the view that he was executed there [Rome] (1 Clement 5:1–7), perhaps as part of the executions of Christians ordered by the Roman emperor

Nero following the great fire in the city in AD 64 (*Encyclopedia Britannica*; "Saint Paul, the Apostle").

The executions of Paul, along with Peter, under Nero are recorded by Eusebius in his *Ecclesiastical History*:

> When the government of Nero was now firmly established, he began to plunge into unholy pursuits, and armed himself even against the religion of the God of the universe.... Thus, publicly announcing himself as the first among God's chief enemies, he was led on to the slaughter of the apostles. It is, therefore, recorded that Paul was beheaded in Rome itself, and that Peter likewise was crucified under Nero. This account of Peter and Paul is substantiated by the fact that their names are preserved in the cemeteries of that place even to the present day (quoted on Bible Hub; "The Persecution under Nero").

With these dates, we can then address other objections to the Pauline authorship of these letters.

First, it is said the writing style of these epistles are different from other Pauline writings. And this is true to a degree. When translating these epistles, I noticed a somewhat different style to them than for the other ten. But it is not so pronounced so as not to be able to be explained by points that have been mentioned before in this regard.

These are the last three letters Paul wrote; Thus, it is understandable that his writing style would change as he neared the end of his life. Moreover, nine of the other ten epistles were written to churches. Philemon was the only exception. But it is unclear how much of a personal relationship Paul had with Philemon given that he is not mentioned elsewhere by Paul. But Paul had close relationships with Timothy and Titus, as can be seen from Acts and their mention elsewhere in Paul's writings. Thus, it is logical that Paul would use a different writing style when writing to two close and longtime friends than when writing to a church or someone he only knew in passing.

Related to this is there are unique words in the Pastorals that are not seen in other Pauline writings, but these words are seen in the writings of the Apostolic Fathers. Thus, it is said these books had to be written at the same time as those books.

But it has been mentioned before that the use of unique words is often due to unique subject matters. And these books are the only ones in which Paul deals with the issue of appointing of church leaders. Thus, it makes sense he would use words he had not used previously. And the Apostolic Fathers were familiar with these books, as seen by their

Translator's Perspective on the Canon of the NT

references to them, Thus, they would have picked up their terminology from Paul. Moreover:

> ... every one of Paul's Epistles has a number of peculiar words, even the little Epistle of Philemon. The most characteristic words were required by the nature of the new topics handled and the heresy combated (Schaff; 11146-11150).

The mention of church leaders is another reason it is said these books were written in the second century. It is said the style of church government indicated in these books is reflective of that of the second not first century. But in fact, by the second century there is more of a hierarchical structure to the Church than seen in the Pastorals.

To explain, Paul mentions overseers (or, bishops, Gr. *episcope* – 1Tim 3:1), ministers (or, deacons, Gr., *diakonos* - 1Tim 3:8), and elders (or, presbyters, Gr., *presybterian* – 1Tim 4:14). These positions are not in a hierarchical structure, but are used interchangeably. This is seen by the same requirements being given for each. But by the time of the Apostolic Fathers, there is a hierarchy, especially in the letters of Ignatius, with much greater veneration given to the overseer, "it is necessary to be looking upon the overseer as the Lord Himself" ... "be obeying the overseer and the body of elders with an undistracted mind" (Ignatius to the Ephesians 6:1; 20:2).

In addition:

> The Epistles have been charged with want of logical connection, with abruptness, monotony, and repetitiousness, unworthy of such an original thinker and writer as Paul. But this feature is only the easy, familiar, we may say careless, style which forms the charm as well as the defect of personal correspondence (Schaff; 11158-11160).

We saw this with Philippians. When writing to friends, less care is taken to present thoughts in a logical manner than when writing to strangers.

Finally, it is said the theology of these epistles is more advanced than that of the other Pauline letters, as is the Gnostic heresy Paul is combating. But it is that very heresy that forces Paul to articulate correct Christian doctrine in a more precise manner. And the heresy is not necessarily more advanced. Paul is simply confronting aspects of it here that he did not in Ephesians or Colossians.

> The Pastoral Epistles, like Colossians, oppose the Gnostic heresy which arose in Asia Minor during his first Roman captivity, and appears more fully developed in Cerinthus, the contemporary of John. This was acknowledged by the early Fathers, Irenaeus and Tertullian, who used these very Epistles as Pauline testimonies against the Gnosticism of their day....
>
> As to the origin of the Gnostic heresy, which the Tübingen school would put down to the age of Hadrian, we have already seen that, like its counterpart, the Ebionite heresy, it dates from the apostolic age, according to the united testimony of the later Pauline Epistles, the Epistles of Peter, John, and Jude, the Apocalypse, and the patristic tradition (Schaff; 11106-11109; 11121-11123).

The point being, with so many NT books by different authors being written to combat an early or incipit form of Gnosticism, it becomes incredulous to time and again claim these books must be "late" due to this heresy being "late." It makes more sense and better fits with all of the evidence that both the letters and the heresy were "early."

Thus, overall, there are sound answers to each of the modern-day objections. "The linguistic and other objections are by no means insurmountable and are overborne by the evidence of the Pauline spirit which animates these last productions of his pen" (Schaff, 4965-4966).

And they are just that—modern-day objections. None of these objections were ever raised in the early Church by people who spoke Greek as their native language, who were part of the early Church and thus knew its structure and the history thereof, and who were aware of the developing Gnostic heresies around them. None of this can be said of today's critics.

Doctrine of God:

These epistles contain many references to the nature of God. Paul opens 1Timothy by calling God "our Savior" and "our Father" (1Tim 1:2f). He then refers to "the glory of the blessed God" (1Tim 1:11). He then breaks out in a praise of God:

[17]Now to the King of the ages [fig., the King eternal], immortal, invisible, [the] only wise God, [be] honor and glory into the ages of the ages! [fig., forever and ever!] So be it! (1Tim 1:17).

Paul emphatically declares, "For [there is] one God: (1Tim 2:5), and he refers to "the living God" three times (1Tim 3:15; 4:10; 6:17). He then writes:

Translator's Perspective on the Canon of the NT

⁴Because every[thing] created by God [is] good, and nothing [is to be] rejected, [if] being received with thanksgiving. ⁵For it is sanctified through [the] word of God and prayer (1Tim 4:4f).

Paul refers to "God, the One giving life to all [things]" (6:13).

Lastly in 1Timothy, Paul proclaims

the blessed and only Sovereign, the King of the ones reigning as kings and Lord of the ones exercising lordship, ¹⁶the only One having immortality, dwelling in unapproachable light, whom no one of people saw nor is able to see, to whom [is] honor and eternal might [or, dominion]! So be it! (6:15b-16).

Putting this together, the God in 1Timothy is a personal God who is close enough for us for us to call Him "Father." He is our Savior. He is not dead like idols, but living. He is the King of kings, eternal, incorporeal, the Creator of all good things, the source of life, and the only One who is in control of all things, while nature is good.

Paul opens his letter to Titus by mentioning "in [the] hope [or, confident expectation] of eternal life, which, the incapable of lying God promised before eternal times (Tit 1:2). He prays for Titus to have "Grace, mercy, [and] peace from God [the] Father" (Tit 1:4). He refers to "God our Savior" (Tit 2:10) and "the saving grace of God" (Tit 2:11). And he mentions, "when the goodness [or, kindness] and the love for humanity of God our Savior appeared" (Tit 3:4).

Thus, God in Titus is trustworthy, existed before time began, the source of grace, mercy, and peace, is our Savior, and is good and love.

Paul opens 2Timothy by praying for Timothy as he did for Titus, "Grace, mercy, [and] peace from God [the] Father" (2Tim 1:2).

He then writes, "I thank God, whom I sacredly serve [as my] forefathers [did] with a pure conscience, as I have unceasing remembrance concerning you in my petitions night and day" (2Tim 1:3), and, "For God did not give us a spirit of cowardice, but of power and of love and of a sound mind [or, of self-discipline]" (2Tim 1:7).

Thus, in 2Timothy, God is the source of grace, mercy, and peace. He is to be thanked for friendships, can be payed to, and gives us power, love, and soundness of mind (or self-disciple). This all fits with the OT conception of God.

Essential Tenets:

Many early essential tenets are affirmed in these three letters. In 1Timothy, Paul refers to the "Lord Jesus Christ" four times (1:1. 5:21;

6:3,14). He calls Jesus "Lord" at least two more times (1:2,12) and "Christ" 13 more times (e.g. 1:1f,14,16). In Titus, Paul calls Jesus the "Lord Jesus Christ" once (1:4). He calls Jesus "Christ" three more times (1:1; 2:13; 3:4). In 2Timothy Paul calls Jesus the "Lord Jesus Christ" twice (4:1,22). He calls Jesus "Lord" at least one more time (1:2) and "Christ" a dozen more times (e.g. 1:1,9,10,13).

In Chapter One of this book, three passages from 1Timothy were quoted as containing early Christian creeds or hymns. They were 1Timothy 2:5f; 3:16; 6:13-16. Those will not be repeated here, except to note that those passages contained a wealth of affirmations of essential doctrines of the early Church. The following is one other important passage from 1Timothy affirming early essential tenets:

[15]Trustworthy [is] the word and worthy of all acceptance, that Christ Jesus came into the world to save sinful [people], of whom I am first [fig., the foremost of all]. [16]But because of this, I was shown mercy, so that in me first [fig., as the foremost of all] Jesus Christ should demonstrate all His patience, as a pattern for the ones about to be believing on [or, trusting in] Him to life eternal (1Tim 1:15f).

Here Paul affirms Jesus saves sinners, using himself as a foremost example. This was due to Paul having persecuted the early Church, but he was converted and saved and then preached the very Gospel he persecuted. As such, no matter what a person has done, he or she can be forgiven by believing in Jesus and thus receive eternal life.

In Titus, Paul writes:

Grace, mercy, [and] peace from God [the] Father and [the] Lord Jesus Christ our Savior!" (Titus 1:2b).

[13]waiting for the blessed hope [or, confident expectation] and appearance of the glory of our great God and Savior Jesus Christ, [14]who gave Himself on our behalf, so that He shall redeem us from all lawlessness and purify for Himself a people as His own special possession, zealous of good works! (Titus 2:13f).

[3]For we also were once foolish, disobedient, being led astray [fig., deceived], serving as bondservants to lusts and various passions [or, desires for pleasure], living in malice and envy [or, jealousy], hateful, hating one another. [4]But when the goodness [or, kindness] and the love for humanity of God our Savior appeared [5](not by means of works, the [ones] in righteousness which we did, but according to His mercy), He saved us, through a bathing of regeneration and a renewing of [the] Holy

Translator's Perspective on the Canon of the NT

Spirit, ⁶whom He poured out upon us richly, through Jesus Christ our Savior, ⁷so that having been justified [or, declared righteous] by the grace of that One [or, by His grace], we shall become heirs according to [the] hope [or, confident expectation] of eternal life! (Titus 3:3-7).

In these three passages, Paul associates God, Jesus, and the Holy Spirit together, while calling Jesus "our Savior." It should be noted that Paul had previously called God "our Savior." Then to make it clear, Paul refers to "our great God and Savior Jesus Christ." Thus, Paul affirms the deity of Jesus.

> The terms "God and Savior" both refer to the same person, Jesus Christ. This is one of the clearest statements in the NT concerning the deity of Christ. The construction in Greek is known as the Granville Sharp rule, named after the English philanthropist-linguist who first clearly articulated the rule in 1798. Sharp pointed out that in the construction article-noun-*kai*-noun (where *kai* = "and"), when two nouns are singular, personal, and common (i.e., not proper names), they *always* had the same referent. Illustrations such as "the friend and brother," "the God and Father," etc. abound in the NT to prove Sharp's point. The only issue is whether terms such as "God" and "Savior" could be considered common nouns as opposed to proper names. Sharp and others who followed (such as T. F. Middleton in his masterful *The Doctrine of the Greek Article*) demonstrated that a proper name in Greek was one that could not be pluralized. Since both "God" (*theos*) and "savior" (*soÒteÒr*) were occasionally found in the plural, they did not constitute proper names, and hence, do fit Sharp's rule. Although there have been 200 years of attempts to dislodge Sharp's rule, all attempts have been futile. Sharp's rule stands vindicated after all the dust has settled (NET Bible footnote on Titus 2:13).

In these passages, Paul also affirms Jesus' Second Coming and His death for our sins. We Thus, can be purified, righteous, and have eternal life. These are all aspects of the renewal of the Holy Spirit.

In 2Timothy 2:8-13, Paul quoted another early creed. It will not be repeated here, except to say it also is filled with affirmations of essential Christian doctrines. But following are other important passages:

¹⁴Guard the good [thing] entrusted to you through [the] Holy Spirit, the One dwelling in us (2Tim 1:14).

²To Timothy, beloved child: Grace, mercy, [and] peace from God [the] Father and Christ Jesus our Lord! (2Tim 1:2).

⁸Therefore, you shall not be ashamed of the testimony of our Lord nor of me His prisoner, <u>but</u> endure hardship along with [me in] the Gospel [or, Good News] according to [the] power of God, ⁹the One having saved us, having called [us] with a holy calling, not according to our works, <u>but</u> according to His own purpose and grace, the one having been given to us in Christ Jesus before eternal times [or, before time began], ¹⁰but having been revealed now through the appearance of our Savior Jesus Christ, on the one hand having abolished death, on the other hand having brought to light life and immortality through the Gospel, ¹¹to which I was appointed a preacher and an apostle and a teacher of Gentiles (2Tim 1:8-10).

¹⁴But <u>you</u>, be remaining in the [things] you learned and were entrusted with, knowing from whom you learned [them], ¹⁵and that from childhood you know the Sacred Writings, the ones being able to make you wise to salvation through faith, the [faith] in Christ Jesus (2Tim 3:14f).

¹Therefore, I strongly urge [you] before God and the Lord Jesus Christ, the One being about to be judging [the] living and [the] dead at His appearing and His kingdom (2Tim 4:1).

Paul first mentions the reception of the Spirit. He then links God the Father and Jesus. He then refers to "the testimony of our Lord." This is probably a reference to Jesus' trial before Pilate that was discussed in Chapter One. Paul then affirms that Jesus saves us to eternal life. He then reiterates this idea by saying we are saved by faith in Jesus, while indicating the way to salvation is known from "the Sacred Writings." This is similar to a creed saying it is "according to the Scriptures" as seen in Chapter One. Both phrases are references to the Old Testament. Finally, Paul affirms that Jesus is coming again to judge the living and the dead, a line that would later be incorporated into the Apostles' Creed.

Appeal and Mark of Inspiration:

There is much appeal to these three letters. They provide personal information about Paul, and it is fitting for the NT to include his final letter before his death, with his very personal comment about "being poured out." These letters also provide important information about the

Translator's Perspective on the Canon of the NT

requirements for church leaders that are not found elsewhere in the NT. And they are filled with important doctrinal affirmations. They also contain two very important passages:

[16]All Scripture [is] God-breathed and [is] beneficial for teaching [or, doctrine], for verification [or, reproof], for correcting faults, for instruction in righteousness [fig., the behavior that God requires], [17]so that the person of God shall be fully qualified [or, perfectly fit], having been completely equipped for every good work (2Tim 3:16f).

[17]But the Lord stood by me and gave me strength (2Tim 4:17).

The first passage is a strong affirmation of the importance of the Bible. The latter is this writer's favorite Bible verse and life motto. As someone who has suffered through many difficulties in my life and as a powerlifter, this verse has a duel meaning for me and has pulled me through many struggles. I even have this verse printed up on a T-shirt, which I wear to keep warm between lifts at powerlifting contests.

In any case, with their sound doctrine and practical advice, these epistles bear the marks of inspiration.

Conclusion on the Pastoral Epistles:

Some today might doubt the Pauline authorship of these three epistles, but only heretics did so in the time of the early Church. All of those within the Church accepted them as Pauline and authoritative from the start. They preserve several early Christian creeds and hymns, and they present many doctrinal affirmations and important practical prescriptions otherwise. They Thus, were rightly included in the canon of the NT.

Conclusion on the Pauline Epistles

From the earliest times down through the 19th century, it was universally accepted that these thirteen letters were genuine Pauline epistles. It has only been since the 1800s that this affirmation has been doubted. But after more radical assertions were shown to be false, even liberal scholars now accept that at least seven of these thirteen epistles are genuine. The seven are: Romans, 1Corinthians, 2Corinthians, Galatians, 1Thessalonians, Philippians, and Philemon. The six epistles doubted by liberals are: 2Thessalonians, Ephesians, Colossians, 1Timothy, 2Timothy, and Titus.

Even if we only accept the seven undoubted epistles, that would not change any major Christian doctrine, as these seven epistles contain affirmations of all of these doctrines. This is not to say the six doubted letters are not important; it's just that for the most part what is found in them is found elsewhere in the NT. Thus, their elimination from the canon of the NT would not fundamentally change the Christian faith.

However, this and the previous chapter have shown there is no reason to eliminate them. The early Church did its job in analyzing books before accepting them into the canon, and they knew all thirteen of these letters, the six now doubted ones included, were written by the Apostle Paul. They were all Thus, rightly included in the canon of Scripture. This universal early acceptance can be seen in the early lists of canonical books and in these thirteen letters circulating very early as a unit, as demonstrated by manuscript evidence. Moreover, the modern-day liberal arguments do not hold water when they are closely examined. As such, all thirteen of these epistles are rightly included in the canon of the NT.

Translator's Perspective on the Canon of the NT

Chapter Eight
The General Epistles
Part One

The eight general epistles are all of the letters in the NT not written by Paul. They are also not addressed to a specific church or person (except for 2,3John) as Paul's letters are. They are instead intended for a general audience, hence the moniker of "general" or "catholic" (with a small "c" meaning "universal").

We already covered the three epistles by John in Chapter Five, so in this and the next chapter we will study the remaining five general epistles. Out of these five, only one is among the *homologoumena*, or the books universally accepted in the early Church as canonical. The other four are among the *antilegomena*, or the books about which there were disagreements. We will see that the early Church was not uncritical in its acceptance of books, but it instead carefully analyzed each book before accepting it into the canon of Scriptures.

> In the oldest manuscripts except the *Sinaiticus* manuscript they [the general epistles] stand before Paul's epistles. Two were "universally acknowledged" (*homologoumena*, Eusebius): 1 Peter and 1 John. All are found in every existing manuscript of the whole New Testament (Fausset's; James, Epistle of").

> The seven Epistles of James, 1st and 2d Peter, 1st, 2d, and 3d John, and Jude usually follow in the old manuscripts the Acts of the Apostles, and precede the Pauline Epistles, perhaps as being the works of the older apostles, and representing, in part at least, the Jewish type of Christianity. They are of a more general character, and addressed not to individuals or single congregations, as those of Paul, but to a larger number of Christians scattered through a district or over the world. Hence they are called, from the time of Origen and Eusebius, Catholic. This does not mean in this connection anti-heretical (still less, of course, Greek Catholic or Roman Catholic), but encyclical or circular....

> Only two of these Epistles, the 1st of Peter and the 1st of John, belong to the Eusebian *Homologumena*, which were universally accepted by the ancient church as inspired and

Translator's Perspective on the Canon of the NT

canonical. About the other five there was more or less doubt as to their origin down to the close of the fourth century, when all controversy on the extent of the canon went to sleep till the time of the Reformation. Yet they bear the general imprint of the apostolic age, and the absence of stronger traditional evidence is due in part to their small size and limited use (Schaff; 10324-10329; 10340-10344).

Hebrews

Hebrews is probably the most important book among the *antilegomena*, as it is filled with important doctrinal information. Its primary purpose is to show that the Person and work of Jesus are "according to the Scriptures." In other words, it shows that Jesus was the fulfillment of OT declarations and types. The title reflects its purpose of bringing Hebrews (Jews) to faith in Christ. But there is also much in it of importance for us Gentiles. Why then was it disputed?

Author:

The primary reason Hebrews was disputed was questions as to its author. Unlike most other NT epistles, there is no salutation indicating the author's name. It jumps right into its presentation of theology:

¹In various parts [or, Bit by bit] and in various ways in time past, God having spoken to the fathers by the prophets, in these last days He spoke to us by [His] Son (Heb 1:1).

Who then wrote this epistle?

A considerable variety of opinions on this subject has at different times been advanced. Some have maintained that its author was Silas, Paul's companion. Others have attributed it to Clement of Rome, or Luke, or Barnabas, or some unknown Alexandrian Christian, or Apollos; but the conclusion which we think is best supported, both from internal and external evidence, is that Paul was its author (Fausset's; Hebrews; Epistle to the").

In addition to Paul, some have suggested Paul's companion Silas, Clement of Rome, Luke, or some unknown Alexandrian Christian. Some modern scholars have also proposed Priscilla as a possible author. A leading candidate is Barnabas, first suggested around AD 300 by Tertullian. Barnabas is considered a leading candidate because his association with Paul may explain some of the Pauline ideas contained within the epistle. He was also proposed early (AD 300) as a possible author. The second leading candidate is Apollos, first suggested by Martin Luther. An association with Pauline thought helps Apollos to stand out as a possible candidate for the author of the epistle. Furthermore, some of the Hellenistic "coloring" of the epistle could be accounted for since Apollos was from Alexandria (Theopedia; "Epistle to the Hebrews").

There are some references in the last chapter of this letter as to the situation of the author that support the view that Paul wrote it:

[34]For indeed you* sympathized with [me] in my chains [fig., imprisonment] (10:34a).

[23]Be knowing [that] the brother Timothy has been released, with whom, if he is coming quickly, I will see you*.
[24]Greet all the ones leading you* and all the holy ones [or, saints]. The [holy ones] from Italy greet you*. (13:23f).

Thus, the author was in prison in Italy and knew Timothy. This fits with this epistle being written during Paul's first Roman imprisonment. But the way the first verse is worded, it could be he had been imprisoned earlier in the location of the recipients but was now free and in Italy. Moreover, verse 23 seems to indicate Timothy had been imprisoned with the author, but there is no indication of Timothy being imprisoned with Paul in Acts or in Paul's letters.

Another claim to support Pauline authorship is that there are many affinities between this letter and Paul's letters. Below are some possible parallels.

---

[2]For we also have had the Gospel [or, Good News] proclaimed [to us], even as they; <u>but</u> the word [which they] heard was of no use to them, it not having been mixed with faith by the ones having heard. [3]For we, the ones having believed, enter into that rest, just as He has said, *"So in My anger I took an oath: 'They will not enter into My rest'"* [Psalm 95:11]—His works were done from [the] laying of the foundation of [the] world [or, from [the] beginning of the creation of [the] universe] (Heb 4:2f).

Translator's Perspective on the Canon of the NT

⁴just as He chose us in Him before [the] laying of the foundation of [the] world [or, from [the] beginning of the creation of [the] universe], so that we shall be holy and unblemished [fig., without fault] before Him, in love (Eph 1:4).

⁸For by grace you* have been saved, through faith, and this [is] not from you*; [it is] the gift of God, ⁹not by works, so that no one shall boast (Eph 2:8).

---

¹⁶Therefore, let us be approaching with boldness [or, a joyful sense of freedom] to the throne of grace, so that we shall receive mercy and find grace for well-timed help (Heb 4:16).

²²let us be approaching with a true heart [fig., pure inner desire], in full assurance of faith, our hearts having been sprinkled [clean] [fig., purified] from an evil conscience and the body having been bathed with pure water (Heb 10:22).

¹²in whom we have the boldness [or, joyful sense of freedom] and the access [or, privilege to enter] in assurance by means of faith in Him (Eph 3:12).

---

⁹Stop being carried away by varied and strange teachings, for [it is] good [for] the heart to continue being established by grace, not by foods, in which the ones having been walking about [in] [fig., having been occupied with] were not benefited (Heb 13:9).

¹⁷For the kingdom of God is not eating and drinking, but righteousness and peace and joy in [the] Holy Spirit (Rom 14:17).

⁸But food does not present [or, commend] us to God, for neither if we eat do we excel [or, are we better off]; nor if we do not eat do we fall short [or, are we inferior] (1Cor 8:8).

---

¹⁴how much more will the blood of Christ (who through [the] eternal Spirit offered Himself unblemished to God) purify [or, purge] your* conscience from dead works for [you*] to be sacredly serving the living God? (Heb 9:14).

¹⁰For we are His workmanship, having been created in Christ Jesus for good works, which God prepared beforehand so that we should walk about [fig., conduct ourselves] in them (Eph 2:10).

---

²⁵Grace [be] with you* all! So be it! (Heb 13:24f).

²⁴The grace of our Lord Jesus Christ [be] with you* all. So be it! (Rom 16:24).

²³The grace of the Lord Jesus Christ [be] with you*. ²⁴My love [is] with you* all in Christ Jesus. So be it! (1Cor 16:23).

²⁴Grace [be] with all the ones loving our Lord Jesus Christ in incorruptibility! [or, with an incorruptible [love]!] So be it! (Eph 6:24).

However, these affinities are not strong enough to prove Pauline authorship. They could indicate the author was a companion of Paul and thus picked up his ideas and terminology. This would be similar to the possible relationship between John the elder and John the apostle discussed previously. Also, the mention of Timothy would be due to him being a mutual friend of both Paul and the author.

Moreover, there are many arguments against Pauline authorship. First, in all of Paul's letters, he names himself in the first verse, but as we just saw, there is no such superscripting here. Now some say that was because Paul was in disfavor with the Hebrews, so they would have rejected the book if they knew it was by him. That's possible, but Paul is so emphatic about claiming his apostolic authority elsewhere, it is doubtful he would refrain from it here.

Second, there is no subscription written by the author's own hand as in Paul's epistles.

Third, a couple of passages argue against Pauline authorship. The first was already quoted. In part it reads, "For **we** also have had the Gospel [or, Good News] proclaimed [to us]" (Hebrews 4:2a). Notice Paul says "we" had the Gospel proclaimed to us. But Paul received the Gospel directly and alone from Jesus Himself, not by hearing it being proclaimed to a group of people.

The second passage reads:

³how will <u>we</u> escape having disregarded so great a salvation? Which having received a beginning [by] being spoken by the Lord, was confirmed **to us** by the ones having heard, ⁴God adding further

277

Translator's Perspective on the Canon of the NT

testimony both with signs and wonders and with various miraculous powers and distributions [fig., gifts] of [the] Holy Spirit, according to His will (Heb 2:3f).

Notice that the author says the message of Jesus "was confirmed *to us* by the ones having heard." Thus, the writer seems to be saying he had not heard Jesus speak and had to have Jesus' message "confirmed" to him. But Paul in his writings emphatically declares that he had seen the Lord and had been directly commissioned by Him:

¹I am an apostle, am I not? I am free, am I not? I have seen Jesus Christ our Lord, have I not? You* are my work in [the] Lord, are you* not? ²If to others I am not an apostle, but yet doubtless I am to you*. For you* are the seal [fig. proof] of my apostleship in [the] Lord (1Cor 9:1f).

¹⁵But when God, the One having separated [or, appointed] me from [the] womb of my mother and having called [me] by His grace, was well pleased ¹⁶to reveal His Son in me, so that I should be proclaiming the Gospel [of] Him among the nations, I did not immediately confer with [or, ask advice from] flesh and blood [fig., any human being]; ¹⁷nor did I go up to Jerusalem to the [ones who were] apostles before me, but I went away to Arabia and returned again to Damascus (Gal 1:15-17).

In the next paragraph, Paul mentions about his visit with James that was discussed in Chapter One as being when he received the creed recorded in 1Cor 15:3-6. But still, Paul had already been preaching the Gospel for three years which he received directly from Jesus in his vision of Him. As such, it is unlikely he would separate himself from those who heard.

Moreover, the next verse says it was those who heard who were performing miracles that confirmed their message. But again, Paul performed miracles and thus would not separate himself from those who did so:

¹²Indeed the signs of the apostle were performed among you* with all perseverance, in signs and wonders and miraculous works (2Cor 2:12).

Fourth is the writing style. It was mentioned in Chapter Two that Luke/ Acts contain the most stylistic (which is to say difficult) Greek of the NT. Hebrews is right behind those books in this regard. But Paul's epistles are considerably less stylistic and easier to translate than Hebrews. Having translated the Pauline letters and this epistle, there is no doubt in this writer's mind they are by different authors. "Hebrews is written in purer Greek than any book of the New Testament, except those portions of Luke where he is independent of prior documents" (Schaff; 11255).

One way some try to evade this is by saying Paul originally wrote Hebrews in Hebrew, but it was translated into Greek, possibly by Luke:

> Pantaenus of Alexandria (in the middle of the second century) saying that as Jesus is called the "apostle" to the Hebrews, Paul does not in it call himself so, being apostle to the Gentiles; also that Paul prudently omitted his name at the beginning, because the Hebrews were prejudiced against him; that it was originally written in Hebrew for the Hebrews, and that Luke translated it into Greek for the Greeks, whence the style resembles that of Acts (Fausset's; Hebrews, Epistle to the").

We see here three of the arguments already mentioned. To respond to the one new point; the only place in the NT Jesus is called an "Apostle" is in this book (Heb 3:1), but He is not called the "Apostle to the Hebrews." And nowhere is He called an Apostle let alone the Apostle to the Hebrews in the Apostolic Fathers.

But on a supposed Hebrew original of Hebrews, there is no mention of such anywhere else in the early literature, and there are no extant Hebrew manuscripts. All the earliest copies of Hebrews are in Greek. Moreover, the style of Greek does not reflect something that was translated from Hebrews.

Fifth, and related to the preceding, the tone of this book differs from the letters of Paul:

> As compared with the undoubted Epistles of Paul, the style of Hebrews is less fiery and forcible, but smoother, more correct, rhetorical, rhythmical, and free from anacolutha and solecisms. There is not that rush and vehemence which bursts through ordinary rules, but a calm and regular flow of speech. The sentences are skillfully constructed and well rounded. Paul is bent exclusively on the thought; the author of Hebrews evidently paid great attention to the form. Though not strictly classical, his style is as pure as the Hellenistic dialect and the close affinity with the Septuagint permit. All these considerations exclude the idea of a translation from a supposed Hebrew original (Schaff; 11259-11264).

Translator's Perspective on the Canon of the NT

Sixth, "The Muratorian Canon enumerates only thirteen Epistles of Paul and omits Hebrews" (Schaff; 11324).

Seventh and finally, there were debates very early as to the author of this book. Some said it was written by Paul, but many other suggestions were also made:

> The passage that is most conclusive against the Pauline authorship (Heb 2:3) is equally conclusive against any other apostle being the author. But almost every prominent name among the Christians of the second generation has been suggested. The epistle itself excludes Timothy (Heb 13:23), and Titus awaits his turn. Otherwise Luke, Clement of Rome, Barnabas, Silas, Apollos, Priscilla and Aquila, Philip the Deacon, and Aristion have all had their champions (ISBE; "Hebrews, Epistle to the").

> Ancient and modern writers mention various pupils of the Apostle [Paul], especially Luke, Clement of Rome, Apollo, lately also Priscilla and Aquila (New Advent; "Epistle to the Hebrews").

To comment on these possible authors, the highly stylistic Greek would give credence to the Luke theory, but the style is still considerably different from Luke/ Acts. But he and Barnabas were traveling companions of Paul; Thus, if either of them were the author then that would account for the affinities between Hebrews and the genuine Pauline letters.

However, arguing against Barnabas is there is an epistle purported to have been written by Barnabas among the Apostolic Fathers. That epistle will be addressed in Volume Three. But here, as will be detailed there, there are vast differences between Hebrews and the Epistle of Barnabas. As such, it is certain the same person did not author both. But it was the common belief in the second century that Barnabas authored that epistle, which would not have been so if it had been thought he authored this book.

Apollos is an interesting option given the description of him in Acts:

[24]Now a certain Jew, Apollos by name, an Alexandrian by race [or, a native of Alexandria], an educated man [or, a man skilled in speech], being mighty in the Scriptures, arrived at Ephesus. [25]This [man] had been instructed [in] the way of the Lord, and boiling [fig., being fervent] in his spirit [or, in the Spirit], he was speaking and teaching accurately the [things] concerning the Lord, knowing only the baptism of John.

²⁶And this [man] began to be speaking boldly in the synagogue. But Aquila and Priscilla having heard of him, they took him aside and explained to him the way of God more accurately.

²⁷Now when he wanted to cross over into Achaia, having encouraged [him], the brothers [and sisters] wrote to the disciples [there] to welcome him, who, having arrived, greatly assisted the ones having believed by grace [or, by the grace [of God]]. ²⁸For he was powerfully refuting the Jews publicly, demonstrating by the Scriptures Jesus to be the Christ (Acts 18:24-28).

Since the purpose of Hebrews is to show Jesus is the fulfillment of OT types, Apollos' preaching in Achaia as described here fits this theme. However, being an Alexandrina, if he were the author, then the Alexandrina church would have trumpeted this idea. But that branch of the church favored Pauline authorship. Moreover, "this hypothesis has not a shadow of support in tradition" (Schaff; 11361).

Even more intriguing is Apollos' teachers Aquila and Priscilla. They were also associated with Paul. But a theological letter written by a woman would not be very well accepted, so if Priscilla was involved in the authorship, that might explain why the author was omitted. But some say you would think her husband's name would have been attached to it even if hers wasn't.

But in favor of this view is sometimes when this couple is mentioned, Aquila is mentioned first, as would be expected and as seen in the preceding passage and in 1Corinthians 16:9. But Priscilla is mentioned first in Acts 18:18 and Romans 16:3. This order is strange for the times but might indicate Priscilla was more prominent in the early Church. Thus, she could have written Hebrews alone, without her husband. In that case, there would have been that much more reason to omit her name; and with her being a companion of Paul, that would explain the affinities between Hebrews and Paul's letters.

Moreover, consider the following:

> However, unlike other contemporaneous letters, the letter to the Hebrews has no prescript with the author's name. Never was an opening sentence so conspicuous by its absence. Was it left out intentionally? If so, by whom and why? Did someone decide to do away with the prescript? A motive would not be hard to find. By suppressing the name of the author, the letter could be assigned to Paul—much to the liking of certain elements in the church. Or did the author or friends of the author omit the prescript when copies were circulated, in order to

Translator's Perspective on the Canon of the NT

secure acceptance for the letter? In a completely different scenario, could the loss of the prescript be accidental?

The latter possibility is too remote to be taken seriously. This is the scholarly consensus. The facts in the case are simple and clear. We have about 14,000 letters from the ancient world. Many are originals. Not one lacks the usual greetings. There is no record of the prescript alone becoming lost from any papyrus roll. ...

Although the author was known to the first recipients, we have seen that when copies were circulated from Rome, at a certain time, the name was omitted. The prominence of women in the church was falling out of favor, and the name was omitted either to suppress its female authorship, or to protect the letter itself from suppression. A telling circumstance is that Clement, Bishop of Rome, made extensive use of Hebrews in his Epistle to Corinthians, 95-96 A.D., but never said who he was quoting. By contrast, Clement did mention Paul when quoting him (God's Word to Women; "Ruth Hoppin").

Clement was another disciple of Paul, whose letter will be discussed in Volume Three. But the style of his epistle is far different from that of Hebrews. But he does reference passages from Hebrews in his letter, as does the Shepherd of Hermas, which will also be discussed in Volume Three:

> Clement of Rome (1st century A.D.) refers to it [Hebrews] oftener than any other canonical New Testament book, adopting its words as on a level with the rest of the New Testament. As the writer of this epistle claims authority Clement virtually sanctions it, and this in the apostolic age (Fausset's; Hebrews, Epistle to the").

> In Western Europe the First Epistle of St. Clement to the Corinthians shows acquaintance with the text of the writing (chs. ix, xii, xvii, xxxvi, xlv), apparently also the "Pastor" of Hermas (Vis. II, iii, n.2; Sim. I, i sq.). (New Advent; "Epistle to the Hebrews").

The only conclusion on the author of Hebrews that can be made is:

> ... the author of Hebrews was a Jew by birth; a Hellenist, not a Palestinian; thoroughly at home in the Greek Scriptures (less so, if at all, in the Hebrew original); familiar with the

Alexandrian Jewish theology (less so, if at all, with the rabbinical learning of Palestine); a pupil of the apostles (not himself an apostle); an independent disciple and coworker of Paul; a friend of Timothy; in close relation with the Hebrew Christians of Palestine, and, when he wrote, on the point of visiting them; an inspired man of apostolic insight, power, and authority, and hence worthy of a position in the canon as "the great unknown."

Beyond these marks we cannot go with safety. The writer purposely withholds his name. The arguments for Barnabas, Luke, and Apollos, as well as the objections against them, are equally strong, and we have no data to decide between them, not to mention other less known workers of the apostolic age. We must still confess with Origen that God only knows the author of the Epistle to the Hebrews (Schaff; 11365-11373).

However, all of these quotes together show Hebrews was known and considered authoritative by the end of the first century. But given that the author was unknown, why was Hebrews eventually included in the canon of Scripture?

> The chief importance of the Epistle is in its content of theological teaching. It is, in complete agreement with the other letters of St. Paul, a glorious testimony to the faith of the Apostolic time; above all it testifies to the true Divinity of Jesus Christ, to His heavenly priesthood, and the atoning power of His death (New Advent; "Epistle to the Hebrews").

> Two facts account for the ultimate acceptance of that view [Pauline authorship] by the whole church. The spiritual value and authority of the book were seen to be too great to relegate it into the same class as the Shepherd [of Hermas] or the Epistle of Barnabas. And the conception of the Canon developed into the hard-and-fast rule of apostolicity. No writing could be admitted into the Canon unless it had an apostle for its author; and when Hebrews could no longer be excluded, it followed that its apostolic authorship must be affirmed. The tradition already existing in Alexandria supplied the demand, and who but Paul, among the apostles, could have written it? (ISBE; "Hebrews, Epistle to the").

The point of these quotes is; Hebrews is so filled with sound theology it just had to be included. Since Paul's name was associated

Translator's Perspective on the Canon of the NT

with it in some traditions, it was ultimately accepted on that basis. But even if that is not the case, as most likely is the case, Hebrews was written in the first century. And with the affinities to Paul's epistles, it most likely was written by an associate of Paul. And since it does not contain any theology counter to previously accepted books, there was ultimately no reason to exclude it.

Date of Writing:

As just indicated, Hebrews is referred to by at least two Apostolic Fathers. It was Thus, most certainly written in the first century. There is little doubt on this. But dating it more exactly is difficult.

Timothy is still alive, but that still just places it in the first century.

The biggest debate is if the temple is still standing. Since the author refers to the tabernacle not the temple, some say this shows he was writing after the temple was destroyed. But if he was, then it would seem logical that he would have mentioned its destruction as the final proof that the OT covenant with its temple rituals were passing away, but he does not:

[1]Now [this is the] main point about the [things] being said: we have such a High Priest who sat down at [the] right hand of the throne of the Majesty in the heavens, [2]a Minister of the holy [places] [fig., the sanctuary] and of the true tabernacle, which the Lord pitched and not humanity [fig., and not by human hands]. [3]For every high priest is appointed to be offering both gifts and sacrifices. Therefore, [it is] necessary for this One also to be having something which He should offer.

[4]For indeed if He were on earth, He would not be a priest, there being the priests, the ones offering the gifts according to the Law, [5]who sacredly serve a copy and shadow of the heavenly [things], just as Moses had been divinely warned, being about to be erecting the tabernacle, *"See,"* for He says, *"you will make all [things] according to the pattern, the one having been shown to you in the mountain."* [Exod 25:40] [6]But now He has obtained a far superior sacred service, to the degree that He is also Mediator of a better covenant, which has been enacted on better promises.

[7]For if that first [covenant] was faultless, a place would not have been sought for a second. ...

[13]By the saying "new," He has made the first obsolete. Now the one becoming obsolete and growing old [is] on the verge of disappearing (Heb 8:1-7,13).

There are indications that the intended readers were beginning to experience persecution:

⁴You* did not yet resist to the point of [shedding] blood struggling against sin (Heb 12:4).

Some date this to the Domitian persecutions of the 90s AD, but it could have been persecutions under Nero or even of Jewish Christians by Claudius in 49 AD. The latter in fact makes the most sense as Jews were not killed at that time, just forced out of Rome:

> According to Suetonius, Claudius banished the Jews from Rome, but the details are obscure. Disputes between Jews and members of the Christian sect in Rome had caused disturbances and Claudius apparently either banished certain Jews or prohibited them from assembling, which led to their voluntary departure, sometime between 41 and 50 C.E. It is generally accepted that the emperor's aim was the preservation of peace and not an act of hostility toward the Jews (Jewish Virtual library; "Claudius").

It was because of this event that Paul first met Aquila and Priscilla:

²And having found a certain Jew by name Aquila, of Pontus by race [or, a native of Pontus], recently having come from Italy, and Priscilla his wife (because of Claudius ordering all the Jews to depart out of Rome [ca. 49 A.D.]), he came to them (Acts 18:2).

It should be noted that Rome at this time would not have made a distinction between Jews and Christians:

> And here we should remind ourselves that, while we with our hindsight can distinguish between Jews and Christians as early as the reign of Claudius, no such distinction could have been made at that time by the Roman authorities (Bruce, "Christianity Under Claudius").

If this banishment is the event the author of Hebrews is referring to, then this letter would be dated shortly afterwards, Thus, in the early 50s AD. However, some see a dependence of this epistle on some Pauline letters, especially Galatians, 1 Corinthians, and Romans. But if this book was written by an associate of Paul, then those affinities could be due to him (or her) having learned those points directly from Paul rather

Translator's Perspective on the Canon of the NT

than from reading his letters. Thus, overall, the evidence favors a date before 70 AD, possibly as early as the 50s.

Since the letter of Clement of Rome to the Corinthians, written about A.D. 96, most probably cites Hebrews, the upper limit for the date of composition is reasonably certain. While the letter's references in the present tense to the Old Testament sacrificial worship do not necessarily show that temple worship was still going on, many older commentators and a growing number of recent ones favor the view that it was and that the author wrote before the destruction of the temple of Jerusalem in A.D. 70. In that case, the argument of the letter is more easily explained as directed toward Jewish Christians rather than those of Gentile origin, and the persecutions they have suffered in the past (cf. Heb 10:32–34) may have been connected with the disturbances that preceded the expulsion of the Jews from Rome in A.D. 49 under the emperor Claudius. These were probably caused by disputes between Jews who accepted Jesus as the Messiah and those who did not (Bishops; the Letter to the Hebrews").

Doctrine of God:

This letter is so filled with theology that some have claimed it is not really a letter but a theological treatise. But the very personal nature of the final chapter precludes that suggestion. To evade that, the treatise advocates claim the final chapter was a later addition, but there is no manuscript evidence supporting that assertion. But still, this book is filled with assertions about the nature of God, starting with the opening verse, which was quoted previously but bears repeating:

¹In various parts [or, Bit by bit] and in various ways in time past, God having spoken to the fathers by the prophets, in these last days He spoke to us by [His] Son (Heb 1:1).

¹⁰And, *"You, LORD, in [the] beginning founded the earth, and the heavens are works of Your hands. ¹¹They will perish, but You remain; and they will all wear out like a garment, ¹²and You will roll them up like a cloak, and they will be changed. But You are the same, and Your years will not fail."* [Psalm 102:25-27] (Heb 1:10-12).

⁴For every house is built by someone, but the One having built all [things is] God (Heb 3:4).

⁴For He has said somewhere concerning the seventh [day] thus, *"And God rested on the seventh day from all His works."* [Gen 2:2] (Heb 4:4).

¹³And no creature is unseen before Him, but all [things are] naked and have been exposed to His eyes to whom we [must give] an account (Heb 4:13).

³And this let us do, only if God shall be permitting (Heb 6:3).

¹³For when God made a promise to Abraham, since He was having no one greater to take an oath by, He took an oath by Himself, ¹⁴saying, *"Surely blessing I will bless you, and multiplying I will multiply you."* [Gen 22:15-17] ¹⁵And so, having waited patiently, he obtained the promise.
¹⁶For people indeed take an oath by the greater, and with them the oath [given] as confirmation [is] an end of every dispute, ¹⁷in which God wanting to show even more [clearly] to the heirs of the promise the unchangeable nature of His purpose, guaranteed [it] by an oath, ¹⁸so that through two unchangeable things, in which [it is] impossible for God Himself to lie, we shall be having a strong encouragement, the ones having fled for refuge to take hold of the hope [or, confident expectation] being set before [us] (Heb 6:13-18).

³⁰For we know the One having said, *"Vengeance [is] Mine; I will repay,"* says [the] Lord. And again, *"[The] LORD will judge His people."* [Deut 32:35,36] ³¹[It is] dreadful [or, terrifying] to fall into [the] hands of [the] living God! (Heb 10:30f).

³By faith we understand the ages [fig., universe] to have been prepared by a word of God, for the [things] being visible not to have come from the [things] being seen. [see Gen 1:1-27] (Heb 11:3).

⁴By faith Abel offered to God a better sacrifice than Cain, through which he was testified to be righteous, God testifying concerning his gifts, and through it [i.e., his faith], having died, he himself still speaks. [see Gen 4:3-10] ⁵By faith Enoch was taken up [so as] not to see death, *"and he was not being found because God took him up;"* for before his removal he had been testified to [as] having been pleasing to God. [see Gen 5:21-24, LXX] ⁶But without faith [it is] impossible to please [Him], for it is necessary [for] the one approaching God to believe that He is and [that] He becomes a rewarder to the ones diligently seeking Him (Heb 11:4-6).

Translator's Perspective on the Canon of the NT

[19]having taken into account that God [was] able to raise [him] up even from [the] dead (Heb 11:19).

to God, [the] Judge of all [people] (Heb 12:23b).

[4]Marriage [is to be] honorable [or, respected] among all, and the marriage bed undefiled, but fornicators and adulterers God will judge (Heb 13:4).

[20]Now may the God of peace (Heb 13:20a).

Thus, in Hebrews, God spoke through the OT prophets. He is the Creator and eternal. He is omniscient. We can only do things if God permits us. He is responsible for population growth. There is none greater than God, and He is unchangeable, so His promises are trustworthy. He will judge sin. He is living, not dead like idols. He is the God of prominent OT people (Only the paragraph about Abel and Enoch are quoted in this regard, but the author goes on to mention many additional OT figures). God rewards those who seek Him. He can raise the dead. He is the God of peace. All of this fits with the OT conception of God.

Essential Tenets:

This letter is so filled with affirmations of essential tenets it will be difficult to quote them all. But it is worthwhile to try, starting once again with the first verse:

[1]In various parts [or, Bit by bit] and in various ways in time past, God having spoken to the fathers by the prophets, in these last days He spoke to us by [His] Son, [2]whom He appointed heir of all [things], through whom also He made the ages [fig., universe]; [3]who being [the] outshining of His glory and [the] exact expression of His essence, and sustaining all the [things] by the word of His power, having Himself made by Himself a purification [or, purgation] of our sins, sat down at [the] right [hand] of the Majesty on high, [4]having become so much better than the angels [or, messengers [of the Lord]], as He has inherited a more excellent name than they (Heb 1:1-4).

Here the author says Jesus is God's Son. Jesus is called the "Son of God" eleven more times in this epistle (1:5, 2x; 1:8; 3;6; 4:14; 5;5,8; 6:6; 7:3,28; 10:29). Jesus is called "Christ" thirteen times (e.g. 3;1,6,14) and "Lord" at least twice (e.g. 7:14; 13:20).

Going back to the opening paragraph, it was through Jesus that God made the universe, just as John and Paul assert. Jesus is the "outshining of His glory and [the] exact expression of His essence." As such, in no uncertain terms the author is declaring the full deity of Jesus. Jesus purified our sins (implying His death given the OT sacrificial system), and He sat down at the right hand of God (implying His ascension).

In the succeeding paragraphs in the first chapter, all of which are OT quotes, the author asserts that Jesus is the "God' and "LORD" mentioned in the quotes, so He is worthy of worship. The author then associates the Father, Son, and Spirit together, while indicating the importance of the Spirit's working:

³how will <u>we</u> escape having disregarded so great a salvation? Which having received a beginning [by] being spoken by the Lord, was confirmed to us by the ones having heard, ⁴God adding further testimony both with signs and wonders and with various miraculous powers and distributions [fig., gifts] of [the] Holy Spirit, according to His will (Heb 2:3f).

The author then writes:

⁹But we see Jesus, the One having been made only a little lower [or, only for a short while lower] than [the] angels because of the suffering of death, having been awarded the victor's wreath [of] [or, having been crowned with] glory and honor, in order that by [the] grace of God He should taste [fig., experience] death on behalf of all.
¹⁰For it was fitting for Him, because of whom [are] all [things], and through whom [are] all [things], having brought many sons [and daughters] to glory, to make the Originator of their salvation perfect through sufferings (Heb 2:9-10).

Here Jesus is said to have been made a little lower than the angels, Thus, implying He had been higher. And very clearly, Jesus died for our sins so that we might be saved. Having asserted Jesus' full deity, the author next asserts the full humanity of Jesus, while re-asserting His death for our sins:

¹⁴Therefore, since the young children have shared of flesh and blood, He Himself also likewise shared in the same, so that through death He should destroy [or, render powerless] the one having the power of death, that is, the Devil, ¹⁵and release those, as many as [due to] a fear of death, throughout all the [time] to live [fig., all their lives], were subjects of servitude. ¹⁶For surely He does not take hold of [fig., give

Translator's Perspective on the Canon of the NT

aid to] angels, <u>but</u> He takes hold of [fig., gives aid to] [the] seed of Abraham. ¹⁷Therefore, it was necessary [for] Him to become like His brothers [and sisters] in all [respects], so that He should become a merciful and faithful High Priest [in] the [things pertaining] to God, [in order] to make propitiation [or, an appeasing sacrifice] for the sins of the people. ¹⁸For He Himself having been tempted in what He suffered, He is able to help the ones being tempted (Heb 2:14-18).

Then in one of this writer's favorite passages of Scripture, the author asserts Jesus is our High Priest and thus Mediator before the Father. As such, we have direct access to God. This is a glorious promise and so unlike false religions that separate people from God:

¹⁴Therefore, having a great High Priest [who] has passed through the heavens—Jesus, the Son of God—let us be holding fast our confession. ¹⁵For we do not have a High Priest [who is] unable to sympathize with our weaknesses, but [One] having been tried in all [respects] in the same way [we are, yet] without sin. ¹⁶Therefore, let us be approaching with boldness [or, a joyful sense of freedom] to the throne of grace, so that we shall receive mercy and find grace for well-timed help. (4:14-16).

Next, the author refers to the reception of the Spirit by saying believers have become "sharers of [the] Holy Spirit" (Heb 6:4).

We then see the author's main purpose for the letter. He is showing that Jesus is the fulfillment of the OT sacrificial rituals. Jesus offers Himself once for all time for our sins, so He is forever our High Priest and able to intercede before God for us. As such, the continual sacrifices of the sanctuary with its succession of priests are no longer necessary. Note that this would have been a fitting place to mention the destruction of the temple if that event had already occurred:

²³And on the one hand many have become priests because they are being prevented by death from continuing; ²⁴on the other hand the One because of His remaining into the age [fig., forever] has the priesthood permanently. ²⁵Therefore, He is also being able to be saving to the [very] end [fig., completely] the ones coming through Him to God, [since] He is always living to be making the intercession on their behalf.

²⁶For such a High Priest was fitting for us: devout [or, holy], innocent, undefiled, having been separated from the sinful [people] and having become higher [than] the heavens, ²⁷who does not have a daily need like the high priests to be first offering up sacrifice on behalf of His own sins then for the [sins] of the people [see Lev 9:7; 16:6]; for

this He did once and for all [fig., once and never again], having offered up Himself. ²⁸For the Law appoints men having weakness [as] high priests, but the word of the oath, the [one] after the Law, [appoints] the Son having been perfected into the age [fig., forever] (Heb 7:23-28).

The author now quotes the passage about the New Covenant from Jeremiah that was quoted in Chapter One. This New Covenant of an inner change rather than an outward Law comes about due to Jesus' death for our sins just discussed:

⁷For if that first [covenant] was faultless, a place would not have been sought for a second. ⁸For finding fault with them [i.e., the people], He says:

> *Listen! [The] days are coming, says [the] LORD, and I will establish a New Covenant over the house of Israel and over the house of Judah, ⁹not according to the covenant which I made with their fathers, in [the] day of My having taken hold of their hand to bring them out of [the] land of Egypt, because they did not remain in [fig., carefully obey] My covenant, and I disregarded them, says [the] LORD.*
> *¹⁰Because this [is] the covenant which I will covenant with the house of Israel after those days, says [the] LORD, giving My laws into their mind, and I will inscribe them on their hearts, and I will be to them for a God, and they will be to Me for a people. ¹¹And by no means shall they teach each his fellow-citizen, and each his brother [and sister], saying, "Know the LORD," because all will know Me from [the] least of them to [the] greatest. ¹²For I will be merciful to their unrighteousness, and their sins and their lawless deeds I shall by no means remember anymore.* [Jer 31:31-34 (verse 32, LXX)]

¹³By the saying "new," He has made the first obsolete. Now the one becoming obsolete and growing old [is] on the verge of disappearing (Heb 8:7-13).

The author continues to discuss the effects of Jesus' death. Jesus offered His blood for our redemption and to purify us to good works. He is thus our Mediator, and we have assurance of an eternal inheritance. This is part of the New Covenant God makes with believers. Note also in this passage the association of the Father, Son, and Spirit and that the Spirit is called "Eternal" just as the Father and Son are:

Translator's Perspective on the Canon of the NT

[11]But Christ having appeared [as] High Priest of the good [things] coming, through the greater and more perfect tabernacle not made with human hands (that is, not of this creation), [12]and not through [the] blood of goats and calves, but through His own blood, entered in once and for all [fig., once and never again] into the Holy [Places], [He] Himself [or, by Himself] having secured eternal redemption. [see Lev 4:3; 16:6-15; Isaiah 53:12]

[13]For if the blood of bulls and goats and ashes of a heifer [i.e., a young cow] sprinkling the ones having been defiled sanctifies to the purifying of the flesh, [see Lev 16:14f; Numb 19:2,17f] [14]how much more will the blood of Christ (who through [the] eternal Spirit offered Himself unblemished to God) purify [or, purge] your* conscience from dead works for [you*] to be sacredly serving the living God?

[15]And because of this, He is Mediator of a New Covenant, in order that (a death having [or, since a death] occurred for redemption of the transgressions under the first covenant) the ones having been called shall receive the promise of the eternal inheritance (Heb 9:11-15).

Next, the author again affirms Jesus' death for our sins, but he now adds a reference to His Second Coming:

[27]And just as it is laid up [fig., destined] for people to die once for all time [or, only once], and after this [comes] judgment, cp. Gen 3:19; Eccl 3:2,20] [28]so also Christ, having been offered once for all time to bear [or, take away] the sins of many, will appear a second time without [reference to] sin to [bring] salvation to the ones eagerly waiting for Him! (Heb 9:27f).

The author affirms Jesus' death on the cross and His ascension to the right hand of God:

[2]looking with undivided attention to the Originator and Perfecter of [our] faith—Jesus—who, because of the joy being set before Him, endured a cross, having disregarded [the] shame, and has sat down at [the] right [hand] of the throne of God (Heb 12:2).

The author once again affirms Jesus' death for our sins and that this is a fulfillment of the OT sacrifices:

[11]For of which living creatures the blood is brought concerning sin into the holy [places] by the high priest, the bodies of these are burned outside the camp. [see Lev 4:11,12,21; 16:27] [12]And so Jesus, so that

He should sanctify the people through [His] own blood, suffered outside the gate (Heb 13:11f).

The author closes his epistle with an affirmation of the resurrection of Jesus and His ability to change us, in order that we are able to do works acceptable to God:

[20]Now may the God of peace, the One having brought up from [the] dead the great Shepherd of the sheep by [the] blood of an eternal covenant—our Lord Jesus, [21]equip you* in every good work in order to do His will, doing in you* the acceptable [thing] before Him, through Jesus Christ, to whom [is] the glory into the ages of the ages! [fig., forever and ever!] So be it! (Heb 13:20f).

Putting this all together, the author affirms just about all of the essential tenets of the early Church, and he (she?) does so by way of an outstanding exposition of the OT sacrificial system and its fulfillment in Jesus Christ.

Appeal and Mark of Inspiration:

The preceding sentence explains the appeal of this letter and why it just "had to" be included in the canon. The doctrines asserted in this letter are found elsewhere in the NT, but they are not presented in the exceptional way they are in this letter. Most of all, this letter shows the idea of Jesus dying for our sins did not originate in NT times. God had been preparing people for this idea for centuries, ever since the OT sacrificial system was instituted. Those sacrifices foreshadowed the greater work of Christ on the cross. As such, this essential teaching of the early Church was grounded in an idea that had been around since antiquity. This book Thus, clearly bears the mark of inspiration.

> The chief importance of the Epistle is in its content of theological teaching. It is, in complete agreement with the other letters of St. Paul, a glorious testimony to the faith of the Apostolic time; above all it testifies to the true Divinity of Jesus Christ, to His heavenly priesthood, and the atoning power of His death (New Advent; "Epistle to the Hebrews").

Conclusion on Hebrews:

Much time has been spent on Hebrews as the issues surrounding it are rather complex, as is the book itself. But the book is so important it was worth looking at in detail. There are questions as to its author, but there is no doubt it was written very early and by someone who

Translator's Perspective on the Canon of the NT

understood and could present essential early Church teachings in a phenomenal way. It was Thus, rightly included in the canon of the NT.

> Though not of Paul's pen, it has, somehow, the impress of his genius and influence, and is altogether worthy to occupy a place in the canon, after his Epistles, or between them and the Catholic Epistles. Pauline in spirit, it is catholic or encyclical in its aim (Schaff; 11221-11223).

James

Like Hebrews, James was among the *antilegomena*, but the reason for there being disputes about it was far different than for Hebrews.

Author:
The salutation to this letter is as follows:

¹James, a bondservant of God and of [the] Lord Jesus Christ, To the Twelve Tribes who are in the Dispersion [i.e., the scattering of Jews outside of Judea]: Greetings!

There are several men with the name of James in the NT. James the brother of John the apostle and son of Zebedee is the first that comes to mind. He was not only one of the original twelve apostles but one of the central three or four that accompanied Jesus when others did not, as was discussed in Chapter Four. But that James most likely is not the James who wrote this epistle as he was martyred very early in Church history:

¹Now about that time [ca. 44 AD] Herod the king [i.e., Herod Agrippa I, grandson of Herod the Great] put his hands to mistreat [or, persecute] some of the [believers] from the assembly. ²Then he executed James the brother of John with [the] sword (Acts 12:1f).

As the note in the ALT indicates, this was in 44 AD, before this epistle was most likely written.

The second James is another of the original twelve apostles, James the son of Alphaeus. He is mentioned in the lists of apostles in all three synoptic Gospels:

²Now the names of the twelve apostles are these: first Simon, the one being called Peter, and Andrew his brother, James the [son] of Zebedee and John his brother, ³Philip and Bartholomew, Thomas and

Matthew the tax collector, **James the [son] of Alpheus** and Lebbeus, the one having been surnamed Thaddeus, ⁴Simon the Canaanite and Judas Iscariot, the one also having betrayed Him (Matt 10:2-4, also Mark 3:16-18; Luke 6:13-16).

This James was the brother of Matthew/ Levi:

¹⁴And passing by, He saw **Levi, the [son] of Alphaeus**, sitting at the tax-office (Mark 2:14).

This James is mentioned as being with the rest of the remaining apostles in the upper room before the day of Pentecost:

¹³And when they entered [Jerusalem], they went up into the upstairs room where they were staying: both Peter and James and John and Andrew, Philip and Thomas, Bartholomew and Matthew, **James [the son] of Alphaeus** and Simon the Zealot, and Judas [the son; or, the brother] of James (Acts 1:13).

That is all that is certain about this James. That means this James was not well-known, while the author of this epistle assumes his readers will know who he is, despite this being a general letter written to Jewish Christians dispersed throughout the Roman Empire. That makes this James an unlikely candidate for the author.

The third James in the NT is much more likely. He is James the brother (or more correctly, half-brother) of Jesus.

⁵⁴And having come into His hometown [i.e., Nazareth, see Matt 2:23], He was teaching them in their synagogue, with the result that they are being astonished and are saying, "From where to this One [or, Where [did] this One [get]] this wisdom and these miraculous powers? ⁵⁵This is the Son of the craftsman, is it not? His mother is called Mary, and His brothers [are] **James** and Joses and Simon and Judas, are they not? ⁵⁶And His sisters are all with us, are they not? So from where to this One all these [things]?" [or, where then [did] this One [get] all these [things]?"] (Matt 13:54-56).

Since James is mentioned first, he was probably the next oldest son after Jesus. But he and his brothers were not believers in the Messiahship of their oldest Brother at this time:

Translator's Perspective on the Canon of the NT

²¹And the [ones] from His side [fig., His relatives] having heard, they went out to take hold of Him, for they said that He was out of His mind (Mark 3:21).

²But the feast of the Jews was near, the Feast of Tabernacles. ³So His brothers said to Him, "Depart from here and be going into Judea, so that Your disciples also will watch Your works which You are doing. ⁴For no one does anything in secret and himself seeks to be in public. If You do these things, show Yourself to the world." ⁵For His brothers were not believing in Him (John 7:2-5).

The first passage might not be referring to Jesus' brothers per se as they are specifically mentioned in Mark 3:31, but the second passage is clearly referring to Jesus' four brothers. But something happened that caused His brothers to believe in Him later. That something was His resurrection and appearance to His brother James. That appearance is not recorded in the Gospels but by Paul at the end of the creed he presents that was discussed in Chapter One:

⁵and that He appeared to Cephas [i.e., Peter], then to the twelve. ⁶Afterwards, He appeared to over five hundred brothers [and sisters] at once, of whom the greater part remain until now, but some also fell asleep [fig., have died]. ⁷Afterwards, He appeared to James, then to all the apostles (1Cor 15:7f).

Thus, Jesus appeared to His brother James before His final appearance to the apostles. This almost certainly was when James became a believer. He most likely told his other three brothers, and they believed also. All four brothers were with the apostles in the upper room before the day of Pentecost:

¹⁴These all were continuing with one mind in prayer and petition, together with [the] women [cp. Luke 8:2-3; 23:55-24:10] and Mary the mother of Jesus, and with His brothers (Acts 1:14).

The "these" were the apostles. With them were some prominent women in the early Church, plus Mary the mother of Jesus and Jesus' brothers. Being the oldest remaining brother, James would have the prominence in the family, and he took that role rather early in the Church as well:

Then he said, "Report these [things] to James and to the brothers [and sisters]" (Acts 12:17b).

The "he" here is Peter who had just been miraculously delivered from prison. Thus, even Peter felt a need to report to James what had happened to him, indicating James' prominent role. This is seen again by James' role at the Jerusalem council:

[13]Now after they became silent, James answered, saying, "Men, brothers, listen to me. [14]Simon [i.e., Peter] explained how God first visited [them] to take out of [the] Gentiles a people for His name. [15]And with this the words of the prophets agree, just as it has been written:

[16]*After these [things] I will return, and I will rebuild the tabernacle of David, the one having fallen down, and the [things] having been torn down from it I will rebuild, and I will restore it,* [17]*in order that the remaining peoples* [i.e., non-Jews] *shall diligently seek the* LORD, *even all the Gentiles on whom My name has been called on them, says the* LORD, *the One doing all these things.* [Amos 9:11,12, LXX]

[18]"Known from [the] ages [fig., from eternity] to God is all His works.
[19]"For this reason, I judge not to be troubling the [ones] turning to God from the Gentiles, [20]but to write instructions to them to be abstaining from the pollutions of the idols and from fornication and from the strangled [animal] and from blood. [21]For Moses from ancient generations has in every city the ones preaching him, being read aloud in the synagogues every Sabbath" (Acts 15:13-21).

This passage has been quoted in full as it is the only recorded words of this James, although he might also have been the primary author of the following letter sent by "The apostles and the elders and the brothers" (Acts 15:22-29). In this passage James can be seen to be knowledgeable in the OT Scriptures and to have a sound concept of the nature of God. God is concerned with both Jews and Gentiles and is omniscient and eternal. James is also concerned with upright living. Idols are not to be worshipped, fornication is to be avoided, and OT food regulations are to be followed. Moreover, the following observations are important:

> James' speech in Acts 15 contains many striking parallels in language with the epistle of James. For example, (*chairo*) χαίρω [greetings] is found in Jas. 1:1 and Acts 15:23 (and elsewhere in Acts only in 23:26); Acts 15:17 and Jas. 2:7 invoke God's name in a special way; the exhortation for the brothers

Translator's Perspective on the Canon of the NT

(*adelphoi*) (ἀδελφοι) to hear is found both in Jas. 2:5 and Acts 15:13. Further, not-so-common individual words are found in both: *episkeptesthe* ἐπισκέπτεσθε (Jas. 1:27; Acts 15:14); *epistrepsein* ἐπιστρέφειν (Jas. 5:19 and Acts 15:19); *terein* τηρεῖν (or *diatewein* διατηρεῖν) *eauton* ἑαυτόν (Jas. 1:27; Acts 15:29); *agatetos* ἀγαπητός (Jas. 1:16, 19; 2:5; Acts 15:25). Though short of conclusive proof, this is nevertheless significant corroborative evidence (Bible.org; "James: Introduction, Outline, and Argument").

This James is mentioned once more in Acts:

[17]Now we having come to be [fig., having arrived] in Jerusalem, the brothers [and sisters] received us gladly. [18]Then on the next [day] Paul had gone in with us to James, and all the elders were present. [19]And having embraced them, he began reporting one by one each of [the things] which God did among the Gentiles through his ministry (Acts 21:17-19).

The "we/us" is Luke, Paul, and other traveling companions. The important point is Paul is mentioned as meeting with James on his arrival. It is to him and "all the elders" that Paul reports about his missionary journey.

Interestingly, James (along with others) encourages Paul to pay the expenses for four men who had taken a vow, which Paul does and goes through the purification ceremony himself:

[23]"Therefore, do this which we say to you: [there] are four men with us having [taken] a vow upon themselves; [24]these having taken, be purified with them and pay their expenses for them, so that they shall shave the head, and all may know that [the things] of which they have been informed about you are nothing, but you are keeping in line with [fig., living in conformity with] and you yourself are keeping the Law. [25]But concerning the ones having believed of [the] Gentiles, we wrote, having judged [that they need] to be observing no such [thing], except to be keeping themselves both [from] the meat sacrificed to idols and [from] blood and [from anything] strangled and [from] fornication." [see Acts 15:28,29]

[26]Then Paul, having taken the men on the following day, having been purified with them, had gone into the temple announcing the completion of the days of the purification, until which [time] the offering was offered on behalf of each one of them (Acts 21:23-26).

Thus, James is thus shown to be stickler for the Law, to which Paul consents. This is probably why this James came to be known as James the Just. But it also brought James and Paul into some conflict. This is seen when Paul mentions James in Galatians:

> [18]Then after three years I went up to Jerusalem to visit with Peter and stayed with him fifteen days. [19]But I did not see [any] other of the apostles, except James, the brother of the Lord (Gal 1:18f).

> [9]and having known the grace, the one having been given to me, James and Cephas [i.e., Peter] and John, the ones highly regarded to be pillars, gave to me and to Barnabas [the] right [hand] of fellowship, so that we indeed [should go] to the Gentiles, but they to the circumcision [i.e., Jews] (Gal 2:9).

> [11]But when Peter came to Antioch, I opposed him to [his] face, because he had been condemned. [12]For before certain [Jews] came from James, he was eating with the Gentiles, but when they came, he began drawing back and separating himself, fearing those from [the] circumcision [i.e., legalist Jews]. [13]And the other Jews also joined him in hypocrisy, with the result that even Barnabas was carried away by their hypocrisy [or, insincerity] (Gal 2:11-13).

The first two passages show again that James was a leader of the early Church, while the latter shows James still believed in separation from Gentiles, at least during meals. This could be due to the aforementioned believed need to follow OT food regulations, which the Gentiles would not have been following. This issue is outside of the scope of this book, but this passages shows James believed this was important while Paul did not, as seen in subsequent paragraphs in Galatians. But here, what matters is Paul considered James to be a pillar of the early Church, and even Peter seems concerned about what James would think of his actions.

The point of all of this is this James, the brother of Jesus, was well-known in the early Church and was one of its early leaders. As such, he could identify himself as simply "James," and his widely scattered readers would know who he is and accept his authority. This fits with the tone of the Epistle of James:

> The writer of this epistle speaks as one having authority. He is not on his defense, as Paul so often is. There is no trace of apology in his presentation of the truth. His official position must have been recognized and unquestioned. He is as sure of

Translator's Perspective on the Canon of the NT

his standing with his readers as he is of the absoluteness of his message (ISBE; "James, Epistle of").

The assignment of this James (also known in later church traditions, starting with Hegesippus, as "James the Just") as author of the letter has been the traditional view (Bible.org; "James: Introduction, Outline, and Argument").

[The Epistle of James] has strong internal evidence of genuineness. It precisely suits the character and position of the historical James as we know him from Paul and the Acts, and differs widely from the apocryphal James of the Ebionite fictions. It hails undoubtedly from Jerusalem, the theocratic metropolis, amid the scenery of Palestine. The Christian communities appear not as churches, but as synagogues, consisting mostly of poor people, oppressed and persecuted by the rich and powerful Jews. There is no trace of Gentile Christians or of any controversy between them and the Jewish Christians (Schaff, 4152-4156).

Before continuing, it should be mentioned there are possibly one or two other men named James in the NT, but it is uncertain if these are to be identified with one or more of the previously mentioned men named James. Also, there are some who do not believe James was a biological half-brother of Jesus. But these issues get rather complicated and are outside the scope of this book. Thus, here it will just be said the evidence points to James the half-brother of the Lord as being the author of this epistle.

The address of the epistle states that the writer is "James, a servant of God and of the Lord Jesus Christ" (Jas 1:1). The tradition of the church has identified this James with the brother of our Lord. Clement of Alexandria says that Peter and James and John, who were the three apostles most honored of the Lord, chose James, the Lord's brother, to be the bishop of Jerusalem after the Lord's ascension (Euscb., *HE*, II, 1). This tradition agrees well with all the notices of James in the New Testament books (ISBE; "James, Epistle of").

Despite this evidence, there were a few in the early Church who questioned the genuineness of this epistle, but for the most part it was accepted as a genuine writing of James the brother of the Lord.

Although, therefore, the canonicity of the Epistle of St. James was questioned by a few during the first centuries, there are to be found from the very earliest ages, in different parts of the Church, numerous testimonies in favour of its canonicity. From the end of the third century its acceptance as inspired, and as the work of St. James, has been universal, as clearly appears from the various lists of the Sacred Books drawn up since the fourth century (New Advent, Epistle of St. James").

However, today there are many who doubt that James the brother of Jesus wrote this letter. There are several reasons for this doubt.

First, it is said the Greek is too stylistic for a Galilean to have written it. And it is true the literary style of Greek of this letter is probably just below Luke/ Acts and Hebrews. But we know very little of the background of James and what schooling he had. Moreover, it is possible he dictated this epistle to a scribe, who would have "cleaned up" any roughness to his Greek.

There is the greatest probability that James used an amanuensis [secretary]. The use of an amanuensis for all the New Testament epistles, except for Philemon, 2 Peter, 2 John and 3 John, is indeed quite likely. Longenecker points out that:

> The Greek papyri . . . indicate quite clearly that an amanuensis was frequently, if not commonly, employed in the writing of personal letters during the time approximating the composition of the NT epistles. They also suggest that at times a letter was composed without secretarial help, particularly when sent from one member of a family to another and/or where the contents were of a more intimate or informal nature (Bible.org; "James: Introduction, Outline, and Argument").

Second, the author does not indicate that he is the brother of Jesus. But this was probably because he was well-known as being the Lord's brother and thus to constantly mention it would be a sign of arrogance. But with James being nicknamed "the Just" such arrogance would not befit him, so it was due to humbleness that James only gives his name.

Third, in this epistle, James refers to "[the] perfect law, the [law] of liberty" (1:24). It is said this does not fit with someone who was a stickler for OT regulations, as the James of Acts 15 seems to be. But this argument assumes that following the Law was considered to be

Translator's Perspective on the Canon of the NT

restrictive. But in fact, doing so can be liberating, as it frees one from the adverse effects that breaking the Law can cause. Thus, by following the OT food regulations, one does not have to be concerned about say trichinosis from eating pig meat.

Fourth, and along these lines, the author only mentions the ethical considerations of the law, not the ritual ones. But such a criticism assumes a purpose for the letter other than James intended it. He was following in the footsteps of Proverbs and more so of Jesus in focusing on correct ethics rather than correct ritual observances.

Other objections concern the dating and theology of this book. We will look at the each of these in turn

Date of Writing:

There is some indication this epistle was known to the author of the Apostolic Fathers work of 1Clement. That book will be discussed in Volume Three. But here, it was probably written in 96 AD. Compare the following passages:

[23]And [so] was fulfilled the Scripture, the one saying, *"But Abraham believed* [or, *trusted*] *God, and it was accounted to him for righteousness."* [Gen 15:6] And he was called a friend of God. [see Isaiah 41:8] (James 2:23).

[1]Abraham, having been designated "the friend," was found faithful in him to become obedient [fig., when he was obedient] to the sayings of God. [James 2:23; Isaiah 41:8 (1Clement 10:1).

[2]Abraham was greatly testified [to] and was called a friend of God [James 2:23; Isaiah 41:8]; yet he said, steadfastly gazing into the glory of God, being modest, "But I am earth and ashes." [Gen 18:27] (1Clement 17:2)

As seen, both Clement and James refer to Isaiah 41:8. That verse reads in the Hebrew text, "[8]But you, Israel, are My servant, Jacob whom I have chosen, The descendants of Abraham My friend" (Isa 41:8 NKJV). But the Septuagint reads, "[8]But you, O Israel, [are] My bondservant, Jacob whom I chose, [the] seed of Abraham, whom I loved" (Isa 41:8; ALT).

Thus, both James and Clement refer to Isaiah 41:8 in the same manner and both use the Hebrew text, not the LXX. It could be that they independently do so, or it could be that Clement copied from James.

Then there are the following possible parallel passages:

>²¹Abraham our father, he was justified [or, shown to be righteous] by means of works, having offered Isaac his son upon the altar, was he not? [see Gen 22:9] (James 2:21).

>²For what reason was our father Abraham blessed? [Because of] having done righteousness and truth through faith, was it not? ³Isaac with confidence, knowing the [thing] being about to [happen], gladly yielded himself [as] a sacrifice. [see Gen 22:9; cp. James 2:21] (1Clement 31:2,3).

Again, Clement could be independent of James or basing his ideas on James. But if the latter is true in one or both cases, then the Epistle of James had to be written before Clement and thus before 96 AD.

There is also a possible connection between the Shepherd of Hermas (another Apostolic Father) and James:

>⁷Therefore, be subjected to God, but stand up against [or, resist] the Devil, and he will flee from you* (James 4:7).

>²But you shall not fear the devil, for fearing the Lord, you will exercise lordship over the devil, for there is not power in him, {nor fear}. [cp. James 4:7] (Hermas; Mandate 7; 1:2a).

The dating of the Shepherd of Hermas will also be discussed in Volume Three. But here is will be said it was possibly around the same time as 1Clement. Thus, again, James has to be before that time. But moving the writing of James even earlier is the strong tradition that this James was martyred in the early 60s:

> James remained the leader of the Jerusalem church until his death around A.D. 62… Eusebius gives three versions of the death of James: one from Clement of Alexandria, one from Hegesippus, and one from Josephus (Christian History; "The Death of James the Just").

These accounts of James death are rather legendary and contradictory, making it hard to determine the truth of what really happened. But it is rather certain that he died in 62 AD. That Thus, gives an end-date for when this epistle could have been written, if it was in fact written by James the brother of Jesus. The earliest date would probably be after the death of James the brother of John and son of Zebedee, as it was after his death that James the Lord's brother rose to prominence. Thus, we have a range of 44-62 AD.

Translator's Perspective on the Canon of the NT

This epistle does not mention the Council at Jerusalem, which occurred in 50/ 51 AD. But the issues addressed there are similar to those address in this letter. As such, if that council had already occurred, it seems logical that James would mention it to buttress his arguments, but he does not. If that is the case, that would move this epistle to the early part of the preceding range or in the late 40s.

However, some claim it was written near the end of James' life due to the issues it addresses needing time to develop. It is for this reason that liberals try to date this letter to the late first century and thus eliminate James as the possible author. But the problems James refers to could occur anytime in the early Church.

The issues being referred to are social and theological. The social issue is the relationship of the rich and poor in the Church:

¹My brothers [and sisters], stop holding the faith of [or, in] our Lord Jesus Christ, the [Lord] of Glory [or, our Lord of Glory, Jesus Christ], with accepting of faces [fig., with a prejudiced attitude]. [cp. Acts 10:34,35; Eph 6:9] ²For if a man comes into your* synagogue with a gold ring, in elegant clothing, and there comes in also a poor [man] in filthy clothing, ³and you* look with care upon the one wearing the elegant clothing and say to him, "You be sitting here, please [or, here in this good seat]," and to the poor [man] you* say, "You stand there," or, "Be sitting here under my footstool," ⁴and [so] did you* not make distinctions among yourselves and [so] became judges with evil thought processes [or, motives]?

⁵Pay attention, my beloved brothers [and sisters]: God chose the poor [people] of the world [to be] rich in faith and heirs of the kingdom which He promised to the ones loving Him, did He not? ⁶But you* dishonored the poor [person]. The rich [people] oppress you*, and they drag you* into [the] courts, do they not? ⁷They blaspheme the good Name by which you* were called, do they not?

⁸If you* indeed fulfill [the] royal Law according to the Scripture, *"You will love your neighbor as yourself,"* you* are doing well. [Lev 19:18] ⁹But if you* accept faces [fig., are prejudiced], you* are committing sin, being convicted by the Law as transgressors (James 2:1-9).

¹Now listen! The rich [people], weep, wailing over your* miseries, the ones coming upon [you*]! ²Your* riches have rotted, and your* clothes have become moth-eaten. ³Your* gold and silver have corroded, and their rust will be for a testimony against you* and will consume your* flesh as fire. You* stored up [treasure] in [the] last days!

⁴Listen! The pay of the laborers, of the ones having cut down grain [in] your* fields, their [pay] having been kept back by you* cries out, and the shouts [or, outcries] of the ones having reaped have entered into the ears of [the] Lord of Armies [fig., [the] Lord Almighty]. ⁵You* lived in luxury on the earth and were self-indulgent; you* nourished [fig., fattened] your* hearts as in a day of slaughter. ⁶You* condemned, you* murdered the righteous [person]; he does not resist you* (James 5:1-6).

First, it should be noted that James says "if a man comes into your* synagogue" not "into your church" Thus, this letter was clearly written before the split between the early Christian movement and Judaism. That began to occur in 49 AD, as mentioned in the discussion on the date of Hebrews. It is uncertain how widespread the split was due to Claudius' edict, but still this argues against a late date for the letter.

> [James] was written without any reference to Paul, probably before the Council of Jerusalem [in 50 AD] and before the circumcision controversy, in the earliest stage of the apostolic church as it is described in the first chapters of the Acts, when the Christians were not yet clearly distinguished and finally separated from the Jews (Schaff; 7418-7420).

Second, the rich began to come into the Church very early. This can be seen in Barnabas and Ananias and Sapphira donating land to the early Church (Acts 4:26f; 5:1f). Moreover, the Church began with a communal arrangement:

⁴⁴Now all the ones believing were at the same [place], and they were having all [things] in common. ⁴⁵And they were selling their possessions and their belongings, and they were distributing them to all, to the extent which anyone was having need (Acts 2:44f).

With this arrangement, it can be seen why a rich person would be especially welcomed. Thus, the favoring of the rich if anything argues for an early not late date.

> "The community appears to belong to the period before the fall of Jerusalem. The oppressors are wealthy landowners, who, after the siege of Jerusalem, virtually ceased to exist in Judaea" (Bible.org; "James: Introduction, Outline, and Argument").

The theological issue is the relationship of faith versus works.

Translator's Perspective on the Canon of the NT

¹⁴What [is] the advantage, my brothers [and sisters], if someone is saying he has faith but is not having works? Such faith is not able to save him, is it? ¹⁵Now if a brother or sister is naked [or, poorly dressed] and is lacking of the daily food, ¹⁶yet any of you* says to them, "Be going away in peace; be keeping yourselves warm and well fed," but does not give to them the necessary [things] of the body, what [is] the advantage? ¹⁷So also faith, if it is not having works, is dead [fig., utterly useless] by itself.

¹⁸But someone will say, "You have faith and I have works." [But I say], "Show to me your faith [apart] from your works, and I will show to you my faith by means of my works." ¹⁹You believe [or, are convinced] that God is one; you do well. The demons also believe—and they shudder [with fear]!

²⁰But are you willing to recognize, O empty [fig., foolish] person, that such faith without such works is dead? ²¹Abraham our father, he was justified [or, shown to be righteous] by means of works, having offered Isaac his son upon the altar, was he not? [see Gen 22:9] ²²Do you see that his faith was working together with his works, and by means of the works his faith was perfected? ²³And [so] was fulfilled the Scripture, the one saying, *"But Abraham believed* [or, *trusted*] *God, and it was accounted to him for righteousness."* [Gen 15:6] And he was called a friend of God. [see Isaiah 41:8] ²⁴So you* see that a person is justified [or, shown to be righteous] by means of works and not by means of faith only (James 2:14-24).

It is said this is a clear polemic against Paul's teaching of salvation being by faith apart from works:

⁸For by grace you* have been saved, through faith, and this [is] not from you*; [it is] the gift of God, ⁹not by works, so that no one shall boast (Eph 2:8f).

It is thus said that the Epistle of James had to be written after Pauls' letters, so as to be a counteraction to them. But this assumes the idea of salvation by faith alone originated with Paul, but it most certainly did not! As we saw in Chapter One, the idea that Jesus' death on the cross paid for our sins was a part of the earliest creeds of the Church. A natural outgrowth of that doctrine is that salvation is by faith in that atoning work. It is true Paul articulated this idea better than any other, but it did not originate with him. It was probably because some were not explaining it as well as Paul did that they misunderstood the doctrine. But Paul himself made a point of always coupling works with faith. After the preceding two verses, Paul writes:

[10]For we are His workmanship, having been created in Christ Jesus for good works, which God prepared beforehand so that we should walk about [fig., conduct ourselves] in them (Eph 2:10).

There is thus no conflict between James and Paul but one of emphasis. Paul focused on the way of attaining salvation, by faith, while James focuses on the results of that salvation, good works. But both recognize the need for both. Thus, James writes, "I will show to you my faith by means of my works" (2:18). Faith comes first, then works. Thus, if anything, this passage shows an early date of this book, before Paul began to more precisely articulate the doctrine.

But the contradiction between James and Paul is verbal rather than logical and doctrinal, and admits of a reconciliation which lies in the inseparable connection of a living faith and good works, or of justification and sanctification, so that they supplement and confirm each other, the one laying the true foundation in character, the other insisting on the practical manifestation. James wrote probably long before he had seen any of Paul's Epistles, certainly with no view to refute his doctrine or even to guard it against antinomian abuse; for this was quite unnecessary, as Paul did it clearly enough himself, and it would have been quite useless for Jewish Christian readers who were exposed to the danger of a barren legalism, but not of a pseudo-Pauline liberalism and antinomianism…
The one insists on a working faith, the other on faithful works. Both are right: James in opposition to the dead Jewish orthodoxy, Paul in opposition to self-righteous legalism (Schaff; 7385-7390).

Thus, overall, the issues addressed in the book argue for an early not late date and thus easily in the lifetime of James the brother of Jesus.

The Epistle was probably written about A.D. 47. The reference to the persecutions (ii, 6) is in the present tense, and indicates a stage of suffering which has not yet receded into the past of history. Now, in A.D. 44 the Churches of Judea were exposed to the persecution inflicted by Herod Agrippa, in which James, the son of Zebedee, was murdered (Acts 12:1 sqq.). Moreover, the author could not have written after the Council of Jerusalem (A.D. 51), where James acted as president, without some allusion to his decision unanimously accepted (Acts 15:4

Translator's Perspective on the Canon of the NT

sqq.). Another indication also derived from indirect internal evidence, is an allusion to the hungry and naked poor (of Jerusalem, ii, 15 sqq.); they suffered probably from the famine foretold by Agabus (Acts 11:28-30), and usually identified with one mentioned by Josephus (*Antiq.*, XX, ii, 5), A.D. 45 (New Advent; "Epistle of James").

Doctrine of God:

James has much to say about the nature of God, but it is mostly of a practical nature:

[5]Now if any of you* lacks wisdom, let him be asking from God, the One giving generously to all and not denouncing [or, without criticizing], and it will be given to him (Jam 1:5).

[13]Let no one say, when tempted, "I am being tempted by God," for God is incapable of being tempted by evil, and He Himself tempts no one (Jam 1:12).

[20]for [the] anger of a man does not produce the righteousness of God (Jam 1:20).

[19]You believe [or, are convinced] that God is one; you do well. (Jam 2:19a).

And he was called a friend of God (Jam 2:23b).

[9]With it [the tongue] we praise the God and Father, and with it we curse the people having been created according to the likeness of God (Jam 3:9).

[13]Is anyone enduring hardship among you*? Let him be praying. Is anyone being cheerful? Let him be singing praises (Jam 5:13).

To sum this up, God can be called upon for wisdom, He is separate from evil, He is righteous, God is one, we can be friends with God, God is the Father, and we are to praise Him for good things in life and pray to Him for help in hard times, and people are created in the image of God. These affirmations are all in line with the OT conception of God. These affirmations are interposed with injunctions for righteous living or are given as the basis of righteous living.

Essential Tenets:

We now come to another reason some doubts were raised about this epistle in the early Church. There is very little of a specific Christian nature to it. It is mostly a Jewish document, with Jesus being mentioned in just two verses:

¹James [cp. Matt 13:55; Acts 1:14; 15:13], a bondservant of God and of [the] Lord Jesus Christ (Jam 1:1a).

¹My brothers [and sisters], stop holding the faith of [or, in] our Lord Jesus Christ, the [Lord] of Glory [or, our Lord of Glory, Jesus Christ], with accepting of faces [fig., with a prejudiced attitude] (2:1).

These two verses affirm that Jesus is Lord and Christ. Then is a very difficult to translate verse, James affirms the reception of the Spirit, "Do you* think that the Scripture speaks in vain? Does the Spirit which [has] dwelt in us yearn to [the point of] envy?" (James 4:5). But that is it as far as affirmations of essential tenets go. This lack of Christian affirmations left this letter questionable in the minds of some early Christians. It seemed more in place in the OT than in the NT:

> The Epistle of James is the most Jewish writing in the New Testament. The Gospel according to Matthew was written for the Jews. The Epistle to the Hebrews is addressed explicitly to them. The Apocalypse is full of the spirit of the Old Testament. The Epistle of Jude is Jewish too. Yet all of these books have more of the distinctively Christian element in them than we can find in the Epistle of James. If we eliminate two or three passages containing references to Christ, the whole epistle might find its place just as properly in the Canon of the Old Testament as in that of the New Testament, as far as its substance of doctrine and contents is concerned. That could not be said of any other book in the New Testament (ISBE; "James, Epistle of").

However, there is nothing in the book that is contradictory to the Christian Gospel, and it contains much practical advice that is perfectly in line with how Christians are to live. Thus, this doctrinal lack was not sufficient to keep this book out of the canon of the NT.

Appeal and Mark of Inspiration:

This book was little known in the early Church. That is another reason it was among the *antilegomena*. The reason for this was two-

Translator's Perspective on the Canon of the NT

fold. First, it is rather short as compared to many other NT books, though longer than a few. Second, it was written to and for Jewish Christians, while very early in the history of the Church the Church had become mostly composed on Gentile converts. But it was not unknown either:

> The epistle of James, being addressed to the scattered Israelites, naturally was for a time less known. Origen, who lived between A.D. 185 and 254, first expressly mentions it (*Commentary on John*, 1:19). Clement of Rome quotes from it a century earlier (1 Ep. to Cor. 10: James 2:21,23). The Shepherd of Hermas soon after quotes James 4:7. Irenaeus (*Haer*. 4:16, section 2) refers to James 2:23. The old Syriac version has it and the Epistle to Hebrews alone of the books which were "disputed" (*antilegomena*, Euseb. 3:25) yet "acknowledged by the majority" (Euseb.). No Latin father of the first three centuries quotes it. It is specified as canonical both in the East and West in the councils of Hippo and Carthage, A.D. 397. Known only partially at first, it subsequently obtained a wider circulation; and the proofs becoming established of its having been recognized in apostolic churches, which had men endowed with the discernment of spirits to discriminate inspired utterances from uninspired (1 Cor. 14:37), it was universally accepted (Fausset's; James, Epistle of").

With its sound practical advice, there is much to commend this epistle. It is also important other reasons:

> The Epistle of James the Brother of the Lord was written, no doubt, from Jerusalem, the metropolis of the ancient theocracy and Jewish Christianity, where the author labored and died a martyr at the head of the mother church of Christendom and as the last connecting link between the old and the new dispensation. It is addressed to the Jews and Jewish Christians of the dispersion before the final doom in the year 70...
>
> It is probably the oldest of the New Testament books, meagre in doctrine, but rich in comfort and lessons of holy living based on faith in Jesus Christ, "the Lord of glory." It contains more reminiscences of the words of Christ than any other epistle. Its leading idea is "the perfect law of freedom," or the law of love revealed in Christ (Schaff; 10345-10357).

Despite a lack of specifically Christian theology, for these reasons James came to be seen as a valuable book. As such, it was accepted as bearing the mark of inspiration and included in the canon of the NT.

Conclusion on James:

Of all of the books we have investigated so far, this is the one with the greatest number of arguments against its inclusion in the canon. There is some uncertainly as to its author. It was not well known in the early Church, and it lacks the wealth of essential affirmations seen in other NT books. Given its lack of doctrine, if it were not included in the NT, that would not in any way change Christian doctrine. And all of the ethical appeals in it appear elsewhere in the Bible. Thus, nothing would change in that regard either. However, there is nothing doctrinal or ethically that conflicts with Biblical teaching elsewhere either.

In addition, it was certainly written in the first century, most likely in the first half thereof. There is good evidence that it was written by James the brother of Jesus, a pillar of the early Church, and it contains much practical advice that is in line with Christian ethics. For these reasons, it was appropriate for the early Church to have ultimately accepted its canonical status.

The next chapter will continue this discussion on the general epistles.

Translator's Perspective on the Canon of the NT

Chapter Nine
The General Epistles
Part Two

The previous chapter overviewed the general epistles and looked at Hebrews and James. This chapter will study 1Peter, 2Peter, and Jude.

1Peter

The First Epistle of Peter is the only book to be investigated in this chapter to be among the *homologoumena*, meaning there were no doubts as to its genuineness in the early Church. But we will take a look at the issues surrounding it.

Author:

The salutation to this letter is as follows:

¹Peter, an apostle of Jesus Christ, To the chosen [or, elect] sojourners of the Dispersion [i.e., the scattering of Jews outside of Judea] of Pontus, Galatia, Cappadocia, Asia, and Bithynia (1Pet 1:1).

Thus, the author identifies himself as Peter. However, this letter is of a high literary quality that seems too stylistic for a fisherman. It is right up there with James in this regard. But that can be explained by a statement near the end of the letter:

¹²By Silvanus, the faithful brother as I consider [him], through [whom] I wrote a few [words] encouraging and testifying this to be [the] true grace of God in which you* have stood firm (1Pet 5:12).

Thus, once again we see the use of a scribe. Peter dictated this epistle to Silvanus. This explains why the Greek is so stylistic. Silvanus probably cleaned up Peter's crude Greek. Going to back to James, this could also explain why his epistle is also of a high literary quality. He probably also used a scribe, even though his letter doesn't specifically say so, but it was a common practice for the time. It should also be noted that Silvanus was also a companion of Paul (1Cor 1:19; 1Th 1:1; 2Th 1:1).

Back to Peter, so much is said about him in the NT it would be impossible to reiterate it all here. But it has already been said that he

Translator's Perspective on the Canon of the NT

was one of the inner circle of three apostles that were closest to Jesus, he preached the sermon on the Day of Pentecost (Acts 2), most of the first half of Acts is about him, and Paul refers to him as a pillar of the early Church (Gal 2:9). He was Thus, a very prominent figure in the early Church.

Adding to all of this is Peter was most likely martyred under Nero in 64-68 AD:

> The tradition is that he died a martyr at Rome about 67 AD, when about 75 years old. His Lord and Master had predicted a violent death for him (Jn 21:18,19), which it is thought came to pass by crucifixion under Nero. It is said that at his own desire he was crucified head downward, feeling himself unworthy to resemble his Master in his death (ISBE; "Peter, Simon").

> Words of John 21:18, 19 clearly allude to the death of Peter and are cast into the literary form of prophecy. The author of this chapter is aware of a tradition concerning the martyrdom of Peter when the Apostle was an old man. And there is a possible reference here to crucifixion as the manner of his death. But as to when or where the death took place there is not so much as a hint.

> The strongest evidence to support the thesis that Peter was martyred in Rome is to be found in the Letter to the Corinthians (c. ad 96; 5:1–6:4) of Clement of Rome ...

> These sources, plus the suggestions and implications of later works, combine to lead many scholars to accept Rome as the location of the martyrdom and the reign of Nero as the time (Encyclopedia Britannica, "Saint Peter the Apostle").

The referenced passage from John reads:

[18]"Most positively, I say to you, when you were younger, you were fastening a belt on yourself and were walking about where you would desire. But when you become old, you will stretch out your hands, and another will fasten a belt on you and will lead [you] where you do not desire." [19]But this He said signifying by what sort of death he will glorify God. And having said this, He says to him, "Be following Me!"

The relevant part of the passage from 1Clement reads:

[3]Let us take before our eyes the good Apostles. [4]Peter, who through unjust jealousy, endured not one or two, <u>but</u> many toils, and in this way

having born witness [or, martyrdom; Gr., *martureo*], he went into the being owed place of glory (1Clement 5:3f).

Nero reigned from 54–68 AD, but persecutions of Christians did not begin until after Rome burned in 64 AD. To divert suspicion from himself, Nero put the blame on the Christians and began to have them burned to death. This occurred near the end of his reign, in about 64-68 AD. Thus, Peter and Paul would have been executed during this time period.

> Firstly, the Neronian Persecution (64-68 CE) which began after a vast conflagration destroyed a considerable area of Rome on 19th July 64. After an exemplary start to his reign, Nero had become unpopular and much feared; as much by his family as by the people. He led a life of excess and had carelessly drained the treasury. He then resorted to subterfuge, extortion and many dubious devices to replenish his much depleted funds. So it is of little surprise that after the fire of Rome a rumour spread alleging that Nero was the author of it. It is generally held that it was Nero's agents who started the fire to clear space for his proposed Golden Palace.
>
> As Tacitus records: "To suppress this rumour, Nero fabricated scapegoats..." that is, he apportioned the blame upon the Christian community. Nero had known Christians arrested and tortured into confessing the names of their brethren so they could be rounded up. Tacitus writes of an immense multitude who persisted at this time, indicating the size of the Roman Church: he also records the cruel and horrific deaths that the martyrs suffered (EarlyChurch.org.uk. "Roman Persecution of the Early Church").

1Peter was among the *homologoumena* in the early Church, meaning all of the Church spoke the same about it, that it was a genuine epistle of the apostle Peter. There is no record of his authorship ever being doubted and much evidence of it being affirmed.

The historical attestation to its authority as an apostolic document is abundant. Polycarp, disciple of the apostle John, martyred in 156 AD at 86 or more years of age, refers to the Epistle in unmistakable terms. Irenaeus, a man who may well be said to represent both the East and the West, who was a disciple of Polycarp, quotes it copiously, we are assured. Clement of Alexandria, born circa 150 AD, died circa 216 AD,

Translator's Perspective on the Canon of the NT

cites it many times in his Stromata, one passage (1 Pet 4:8) being quoted five times by actual count. "The testimony of the early-church is summed up by Eusebius (*Historia Ecclesiastica*, III, xxiii, 3). He places it among those writings about which no question was ever raised, no doubt ever entertained by any portion of the catholic church" (Professor Lumby in Bible Comm.) (ISBE; "Peter, The First Epistle of").

Polycarp's epistle will be discussed in Volume Three, where it will be dated to 107-117 AD. The quotes from 1Peter in Polycarp's epistle occur in chapters two, five, and eight:

[1]"For this reason, having tied up your* clothes at the waist [fig., having prepared yourselves for action]" [1Pet 1:13], serve as a bondservant to God in fear and truth, having forsaken the empty, futile discourse and the error of the many, "having believed in the One having raised up our Lord Jesus Christ from dead [ones] and having given glory to Him," and a throne at His right parts [fig., hand]. [1Pet 1:21], to whom all the heavenly and earthly [things] are subjected, to whom every breath sacredly serves, who is coming [as] Judge of living [ones] and of dead [ones], whose blood God will require from the ones being disobedient to Him.

[2]But the One having raised Him up from dead [ones] will raise up us also, if we do His will and walk in His commandments and love what He loved, keeping distant from all unrighteousness, covetousness, love of money, evil speaking [or, slander], false witness; "not returning evil for evil, or insult for insult," or blow for blow, or curse for curse, [1Pet 3:9], [3]but remembering what the Lord said, teaching, "Stop judging, so that you* shall not be judged; forgive, and it will be forgiven to you*; be showing mercy, that you* shall be shown mercy; with what measure you* measure, it will be measured back to you*." And, "Blessed [are] the poor [people] and the ones being persecuted for the sake of righteousness, for theirs is the kingdom of God." [Matt 7:1f; 6:14; 5:3,10] (Polycarp 2:1-3).

[3]Likewise also, [let] young men [be] blameless in all [things], above all thinking of [or, planning for] purity beforehand and bridling [or, restraining] themselves from every evil; for [it is] good to be hindered from the lusts in the world, since "every lust serves as a soldier [or, wages war] against the spirit" [1Pet 2:11], and "neither fornicators, nor passive partners in male-male sex, nor active partners in male-male sex will inherit the kingdom of God" [1Cor 6:9], nor the ones doing the improper [things]. Because of which, it is being necessary to be keeping

distant from all of these [things], being subjected to the elders [or, presbyters] and ministers as to God and to Christ. The virgins [are] to be walking about with a blameless and pure conscience (Polycarp 5:3).

[1]Therefore, let us continue constantly in our hope and by the down payment [or, guarantee] of our righteousness, who is Jesus Christ, [see 2Cor 1:22; 5:5; Eph 1:14] "who carried our sins in His own body upon the tree," "who did not sin, nor was deceit found in His mouth," but He endured all [things] for us, that should might live in Him. [1Pet 2:24,22; Isa 53:9] [2]Therefore, let us become imitators of His patient endurance, and if we should suffer on account of His Name, let us glorify Him. For this [One] set the example to us through Himself, and we believed this (Polycarp 8:1f).

Notice how words from 1Peter are placed beside words of Jesus as recorded in the Gospel of Matthew and the words of Paul, with the latter quoted as authoritative as both of the former.

Further evidence for Petrine authorship can be gathered by comparing this letter to the sermons of Peter recorded in the Book of Acts. Consider the following sets of passages:

---

[18]But what [things] God announced beforehand by [the] mouth of all His prophets, [that] the Christ [would] suffer, He fulfilled in this manner (Acts 3:18).

[43]To this One all the prophets bear witness [that] through His name every[one] that is believing [or, trusting] in Him receives forgiveness of sins" (Acts 10:43).

[10]Concerning which salvation [the] prophets sought diligently and carefully searched, the [prophets] having prophesied concerning the grace [coming] to you* (1Pet 1:10).

---

[32]And we are His witnesses of these matters, and also the Holy Spirit, whom God gave to the ones being obedient to Him" (Acts 5:32).

[12]To whom it was revealed that not to themselves but to you* they were serving these [things], which now were announced to you* by the ones having proclaimed the Gospel [or, Good News] to you* by [the] Holy Spirit having been sent from heaven, into which [things] angels [or, messengers [of the Lord]] desire to look (1Pet 1:12).

Translator's Perspective on the Canon of the NT

³⁴Then Peter having opened his mouth, said, "Truly, I comprehend that God is not One to accept faces [fig., to be prejudice] (Acts 10:34).

¹⁷And if you* call on the Father, the One judging impartially according to the work of each [person], conduct yourselves in fear [during] the time of your* sojourn [fig., life on earth] (1Pet 1:17).

---

³²This Jesus God raised up, of which we are all witnesses! ³³"Therefore, having been exalted to the right hand of God, and having received the promise of the Holy Spirit from the Father, He poured out this which you* now see and hear. ³⁴For David did not ascend into the heavens, but he says himself, *'The LORD said to my Lord, "Sit at My right [parts]* [fig., *on My right side*], ³⁵*until I put Your enemies [as] Your footstool for Your feet."'* [Psalm 110:1] ³⁶Therefore, let all the house of Israel know securely [fig., without a doubt] that God made Him both Lord and Christ—this Jesus whom you* crucified!" (Acts 2:32-36).

²¹the ones through Him believing in God, the One having raised Him from [the] dead and having given glory to Him, in order that your* faith and hope [or, expectation] are in God (1Pet 1:21).

---

¹⁰let it be known to you* all and to all the people of Israel that by the name of Jesus Christ the Nazarene, whom you* crucified, whom God raised from [the] dead, by Him has this [man] stood before you* healthy! ¹¹This is, *'The stone, the one having been rejected by you* the builders, the one becoming [fig., which has become] [the] head of a corner* [or, *cornerstone*].' [Psalm 118:22] (Acts 4:10f).

⁷Therefore, the honor [is] to you*, the ones believing. But to the ones disobeying [or, refusing to believe], *"[The] stone which the builders rejected, this [one] became for [the] head of [the] corner* [or, *the chief cornerstone*]." [Psalm 118:22] ⁸and *"A stone of tripping and a rock of a stumbling block,"* [Isaiah 8:14] who trip at the word, refusing to believe, to which also they were appointed (1Pet 2:7f).

---

²⁸And he said to them, "You* know how it is unlawful for a man, a Jew, to be associating with or to be visiting one of another race [cp. John

18:28], and [yet] God showed to me to be calling no one common or unclean [or, defiled] (Acts 10:28).

¹⁷Honor all [people]. Love the brotherhood [fig., community of believers]. You* yourselves be fearing God. Be honoring the king. (1Pet 2:17).

---

³⁰The God of our fathers raised up Jesus, whom you* murdered, having hanged [Him] on a tree [or, a cross] (Acts 5:30).

³⁹"And we are witnesses of all [things] which He did, both in the country of the Jews and in Jerusalem; whom they also executed, having hanged [Him] on a tree [or, a cross] (Acts 10:39).

²⁴who Himself carried our sins in His body on the tree [or, cross] (1Pet 2:24a).

---

¹⁹Therefore, repent and turn back [to God] in order for your* sins to be blotted out, in order that times of refreshing shall come from [the] face [fig., presence] of the Lord…
²⁶To you* first, God, having raised up His Servant Jesus, sent Him, blessing you* in the turning away [or, by turning away] each [of you*] from your* wicked ways" (Acts 3:19,26).

so that having died to sins, we shall live to righteousness; of whom *"by His wound[s] you* were healed"* (1Pet 2:24b).

---

¹⁴But you* denied [or, disowned] the Holy and Righteous [One], and demanded a man, a murderer, to be graciously granted to you* (Acts 3:14).

¹⁸For Christ also suffered once for sin for all [time, the] Righteous [One] on behalf of unrighteous [people], so that He should bring you* to God (1Pet 3:18a).

---

⁴²And He gave strict orders to us to preach to the people and to solemnly testify that He is the One having been designated by God [to be] Judge of living [people] and of dead [people] (Acts 10:42).

Translator's Perspective on the Canon of the NT

⁵who will give an account to the One being prepared to judge living [people] and dead [people] (1Pet 4:5).

---

³²This Jesus God raised up, of which we are all witnesses! (Acts 2:32).

¹⁵but you* killed the Prince of Life, whom God raised from [the] dead, of which we are witnesses (Acts 3:15).

I encourage the elders among you* [as] a fellow-elder and a witness of the sufferings of Christ and a partaker of the glory about to be revealed (1Pet 5:1).

Moreover, as seen in the preceding quotes and as will be seen even more later, this epistle is filled with affirmations of the work of work of Christ, as would be expected from someone who witnessed His sufferings and resurrection.

Finally, this epistle is referred to in 2Peter:

¹This [is] now, beloved, [the] second letter I am writing to you*, in which I am stirring up your* pure [or, sincere] mind by reminding [you*] ²to be mindful of the words having been previously spoken by the holy prophets and of the commandment of your* apostles of the Lord and Savior (2Pet 3:1f).

The issues surrounding 2Peter will be discussed shortly, but there is no doubt it was an early document and thus gives an early witness to Peter being the author of 1Peter.

But despite this overwhelming internal and early external evidence, there are many today who doubt that Peter in fact wrote this letter. There are many reasons for this denial.

First is a point already alluded to, the style of the Greek of this letter. It is said to be too stylistic for a Galilean fisherman. But as already noted; Peter used a secretary who would have cleaned up his rough Greek. Thus, this objection holds little water.

Second is a claimed lack of personal references to the life of Jesus. It is said that surely Peter would have buttressed his authority by making references to Jesus that only he as a part of the inner circle would know. Related to this is the lack of an assertion of his authority in the epistle. However, as already indicated, Peter was well-known in the early Church and thus did not need to tout his "references." Christians by and large knew he was an apostle, and not just any apostle but a leader of the early Church. His authority was Thus, unquestioned. Just his name would suffice, as it did for James in his letter. Thus, again, this objection is without basis.

Third is this verse, "¹I encourage the elders among you* [as] a fellow-elder and a witness of the sufferings of Christ and a partaker of the glory about to be revealed" (1Pet 5:1).

It is said Peter would never call himself a mere "elder" since he was an apostle. But Peter did call himself "an apostle" in 1:1, and the early Church did not consider an elder to be "mere" but a very important position. This was seen in our discussions on 2 and 3John. Whether that was John the apostle or John the elder, it shows that an elder was considered authoritative. Note also that Peter says he was "a witness of the sufferings of Christ" Thus, negating the second objection.

The final couple of objections concern the date of this letter, to which we turn next.

Date of Writing:

The date of writing can be determined from internal evidence. The first concerns Peter's attitude toward the Roman authorities:

¹³Therefore, be subject to every human institution [or, authority] for the sake of [or, on account of] the Lord, whether to a king as [the one] having authority, ¹⁴or to governors as [the ones] having been sent by him for [the] punishment of evildoers, but [for the] praise of [the ones] doing good. ¹⁵For such is the will of God, doing good [in order] to be silencing the ignorance of the foolish people. ¹⁶[Live] as free [persons], yet not using such freedom as a covering [or, excuse] for evil, but as bondservants of God.

¹⁷Honor all [people]. Love the brotherhood [fig., community of believers]. You* yourselves be fearing God. Be honoring the king. [cp. Rom 13:1-7] (1Pet 2:13-17).

Note the cross-reference to Paul's epistle to Romans. It is clear that this epistle and Romans were written before the persecutions under Nero began near the end of his reign (c. 64 AD). Otherwise, both Paul and Peter would not have spoken in such glowing terms about obeying human institutions. That leads to the next point:

⁶in which you* are very glad, [though] now [for] a little [while], if it is necessary, you* have been distressed by various trials (1Pet 1:6).

Translator's Perspective on the Canon of the NT

¹²Beloved, stop being surprised by the fiery ordeal [or, painful suffering] taking place among you* to try you*, as [though] a strange [thing] is happening to you* (1Pet 4:12).

⁸Be sober [or, Be clear-headed]; keep watch! Your* adversary [the] Devil walks about as a roaring lion seeking someone to devour, ⁹whom you* [are to] stand up against [or, resist], [being] steadfast in the faith, knowing the same sufferings are being experienced by your* brotherhood [fig., the community of believers] in [the] world (1Pet 5:8f).

In these verses, Peters speaks about Christians being persecuted "in the world." It is for this reason that some claim this epistle was not written until the end of the first century, during the persecutions under Domitian, as the ones under Nero were not widespread. But as just seen, Peter speaks glowingly of human institutions and directs submission to them. Thus, this epistle had to be written before both of these times of persecutions by the Roman government. "This submission would scarcely be pressed if the state had already proscribed Christianity and decreed its total suppression" (ISBE; "Peter, First Epistle of"). The sufferings mentioned here are probably at the hands of Jews, as seen in the Book of Acts. Thus, this letter fits within the time frame of Acts and thus before 62 AD.

Next, it is claimed this letter is dependent of Paul's letters. And there are many parallels. One has already been indicated—the attitude of both Paul and Peter towards the Roman authorities. Add to this the following sets of passages:

---

¹⁸The domestic bondservants, [continue] being subjected [or, submitted] with all fear to your* masters, not only to the good and gentle [or, considerate], but also to the crooked [or, harsh] (1Pet 2:18).

⁵The bondservants, be obeying the masters according to [the] flesh, with fear and trembling, in sincerity of your* heart, as to Christ, ⁶not with eye-service as people-pleasers, but as bondservants of Christ, doing the will of God from [the] soul [fig., wholeheartedly], ⁷serving with goodwill [or, wholehearted zeal] as to the Lord and not to people (Eph 6:5-7

²²The bondservants, be obeying with respect to all [things] your* masters according to [the] flesh, not in eye-service as people-pleasers, but in sincerity of heart, fearing God. ²³And every[thing], whatever

you* shall be doing, be working from [your*] soul [fig., heartily] as to the Lord and not to people, ²⁴knowing that from [the] Lord you* will receive the recompense of the inheritance, for to the Lord Christ you* are serving as a bondservant (Col 3:22-24).

---

¹Likewise, the wives, [continue] being subjected [or, submitted] to your* own husbands, so that even if some are refusing to believe the word, through the conduct of their wives they will be won [for Christ] without a word, ²having observed your* pure conduct with respect (1Pet 3:1f).

¹⁸The wives, be subjecting [or, submitting] yourselves to your* own husbands, as is fitting in [the] Lord (Col 3:18).

¹⁶For how do you know, O wife, whether you will save your husband? Or how do you know, O husband, whether you will save your wife? (1Cor 7:16).

---

⁵For in this way in times past also the holy women, the ones placing their hope on [or, trusting in] God were adorning themselves, being subjected [or, submitted] to their own husbands, ⁶as Sarah was obedient to Abraham, calling him "lord," of whom you* became daughters, doing good, and not fearing any terror (1Pet 3:5f).

²²The wives, be subjecting [or, submitting] yourselves to your* own husbands, as to the Lord, ²³because a husband is head of his wife, as also Christ [is] head of the Assembly, and He is [the] Savior of the body. ²⁴But even as the Assembly is subjected [or, submitted] to Christ, so also the wives [should be] to their own husbands in everything (Eph 5:22-24).

---

⁷The husbands, likewise, [continue] living with [your* wives] according to knowledge, as with a weaker vessel, with the feminine [one], showing respect, as also being joint-heirs of [the] grace of life, for your* prayers not to be hindered (1Pet 3:7).

⁴[for] each of you* to know how to be acquiring his own vessel [fig., wife; cp. 1Pet 3:7] in sanctification and honor (1Th 4:4).

Translator's Perspective on the Canon of the NT

²⁵The husbands, be loving your* own wives, just as also Christ loved the Assembly and gave Himself [or, handed Himself over] on her behalf (Eph 5:25).

¹⁹The husbands, be loving your* wives, and stop becoming bitter towards them (Col 3:19).

---

³For the time of life having past [is] sufficient for us to accomplish the desire of the Gentiles, having gone [fig., lived] in flagrant sexual immorality, lusts, drunkenness, drunken orgies, drinking parties, and unlawful [fig., abominable] idolatries; ⁴in which they are surprised [by] your* not running together with [them] into the same excess of reckless living, speaking evil of [you*], ⁵who will give an account to the One being prepared to judge [the] living and [the] dead (1Pet 4:3-5).

¹⁹Now the works of the flesh are evident, which are: adultery, fornication, impurity [or, immorality], flagrant sexual immorality, ²⁰idolatry, witchcraft, hostilities [or, feuds], quarrels, jealous rivalries, angry outbursts, selfish ambitions, divisions [or, discords], heretical sects, ²¹envies [or, jealousies], murders, drunkennesses [or, drinking bouts], drunken orgies, and the [things] like these; which I forewarn you*, just as I also warned [you*] before that the ones practicing such [things] will not inherit [the] kingdom of God (Gal 5:19-21).

---

¹⁰Just as each [believer] received a spiritual gift, [be] serving [with] it to one another, as good stewards of the manifold [or, widely varied] grace of God (1Pet 4:10).

⁴Now [there] are varieties of spiritual [gifts], but the same Spirit. ⁵And [there] are varieties of ministries, and the same Lord. ⁶And [there] are varieties of divine workings [or, activities], but the same God is the One supernaturally working all such [things] in all. ⁷But to each [one] has been given the manifestation of the Spirit for the advantage [of all] [or, for the common good] (1Cor 12:4-7).

The following is a complete list of possible parallels between Peter and Paul:

1) 1Pet 1:2 / Rom 8:29; 1Thes 5:9; 2Thes 2:13; Eph 1:7
2) 1Pet 1:8 / 2Cor 5:7

3) 1Pet 1:13f / Col 3:5-9; 2Cor 7:1
4) 1Pet 1:18f / Eph 1:7; Col 1:20
5) 1Pet 1:21 / Eph 1:20-22
6) 1Pet 2:13f / Rom 13:1-4
7) 1Pet 2:18 / Eph 6:5-8
8) 1Pet 2:22f / 2Cor 5:21
9) 1Pet 3:1 / 1Cor 7:14; Eph 5:22
10) 1Pet 3:3f / 1Tim 2:9
11) 1Pet 3:18 / Rom 5:6-10; 8:11
12) 1Pet 3:22 / Eph 1:20-22
13) 1Pet 4:1-3 / Rom 6:1-7; Col 3:5-9
14) 1Pet 4:5 / Rom 14:9f
15) 1Pet 4:10f / Rom 12:6-8
16) 1Pet 4:12-16 / 2Cor 1:3-7
17) 1Pet 5:2 / Acts 20:28
18) 1Pet 5:5 / Eph 5:21

It is thus clear that Peter and Paul had much in agreement. This disproves a common notion that these two were in sharp disagreement. But as for our discussion, some claim this proves that 1Peter had to be written after all of these Pauline epistles and even Acts. Even if that were true, it would not discount Petrine authorship, as all of these Pauline letters were written before the time of Peter's death. Given that Pauls' companion Silvanus was with Peter when he wrote this letter, then he could have informed Peter as to the content of Paul's letters and teachings, even if Peter himself had not read all of them. Thus, this letter could be dated after the writing of all of these Pauline letters and of Acts but before Peter's death, or in 62-68 AD.

However, it is just as likely that Peter and Pauls' teachings parallel each other because they are both expounding upon Christians truths that circulated throughout the Church in the early decades. It was seen in the case of the early creeds that many early essentials doctrines were already written down and circulating, and there is every reason to believe common teachings on other matters also circulated. Thus, Peter would not be dependent on Paul, but both independently reflect this tradition.

But whatever the case, these parallels do not prove 1Peter had to be written long after the death of Peter as some claim.

The next issue is the place of composition of this letter, and those with Peter when he wrote it. Peter writes at the end of his letter:

[13]The [woman] [i.e., Peter's wife or your sister-assembly] in Babylon [i.e., possibly a cryptic reference to Rome], chosen together

Translator's Perspective on the Canon of the NT

with [you*], greets you*, and Mark my son [fig., disciple; i.e., the author of the second Gospel] (1Pet 5:12).

Here we see Peter possibly referring to his wife. On a side note; "Clemens Alex [of Alexandria] gives the name of Peter's wife as Perpetua" (Fausset's; "Peter"). But what concerns us is the reference to Babylon. As the note in the ALT indicates, this is possibly a cryptic reference to Rome. I included that note in the ALT as it is what I learned in seminary, and there is a strong early tradition behind it:

> "Babylon" is a cryptic term indicating Rome, and it is the understanding utilized in Revelation 14:8; 16:19; 17:5, 6 and in the works of various Jewish seers (Encyclopedia Britannica, "Saint Peter the Apostle").

> The critics who have denied Peter's sojourn at Rome must necessarily deny that the letter was written from there, but the great majority of critics, with all Christian antiquity, agree that it was written at Rome itself, designated by the metaphorical name Babylon (v, 13). This interpretation has been accepted from the most remote times, and indeed no other metaphor could so well describe the city of Rome, rich and luxurious as it was, and given over to the worship of false gods and every species of immorality. Both cities had caused trouble to the people of God, Babylon to the Jews, and Rome to the Christians. Moreover this metaphor was in use among the early Christians (cf. Revelation 14:8; 16:19; 17:5; 18:2, 10, 21). Finally, tradition has not brought us the faintest memory of any sojourn of Peter at Babylon (New Advent; "Epistles of Saint Peter").

However, now that I have looked into the matter further, it is possible that this letter was in fact written from a city named Babylon:

> It was written from Babylon, on the Euphrates, which was at this time one of the chief seats of Jewish learning, and a fitting centre for labour among the Jews. It has been noticed that in the beginning of his epistle Peter names the provinces of Asia Minor in the order in which they would naturally occur to one writing from Babylon (Easton's, "Peter, First Epistle of").

I have Thus, updated the note in the ALT to reflect this possibility to "i.e., a cryptic reference to Rome, or this is Babylon, on the Euphrates River."

How this affects the dating is those who deny Petrine authorship claim this letter is dependent on The Revelation for this identification of Rome with Babylon (see Rev 14:8; 16:19; 17:5; 18:2,10,21). As such, it was not written until the 90s, long after Peter's death. But if Babylon is not a cryptic reference to Rome, then there is no such dependency. In fact, it would be an argument for 1Peter to have been written before The Revelation and this association became popular. But even if it is a reference to Rome, then it is just as possible The Revelation is dependent on 1Peter as the reverse.

Also in this verse is mention of Mark being with Peter. This letter would Thus, have to be written at a time when Mark was not with Paul, but Mark is mentioned twice by Paul in his later letters.

[10]Aristarchus greets you*, my fellow-prisoner, and Mark, the cousin of Barnabas [see Acts 15:37] (concerning whom you* received instructions; if he comes to you*, receive him) (Col 4:10).

[11]Only Luke is with me. Having picked up Mark, be bringing [him] with yourself, for he is useful to me for ministry [or, service] (2Tim 4:11).

1Peter was probably written between the time of Colossians and 2Timothy. Thus, 1Peter could be dated to the early 60s. It should also be noted that with Mark being another companion of both Paul and Peter, this could account for why each knew of the others' writings and teachings.

Overall, the evidence favors a date in the early to mid-60s, and there is no reason to date it long after the death of Peter and thus to deny the Petrine authorship. And with that dating, it means this book was written near the end of Peter's life, "when his ardent natural temper was deeply humbled, softened, and sanctified by the work of grace" (Schaff; 10361-10362).

Doctrine of God:

Peter mentions God many times in this letter. But he seems to mostly assume his readers had a correct conception of God to begin with. This would be a logical assumption given that his intended audience were Jewish Christians. But still, the following references are instructive.

Translator's Perspective on the Canon of the NT

²according to [the] foreknowledge of God [the] Father (1:2a).

⁵the ones being guarded by [the] power of God (1:5a).

in order that your* faith and hope [or, expectation] are in God (1:21b).

through [the] word of God [which is] living and remaining into the age [fig., forever] (1:23b).

You* yourselves be fearing God (2:17b).

¹⁷For [it is] better to suffer [for] doing good, if the will of God might be willing [it], than [for] doing evil (3:17).

¹⁰Just as each [believer] received a spiritual gift, [be] serving [with] it to one another, as good stewards of the manifold [or, widely varied] grace of God. [cp. 1Cor 12:4-7] ¹¹When someone speaks, [let him speak] as [the] oracles [or, inspired utterances] of God. When someone serves, [let him serve] as from [the] strength [or, ability] as God supplies, so that in all [things] God shall be glorified through Jesus Christ, to whom is the glory and the might [or, dominion] into the ages of the ages! [fig., forever and ever!] So be it! (4:10f).

¹⁵Be making sure none of you* suffer as a murderer, or a thief, or an evildoer, or as a meddler into other's affairs; ¹⁶but if as a Christian, stop being ashamed, but be glorifying God in this matter (4:15f).

¹⁹So also the ones suffering according to the will of God, as to a trustworthy Creator, must be committing [or, entrusting] their souls in good doing (4:19).

Clothe yourselves with humility, for, *"God resists* [or, *sets Himself in opposition against*] *proud [people], but He gives grace to humble [people]."* [Prov 3:34, LXX] ⁶Therefore, be humbled [or, humble yourselves] under the mighty hand of God, so that He shall exalt you* at [the proper] time [cp. Jam 4:10], ⁷having cast all your* anxiety upon Him, for it is a concern to Him about you*! [fig., for He cares for you*!] (5:5b-7).

¹⁰But the God of all grace, the One having called you* into His eternal glory in Christ Jesus, [after] you* have suffered [for] a little while, may He Himself make you* perfect [or, fully adequate]—He will

establish, strengthen, [and] firmly ground [you*] [or, cause [you*] to be unwavering]. ¹¹To Him [be] the glory and the might [or, dominion] into the ages of the ages! [fig., forever and ever!] So be it!

¹²By Silvanus, the faithful brother as I consider [him], through [whom] I wrote a few [words], encouraging and testifying this to be [the] true grace of God in which you* have stood firm (5:10-12).

Putting this all together, to Peter, God's foreknowledge directs our actions, we are guarded by God's power, we can place our trust in God, God's word is eternal, we are to fear God, we are to accept God's will for our lives, God is mighty, God gives each of us a gift, and we are to use it, we are to glorify God even in hard times, God is graceful and cares for us, God will make us better people, God is to praised, and God is full of grace. All of this is in perfect accordance with the OT conception of God.

Essential Tenets:

Not unexpectedly, this epistle is filled with many affirmations of the work of Christ and of other early essential tenets. Peter begins by associating the Father, Son, and Spirit together:

²according to [the] foreknowledge of God [the] Father, in sanctification of [the] Spirit, for obedience and sprinkling of [the] blood of Jesus Christ: May grace and peace be multiplied to you*! (1Pet 1:2).

Peter then refers to "our Lord Jesus Christ" (1:3). He calls Jesus "Christ" 24 more times (e.g., 1:1,2,3,7). Then are the following:

for obedience and sprinkling of [the] blood of Jesus Christ (1:2b).

³Blessed [be] the God and Father of our Lord Jesus Christ, the One according to His great mercy having regenerated us to a living hope [or, confident expectation], through [the] resurrection of Jesus Christ from [the] dead (1:3).

⁹receiving the end of your* faith, [the] salvation of [your*] souls (1:9).

¹⁰Concerning which salvation [the] prophets sought diligently and carefully searched, the [prophets] having prophesied concerning the grace [coming] to you*, ¹¹searching for who or what time the Spirit of Christ in them was clearly showing, predicting the sufferings of Christ and the glory after these (1:10).

Translator's Perspective on the Canon of the NT

¹⁸knowing that not with corruptible [things like] silver or gold were you* redeemed from your* futile way of life handed down by your* fathers, ¹⁹but with [the] precious blood of Christ, as of a lamb unblemished and spotless, ²⁰having been foreknown, on the one hand before [the] laying of the foundation of [the] world [or, from [the] beginning of the creation of [the] universe], on the other hand having been revealed in [the] last times for the sake of you*, ²¹the ones through Him believing in God, the One having raised Him from [the] dead and having given glory to Him, in order that your* faith and hope [or, expectation] are in God (1:18-21).

²¹Because, for this [reason] you* were called, because Christ also suffered on our behalf, leaving behind an example for you*, so that you* should follow in His footsteps, ²²who *"Did not commit sin, nor was deceit found in His mouth,"* [Isaiah 53:9] ²³who being verbally abused, was not returning verbal insults, suffering, was not threatening, but was entrusting Himself to the One judging righteously; ²⁴who Himself carried our sins in His body on the tree [fig., cross], so that having died to sins, we shall live to righteousness; of whom *"by His wound[s] you* were healed."* [Isaiah 53:5] (1Pet 2:21-24).

¹⁸For Christ also suffered once for sin for all [time, the] Righteous [One] on behalf of unrighteous [people], so that He should bring you* to God, [Christ] having been put to death on the one hand in flesh [fig., in the physical realm], on the other hand having been made alive in spirit [fig., in the spiritual realm via resurrection], ¹⁹in which [state of resurrection] also having gone, He proclaimed [His victory] to the spirits in prison, ²⁰having formerly refused to believe, when the patience of God kept eagerly waiting in [the] days of Noah, while an ark was being prepared, in which a few, that is, eight souls, were saved through water; ²¹which [as] an antitype baptism [or, immersion] now also saves us (not [the] removal of [the] filth of [the] flesh, but an appeal to God for [or, a pledge to God from] a good conscience) through [the] resurrection of Jesus Christ, ²²who is at [the] right hand of God, having gone into heaven, angels [or, messengers [of the Lord]] and authorities and powers having been subjected to Him (3:18-22).

¹Therefore, Christ having suffered [or, since Christ suffered] on our behalf in [the] flesh (4:1a).,

¹³But according as you* are sharing in the sufferings of Christ, be rejoicing, so that also in the revelation of His glory you* shall rejoice, being very glad (4:13).

¹I encourage the elders among you* [as] a fellow-elder and a witness of the sufferings of Christ and a partaker of the glory about to be revealed (5:1).

⁴And when the Chief Shepherd appears, you* will receive the unfading victor's wreath [or, crown] of glory (5:4).

In these many passages, Peter affirms the death of Jesus in the flesh and His shed blood, Thus, also affirming His full humanity. Salvation is by faith. He affirms His death was for our sins and was according to the Scriptures. He affirms the resurrection, ascension to the right hand of God, and Second Coming of Jesus. He affirms salvation is by faith in Christ's death and that this salvation will enable us to live righteous lives and to be rejoicing. Thus, all of the essential aspects of the work of Christ are affirmed.

Peter also has much to say about the Holy Spirit. In addition to associating the Spirit with the Father and Son, he affirms the work of the Spirit in believers and the renewal of believers:

²²Having [or, Since you* have] purified your* souls in obedience to the truth through [the] Spirit in sincere brotherly love [fig., affection for fellow-believers], love one another earnestly from a pure heart, ²³having been [or, because you* have been] regenerated [or, born again] not from corruptible seed but incorruptible, through [the] word of God [which is] living and remaining into the age [fig., forever] (1Pet 1:22f).

Peter also discusses how the Spirit works in the lives of believers:

¹²Beloved, stop being surprised by the fiery ordeal [or, painful suffering] taking place among you* to try you*, as [though] a strange [thing] is happening to you*. ¹³But according as you* are sharing in the sufferings of Christ, be rejoicing, so that also in the revelation of His glory you* shall rejoice, expressing great happiness. ¹⁴When you* are being insulted for the name of Christ, [you* are] fortunate [or, blessed], for the Spirit of the glory and of God [fig., the glorious Spirit of God] rests on you*. On the one hand according to them, He is being blasphemed, on the other hand according to you*, He is glorified (1Peter 4:12-14).

Translator's Perspective on the Canon of the NT
Appeal and Mark of Inspiration:
With its strong teaching of the essentials of the Gospel, this letter has much appeal to both the saved and unsaved person. It is an encouragement to the former in the soundness of his or her faith, and it is an encouragement to the latter to trust in Christ for salvation.

With the focus on the persecutions the readers are experiencing, this letter is an encouragement to those who are suffering in any way that God will give them strength to endure. This letter is also filled with much practical advice for everyday living. With all of this sound doctrine and practical advice, this epistle bears the mark of inspiration.

> It consists of precious consolations and exhortations to a holy walk after the example of Christ, to joyful hope of the heavenly inheritance, to patience under the persecutions already raging or impending. It gives us the fruit of a rich spiritual experience, and is altogether worthy of Peter and his mission to tend the flock of God under Christ, the chief shepherd of souls (Schaff; 10364-10366).

Conclusion on 1Peter:
This epistle was universally accepted in the early Church as being written by the apostle Peter, a leader of the early Church. Thus, its authority was unquestioned. It is only today's critics that have tried to cast doubts on its authenticity, but their arguments are without basis. As such, this letter was rightly included in the canon of the NT.

2Peter

The issues surrounding 2Peter are much more complicated than for 1Peter, as unlike 1Peter, 2Peter was among the *antilegomena* in the early Church.

> The Second Epistle of Peter comes to us with less historical support of its genuineness than any other book of the New Testament. In consequence, its right to a place in the Canon is seriously doubted by some and denied by others. There are those who confidently assign it to the Apostolic age and to the apostle whose name it bears in the New Testament, while there are those who as confidently assign it to post-apostolic times, and repudiate its Petrine authorship (ISBE; "Peter, Second Epistle of").

Author:

The salutation to this letter is, "¹Simon Peter, a bondservant and an apostle of Jesus Christ" (2Pet 1:1). Thus, this letter clearly claims to be written by Peter the apostle. This claim is reaffirmed later, "¹This [is] now, beloved, [the] second letter I am writing to you*" (2Pet 3:1).

Thus, the author claims to be the same person who wrote 1Peter. However, there were many doubts about this claim in the early Church, and more so today. In the early Church, 2Peter seems to have been known in the late first to second century, but this is not certain.

> In the first two centuries there is not in the Apostolic Fathers and other ecclesiastical writers, if we except Theophilus of Antioch (180), a single quotation properly so called from this Epistle; at most there are some more or less probable allusions in their writings, e.g., the First Epistle of St. Clement of Rome to the Corinthians, the "Didache", St. Ignatius, the Epistle of Barnabas, the "Pastor" of Hermas, the Epistle of Polycarp to the Philippians, the Dialogue of St. Justin with Trypho, St. Irenæus, the Clementine "Recognitions", the "Acts of Peter", etc. The Epistle formed part of the ancient Itala, but is not in the Syriac. This proves that the Second Epistle of Peter existed and even had a certain amount of authority. But it is impossible to bring forward with certainty a single explicit testimony in favour of this authenticity (New Advent; "The Epistles of Saint Peter").

Given that 1Peter was well-known, and that 2Peter was written shortly after 1Peter, from the same location and to the same recipients, it is said by the critics that it is very strange 2Peter would not also be well-known. You would think the two letters would have circulated as a unit, like the letters of Paul did.

That does sound reasonable, except for one issue. During the first two centuries, there were many spurious Gnostic writings written under the name of Peter. This will be seen in Volume Three. But here; this plethora of pseudepigraphical or forged Petrine writings made the early Church leaders very hesitant about accepting or quoting from any documents purported to be written by the apostle Peter, and they spoke out strongly against such spurious documents. But despite this pattern:

> Even though all other works attributed to Peter were rejected by the church (save 1 Peter), "there is no evidence from any part of the early church that this epistle was ever rejected as spurious, in spite of the hesitancy which existed over its

Translator's Perspective on the Canon of the NT

reception" (Bible.org; "Second Peter: Introduction, Argument, and Outline).

Thus, the early Church strongly rejected most claimed Petrine documents, knowing they were forgeries; but they accepted 1Peter without question as being genuine and held 2Peter somewhat in limbo. They seemed to be unsure one way or the other about it. This shows the early Church was very cautious when it came to claimed Petrine writings. The fact that this letter was not outright rejected like most other Petrine writings needs an explanation. That is probably to be found in its sound theology as opposed to the very unsound theology found in Gnostic pseudepigraphical Petrine writings.

That issue will be addressed in Volume Three, but here the main reason for the early hesitancy over this letter is the style of Greek of it is vastly different than that of 1Peter. Of this there is little doubt. As discussed previously, the Greek of 1Peter is among the most stylistic of the NT, while the Greek of 2Peter is among the least literary of the NT. Simply put, 2Peter is very easy to translate while 1Peter is very difficult. This could argue for different authors, if it were not for an issue that has been mentioned several times before.

In our discussion of 1Peter it was seen that Peter used a scribe in writing it, Silvanus to be exact, as mentioned at the end of that letter. But 2Peter has no such subscription to it. Thus, it is very possible that Peter wrote 2Peter himself, in his own fisherman's Greek, while Silvanus cleaned up Peter's crude Greek for 1Peter. It is also possible Peter used a scribe other than Silvanus for 2Peter, one who was not as skilled as Silvanus. Either way, the difference in style can be explained, while still having Peter as the ultimate author of both letters. Moreover, despite the obvious dissimilarity of writing style, there are many similar expressions between the two letters that are not found at all or only rarely elsewhere in the NT. In the following sets of verses, the English translation of the same Greek word(s) is marked with a hashtag (#).

---

⁷so that the genuineness of your* faith, [being] much more #precious [than] gold (1Pet 1:7a).

¹⁹but with [the] #precious blood of Christ, as of a lamb unblemished and spotless (1Pet 1:19b).

¹Simon Peter, a bondservant and an apostle of Jesus Christ, To the ones having obtained [or, having been chosen to have] an equally

#precious faith with us (2Pet 1:1a). (Found elsewhere in the NT only in Acts 5:34; 20:24; 1Cor 3:14; Heb 13:4; Rev 17:4; 18:12,16; 21:11,19).

---

⁹But you* [are] "*a chosen race, a royal priesthood, a holy nation, a people for [God's own] possession,*" [Exod 19:5,6; Isaiah 43:20,21; 61:6] in order that you* shall proclaim the #excellencies of the One having called you* out of darkness into His marvelous light (1Pet 2:9).

³as [fig., seeing that] His divine power has given to us all the [things] pertaining to life and godliness through the full [or, true] knowledge of the One having called us by glory and #excellence (2Pet 1:3).

⁵But also [for] this very [reason], having applied all diligence, provide with your* faith moral #excellence [or, virtue], and with moral #excellence knowledge (2Pet 2:15). (Found elsewhere in the NT only in Phil 4:8).

---

²²Having [or, Since you* have] purified your* souls in obedience to the truth through [the] Spirit in sincere #brotherly love [fig., affection for fellow-believers], love one another earnestly from a pure heart (1Pet 1:22).

⁷and with godliness #brotherly love [fig., affection for fellow-believers], and with #brotherly love [Gr., *philadelphia*] love [Gr., *agape*] (2Pet 1:7). (Found only in these verses in the NT).

---

¹²having your* conduct good [or, honorable] among the Gentiles, so that in what they speak against you* as evildoers, having #observed your* good works, they shall glorify God in [the] day of visitation (1Pet 2:12).

²having #observed your* pure conduct with respect (1Pet 3:2).

¹⁶For not having followed having been cleverly made-up myths, we made known to you* the power and Arrival [or, Coming] of our Lord Jesus Christ, but having become #eyewitnesses of the magnificence of that One (2Pet 1:16). (Note: "having observed" is the verbal form of "eyewitnesses." Both forms only occur in these verses in the NT.)

Translator's Perspective on the Canon of the NT

¹⁹but with [the] precious blood of Christ, as of a lamb unblemished and #spotless (1Pet 1:19).

¹⁴For this reason, beloved, waiting for these [things], be eager [or, diligent] to be found by Him in peace, #spotless and blameless (2Pet 3:14). (Found elsewhere in the NT only in 1Tim 6:14; Jam 1:27)

¹³receiving back a reward of unrighteousness, counting [it as] a pleasure [to be engaging in] self-indulgence in the day; [they are] #spots and blemishes [fig., a disgrace], openly indulging in their deceitful ways while they feast with you* (2Pet 2:13). (Note: "unblemished and spotless" are the negative forms of "spots and blemishes." Both sets of words are only found here in the NT).

---

¹⁸And, "If the righteous [person] is scarcely [or, with difficulty is] saved, where will the #ungodly and sinful [person] appear? [fig., what will become of the #ungodly and sinful [person]?]" [Prov 11:31, LXX] (1Pet 4:18).

⁵and He did not spare the ancient world, but kept Noah, [the] eighth [person] [fig., with seven others], a preacher of righteousness, having brought a Flood upon the world of #ungodly [people] (2Pet 2:5).

⁷But the present heavens and the [present] earth having been stored up [or, reserved] for fire by His word are being kept for [the] day of judgment and of destruction of the #ungodly people (2Pet 3:7). (Found elsewhere only in the NT in Rom 4:5; 5:6; 1Tim 1:9; Jude 1:4,15).

That is not a lot of evidence, but it does show some consistency of the language of these two letters.
The next objection to Petrine authorship is that this letter pushes too hard to show it is by Peter by relating Peter's personal experiences with Jesus, most notably in the following passage about the Transfiguration:

¹⁶For not having followed having been cleverly made-up myths, we made known to you* the power and Arrival [or, Coming] of our Lord Jesus Christ, but having become eyewitnesses of the magnificence of that One. [cp. Luke 9:43] ¹⁷For having received from God [the] Father honor and glory, such a voice being brought [fig., uttered] to Him by the Majestic Glory, "This is My Son—the Beloved—in whom I am

well-pleased." [Matt 17:5] ¹⁸And this voice we heard, being brought [fig., uttered] out of heaven, being with Him on the holy mountain (2Pet 1:16-18).

Two points on this objection. First, remember in the discussion on 1Peter that one of the liberals' objections to Petrine authorship was the author did not make references to his personal experiences with Jesus, but here the liberals are saying Peter did not write this letter because he makes references to his personal experiences with Jesus! They cannot have it both ways.

Second, the manner in which Peter relates his experience here is rather muted as compared to the elaborate descriptions of this event seen in apocryphal books. Also, Peter relates this experience to introduce his discussion on the authority of Scripture in the next paragraph, so there is a point to it other than him "bragging" about this experience.

The next objection to Petrine authorship is the similarity of 2Peter 2:1-3:4 and Jude 1:4-19. It is rather clear one writer copied from the other. But who copied from whom? Liberals claim 2Peter copied from Jude, and they claim Jude was written about 80 AD. Thus, they reason, 2Peter had to be written well after that date and thus after the lifetime of Peter.

The dating of Jude will be dealt with shortly, but here it will be said it is just as likely Jude copied from 2Peter. In fact, that is more likely given that 2Peter predicts that false teachers will come into the Church, while Jude reports they have come in. In other words, 2Peter uses the future tense while Jude uses past and present tenses:

¹But also false prophets came to be among the people, as also false teachers **will be** among you*, who **will** secretly bring in destructive, heretical sects, and denying the Master having redeemed them, bringing swift destruction upon themselves. ²And many **will** follow their flagrant sexually immoral ways, because of whom the way of truth **will be** blasphemed. ³And in covetous desire [or, greed], with fabricated words, they **will** exploit you*, for whom their judgment of old is not idle, and their destruction will not sleep (2Pet 2:1-3).

⁴For certain people **wormed their way in**, the ones having been marked out long ago for this judgment, ungodly [people], **perverting** the grace of our God into flagrant sexual immorality and **denying** our only Master, God, and Lord—Jesus Christ [or, the only Master God and our Lord Jesus Christ] (Jude 1:4).

Translator's Perspective on the Canon of the NT

It makes little sense for a pseudo-Peter to read Jude and its mentions of false teachers currently operating and to change that to a prediction of future false teachers, when they were already present! However, it makes perfect sense for Jude, having read 2Peter and its predictions of false teachers, to have seen the false teachers operating in his somewhat later time and to change Peter's future tenses to present tenses.

> If 2 Pet is dependent on Jude, if the apostle cited from Jude, how explain the strong predictive element in his opening verses (2 Pet 2:1-3)? If as Peter wrote he had lying before him Jude's letter, which represents the corrupters as already within the Christian community and doing their deadly work, his repeated use of the future tense is absolutely inexplicable. Assuming, however, that he wrote prior to Jude, his predictions become perfectly intelligible. No doubt the virus was working when he wrote, but it was latent, undeveloped; far worse would appear; but when Jude wrote the poison was widely diffused, as 1:12,19 clearly show. The very life of the churches was endangered (ISBE, "Jude, Epistle of").

The following footnote in the NET Bible on Jude 1:4 is also relevant here:

> The Greek term for Master (*despoteÒs*) is the same term the author of 2 Peter used (2 Pet 2:1) to describe his Lord when he prophesied about these false teachers. Since *despoteÒs* is used only ten times in the NT, the verbal connection between these two books at this juncture is striking. This is especially so since both Peter and Jude speak of these false teachers as denying the Master (both using the same verb). The basic difference is that Peter is looking to the future, while Jude is arguing that these false teachers are here now.

The next couple of objections are more directly related to the dating of this letter, to which we now turn.

Date of Writing:

Another reason for denial of Petrine authorship it is said this letter dates to well after the lifetime of Peter, as seen is the following passage:

[14]For this reason, beloved, waiting for these [things], be eager [or, diligent] to be found by Him in peace, spotless and blameless. [15]And consider the patience of our Lord [to be] salvation, just as also our

beloved brother Paul, according to the wisdom having been given to him, wrote to you*, ¹⁶as also in all his letters, speaking in them concerning these [things], in which are some [things] difficult to be understood, which the untaught and unstable twist [fig., distort] to their own destruction, as [they do] also the rest of [the] Scriptures (2Pet 3:14-16).

It is said it was not until the late first century to early second century that all of Paul's letters circulated as a unit. Since the author seems to be aware of this complete Pauline corpus, then this letter could not have been written until that time period.

However, in our study of Ephesians it was seen that Ephesians was a circular letter, being sent first to Ephesus, then to Laodicea, then to Colossae, while Colossians was sent to Colossae and was then to go to Laodicea. It is safe to assume that other letters by Paul were circulating between cities during the lifetimes of both Peter and Paul. And that circulating of individual Pauline letters is what Peter is referring to here. It is not necessary for all of the Pauline epistles to have been written by this time, let alone to be circulating as a unit, but only that Paul's letters in general were well-known, which this evidence shows they were.

On a side note, in this passage Peter places Paul's writings on the same level as the OT Scriptures and the NT books that had been written by this time. Even if Peter did not write this letter, this shows that Paul's letters were accepted as Scripture very early. And if this letter was written by Peter, then we have his authority about the authority of the letters of Paul.

It is also said the theological situation reflected in 2Peter is from the later first to first half of the second century and not from the mid-first century as a Petrine authorship would require. Specifically, it is said the heresy being argued against is Gnosticism, which did not become full-blown until the second century.

However, there really is nothing distinctively Gnostic about the heresy Peter is combatting. In fact, it is hard to identify much about it given the paucity of what Peter provides. And even if it were Gnosticism, it would not be necessary for it to be full-blown. We have already seen that Paul combatted an early or incipit form of Gnosticism in Colossians and Ephesians.

Next is supposed problems in the following paragraph:

¹This [is] now, beloved, [the] second letter I am writing to you*, in which I am stirring up your* pure [or, sincere] mind by reminding [you*] ²to be mindful of the words having been previously spoken by the holy prophets and of the commandment of your* apostles of the

Translator's Perspective on the Canon of the NT

Lord and Savior, ³knowing this first, that scoffers will come at [the] last of the days [or, at [the] end of time], going [fig., living] according to their own desires, ⁴and saying, "Where is the promise of His Arrival [or, Coming]? For since the fathers fell asleep [fig., died], all [things] continue in the same manner [as] from [the] beginning of creation" (2Pet 3:1-4).

First here is the reference to "the second letter." It is said this was a common practice of apocryphal writers, to associate their books with books known to be written by notable figures. But Paul does the same thing when he writes twice to the same people, as seen in 1,2Corinthians. And when apocryphal writers use this practice, they deal with similar topics as the original but give it their own heretical slant. But 2Peter deals with completely different topics than 1Peter, another reason, by the way, for its much different writing style.

Second is the reference to "your* apostles of the Lord and Savior." It is said this is a strange expression for an apostle to make. But I really do not understand why. I guess the critics want Peter to have said "us your* apostles." But that would be self-evident if the readers knew who was writing to them.

Lastly on this paragraph is the statement "since the fathers fell asleep [fig., died]." It is said this is a reference to the apostles who have already died. But it actually is a reference to the OT patriarchs, as the context clearly shows.

Next, it is said there is too high of a Christology in this book for it to have been written in the mid-first century. It instead reflects Christological development of the second century. The basis for this claim is the following verse.

¹Simon Peter, a bondservant and an apostle of Jesus Christ, To the ones having obtained [or, having been chosen to have] an equally precious faith with us [or, a faith as valuable as ours] by [the] righteousness of our God and Savior Jesus Christ (2Pet 1:1).

The note in the ALT after this verse reads, "one Person is referred to here; cp. the same construction in 1:11; 2:20; 3:2,18." The first referenced verse reads:

¹¹For in this way, the entrance into the eternal kingdom of our Lord and Savior Jesus Christ will be richly supplied to you* (2Pet 1:1).

It is clear here that "Lord" and "Savior" both refer to the one Person of Jesus Christ. Since the same construction appears in 1:1, it clearly

Why Are These Books in the Bible? Volume Two

means "God" and "Savior" both refer to the one Person of Jesus Christ. This is another example of the Granville Sharp rule that was explained in Chapter Seven in the discussion on Titus 2:13. It is thus said these books must be "late" as the idea of the deity of Christ was a later theological development.

However, these two verses are by no means the only affirmations of the deity of Christ in the NT. Many references have already been made to verses in various books that uphold this doctrine, many of which are "early." In fact, the affirmation of the deity of Christ was shown to be was one of the early essential tenets. Thus, having a clear reference to the deity of Jesus in no way argues against a mid-first century date for this letter.

Finally, it is said the author is aware of the prediction of the death of Peter recorded in the Gospel of John, and thus this letter had to have been written after that book. The passage from John reads:

[18]"Most positively, I say to you, when you were younger, you were fastening a belt on yourself and were walking about where you would desire. But when you become old, you will stretch out your hands, and another will fasten a belt on you and will lead [you] where you do not desire." [19]But this He said signifying by what sort of death he will glorify God. And having said this, He says to him, "Be following Me!" (John 21:18f).

The "you" here is Peter, whom Jesus is talking to. 2Peter refers to this conversation in the following paragraph:

[12]For this reason, I will not neglect to be always reminding you* concerning these [things], although you* know [them] and have been established in the present truth. [13]But I consider [it] right, as long as I am in this tent-like dwelling [fig., this body] to be waking [fig., stirring] you* up by way of reminder, [14]knowing that the taking down of my tent-like dwelling [fig., that my death] is soon, even as also our Lord Jesus Christ made clear to me. [see John 21:18,19] [15]But I will be eager [or, will make every effort] also to cause you* to be having at all times after my departure [Gr., *exodus*] a remembrance of these [things] (2Pet 1:12-15).

However, if in fact Jesus spoke the words recorded in the Gospel of John to Peter, and Peter wrote this letter, then there is no need for the Gospel of John to have already been written for Peter to known this prediction as Jesus spoke it to him! Peter was simply reminded of this

341

Translator's Perspective on the Canon of the NT

prediction with his death now coming near and thus he mentions about it to his readers.

Before closing this discussion, I cannot resist commenting on a couple of lines from liberal sources evaluating this book:

> Kummel presents the arguments that make all critical scholars recognize that II Peter is a pseudepigraph (Introduction to the New Testament, pp. 430-4):

> Nearly all scholars would agree with a date sometime in the second century, probably in the second quarter (Early Christian; "2 Peter").

These statements remind me of claims that "all reputable scientists believe in evolution" or "all reputable scientists agree with human-made global warming." The implication being that anyone who disagrees with evolution or human-made global warming is not true scientist, no matter what their qualifications are. Here the implication is that if someone has the "audacity" to agree with the ultimate conclusion of the early Church and to accept Peter as being the author of this epistle, having written it shortly before his death in the mid-60s AD, then he or she is not a "scholar." But the fact is that after much investigation, the early Church came to this conclusion as did I and many conservative scholars.

> Although a very strong case has been made against Petrine authorship of 2 Peter, we believe it is deficient. Not only is there very good evidence that this epistle was utilized in the late first and early second century by a variety of writers (as Picirilli has recently pointed out), but the occasion for the letter fits the lifetime of Peter better than later. Further, once some kind of amanuensis [use of a scribe] hypothesis is seriously taken into consideration (in our view, an amanuensis was used for 1Peter but probably not for 2Peter), then many of the objections against Petrine authorship are found wanting. Taken together, these external and internal arguments strongly suggest the traditional view, viz., that Peter was indeed the author of the second epistle which bears his name....

Hence, 2Peter was probably written late in 64 CE or sometime in 65 CE, if Peter actually lived till that year (Bible.org; "Second Peter: Introduction, Argument, and Outline").

Doctrine of God:

It was stated previously that this epistle is sound in its theology. This can be seen in its teachings on the nature of God.

God [the] Father (2Pet 1:17b).

⁴For if God did not spare angels having sinned, but having hurled [them] down to the deepest pit of gloom [Gr. *tartarus*], He delivered [them] to chains of thick darkness, being kept for judgment; ⁵and He did not spare the ancient world, but kept Noah, [the] eighth [person] [fig., with seven others], a preacher of righteousness, having brought a Flood upon the world of ungodly [people] … (2Pet 2:4f).

⁹[the] Lord knows [how] to be rescuing godly [people] out of temptation, but to be keeping [the] unrighteous being punished for [the] day of judgment (2Pet 4:9).

⁵For this they willingly forget [or, ignore], that [the] heavens were from of old, and [the] earth having existed out of water and through water by the word of God, ⁶through which the then world, having been flooded by water, was destroyed. [see Gen 1:6,7; 9:11,12] (2Pet 2:5f).

⁸But stop letting this one [fact] be forgotten [or, ignored] by you*, beloved, that one day with [the] Lord [is] as a thousand years, and a thousand years as one day. [see Psalm 90:4] (2Pet 3:8).

¹⁵And consider the patience of our Lord [to be] salvation (2Pet 3:15a).

Thus, in 2Peter, God is Father and thus a personal, reachable Being. He is judge and will punish evildoers, but He will spare righteous people. He created the world and later flooded it in judgment. God's conception of time is different than ours, indicating He is eternal. He is patient with us. All of this is in accordance with the OT conception of God.

Essential Tenets:

The sound theology of this letter is also seen in its affirmations of essential tenets. The phrase 'Lord Jesus Christ" occurs three times (1:8,14,16). Jesus is called "Lord" at least five more times (1:2,11; 2:20; 3:2,18). He is also called "Christ" five more times (1:1, 2x, 1:11; 2:20; 3:18). We already saw that Jesus is called "God" in 1:1 and God's Son

343

Translator's Perspective on the Canon of the NT

in the Transfiguration scene previously quoted. There is also an affirmation of the Second Coming:

[10]But the day of [the] Lord will come like a thief in [the] night, in which the heavens with a loud roar [or, with roaring speed] will pass away, and [the] elements being consumed by intense heat will be destroyed, and [the] earth and the works in it will be burned up (2Pet 3:10).

Peter acknowledges the work of the Spirit in inspiring Scripture, "for prophecy never came by [the] will of a person, but holy men of God spoke being moved along by [the] Holy Spirit" (2Pet 1:21).

Peter closes this letter by praising Jesus, Thus, showing He is worthy of worship:

[18]But be increasing in [the] grace and knowledge of our Lord and Savior Jesus Christ. To Him [be] the glory both now and to [the] day of [the] age! [fig, to eternity!] So be it! (2Pet 3:18).

That is not a lot of doctrine, but it is a short epistle, just three chapters. And this is the second letter Peter wrote to the same recipients, so he could assume they would know the contents of his doctrinally filled first letter.

Appeal and Mark of Inspiration:

The main appeal of this letter is its warnings about false teachers. This is important for Christians of all ages. Otherwise, being written shortly before Peter's death makes it of personal interest. It also has limited but sound doctrine. This all gives it the mark of inspiration.

Conclusion on 2Peter:

There is probably less support for the canonicity of 2Peter than for any other NT book, but that does not mean such support does not exist. The early Church was aware of possible problems with this book, but they were eventually resolved in favor of acceptance. And they were most likely right in that conclusion, as there is no conclusive evidence against it. Moreover:

> … the Epistle, at least the first and third chapters, contains nothing which Peter might not have written, and the allusion to the scene of transfiguration admits only the alternative: either Peter, or a forger. It seems morally impossible that a forger should have produced a letter so full of spiritual beauty and

unction, and expressly denouncing all cunning fabrications. It may have been enlarged by the editor after Peter's death. But the whole breathes an apostolic spirit, and could not well be spared from the New Testament. It is a worthy valedictory of the aged apostle awaiting his martyrdom, and with its still valid warnings against internal dangers from false Christianity, it forms a suitable complement to the first Epistle, which comforts the Christians amidst external dangers from heathen and Jewish persecutors (Schaff; 10386-10391).

Jude

The Book of Jude is the last NT book to be studied. Like 2Peter that it parallels, it also was among the *antilegomena* for similar reasons as for 2Peter

Author:

The salutation to this letter is:
¹Jude, a bondservant of Jesus Christ and a brother of James, To the called [ones], having been sanctified by God the Father and having been kept in Jesus Christ (Jude 1:1).

Thus, the writer identifies himself as "Jude, brother of James." If this is the same James who wrote the Epistle of James, then this would be another half-brother of Jesus. Jesus' brothers are listed as: James and Joses and Simon and Judas in Matthew 13:55, but as James and Joses and Judas and Simon in Mark 6:3. Jude would be the same as Judas and thus would be either the youngest or second youngest brother.

By identifying himself only as "the brother of James" Jude is assuming his brother is well-known. This takes us back to the discussion of the Epistle of James and the fact the author of that epistle had to be well-known to identify himself as simply James. Thus, Jude and James go together in terms of assuming the readers will know who James is, and as we saw then, only James the brother of the Lord fits that bill. Thus, the internal evidence is that this is Jude, the youngest or second youngest brother of Jesus.

This identification was for the most part accepted in the earliest stages of the Church, as was the authority of this letter in general. But somewhat later, its authenticity was questioned, or at least its authority. The main reason for these doubts was Jude's use of apocryphal material:

Translator's Perspective on the Canon of the NT

The chief reason why it was rejected by some and regarded with suspicion by others in primitive times is its quotation from the apocryphal Book of Enoch, so Jerome informs us (Vir. Ill., 4). It is possible that Jude had in mind another spurious writing, namely, the Assumption of Moses, when he spoke of the contention of Michael the archangel with the devil about the body of Moses (1:9) (ISbe, "Jude, Epistle of").

The passages in question are the following:

⁹But Michael the archangel [or, the chief messenger [of the Lord]], when contending with the Devil, he was arguing about the body of Moses, did not dare to bring a slanderous judgment, <u>but</u> he said, "May [the] Lord rebuke you!" [i.e., a scene from the apocryphal book *The Assumption of Moses*, ca. early 1st century AD.] (Jude 1:9).

¹⁴Now Enoch, [in] the seventh [generation] from Adam [see Gen 5:18-24], also prophesied about these [people], saying, "Look! [The] Lord came with countless thousands of His holy ones, ¹⁵to execute judgment upon all and to convict every soul concerning all of the works of ungodliness which they committed in an ungodly manner and concerning all of the harsh [words] which sinful, ungodly [people] spoke against Him." [i.e., a quote from the pseudepigraphical *Book of Enoch* 2:1, ca. 165 BC.] (Jude 1:14).

The bracketed notes in the ALT indicate the sources for these quotes. These books were discussed in Volume One. There it was seen that both were pseudepigraphical, which is to say, they were not written by the names associate with them and thus were rightly rejected from being included in the canon of the OT. Given that rejection, it makes Jude's use of them suspect. He seems to have thought they were genuine or at least authoritative. And Thus, if Jude was accepted as canonical it might get people thinking these books should be also.

However, just because a Biblical writer or personality quotes from a book, it does not mean he thinks it is inspired by God and thus should be included in the Bible. We saw in Volume One that OT book writers often refer to extra-biblical books and even used them as sources. This means they accepted that particular portion as recording reliable history or as presenting some truth. Thus, the writer of the Books of Kings could refer to "the scrolls of the kings of Israel and Judah" without indicating that journal should be in the Bible.

Maybe a closer example would be Paul's use of Grecian writers in his sermon in Athens:

²⁸'For in Him we live and move and are [fig., exist],' as also some of your* poets have said, 'For we are also His offspring' [i.e., quoting Epimendes (ca. 600 BC) and Aratus of Cilia (ca. 270 BC), respectively] (Acts 17:8).

As the notes in the ALT indicate, Paul is quoting from two different non-biblical Greek sources. But in no way does this mean Paul thought these books were inspired and should be included in the Bible. But still, it was these non-biblical quotes in Jude that gave the Church Fathers pause, not doubts that Jude actually wrote the letter. But today it is the exact opposite for liberals. They deny the genuineness of Jude due to doubts that Jude actually wrote it, with little care for its use of apocryphal material, except as it relates Jude actually being the author.

One argument of liberals against Judean authorship is one we have seen before—the Greek of this letter is too stylistic for a peasant Galilean. But as was asserted when this claim was made against James writing the Epistle of James, we know very little of the background of Jude and what schooling he had. Moreover, it is possible he dictated this epistle to a scribe, who would have "cleaned up" any roughness to his Greek.

Similar to this is the claim that Jude quoted from the Greek text of Enoch, something a Galilean it is said would not do. But if Jude knew Greek, then this argument is without basis.

Additional arguments are based on the dating of this book, to which we now turn.

Date of Writing:

Jude was the youngest or second youngest brother of Jesus, with two or three brothers in-between them. Jesus also had at least two sisters. This is seen in the phrase "And His sisters are all with us, are they not?" (Mat 13:56a). The plural "sisters" means there were at least two sisters, and the word "all" makes it most likely there were more than two. But there is no indication of the birth order of these sisters. But it is safe to assume one or two were born in-between Jesus and Jude and thus at least four children were born in-between them. Thus, Jude had to be born several years after Jesus and possibly a decade or so later.

If Jesus was born in 5 BC as most believe, this would place the birth of Jude in the latter half of the first decade AD, or about 6-10 AD. We have no idea how long Jude lived, but assuming an average lifespan of about 70 years, then 80 AD would be the outside date for his death. Thus, if Jude wrote this epistle, it had to be before that date. However, today's critics date Jude to after that date, as late as 90-120 AD, too late

Translator's Perspective on the Canon of the NT

for Jude to have written it. There are several reasons for this claimed late date.

First, the writer seems to assert that the apostolic age has passed and "the faith" is now complete:

> ³Beloved, making all diligence [or, while I was making every effort] to be writing to you* concerning the common salvation, I had necessity to write to you* urging [you*] to be contending earnestly for the faith [or, the essential doctrines] having been handed down once for all time to the holy ones [or, saints] (Jude 1:3).

The claim is that by declaring the faith has "been handed down once for all time" Jude says the apostles have all died and thus there is no new revelation or doctrines forthcoming. But that is far from what the phrase "the faith" means. This phrase is used in the Apostolic and later Church Fathers to refer to the essential doctrines of the Christian faith, or the essential tenets as they have been termed in this book. These are the central and unchangeable doctrines of the Christian faith, but they do not constitute the full expression of Christian doctrine, just that all Christian doctrines must be in accordance with these essentials. Even the apostles would not change these essentials, and thus there is no contradiction to this phrase if the apostle are still alive.

Similar to this is a claim based on the following verse:

> ¹⁷But you*, beloved, remember the words, the ones having been spoken previously by the apostles of our Lord Jesus Christ (Jude 1:17).

Here again the claim is the writer seems to be separating himself from the apostles and calling himself a second generation Christian. But the critics are completely missing Jude's point. It is that the recipients had previously been taught by the apostles and need to abide by those words, not those of the false teachers now among them. And it should be noted that the word "apostles" is plural, indicating more than one apostle had visited the recipients of this letter.

One last liberal argument is based on the following passage:

> ²⁰But you*, beloved, building yourselves up in your* most holy faith, praying in [the] Holy Spirit, ²¹keep yourselves in [the] love of God, waiting for [or, expecting] the mercy of our Lord Jesus Christ to eternal life (Jude 1:20f).

A liberal site comments on this passage:

> In verses 20-21 … testifies to the liturgical development of a trinitarian formula. The closing benediction is a magnificent piece of liturgical language, so different in style and tone from the remainder of the letter that the writer has probably taken it from the liturgy of his church (Early Christian; "Jude").

This passage was quoted in Chapter One as being an early church service benediction Thus, showing the early nature of this theology. But the critics are trying to use this to prove this is "late" theology. But it parallels the following passage from one of Paul's epistles that even liberals accept as being genuine and written in the late 50s.

¹⁴The grace of the Lord Jesus Christ and the love of God and the fellowship of the Holy Spirit [be] with you* all! So be it! (2Cor 13:14).

As such, this Trinitarian formula is not "late" but a part of early Christian doctrine. Since this passage from Jude is taken from an early Christian liturgy, then it predates the writing of Jude and thus represents early Christian doctrine. The point is; liberals are fond of the idea that Christian doctrine developed very slowly over decades and even centuries, but the embedded early creeds and this embedded early church service benediction demonstrate that even "advanced" theology, like a conception of the triune nature of God, existed very early.

All that said, when was this book written? If previous suppositions are correct that Jude copied from 2Peter, that 2Peter was written shortly before Peter's death, and that Jude was born about a decade after Jesus and lived about 70 years, then the date range for this letter would be 65-80 AD. It would be impossible to narrow it down any further.

But if it is the earlier part of this range, then that easily pushes the above mentioned liturgical benediction into the 50s or to about the same time as 2Corinthians and thus further buttresses the idea that a concept of a triune God was part of Christian theology very early.

Doctrine of God:

Along with the liturgical benediction indicating the triune nature of God, there is the following:

God the Father (1:1b).

the grace of our God (1:4).

[the] love of God (1:21).

Translator's Perspective on the Canon of the NT

²⁴Now to the One being able to keep them from stumbling and to make [you*] stand in the presence of His glory unblemished [or, blameless], with great happiness—²⁵to [the] only wise God our Savior, [be] glory and majesty, dominion and authority, both now and to all the ages! [fig., forevermore!] So be it! (Jude 1:24f).

Thus, for Jude, God is Father and thus personal and reachable. He is graceful and the source of love. He enables us to live a righteous life. There is only one God, and He is wise and our Savior, and He is worthy of praise and worship forever.

Essential Tenets:

Jude calls Jesus "our Lord Jesus Christ" twice (1:17,21). He is called "Christ" twice more (1:1, 2x). These counts do not include the last phrase of verse 4: "our only Master, God, and Lord—Jesus Christ."

There are two issues on this phrase, that of a textual variant and of interpretation. The textual variant is in regards to the word "God" (Greek, *theos*). It appears in the vast majority of Greek manuscripts but not in the earliest Greek manuscripts. It Thus, appears in the Byzantine Majority Greek text the ALT is based on and in the *Textus Receptus* the KJV and NKJV are based on, but it is omitted in the Critical Text most other modern day versions are based on, including the NET Bible. But its comment on this verse on the interpretation of the other terms would include *theos* if it is original:

> The terms "Master and Lord" both refer to the same person.
> The construction in Greek is known as the Granville Sharp rule.

This rule was seen before in regards to Titus 2:13 and 2Peter 1:1. But here, if "God" is original it would also be included in this rule, and thus Master, God, and Lord would all be referring to the one Person of Jesus Christ. But even if God is not original, then Jesus is still being called "Master and Lord."

Jude then mentions the work of the Spirit in the lives of believers, first by way of contrast with those who do not have the Spirit, namely false believers, Thus, indirectly affirming the reception of the Spirit by true believers, then by mentioning the Spirit's leading in prayer.

¹⁹These are the ones causing divisions, worldly, not having [the] Spirit. [cp. Matt 24:23-25; 1Tim 4:1-3; 2Tim 3:1-9; 2Peter 2:1-3]

²⁰But you*, beloved, building yourselves up in your* most holy faith, praying in [the] Holy Spirit (Jude 1:19f).

Another essential affirmation would be "waiting for [or, expecting] the mercy of our Lord Jesus Christ to eternal life" (Jude 1:21b). Here Jude says Jesus at His Second Coming will be the source of mercy leading to eternal life.

There would also be the association of the Father, Jesus Christ, and the Holy Spirit that was previously discussed.

As with 2Peter, that is not a lot of doctrine. But remember, Jude knew more than one apostle had taught the recipients of this letter and thus could assume they taught the recipients correct doctrine. The purpose of this short letter was to warn them against the false teachers currently operating among them; they are to reject those doctrines and instead to abide by the doctrines the apostles had taught them.

Appeal and Mark of Inspiration:

The appeal of this book is the same as that for 2Peter—the warning against false teachers. But given that this epistle is mostly copied from that one, this letter is somewhat redundant. But it does contain a couple of verses independent of 2Peter that are meaningful, namely the quoted passages about "contending earnestly for the faith" and the Trinitarian benediction. The former is an important injunction for every age, and the later attests to the early nature of the Christian concept of a triune God. As such, there was a good reason to include this book in the canon, though not a strong one.

Conclusion on Jude:

The evidence for the genuineness of this letter is only slightly better than for 2Peter, and it only contains limited important material given its shortness and dependence on 2Peter. But arguments against its inclusion were settled in its favor in the early Church and thus it was most likely correctly included in the canon. But like 2Peter, if it had been left out, it would not change the Christian faith one iota.

Translator's Perspective on the Canon of the NT

Why Are These Books in the Bible? Volume Two

Chapter Ten
Conclusion on the New Testament

We started this study on the books contained in the New Testament (NT) by noting that 20 of the 27 books were uncontested in the early Church, and it has been shown that universal acceptance was for good reasons. Those 20 books were undoubtedly authored by the names traditionally attached to them, which is to say apostles or direct apostolic associates. They were all written in the first century; they all contain correct and substantial theology in regards to the nature of God and early essential Christian tenets, and they all have wide appeal and bear the marks of inspiration.

Of the seven disputed books, two, James and the Revelation, have strong support for them also being authored by the traditional authors, were written in the first century, have wide appeal, and bear the marks of inspiration. The latter also contains much sound theology, while the former contains sound practical advice. Hebrews is anonymous, but it was shown it most certainly was written by a direct apostolic associate, was unquestionably written in the first century, contains a wealth of important and sound doctrine, and bears the marks of inspiration. Thus, after the disputes were settled, these three books were rightly included in the canon of the NT.

The remaining four disputed books (2John, 3John, 2Peter, and Jude) have less support for their genuineness than for the other 23 books, but there still is a respectable basis to accept their traditional authors and dating. Being very short books, there is not much in them in the way of doctrine, but what they do contain is sound theology. And there is some appeal to them, so there is good reason they were included, but if they had not been, it would not have changed the Christian faith in any way.

Bottom line, the 27 books in the NT all belong in the NT. All 27 books meet all of the standards laid down by the early Church for a book to be accepted into the NT. There is a consistency of thought in regards to all essential doctrinal tenets running through all 27 books, and all of these books bear the marks of inspiration. These 27 books were Thus, rightly included in the NT and can be read for spiritual enrichment.

> The twenty-seven books of the New Testament are better supported than any ancient classic, both by a chain of external testimonies which reaches up almost to the close of the

Translator's Perspective on the Canon of the NT

apostolic age, and by the internal evidence of a spiritual depth and unction which raises them far above the best productions of the second century. The church has undoubtedly been guided by the Holy Spirit in the selection and final determination of the Christian canon (Schaff; 2861-2864).

The New Testament is thus but one book, the teaching of one mind, the mind of Christ. He gave to his disciples the words of life which the Father gave him, and inspired them with the spirit of truth to reveal his glory to them. Herein consists the unity and harmony of the twenty-seven writings which constitute the New Testament, for all emergencies and for perpetual use, until the written and printed word shall be superseded by the reappearance of the personal Word, and the beatific vision of saints in light (Schaff; 7329-7333).

Appendixes

Translator's Perspective on the Canon of the NT

Appendix One
Bibliography

Sources are cited in the text by being placed in parentheses using the first word or two of the main title of the source. For websites, the name of the website is given, followed by the webpage title in quotation marks. This Bibliography then gives the full biographical information. Since very often more than one page from a given digital reference book or website is cited in this book, only the reference book title or home page URL is given. The specific article can be found using the search engine or directory for the book or on the website.

For all Sections:

Analytical Literal Translation:

Analytical-Literal Translation of the Old Testament: Volume I: The Torah. Copyright © 2012 by Gary F. Zeolla (www.Zeolla.org).

Analytical-Literal Translation of the Old Testament: Volume II: The Historical Books. Copyright © 2013 by Gary F. Zeolla (www.Zeolla.org).

Analytical-Literal Translation of the Old Testament: Volume III: The Poetic Books. Copyright © 2013 by Gary F. Zeolla (www.Zeolla.org).

Analytical-Literal Translation of the Old Testament: Volume IV: The Prophetic Books. Copyright © 2014 by Gary F. Zeolla (www.Zeolla.org).

Analytical-Literal Translation of the Apocryphal/ Deuterocanonical Books: Volume V of the ALT: Copyright © 2014 by Gary F. Zeolla (www.Zeolla.org).

Analytical-Literal Translation of the New Testament: Third Edition. Copyright © 2012 by Gary F. Zeolla (www.Zeolla.org). Previously copyrighted © 1999, 2001, 2005, 2007 by Gary F. Zeolla.

Analytical-Literal Translation of the Apostolic Fathers: Volume Seven of the ALT. Copyright © 2016 by Gary F. Zeolla (www.Zeolla.org).

Note: There are some differences between the text of the ALT as quoted in this book versus the texts in the published volumes. That is because this writer/ translator has been making changes and corrections to the texts in my own files in preparation for new editions of these volumes (see Appendix Three).

Translator's Perspective on the Canon of the NT

Additional Bible Versions:
English Standard Version (ESV). Copyright © July 2001 by Crossway Books/Good News Publishers, Wheaton, IL.

Holman Christian Standard Bible® (HCSB). Copyright © 1999, 2000, 2002, 2003, 2009 by Holman Bible Publishers.

King James Version (KJV). Public Domain.

New American Bible (NAB), revised edition © 2010, 1991, 1986, 1970 Confraternity of Christian Doctrine, Inc., Washington, DC. All Rights Reserved.

New American Standard Bible (NASB). Copyright © 1960-1995. La Biblia de Las Americas. The Lockman Foundation.

New English Translation (a.k.a. *NET Bible*). Version 1.0 - Copyright © 1996-2006 Biblical Studies Press, L.L.C.

New International Reader's Version (NIRV). ® Copyright © 1995, 1996, 1998 by International Bible Society www.ibs.org. All rights reserved worldwide.

New International Version (NIV). Copyright © 1973, 1984, 1987, 2011 by the International Bible Society www.ibs.org. All rights reserved worldwide.

New King James Version (NKJV). Nashville, TN: Thomas Nelson Publishers, 1982.

New Revised Standard Version (NRSV). Copyrighted 1989 by the Division of Christian Education of the National Council of the Churches of Christ in the United States of America. All rights reserved.

New Living Translation (NLT), copyright © 1996 by Tyndale Charitable Trust. All rights reserved.

Software:
BibleWorks™ Copyright © 1992-2015 BibleWorks, LLC. All rights reserved. BibleWorks was programmed by Michael S. Bushell, Michael D. Tan, and Glenn L. Weaver. All rights reserved.

BDB. *Hebrew-Aramaic and English Lexicon of the Old Testament* (Abridged BDB-Gesenius Lexicon), by Francis Brown, D.D., D.Litt., S. R. Driver, D.D., D.Litt., and Charles A. Briggs, 1906. As found on *BibleWorks*.

Encarta Dictionary and Thesaurus. On Microsoft *Word 2010*.

Easton's Bible Dictionary. Public domain. On *BibleWorks*.

Fausset's Bible Dictionary. Public domain. On *BibleWorks*.

Friberg, Timothy and Barbara. *Analytical Greek New Testament*. Copyright © 1994 and *Analytical Lexicon to the Greek New Testament*. Copyright © 1994. Both on *BibleWorks*.

Holladay. *Hebrew and Aramaic Lexicon of the OT*. On *BibleWorks*.

ISBE. *International Standard Bible Encyclopedia*, 1915, 1st Edition, from Dr. Stanley Morris, IBT, 1997. Original unabridged edition. James Orr, M.A., D.D. General Editor, et. al. Revision published in 1939 by W. B. Eerdmans Publishing Co. On *BibleWorks*.

LS. *The Abridged Liddell-Scott Greek-English Lexicon*. From the public domain. On *BibleWorks*.

Newman, Barclay M. Jr. *A Concise Greek-English Lexicon of the New Testament*. Copyright © 1971 by United Bible Societies and 1993 by Deutsche Biblelgesellschaft (German Bible Society), Sttugart. On BibleWorks.

Oxford Dictionaries. © Oxford University Press. On Microsoft Word 2016.

Websites:
Bible.org. https://Bible.org
Bible Research by Michael Marlowe. http://www.bible-researcher.com
Blue Letter Bible. https://www.blueletterbible.org/
Christian History for Everyman. http://www.christian-history.orgs
Encyclopedia Britannica. http://www.britannica.com/
Early Christian Writings. http://www.earlychristianwritings.com/
GotQuestions?org. http://www.gotquestions.org/
Merriam-Webster. http://www.merriam-webster.com/
New Advent. The Catholic Encyclopedia. http://www.newadvent.org/cathen/
New World Encyclopedia. http://www.newworldencyclopedia.org
Original Catholic Encyclopedia. http://oce.catholic.com/index.php?title=Home
PBS. http://www.pbs.org
Theopidea. http://www.theopedia.com/
United States Conference of Catholic Bishops. http://www.usccb.org/
Your Dictionary. www.YourDictionary.com. LoveToKnow Corporation.

Other:
Schaff, Philip. *History Of The Christian Church* (The Complete Eight Volumes In One). Kindle Edition. Note that the numbers after "Schaff" refer to the Kindle Locations.

Denver Seminary. Information marked by the source of "Denver Seminary" indicates the source is lessons I learned during various classes while attending Denver Seminary back in 1988-90.

Translator's Perspective on the Canon of the NT
Introductory Pages:

Websites:
CBA News. December 2014. CBA Best-sellers. Bible Translations. http://cbanews.org/wp-content/uploads/sites/3/2014/12/BiblesTranslations201412.pdf

Christian Timelines. Peter and Paul: Two Early Martyrs. http://www.christiantimelines.com/peter_and_paul.htm

Christianity in View. Timeline of Paul's ministry. http://christianityinview.com/paulstimeline.html

Century One Bookstore. 25 Interesting Facts about the Dead Sea Scrolls. http://www.centuryone.com/25dssfacts.html

Deeper Study. Greek New Testament Manuscripts. http://deeperstudy.com/link/manuscript_list.html

GotAnswers?org. http://www.gotquestions.org/

Free Dictionary. Maccabees. http://encyclopedia2.thefreedictionary.com/Maccabean+revolt

Google. Search results top windows. "Date of Exodus" etc.

Interactive Bible. The Date of the Exodus: 1446 BC http://www.bible.ca/archeology/bible-archeology-exodus-date-1440bc.htm

Lambert Dolphin's Library. Kings of Israel and Judah. http://www.ldolphin.org/kings.html

National Catholic Register. 7 clues tell us *precisely* when Jesus died. http://www.ncregister.com/blog/jimmy-akin/when-precisely-did-jesus-die-the-year-month-day-and-hour-revealed

Patheos. What Is The Canon In The Bible? http://www.patheos.com/blogs/christiancrier/2015/08/22/what-is-the-canon-in-the-bible/

Pratt, John P. When Was Judah's 70-Year Babylonian Captivity? http://www.johnpratt.com/items/docs/captivity.html

Septuagint. http://www.septuagint.net/

Timberlake Church. Is There a Difference Between Hebrews, Jews and Israelites? http://www.timberlandchurch.com/faqs/586-is-there-a-difference-between-hebrews-jews-and-israelites-.html

Timeline of Greek & Roman Antiquity. http://people.umass.edu/dfleming/english704-timeline.html

Union college Faculty Website. Roman Judea. http://faculty.ucc.edu/egh-damerow/roman_judea.htm

Books:
KJV/ NKJV Parallel Reference Bible. Nashville: Thomas Nelson, 1991.

McDowell, Josh. *Evidence that Demands a Verdict*. San Bernardino, CA: Here's Life Publishers, 1979.

Zeolla, Gary. F. *Differences Between Bible Versions*. Lulu Publishing. Third Edition. © 2012 by Gary F. Zeolla.

Chapters:

Websites:

Ancient History Encyclopedia. Nero. http://www.ancient.eu/Nero/

Bible Hub. Martyrdom in Behalf of Religion. http://biblehub.com/library/pamphilius/church_history/chapter_xxv_the_persecution_under_nero.htm

Bible Study Tools. http://www.biblestudytools.com/

Bruce, F.F. "Christianity Under Claudius" http://biblicalstudies.org.uk/pdf/bjrl/claudius_bruce.pdf

Christian Classics Ethereal Library. Apostles' Creed. https://www.ccel.org/creeds/apostles.creed.html

Creation.com; Darkness at the crucifixion: metaphor or real history? http://creation.com/darkness-at-the-crucifixion-metaphor-or-real-history

Dependence of Mark upon Matthew. http://www.tjresearch.info/mksecond.htm

EarlyChurch.org.uk. Roman Persecution of the Early Church. http://earlychurch.org.uk/

Easy English Bible. http://www.easyenglish.info/

Evidence for Christianity. http://evidenceforchristianity.org/

Facing the Critics. The Rylands fragment. http://www.facingthechallenge.org/rylands.php

Farmer's Argument For Matthean Priority. http://www.maplenet.net/~trowbridge/farmer.htm

God's Word to Women. http://godswordtowomen.org

Gospel Coalition. Why is the Number of the Best 666? http://www.thegospelcoalition.org/article/why-is-the-number-of-the-beast-666

Good News Inc. Other Bible Books. http://www.goodnewsinc.net/othbooks/othbks.html

Insight. First John. http://www.insight.org/resources/bible/first-john.html

Jewish Virtual Library. Claudius. http://www.jewishvirtuallibrary.org/jsource/judaica/ejud_0002_0004_0_04339.html

Translator's Perspective on the Canon of the NT

Johnston, Edward, A. The First Harmony of the Gospels. http://www.etsjets.org/files/JETS-PDFs/14/14-4/14-4-pp227-238_JETS.pdf

La Vista Church of God. Question and Answer. http://lavistachurchofchrist.org/LVanswers/2007/11-14.html

PBS. http://www.pbs.com

Precept Austin. http://preceptaustin.org/

Religion Facts. Persecution in the Early Church. http://www.religionfacts.com/christianity/history/persecution

Sonic Light. http://soniclight.com/

Vision. How Many Gospels Are There? http://www.vision.org/visionmedia/religion-and-spirituality-new-testament-gospels/53328.aspx

Women Can Be Priests. Several articles named by the book being discussed. http://www.womenpriests.org/

Books:

Bruce. F. F. *The Canon of the New Testament*. As found on Bible Researcher. http://www.bible-researcher.com/bruce1.html

Other:

Various episodes of *The John Ankerberg Show*. Back episodes can be viewed or listen to via his app for smart phones and tablets or the website for his ministry, which also provides additional resources– http://www.jashow.org/.

Appendix Two
Additional Books by the Author

The author of this book (Gary F. Zeolla) is also the author of many additional books and the translator of the *Analytical-Literal Translation of the Bible* (ALT). These books are all available in paperback and various eBook formats (Kindle, Acrobat Reader, and ePUB). Some are also available in hardback format.

These books are available from Amazon (www.Amazon.com) and Lulu Publishing (www.lulu.com). Some are also available from Author House (www.AuthorHouse.com ~ 1-888-280-7715) and other online bookstores. Ordering and further details on all of these books can be found on the author's personal website: www.Zeolla.org.

Christian Books

Analytical-Literal Translation of the Old Testament

The Analytical-Literal Translation of the Old Testament (ALT: OT) is available in five volumes. Most Old Testaments are based on the Hebrew text. But this Old Testament is based on the Greek Septuagint (LXX). The LXX is a third century B.C. Greek translation of the Hebrew Bible. The importance of the LXX is that it was THE Bible of the early Church. The purpose of the ALT: OT is to provide a translation of the Greek Septuagint that will enable the reader to come as close to the Greek text as possible without having to be proficient in Greek.

Analytical-Literal Translation of the Old Testament (Septuagint) - Volume One - The Torah

This first volume contains the Torah (Genesis, Exodus, Leviticus, Numbers, Deuteronomy). These five books are foundational to the rest of the Bible, the Jewish and Christian religions, and God's plan of redemption.

Translator's Perspective on the Canon of the NT

Analytical-Literal Translation of the Old Testament (Septuagint) - Volume Two - The Historical Books

This second volume contains the Historical Books (Joshua, Judges, Ruth, 1Samuel, 2Samuel, 1Kings, 2Kings, 1Chronicles, 2Chronicles, Ezra, Nehemiah, Esther). These books present the LORD's providence in the history of the ancient Israelite nation.

Analytical-Literal Translation of the Old Testament (Septuagint) - Volume Three - The Poetic Books

This third volume contains the Poetic Books (Job, Psalms, Proverbs, Ecclesiastes, Song of Solomon).

These books contain praises to the LORD, honest expressions of personal struggles, wisdom sayings, and a romantic story.

Analytical-Literal Translation of the Old Testament (Septuagint) - Volume Four - The Prophetic Books

This fourth volume contains the Prophetic Books (Isaiah, Jeremiah, Lamentations, Ezekiel, Daniel, Hosea, Joel, Amos, Obadiah, Jonah, Micah, Nahum, Habakkuk, Zephaniah, Haggai, Zechariah, Malachi).

In these books, the LORD, speaking through His prophets, denounces Israel, Judah, and surrounding nations for their sins. These warnings are applicable to us today, as the USA and other nations are now engaging in similar sins. But there is also much uplifting material in these books, with the prophets expressing strong faith in the LORD in the face of hardships.

Analytical-Literal Translation of the Old Testament (Septuagint): Volume Five, Apocryphal/ Deuterocanonical Books

This fifth and final volume of the ALT: OT contains the "extra" books found in Roman Catholic and Eastern Orthodox Bibles as compared to Jewish and Protestant Bibles. There is much debate on whether these books are inspired by God or not. Only by reading them in a literal translation can you make a decision on this controversial issue. These books were written from 200 B. C. to 50 A.D. Therefore, whether inspired or not, they provide insight into Jewish history and thought shortly before and during the time of New Testament events and thus provide important background to the New Testament.

Why Are These Books in the Bible? Volume Two
Analytical-Literal Translation of the New Testament

Analytical-Literal Translation of the New Testament: Third Edition (ALT3)

ALT3 is the only New Testament that is a literal translation of the second edition of the Byzantine Majority Greek Text, brings out nuances of the Greek text, and includes study aids within the text. It promotes understanding of what the New Testament writers originally wrote. No other English translation gets as close to the original text as ALT3. It is truly the ideal version for the serious student of the Bible.

Analytical-Literal Translation of the New Testament: Devotional Version (ALTD)

The main difference between ALTD and ALT3 is that in the ALTD the "analytical" information is footnoted, while in ALT3 such information is included within brackets within the text. That makes the information readily available, but it makes the text awkward to read and to quote from. By putting this information in footnotes, ALTD is a much easier to read and to quote from version.

Additional ALT Books

Analytical-Literal Translation of the Apostolic Fathers: Volume Seven of the ALT (ALT: APF)

This final volume of the ALT contains the writings of Church leaders of the late first to early second centuries (c. 80-150 AD). Some of these books were seriously considered for inclusion in the canon of the New Testament. They were ultimately rejected for the canon, but all of these books were popular in the early centuries of the Church. They provide insight into the mindset of the early Church immediately after the apostles and give background to the New Testament.

Companion Volume to the ALT

This volume provides aid in understanding the translations seen in the *Analytical-Literal Translation of the New Testament* (ALT). It includes a glossary for important words in the ALT, an-eight part

Translator's Perspective on the Canon of the NT

"Grammatical Renderings" section to explain the unique translations in the ALT, along with other background information to the ALT.

Complete Concordance to the ALT

This volume indexes every occurrence of most words in the *Analytical-Literal Translation of the New Testament*. Only minor words are omitted, like: the, a, of, etc. Sufficient context is provided for the reader to recognize the verse or to get the gist of it.

How Were the Books of the Bible Chosen?

Christians claim the Bible is the Word of God, that it is the final authority in all matters relating to Christian faith and practice, and that it is absolutely reliable in all that it teaches. But to put such confidence in the Bible requires that the correct books are in the Bible. But is there? Why are the 66 books in the Bible in the Bible, and why were other books that could have been included not included? This three-volume set answers these and many related questions.

Why Are These Books in the Bible and Not Others? Volume One – A Translator's Perspective on the Canon of the Old Testament

This Volume One of a three volume set studies the books included in the Old Testament (OT) and considers other books that could have been included in it but were not. Each of the 39 books in the OT are reviewed in detail, and it is explained why they were included in the OT. Then the debate about the "extra" books found in Roman Catholic and Eastern Orthodox Bibles as compared to Protestant and Jewish Bibles is addressed. Lastly, other books that some wonder why they are not included in the OT are discussed. It is explained why these books were rejected.

Why Are These Books in the Bible and Not Others? Volume Two - A Translator's Perspective on the Canon of the New Testament

In this Volume Two of a three-volume set, each of the 27 books included in the New Testament are reviewed in detail. Who wrote them and when, their theology, and other pertinent background information are discussed to explain why they were included in the New Testament.

Why Are These Books in the Bible? Volume Two

Arguments against the traditional viewpoints on these books are addressed and refuted.

Why Are These Books in the Bible and Not Others? Volume Three - The Apostolic Fathers and the New Testament Apocrypha

This Volume Three of a three volume set covers books not included in the New Testament. These books include the writings of the Apostolic Fathers, who were Church leaders and writers of the late first to mid-second centuries, along with "apocryphal" books, both orthodox and Gnostic. Among these apocryphal books are some that have received much publicity of late and from which many people derive their ideas of early Christian history.

Sex and the Bible

These three books look in-depth at what the Bible has to say on sexual types of relationships and related issues. By this is meant: dating, premarital sex, marriage, divorce, remarriage, marital sex, extramarital sex, homosexuality, transsexualism, abortion, and birth control.

All three books go through the Scriptures systematically, looking at relevant passages of Scripture in order. The passages are written out, with commentary afterwards.

The first book is an introduction to the various subjects, quoting the most relevant Scriptures and with only short commentary. The next two books are much more detailed, with many more Scripture passages quoted and much more detailed commentary.

The Bible and Sexual Relationships Issues

In this book, explanations and interpretations are provided for each quoted Bible passage to aid the reader in understanding the Scriptures. However, the emphasis is on the Scriptures themselves. This format will enable the reader to draw conclusions about what the Bible as a whole has to teach on these personal and very relevant issues.

God's Sex Plan: Volume One: What the Old Testament Teaches About Human Sexuality

Does God have a sex plan? By that is meant, did God design the human race to function best by following a specific plan for how human

Translator's Perspective on the Canon of the NT

beings are to interact sexually and to reproduce? What happens when this plan is followed, and when it is not followed? Are different varieties of sexual behaviors just as legitimate as God's original sex plan?

God's Sex Plan: Volume Two: What the New Testament Teaches About Human Sexuality

Many issues are discussed in this set that are related to sex, including but not limited to: monogamy, marital sex, polygamy, incest, homo-sexuality, premarital sex (fornication), extramarital sex (adultery), celibacy, transsexualism, reproduction, infertility, contraception, abortion, sexual harassment and assault, masturbation, pornography, gender roles, and school and other mass shootings (yes, those are related to this topic).

Bible Study

The LORD Has It Under Control: What the Bible Teaches About the Sovereignty of God

This book is for the person struggling in life and for the person struggling with how God sovereignly works in people's lives. It goes through the Bible more or less in order. Along the way, I relate examples of how I believe the sovereignty of God has been operating in my life, in hopes that my experiences will help the reader to apply the principles to your life. It also addresses the question of the relationship of God's sovereignty to the human will or volition.

Scripture Workbook: Third Edition: For Personal and Group Bible Study and Teaching the Bible

The doctrinal and ethical teachings of the Bible as presented in this book encompass an overall way of viewing the world that differs greatly from the prevailing secular worldview. It is hoped this book will enable the reader to not only understand this Biblical worldview but also why it is true and thus to come to trust in it, and then to be prepared to defend this Biblical worldview before an unbelieving world (Matt 28:18-20; Luke 24:27,45; Acts 14:14-18; 17:22-31).

Many changes have been made for this Third Edition of this book, but the total number of forty Scripture Studies remains the same.

Why Are These Books in the Bible? Volume Two
Scripture Workbook: For Personal Bible Study and Teaching the Bible: Second Edition

This book contains forty individual "Scripture Studies." It is divided into two volumes. Volume I covers the essential doctrines of the Christian faith. It is these doctrines that separate the true Christian faith from cultic and other deviations. Volume II of this book then covers controversial theologies, cults, and ethics.

This book has been superseded by the Third Edition, but it is still available.

Scripture Workbook: For Personal Bible Study and Teaching the Bible: Edition 1.1

This book contains twenty-two individual "Scripture Studies." Each study focuses on one general area of study. These studies enable individuals to do in-depth, topical studies of the Bible. They are also invaluable to the Bible study teacher preparing lessons for Sunday School or a home Bible study.

This book has been superseded by the Third Edition, but it is still available.

Bible Versions and Translation

Differences Between Bible Versions: Third Edition

Why do Bible versions differ? Why does the same verse read differently in different versions? Why do some versions contain words, phrases, and even entire verses that other versions omit? Which Bible versions are the most reliable? These and many other questions are answered in this book. Forty versions of the Bible are compared and evaluated.

New World Translation: A Reliable Bible Version? Edition 2.1

The NWT is the Bible of Jehovah's Witnesses. This review evaluates the NWT by looking at select passages from Paul's Epistle to the Ephesians. The standards I use are the same standards that I use in my book *Differences Between Bible Versions*. Simply put, does the translation faithfully and accurately render the Greek text into English?

Translator's Perspective on the Canon of the NT

Health and Fitness Books

Nutrition and the Bible

God-given Foods Eating Plan: For Lifelong Health, Optimization of Hormones, Improved Athletic Performance

The approach of this book is to study different foods and food groups, with a chapter devoted to each major classification of foods. First the Biblical evidence is considered, then the modern-day scientific research is reviewed. Foods are then classified as "God-given foods" and "non-God-given foods." The main point will be a healthy eating plan is composed of a variety of God-given foods and avoids non-God-given foods.

Creationist Diet:
Nutrition and God-given Foods According to the Bible

This book has been superseded by the following book, but it is still available.
What did God give to human beings for food? What does the Bible teach about diet and nutrition? How do the Biblical teachings on foods compare to scientific research on nutrition and degenerative disease like heart disease, cancer, and stroke? These and other questions are addressed in this book.

Creationist Diet: Second Edition; A Comprehensive Guide to Bible and Science Based Nutrition

This Second Edition is 2-1/2 times as long and presents a different perspective on diet than the First Edition. The First Edition mostly advocated a vegan diet, while this Second Edition also advocates for a diet that includes animal foods. However, and this is very important, those animal foods are to be what are called "old-fashioned" meats, dairy, and eggs, not the "factory farm" products that most people eat. What is meant by these two terms and the incredible difference between them is explained in this book. In addition, this book covers a wide range of diet related topics to help the reader to understand how to live a healthier lifestyle according to God's design.

Why Are These Books in the Bible? Volume Two
Powerlifting and Back Pain

Starting and Progressing in Powerlifting: A Comprehensive Guide to the World's Strongest Sport

This 350-page book is geared towards the beginner to intermediate powerlifter, along with the person just thinking about getting into the sport. This book presents sound training, competition, dietary, and supplement advice to aid the reader in starting and progressing in the sport of powerlifting. It will also help the reader to wade through the maze of federations, divisions, and supportive gear now found in powerlifting.

Overcoming Back Pain: A Mind-body Solution (Second Edition)

I powerlifted in college, but back pain forced me to stop lifting. Eventually, the back pain worsened to the point where I was crippled by it for six years. I tried various traditional and alternative treatments, but all to no avail. But then by utilizing mind-body techniques I was able to completely overcome the back pain, so much so that I was able to start powerlifting again.

Politics Books

Joe Biden's Failing Presidency

On the day Biden was inaugurated, he took over the @POTUS account on Twitter and began tweeting profusely. This five-book series reproduces Biden's tweets for the first and second years of his presidency. These books also include my comments I posted on Twitter in response to his tweets. Some of my comments were added later and reflect later developments. I have also added an occasional "Extended Comment" to provide further context and commentary to some tweets.

Joe Biden Tweets During the First Year of His Failing Presidency, Volume One: Reversing Trump, while Dividing and Destroying America, January through July 2021

Biden tweets in his first year in office promoted his "Build Back Better" policies. But with them being a reversal of Trump's policies, they were often subtle attacks on Trump and his supporters and on all who believe in conservative and traditional values.

Joe Biden Tweets During the First Year of His Failing Presidency, Volume Two: Reversing Trump, while Dividing and Destroying America, August 2021 through January 2022

Biden can be very disingenuous in his tweets and his claims about his various plans and polices. He thinks they are all grand and good for the country. But in fact, it is those very plans and policies that is causing his presidency to be failing. Those plans and polices are also dividing and destroying American. Biden's early actions set the stage for more failures later in his presidency, so it is important to remember them.

Joe Biden Tweets During the Second Year of His Failing Presidency, Volume One: Promoting Sin and Death, Causing Bidenflation, and Spewing Hate and Division, January through May 2022

In 2022, Biden declared it was his "intention" to run for a second term as President. It is for that reason I continued this series through the second year of his failing presidency. Come 2024, much of the focus will be on his third and fourth years, but this series will remind voters of his failures in his first two years in office.

Joe Biden Tweets During the Second Year of His Failing Presidency, Volume Two: Promoting Sin and Death, Causing Bidenflation, and Spewing Hate and Division, June 1 through October 15, 2022

Biden promotes sin via his support of the sinful and destructive LGBTQ movement and of abortion. He promotes death by his support of abortion and via his open-door southern border policies. The latter has led to the deaths of migrants and of Americans at the hands of those illegal aliens and by the influx of illicit drugs into the USA. He spews hate and division with his lie-filled rhetoric against "MAGA Republicans" and all who believe in conservative and traditional values.

Joe Biden Tweets During the Second Year of His Failing Presidency, Volume Three: Promoting Sin and Death, Causing Bidenflation, and Spewing Hate and Division, October 16, through December 31, 2022, Plus Updates for Early 2023

This series of five books provides the definitive record of Biden's failures in his first two years as President. These failures should not be forgotten, as they laid the foundation for his continual failures in his subsequent years as President. He has been failing miserably on both domestic issues and in foreign policy. Those failures are all chronicled in these five books.

The 2020 Election, the January 6 "Insurrection," and Their Aftermath

The following five books cover every aspect of the 2020 Election, the January 6 "insurrection," and their aftermath. Starting with claims of fraud and irregularities in that election, to the tragic events of January 6, 2021 (J6; the so-called insurrection), the subsequent second impeachment of Donald J. Trump, to the public hearings of the J6 Commission in the summer and fall of 2022. Also reproduced in these books is all Trump had to say about these and related matters during this time.

Alleged Corruption, Bias, and Fraud: Allegations of the Corruption of Joe Biden, Bias of the Media and Big Tech, and Fraud in the 2020 Election

This book covers events from October 2020 to New Year's Day 2021 that are directly related to the 2020 presidential election. Those events include revelations about the alleged corruption of Joseph R. Biden via his son Hunter Biden. However, the mainstream media (MSM) and Big Tech did their best to hide that potential corruption from the American public, so that Biden could win the election. That worked, or so it was said. But allegations of voter fraud and anomalies abounded. This book investigates those claims to determine which are valid or not.

Trump's 2020 Election Tweets, Georgia Phone Call, and January 2021 Speeches: Did Trump's Claims of Election Fraud Lead to the Capitol Building Uprising?

This book reproduces all that Donald J. Trump said publicly from Election Day 2020 to the end of his presidency related to the 2020 presidential election. Many of Trump's claims about fraud or

Translator's Perspective on the Canon of the NT

irregularities in the 2020 election are disputed. This does not necessarily mean they are false. With my comments, I mention which grievances are valid and which are not. But whether valid or not, Trump's claims of election fraud were said to have led to an insurrection in Washington DC on January 6, 2021. Reading this book will help the reader to decide if in fact Trump's comments led to that tragic event.

Tragic Ending to Donald J. Trump's Great Presidency: Capitol Building Uprising Leads to Impeachment 2.0, as Media and Big Tech Bias and Claims of Election Fraud Continues

Democrats claim the events of January 6, 2021 (J6) were "a deadly insurrection incited by Donald J. Trump." But this book demonstrates that J6, though tragic, was not deadly (with one exception), it was not an insurrection, and it was not incited by then President Trump. This book also updates issues covered in a previous book by the author related to the bias of the mainstream media (MSM) and of Big Tech and problems with the 2020 election.

Trump Fights Back with Statements: Against the Lies of Joe Biden, Attacks from Dems, and the Bias of the Media, of Big Tech, and of the J6 Commission

If you enjoyed reading Trump's Tweets on Twitter until January 8, 2021 or are enjoying his Truths on Truth Social since April 29, 2022, then you should enjoy this book. It fills in the gap with all of his email Statements issued between those dates. These Statements were often Trump fighting back against the lies of President Joe Biden. They also reflect Trump fighting back against the ongoing bias of the mainstream media (MSM) and of Big Tech and against the Dem-controlled Commission (which Trump calls the "Unselect Committee") investigating the tragic events of January 6, 2021 (J6).

The Biased J6 Select Committee: The Public Hearings Were Half a Trial; This Book Gives You the Other Half

The public hearings in the summer and fall of 2022 about the tragic events of January 6, 2021 (J6) were the prosecution presenting its case against Donald J. Trump, with the American public as the jury. But he was not afforded a defense. This book provides that defense.

Do not miss how dangerous this precedent was. What if this were you? How would you like it if primetime hearings were held prosecuting you, aired on all major networks, but without you being able to present a defense on such a grand scale? But this book presents the other side, so the reader can make an informed decision about J6 and Trump's role in it.

The First Impeachment of Donald J. Trump

The first impeachment of Donald J. Trump began when he made a phone call on July 25, 2019. A complaint about that phone call led to an impeachment inquiry and proceedings in the US House and a trial in the US Senate. This impeachment and trial was occurring against the backdrop of the 2020 Presidential election, which was already underway in the summer of 2019, even though the election itself was still over a year away. As will be seen, and as the title of this three-volume set implies, that election was in fact the real impetus for the impeachment.

The impeachment inquiry itself began in early September 2019 and ran up until February 5, 2020. This set will also mention additional important events that occurred during that time period. It will mostly conclude two days after the close of the Senate impeachment trial, on February 7, 2020. But several updates after that date will be included in Volume Three.

Dems Cannot Beat Trump, So They Impeach Trump: Volume One: Beginnings Through HIC Hearings (Early September Through Late November 2019)

This three-volume set covers the impeachment of Donald J. Trump that occurred over the fall of 2019 to the winter of 2020. It was yet one more attempt to oust the President from office by Democrats, who never accepted he won in 2016. A complaint about a phone call between President Trump and Ukraine President Zelensky led to an impeachment inquiry to begin in early September 2019. This Volume One covers the beginnings of the impeachment inquiry through the public hearings before the House Intelligence Committee (HIC).

Dems Cannot Beat Trump, So They Impeach Trump: Volume Two: HJC Hearings and Pre-Senate Trial Events (Mid-November 2019 to Mid-January 2020)

This second volume of this three volume set continues the discussion about the impeachment proceedings in the US House. It covers the public hearings before the House Judiciary Committee (HJC) and events that occurred up until the impeachment trial in the Senate. It also directly answers a question the author has often been asked—how can the author, as a conservative Christian, support such a "crude" person as President Donald J. Trump?

Dems Cannot Beat Trump, So They Impeach Trump: Volume Three: Senate Trial and Aftermath (Late January to Early February 2020, Updates Through October 2020)

This third volume of this three volume set covers the impeachment trial in the US Senate in January to February 2020 and its aftermath. In the trial, both sides were given an equal opportunity to present their arguments. This volume also provides updates of related issues up to just before the 2020 election. It focuses on the corruption of Joe Biden that Trump wanted investigated and which led to the impeachment inquiry.

Sexual Harassment Claims and Political Incivility

Tearing the USA Apart: From Kavanaugh, to Incivility, to Caravans, to Violence, to the 2018 Midterm Elections, and Beyond

The United States of American is being torn apart by political differences more than any time since the 1960s and maybe since the Civil War of the 1860s. This division was amplified by political events in the summer to fall of 2018. This time period could prove to be seminal in the history of the United States. This tearing apart came to the forefront and was amplified during the confirmation proceedings for Supreme Court nominee Judge Brett Kavanaugh. This book overviews the Brett Kavanaugh confirmation proceedings in detail. It then overviews these additional major events that occurred up to the end of November 2018.

Why Are These Books in the Bible? Volume Two

Appendix Three
The Author's Websites, Newsletters, and Social Sites

This appendix provides details on my websites, newsletters, and social sites.

Zeolla.org
www.Zeolla.org

Zeolla.org is the personal website of Gary F. Zeolla. He is the author of Christian, fitness, and politics books, websites, and newsletters. He has a B.S. in Nutrition Science (Penn State; 1983) and attended Denver Seminary (1988-90). He is also a powerlifter, holding fifteen All-time world records, plus over a hundred federation records.

This website provides links to all of my writings, along with information about my Christian faith, powerlifting, and other personal details. A detailed autobiography is also available on the site.

Darkness to Light
www.Zeolla.org/Christian

Darkness to Light ministry is dedicated to explaining and defending the Christian faith. Currently available on the website are over 1,200 webpages, over twenty books and eBooks, and a free email newsletter. In these materials, a wide range of topics are covered, including: theology, apologetics, cults, ethics, Bible versions, and much more, so you are sure to find something of interest.

The name for the ministry is taken from the following verse:

"…to open their eyes [in order] to turn [them] back from **darkness to light** and [from] the authority of Satan to God, [in order for] them to receive forgiveness of sins and an inheritance among the ones having been sanctified by faith in Me" (Acts 26:18).

The words "darkness" and "light" have a wide range of meanings when used metaphorically in Scripture, but basically, "darkness" refers to falsehood and unrighteousness while "light" refers to truth and righteousness. People turn from darkness to light when they come to believe the teachings of the Bible and live in accordance with them.

Fitness for One and All
www.Zeolla.org/Fitness

I have a B.S. in Nutrition Science (Penn State; 1983). I competed very successfully in powerlifting in my late teens to early twenties (1978-85), again in my 40s (2003-09), then again in my 50s (2015-2021). But health problems forced me to stop competing each time. Now in my 60s, I am attempting a third comeback.

With all I have been through, dealt with, and accomplished, it is now my passion to help others achieve their health, fitness, and performance goals. To that end, I set up Fitness for One and All website.

Currently available on the website are over 1,000 webpages, hundreds of weightlifting videos, five books and eBooks, and a free email newsletter. These materials are directed towards a wide range of people, including beginning fitness enthusiasts, athletes, powerlifters, and those dealing with health problems. The name "Fitness for One and All" reflects this diversity of covered topics.

Biblical and Constitutional Politics
www.Zeolla.org/Politics

This website presents political articles and commentary from a conservative Christian and politically conservative perspective.

"Conservative Christian" includes the belief that the Bible is God-breathed and fully reliable in all that it teaches, including about politics.

"Politically conservative" refers to the belief in limited government, separation of powers, traditional values, personal and national security, capitalism, freedom and liberty, and most of all, an adherence to the Constitution of the United States, following an originalist interpretation thereof. Currently available on the website are over 300 webpages and fourteen books.

Covid Fearmongering and Lies
https://www.zeolla.org/covid/

Coronavirus Fearmongering on the Left, Covid-19 Lies on the Right: A Layman's View of What the Authorities Got Correct and Incorrect about the SARS-CoV-2 pandemic.

The articles and commentaries on this website are listed in chronological order. In this way, the reader can follow the chronology of the pandemic and the evolution of my thoughts thereupon, from being a Covid-denier to recognizing the seriousness of Covid-19 and the need for the vaccines for high-risk groups.

Social Sites

Facebook: www.Facebook.com/GZeolla

Gab: https://gab.com/GZeolla

Gettr: https://gettr.com/user/GZeolla

Truth Social: https://truthsocial.com/@GZeolla

Twitter (X): https://twitter.com/GZeolla

    I am sure the reader has heard of the first and last of these sites, but you might not have heard of the other three. That is because they are newer sites that were developed by conservatives in reaction to the other two "shadow banning" conservatives.

    I might have been so shadow banned of late, though I am not sure. I just know there have been many times I have posted comments on Facebook or Twitter that I thought would bring a significant reaction, but nothing, no response whatsoever. But even if I haven't already, I am sure to be so in the future, as those sites crack down on conservative speech.

    That is why I set up accounts on Gab, Gettr and Truth Social, to be sure I have a place to voice my opinions. These sites promise not to censor people's comments, beyond what is required by law.

    Note also, if the reader hasn't figured it out by now, I'm not good at being concise in my writings. But by being so exhaustive, I thoroughly cover every topic I address. And if the reader peruses all of my writings on a given subject, you will be well-versed on the topic at hand.

    But that is why I found the 280-character limit on Twitter to be quite restrictive, so I rarely posted to it. But after Elon Musk took it over, renamed it X, and opened it so that "blue check" users could post messages of up to 2,500 characters, I went through the identity confirmation and paid the fee to get a blue check mark. Thus, I now post

Translator's Perspective on the Canon of the NT

to X more often. Also, by getting a blue checkmark, I can edit posts and run advertisements on X.

Otherwise, Gettr has a 777-character limit, Truth Social a 1,000-character limit, Gab a 2,000-character limit, and Facebook has no such limits. I try to keep my posts below the lowest of these of 777 characters or at least below 1,000, so my messages are still not too wordy, and I can post the same message on all of these sites.

On these social pages, I post about new items being posted on any of my four websites: my personal website, my Christian website, my fitness website, and my politics website. I also post personal updates, such as about my powerlifting.

On my social pages, I ignore all comments and replies that utilize "foul" or indecent language. That means, if you reply to one of my posts using such language, I will not even read your comments, let alone respond to them. I also will not respond to ad hominem (personal) attacks.

Simply put, if you cannot respond to the substance of my post in a civil manner, without resorting to name-calling, personal attacks, or foul language, you will not get a response. And if my post is a link to one of my articles or books, then read that item before responding. If you do not, I will just refer you back to it, and that will be that.

Contacting the Author

The translator can be contacted by using the email link on any of my four websites. Click on the "Contact Information" link near the bottom of any page of any site. But my preceding remarks about social media responses apply to emailed comments as well.

Reviews

It would be appreciated if the reader would write a review of this book on Amazon and/ or wherever you purchased it. Such reviews are a benefit to others who might be thinking of purchasing this book, and it is a help to me to know what readers like and do not like about this book. It would also be helpful if you would mention this book on whatever social media sites you participate in. Many thanks in advance for doing so.

Printed in Great Britain
by Amazon